INTERNATIONAL ORGANIZATIONS IN EUROPE AND THE RIGHT TO HEALTH CARE

DOOR

MR. DR. H.D.C. ROSCAM ABBING

KLUWER – DEVENTER/THE NETHERLANDS
ANTWERP. BOSTON
FRANKFURT(M). LONDON

Dit boek werd door de schrijfster verdedigd aan de Universiteit van
Amsterdam

ISBN 90 268 1077 6
Library of Congress Catalog Card Number: 79-20 658

Contents

X

Preface

The idea to undertake a study on international health activities within the framework of intergovernmental co-operation, to analyse its basis (right to health care) and to critically examine present structures of international public health undertakings, particularly in Europe, arose when I was attached to the public health division of the Council of Europe in Strasbourg (France) (1968-1975).

I was then in a position to observe closely the developments in this field. It was out of concern for the actual provision of health care and the uneasiness about the way in which the realization of the right to health care is handled internationally, that I turned to this subject.

When still in Strasbourg, I already started gathering material, which was then fairly an easy matter. However, once returned to the Netherlands, it proved to be extremely difficult to obtain the necessary documentation. Some of the international organizations, but also national libraries were reluctant to provide me with the necessary information. I should, therefore, like to express my most sincere thanks to all those who have assisted me in my efforts, and particularly to the library of the University Institute of Social Medicine in Amsterdam and the library of the Sick Fund Council in Amstelveen.

I am also most grateful to all those who have assisted me either in correcting my English or in typing manuscripts. Without their much appreciated help and assistance this publication could not have been realized in its present form.

In fact I should like to thank everyone who has assisted me some-how in preparing this study, either morally or materially; their assistance, in whatever form, has always been much appreciated. To you, Professor Schermers I express my gratitude for having given of your precious time to discuss with me the various parts of this book. Your experience with, and knowledge of international organizations have been of inestimable value to me. As a supervisor of this work for the purpose of obtaining my doctor's degree you were always a quiet figure in the background, upon whom I could fall back whenever necessary.

Last, but not least, I should like to say a very special word to Professor Leenen. Because of a revision of university rules and for some strictly formal reasons, you were at the last moment unable to take the place you were supposed to take: Professor Schermers is a specialist in international organizations; you, Professor Leenen, should have been the counterpart as an expert in health law. Yet, you have assisted me all the way through, as if you had been a supervisor. Moreover, not only did you give me very valuable scientific support, but you were also always there to give me the moral support I often needed. You have in fact lived through the whole difficult process of preparing this study, without at any time showing that you too were going through a difficult period. I believe this has been the greatest supporting factor for me and the right incentive to carry on even when the going was tough.

The text of this book was completed on 31st December 1978.

XII

'The enjoyment of the highest attainable standard of health is one of the fundamental rights of every human being without distinction of race, religion, political belief, economic or social condition'
(*Preamble of the World Health Organization, second paragraph, 1946*)

Introduction

1. General remarks

The legal basis for the promotion of health care lies in the recognition of the existence of human rights. They include the recognition of the right to protection of the individual against violation of his particular state of physical and mental health (civil and political rights), as well as the recognition of the right to health care as an integral part of the economic, social and cultural rights.

The right to health care is a social human right, in as far as it gives a right to everybody to make use of the possibilities society is able to offer (Leenen, 1978, p. 18).[1] Yet at the same time there are several individual human rights, which are inherent to the right to health care. Of these, the two most important ones are the right to life; the prohibition of torture, maltreatment and medical experimentation without free consent. There are not only some further individual human rights which intervene with the right to health care as a social right, but also some further social human rights. Examples are the respect of privacy, the right to information, the right to an adequate complaint procedure (individual human rights), the right to self-determination (individual and social right) and the right to social security (social human right).

Hence, the right to health care is conditioned both by individual and social human rights, which are complementary to each other; this particular right would be void if no consideration is given to the other human rights involved (Leenen, 1978, p. 17).

The mere recognition of the rights relating to 'physical and mental integrity' and to 'health care' by virtue of human rights instruments would not suffice to attain the World Health Organization's objective of 'an acceptable level of health' for all. The realization of these rights depends entirely on their implementation through operational activities; the attainment of an acceptable level of health is conditioned by economic, political, social and legal conditions, nationally and internationally.

The promotion of health care at a national level is an initial consequence of the recognition of these human rights. International co-operation in this field is logically the next step to their realization.

International organizations have a primary role to play in this field, in particular when one realises that national efforts and undertakings often have

---

1. See also Leenen, 1966, p. 93.

consequences on an international level, that national resources often do not suffice to attain the objective, and that experience gained elsewhere might usefully contribute to national undertakings. International health work is necessary for 'any or all activities for the prevention, diagnosis or treatment of diseases which require the combined consideration and action of more than one country' (Goodman, 1971, p. 3).

To cite but a few examples of fields in which international co-operation is relevant: exchange of experience, personnel and material; drawing up of internationally acceptable standards for pharmaceuticals; co-operative efforts to control communicable diseases; harmonization of training requirements.

Thus, simultaneously with the development of human rights and their formulation in international human rights instruments, 'health' and 'health care' have gradually become the subject of international activities and international legal rules, especially since the twentieth century. At the early stage of international public health work activities at an international level were considered to be necessary for a restricted area only (prevention of communicable diseases). The basis for these undertakings has gradually expanded, simultaneously with the recognition of the right to health care, as well as with the growing awareness of the real significance of this right, and hence the concern with it, also at an international scale.

This international co-operation in the field of health care requires, by necessity, an adequate international structure.

First on a limited scale, through diplomatic conferences, at the end of the nineteenth century in the frame of an international organization with a restricted mandate, the growing concern for international health activities finally resulted in the creation in 1949 of the World Health Organization, while activities in other international settings have also been taken up since.

This work, performed by international organizations or through other forms of intergovernmental co-operation can be seen as a contribution to the practical realization of the right to health care: though it will not always be explicitly mentioned, the ultimate aim remains the fulfillment of this right.[2] Its recognition finds expression in the statutes of various international organizations, as well as in the conventions, agreements, resolutions and directives stemming from the statutory provisions of these organizations.

The usefulness of these international undertakings in the field of health is not contested: political divergencies are mostly no hindrance for international health activities. Notwithstanding the fact that the present subject is closely related to other fields, such as the social, economical and political ones, the latter may explain why there is a certain tendency to deal with health matters as a separate entity within the whole of international co-operation; this may

2. This right is sometimes referred to as a right to 'health protection', as, for instance, in the case of the European Social Charter. Yet, despite this incomplete and not altogether exact formulation, it was meant to cover the 'right to health care', as will be shown when discussing the formulation process of this right in the framework of the Social Charter (see Part A, Ch. II, para. 4.3.).

sometimes stand in the way of the effectiveness of international co-operation in the field of health.

2. *Scope of the present study*

2.1. OBJECTIVE

Bearing in mind the preceeding remarks, the objective of this study is to analyse past and present activities of international organizations in the field of health care, primarily on a European scale[3], with a view to examine possibilities for optimal international European promotion of health care. Because the basis for international activities and international legal rules in the field of health care lies in the recognition of certain human rights as included in international human rights instruments, it is necessary to first review the history of the formulation of these rights, in order to gain understanding of their meaning and scope. Only on the basis of insight in the line of thought and in the decisionmaking process during the various stages of the formulation of these rights, including the problems which were encoutered during this process, will it be possible to critically examine the manner in which international organizations and other forms of international co-operation contribute and, or should contribute to the promotion of health care through the realization of these rights: the functions, tasks, possibilities, limitations and shortcomings of the international co-operation in this respect will become clear.

2.2. HUMAN RIGHTS (PART A)

It is obvious that the right to health care has to be considered in relation to a number of other human rights. Examples of these are: the right to food, clothing, housing, decent living conditions, freedom and privacy. These rights either fall under the category of civil and political rights (the so-called individual rights) or under the category of economic, social and cultural rights (the so-called social rights). Sometimes these rights will complement each other, sometimes they will be conflicting. They will be conflicting when community interests override the individual's interests (privacy, personal freedom) as, for instance, in the case of compulsory vaccination and quarantine. Complementary to the right to health care (and vice versa) are, for instance, the right to life (abortion: right to life and health care of the mother, right to life of the child), the prohibition of torture and the safeguarding against medical experimentation. (Medical experimentation is only permitted with the free consent of the person concerned and with a view to appropriate health care, either individual or more general (advances in treatment methods.)

From the category of civil and political rights, the articles pertaining to

3. See para. 2.3. below.

'physical existence' in particulàr, are directly related to the subject matter, although, as said before, there are also other individual human rights which intervene with this social right. The right to life, for instance, would have no meaning if the individual were not properly protected against illness, or, in case of disease, would not be adequately cared for (right to health care).

Despite the close relationship between both categories of human rights, they will be dealt with separately because their respective scope and implementation differ (see Part A, Ch.I, para. 1.).
  The international instruments which include the individual rights are:
— United Nations Universal Declaration of Human Rights of 10 December 1948 (Articles 3 and 5);
— Council of Europe Convention for the Protection of Human Rights and Fundamental Freedoms of 4 November 1950 (Articles 2 and 3);
— United Nations International Covenant on Civil and Political Rights of 16 December 1966 (Articles 6 and 7).

The right to adequate health care (minimum requirements for undertakings which aim at improvements of the state of health of the individual and the community, as well as at provisions for an adequate health care system, including preventive measures) is included in the following international human rights instruments:
— United Nations Declaration of Human Rights of 10 December 1948 (Article 25);
— Council of Europe European Social Charter of 18 October 1961 (Article 11);
— United Nations International Covenant on Economic, Social and Cultural Rights of 16 December 1966 (Article 12).

2.3. INTERNATIONAL ORGANIZATIONS (PART B)

Having discussed the development of these human rights a review will be given of the tasks of international organizations and other forms of international co-operation on the basis of the recognition of the human rights dealt with in Part A. This will be done on a primarily European basis, because the practical realization of the right to health care can best be performed on a regional basis (with the exception of some activities which should remain on a worldwide basis, such as the efforts in the field of communicable diseases). Prevalent social, economical and political conditions in the world make it almost impossible to develop a common approach to many of the problems inherent to the subject field and controversies are more likely to remain on a worldwide basis than at a regional level.[4]
  Therefore it will be in the regional context that the creation and the objectives of international organizations and other forms of international co-opera-

4. See Part C, Ch. I, para. 3. on regionalization.

tion as well as their functioning with respect to the practical realization and the further elaboration of the right to health care will be examined.

The relations between the various settings in which international co-operation takes place will also be discussed.

The only existing organizations with tasks entirely restricted to the health field, the World Health Organization, will first be given attention. Then other international organizations operating in Europe, as well as other forms of international co-operation, which are of a more general nature, but which have, though not exclusive, functions in this field in the context of their objectives, will be described.

They are the Council of Europe, the European Community, the Organisation for Economic Co-operation and Development, the North Atlantic Treaty Organization and the European Free Trade Association. The latter will be mentioned only briefly, because their significance regarding the present subject is rather limited. Among the regional arrangements, the Benelux Economic Union and the Nordic Council will also receive some attention. It is by no means the intention to give an exhaustive enumeration of activities of the international bodies to be discussed. The purpose is rather to indicate general trends so as to show possibilities, failures and shortcomings of international co-operation in the field of health in Europe.

2.4. SUGGESTIONS (PART C)

Once the background of the right to health care as formulated in the international human rights instruments has been sketched and the international bodies have been reviewed organizationally, structurally and functionally, an analysis will be made of the potentialities and shortcomings of the international settings which are under review in respect of the further elaboration of the human rights discussed, as well as in respect of the putting into practice of the right to health care.

The present co-operation and co-ordination among the various international settings as well as some of the shortcomings in this respect will then be assessed.

On the basis of this critical analysis it will be indicated what an adequate structure could be for international European undertakings in the field of the right to health care (further elaboration of the human rights under discussion as well as the practical realization of the right to health care). Suggestions will be made on a certain repartition of work and areas of action, including aspects of human rights which are suitable for further elaboration at the European level.

The whole will be based on the assumption that, failing an adequate overall structure, prevalent possibilities at the international European level can not be optimally used to fully implement the right to health care.

2.5. LIMITATIONS OF THE STUDY

For various reasons some limitations had to be made to the scope of the present study.

Firstly, as was indicated in para. 2.3., the international undertakings in the field of health care can best be performed on a regional basis. Therefore this study is based on this concept and will, for practical reasons, be limited to one region, namely the European one. Tangent planes on world scale will, however, not be neglected.

A second limitation to this study is that it deals exclusively with international governmental organizations; non-governmental organizations as the League of Red Cross Societies and various professional organizations will not be examined, though sometimes mention will be made of these organizations. It is recognized that these non-governmental organizations may usefully contribute to international health care (through influencing the decision making process), but they are void of any legal authority in this field.

Thirdly, only those human rights, which have a direct bearing on health care will be dealt with. Also various specific subject matters will be excluded from this study. They are, environmental problems, which do touch closely upon the present subject matter, but are as much related to other (policy) fields. Moreover, health care has been the subject of international co-operation for some time. From this international co-operation only recently, specific attention has been derived for the environment. Environmental matters have since, often also organizationally, been dissolved from the international health work. This subject would furthermore require a separate study, because of the extent of the problems involved. Further, social security matters will not be dealt with, as they fall under the right to social security with an angle of incidence which is different from the one used in the present study. Occupational health will not be dealt with, because matters like safety and hygiene at working places primarily fall within the sphere of labour law.

6

Part A - International human rights instruments

I. General introduction

1. Categories of human rights

Human rights are commonly divided into two categories:
a. political and civil rights (the so-called classical, individual or negative rights);
b. economic, social and cultural rights (the so-called modern, positive or social rights).

Vasak (1973, p. 11 a.f.) introduces a third category of rights, the 'rights of solidarity'. As it falls outside the scope of this study to review in detail these various categories[1] only some general remarks will be made here, as far as they are relevant to the subject matter.

a. political and civil rights

These classical rights are formulated with a view to protecting individual freedoms. They group together the political and civil rights of the individual, and include, amongst other principles, the protection of physical integrity and of human dignity (outlawing, for example, medical experimentation without free consent; forced treatment; torture).

In essence, individual rights are of an absolute nature, they do not depend upon surrounding conditions such as the social or economic circumstances in which they are exercised, although the interdependence cannot be denied. For rights can only be exercised in society, and the promotion of political and civil rights will therefore be influenced by the prevailing social and economic conditions of the society in which they are realized (Leenen, 1966, p. 92).

Their achievement depends upon an absence of action, a non-interference with the principles on which these rights are based.

The guarantee of the fundamental human rights lies in the allotment of a subjective right to the individual, which in turn is based on the existence of a certain number of more or less absolute principles and fundamental rules. The rights concerned are therefore mostly defined as a declaration of principle, covering the individual and subjective aspects of these rights.

For this category of rights, legal rules are laid down which form a protective machinery for the individual. This machinery can be put into operation whenever an infraction occurs, and legal sanctions can be requested before the courts. In cases where all available domestic, national sources have been exhausted, procedures for individual petitions and even for jurisdiction by an international court have been elaborated (see below, para. 2.3.3.).

1. See for instance: Jellinek, Die Erklärung der Menschen- und Bürgerrechte (1927); Goslinga, De regten van den Mens en Burger (1936); Cassin, La Declaration universelle et la mise en oeuvre des droits de l'homme (1951) and Gurvitch, La Declaration des droits sociaux (1946).

b. economic, social and cultural rights

It was only in the early period of the 20th century that considerable evolution took place in social awareness, and consequently in the concept of social law (Leenen, 1966, p. 89).

The first instruments for this category of rights had, in their formulation, clearly been inspired by the existing individual human rights instruments. Like in the case of the latter instruments, the first instruments dealing with social rights, enumerate these rights as individual (personal) human rights. Thus, for instance, the terminology used in the UN International Covenant on Economic, Social and Cultural Rights for the formulation of the right to health care is the one commonly applied to individual rights.

By using this specific terminology (Glaser, 1964, p. 8) the impression was given that these rights were individual, subjective rights and, if so, then the fundamental difference between the two categories of rights would be lost. However, the economic, social and cultural rights, though they too have aspects of subjective law, are not understood to be subjective rights concerning the individual alone. These rights are not intended to protect the individual's freedom, but are rather subjective rights in a given community. The existence of this community, and its essence as determined by its economic, social and cultural conditions, makes it possible for the individual to place a 'quality' claim on the community. These rights are, therefore, indirect rights, derived from, and made possible by, the existence of the particular community; social rights and privileges which man may enjoy, not only because of his character as a human being, but also because he contributes to society according to his ability and because he is entitled to receive from that society according to his needs. (Collected edition of the travaux préparatoires, Vol. I, 1975, p. 142; See also Drost, P., Human Rights as Legal Rights, 1951, p. 174.)

Leenen, 1966, p. 169, calls these rights 'rights to participation', which term expresses the mutual relationship of the individual and society; both participate in the whole system of human society in development. They would remain a 'dead language' if the declaration of principles which underly these rights is not followed by implementation. The social discipline involved in the latter imbibe these rights with their positive aspect. It is for this reason that, in contrast to the political and civil rights which, by their more absolute character, are not difficult to define, the present category of rights cannot be described as invariable, absolute rights; this event would render their legal scope doubtful.

The definition of these social rights is of a dual nature; first, it includes the principles accepted by states and recognized as a right incumbant to every one (as is the case for the individual human rights), which is the legal aspect, and secondly, it consists of the social quality part, which involves the measures to be taken for the application of these rights. Their guarantee lies in the (minimum-indispensable) standards and provisions which the states are bound to take.[2]

2. Reflex-Rechte; see: Jellinek, System des Subjectiven Öffentlichen Rechte, 1892, p. 69; Vedel, Les Declarations des droits de l'homme, 1950, p. 70 a.f.; Geney, Methode d'interpretation, 1924, p. 464; Drost, Human Rights as a legal right, 1951, p. 174.

Instruments of economic, social and cultural rights are, by definition, flexible. Gradual rather than immediate and rapid implementation is imposed by the variety of prevalent (economic, social and cultural) conditions. The nature of these conditions, which are in constant fluctuation and (progressive) development, implies that room should be left for the evolution and adaptation of the instruments so that the latter form an optimal frame within which adequate programming is made possible. Furthermore, like the classical rights, the realization of the 'social' ones has direct bearing on international activities. The concerted effort to be undertaken in respect to them is in many cases extended to international co-operation, which forms the ideal framework for creating optimal (quality) conditions for these positive rights.

The claim an individual may put on society for the realization of these rights, among which is the right to health care, will be greater, the more society can offer. On the other hand, we should not overlook the fact that it is not a claim by the individual alone. Society also places a reciprocal claim on the individual, as, for instance, in the case of health care. It is recognized that the individual has a moral obligation (which means a limitation of his freedom) to avoid anything which might be harmful to his own health. This, however, is entirely subject to individual standards. For no one can maintain that a person wanting to spoil his own private physical state without creating danger for his environment would be wronging society.[3] In the present context it is, therefore, not this notion of 'care for ones own health' we are concerned with, but rather the health of the individual in relation to his environment (such as contagious diseases) (i.e. health protection), as well as the efforts states have to deploy to attain an acceptable standard of health (i.e. health promotion).

The very nature of the social rights makes their protection machinery much more complicated than for the 'individual' ones. The implementation of social, economic and cultural rights does not depend on juridical but rather on legislative measures and administrative steps. Respective instruments form a legal frame to be completed with social policy measures.

Decisions on their implementation belong to the social policy of a state and fall outside the scope of the juridical authorities. Hence the control system for instruments dealing with economic, social and cultural rights is not based upon a legal procedure. The existing international control on the implementation of these 'claim rights' consists entirely of an administrative reporting system, which does not put any *direct legal* obligation on states, but is mainly based on the moral pressure the specific system may exercise ('promotional' character).

The individual and social human rights are different in nature and in structure, but they do have a relationship; the modern rights could not exist without the cognisance of individual liberty and freedom. Their realization has to take into account the existence of individual rights so as not to lead to the nega-

---

3. Abstraction is made here of the possible financial implications.

tion of individual freedom.[4] On the other hand, the individual rights are promoted through the exercise of the social rights. A proper balance in the simultaneous realization of these two categories of fundamental rights will ensure the optimal protection of the individual human being.

The significance of this relationship between both categories of rights for the right to health care was pointed out in the introduction (para. 2.2.).

c. rights of solidarity

The so-called solidarity rights have not (yet) been specified as a separate and distinct category alongside of the political and civil rights, and the economic, social and cultural ones. According to Vasak (1973, p. 11 a.f.) this category is thought to be composed of rights resulting from a certain conception of life in community. They can, in that author's opinion, only be obtained through common effort of all components of society: the state, public and private groups and each individual. The rights Vasak aims at are mainly related to aspects of the environment — the right to a healthy one —. He also groups the 'right to peace' under this category.

Vasak states that he is aware that, as the separate identification of these rights is only of recent vintage, international legislation is still almost non-existent. This lack of formalization indicates according to that author that they are therefore not yet recognized as separate entities.

Vasak's arguments for 'introducing' this 'new category' of rights appears to be doubtful for instance in respect to the conception of the existence of solidarity rights. Article 11 of the Social Charter of the Council of Europe well illustrates this objection in stating a desire to impose the 'remov(al) as far as possible (of the) cause(s) of ill-health' as a state's obligation. Vasak's interpretation of 'ill-health' is evidently restrictively narrow. Ill-health can be caused by external biological factors (such as infections), but also by any action or inaction of the individual, the society and its component parts.

The idea that environmental conditions affect the human being living in them has long been recognized. As soon as the margins of the tolerable have been reached, various rights, but above all the right to proper health care, including prevention of conditions detrimental to good health, are impeded. An individual can by addiction or through venereal diseases endanger his direct environment. The enterprise is doing likewise by, for instance, marketing poorly-conceived products whose dangerous side-effects have not been properly checked. Government officials, by inaction on requirements for safety and quality products endanger the well being of the population. Further, it appears that individual states have and will become more and more bound (through international agreements and so forth) to common acceptable quality standards. Inaction as a first stage, thus is followed by action. The supposed distinction,

---

4. See for instance: v.d. Ven, Leenen, Beekman, Human rights and social welfare, National Report, Netherlands Council on Social Welfare, 1968, pp. 10 and 18; Leenen in v. Zonneveld e.a., 1974, p. 102.

12

therefore, which Vasak makes seems imaginary; the rights concerned may better be grouped under the economic, social and cultural rights.

2. International human rights instruments (general review)

2.1. UN UNIVERSAL DECLARATION OF HUMAN RIGHTS (1948)

2.1.1. Brief drafting history

In pursuance of Article 68[5] of the Charter of the United Nations, the Economic and Social Council (ECOSOC; the Council) established the United Nations' commission on human rights (the commission). This commission was assigned the task of submitting proposals, recommendations and reports with regard to, inter alia, an International Bill of Human Rights (Council Resolution 5 (1) of 16 February 1946). Through its subsequent Resolution 9 (II) of 21 June 1946, the Council requested the commission to submit suggestions for the effective implementation of human rights and fundamental freedoms.

A drafting committee[6] of the commission prepared a preliminary draft for such an International Bill of Human Rights, for which use was made of various texts, such as:
— a preliminary draft outline of an International Bill of Human Rights prepared by the secretariat (E/CN.4/AC.1/3);
— a text of a letter from the United Kingdom representative on the commission on human rights, transmitting among other texts a draft International Bill (E/CN.4/AC.1/4);
— proposals by the United States for rewording some items of the secretariat draft outline (E/CN.4/AC.1/8 and Revs. 1 and 2);
— International Declaration of Fundamental Rights and Freedoms of Man ('Declaration of Philadelphia') (A/148).

The drafting committee, when discussing the form the preliminary Bill of Human Rights might take, favoured a declaration with a wide context and general in expression, to be followed by a convention on specific groups of rights. The drafting committee therefore decided to prepare two such texts, leaving it to the commission on human rights to take a final decision on the form the bill should take.

The drafting committee submitted to the commission a text for a draft declaration as well as some suggestions for a draft convention, which were taken from the text of the United Kingdom representative and consisted of three further subjects, among which were 'physical integrity, torture and cruel punishment' (E/CN.4/21 Annex G).

At its second session (2 to 17 December 1947), the commission decided that the Bill of Human Rights should be composed of three sections: a 'Decla-

---

5. Article 68: The Economic and Social Council shall set up commissions in economic and social fields and for the promotion of human rights, and such other commissions as may be required for the performance of its functions.
6. Council Resolution 46 (IV).

ration', a 'Convention or Covenant', and 'Measures for implementation' (E/600, para. 18).

At its third session (24 May to 16 June 1948) the commission completed its work[7] on the Declaration[8], which was then submitted to the Council (E/800). The latter decided at its seventh session (19 July to 28 August 1948) to transmit the text to the General Assembly (Assembly Resolution 151 (VII)).[9] The Assembly adopted unanimously the Universal Declaration of Human Rights on 10 December 1948 (Resolution 217 A (III)) and proclaimed the Declaration as 'a common standard of achievement for all people and all Nations'.

The section of the Universal Declaration which deals with economic, social and cultural rights (Articles 22-28) is the result of a drafting compromise. This compromise was mainly due to a divergency of views which existed on the extent to which the duties and obligations of a state should be formulated. There was also discussion on the question of priority of obligations: those of the individual with regard to the state or vice-versa.

To overcome this deadlock, the commission decided at its third session (24 May to 16 June 1948)[10] to delete any reference to obligations of states throughout the whole section dealing with social rights. This, however, made it necessary to elaborate a general article on the real enjoyment of the economic, social and cultural rights (Verdoodt, 1964, p. 212; de la Chapelle, 1969, p. 100). This Article (28) tends to confirm the rights of each person on a fair social and international order:

'Everyone is entitled to a social and international order in which the rights and freedoms set forth in the Declaration can be fully realised.'

Social (including health) and international order were given the same importance in the text. Social is the general principle, and should be read to include on the one hand, national and international *social* order and, on the other hand, international order.

Article 28 is a very general one, not defining a precise right, but stating a general principle applicable throughout the Declaration. It implies that every state will put into effect the rights and liberties proclaimed by the Declaration.

Besides this Article, there was, however, still a need for a general article to introduce the section of economic, social and cultural rights. Such an article should contain the characteristics common to these rights, as set forth in the following Articles (23-27), and would make these rights distinct from the traditional ones, in that their satisfaction depends upon national resources and

7. Relevant working papers are: E/CN.4/57 and E/CN.4/95 Annexes A and B.
8. For a very detailed and clear description of the elaboration of the Universal Declaration of Human Rights see Verdoodt 'Naissance et signification de la Déclaration des droits de l'homme' (1964), and de la Chapelle 'La Déclaration des Droits de l'homme et le catholicisme' (1967).
9. Third Session, 21 September to 12 December 1948.
10. E/800.

international co-operation which may guide national effort in this respect. The commission, therefore, agreed on a text for an 'umbrella' Article (22), which, as amended on a minor point by the committee on social, humanitarian and cultural affairs (third committee) of the Assembly, reads as follows:

'Everyone, as a member of society, has the right to social security and is entitled to the realisation, through national effort and international co-operation, and in accordance with the organisation and resources of each State, of the economic, social and cultural rights indispensable for his dignity and the free development of his personality.'[11]

On basis of the discussions, which were held on the section dealing with social rights, it becomes clear that the term 'social security' as used in this Article signifies 'social justice'; in other words everyone should enjoy economic, social and cultural rights, indispensable for his dignity and free development of his personality. This means in practice the enjoyment of the rights set forth in the following Articles (23-28). 'Social security' in this Article, therefore, is not used in its usual narrow sense of protection of the individual against need as is the case in Article 25.[12] The present term in Article 22 was inserted solely because the need was felt to insert somehow this idea (Verdoodt, 1964, pp. 210-215).

There are only two limitations which may be valid in respect to the articles in the Declaration dealing with the economic, social and cultural rights: national resources (and as such, feasabilities) and organizational methods (the means), as available in each territory. These 'criteria' or 'principles' are, in fact, generally valid whenever health care is applied at an international level.

2.1.2. Impact of the Declaration
The Universal Declaration is an enumeration of universal human rights, without any concomitant legal obligations. The major obstacle for effectiveness of an instrument for human rights, binding on all member states, is the great diversity of existing values and standards. Therefore the Universal Declaration could not be more than a mere enumeration of principles, not giving any precise definitions. A regional instrument, internationally enforceable, is easier to draw up as the values in a given region will somehow be more similar.

Thus, the Declaration is of primarily political authority, in that it enunciates a political programme for states, which is to be progressively achieved with the support of international legal processes.

2.1.3. Implementation of the Declaration
It was intended to put the Declaration into effect through the second section of the Bill of Human Rights, the 'Convention'. For this reason, a proposal on the insertion of a clause on the implementation of the Universal Declaration was rejected by the Assembly's committee on social, humanitarian and cultural affairs (third committee).

Since 1956, however, member states have been requested to produce every

11. See for instance E/CN.4/SR.67, 71 and 72.
12. See for instance E/CN.4/SR.70.

15

three years reports on human rights. Moreover various specialised agencies of the UN, one of them being the World Health Organization (WHO), though not being entrusted with safeguarding legal rights, submit information on human rights as far as governments in their reporting to these specialised agencies refer to specific matters in this context (see for instance documents E/CN.4/ 776 add. 2 and E/CN.4/758). Although the value of this type of reporting system appears to be of little consequence, it does regularly draw attention to the Universal Declaration.

In 1970 a procedure was adopted for dealing with communications relating to violations of human rights and fundamental freedoms. For this purpose the subcommittee on prevention of discrimination and protection of minorities has been given a specific mandate for referring particular situations to the commission (E/RES.1503 (XLVIII) of 19 June 1970).

2.2. UN INTERNATIONAL COVENANTS ON CIVIL AND POLITICAL RIGHTS, AND ON ECONOMIC, SOCIAL AND CULTURAL RIGHTS (1966)

2.2.1. Brief drafting history

When adopting the Universal Declaration of Human Rights, the Assembly requested the Council to ask the commission to prepare a 'Convention' on human rights (Council Resolutions 217 E and B (III) and 191 (VIII)). The purpose of the 'Convention' was to implement, under international control, the general principles proclaimed by the Universal Declaration.

The commission's first draft of the 'Convention' (sixth session, 27 March to 19 May 1950; E/1681) contained only civil and political rights, including an Article on 'torture' and another on 'medical experimentation'. [13]

The Assembly decided in 1950 (fifth session, 19 September to 15 December 1950), that the 'Convention' on human rights should also contain provisions on economic, social and cultural rights (Assembly Resolution 421 E (V) [14] of 4 December 1950 and Council Resolution 349 (XII) of 23 February 1951)).

During the seventh session of the commission (16 April to 19 May 1951) the representative of India presented a draft resolution in 'considering that economic, social and cultural rights, though equally fundamental, and therefore important, formed a separate category of rights from that of the civil and political rights, in that they were not justifiable rights and considering that the method of their implementation was, therefore, different', proposed recon-

13. For previous discussions in the commission (1949) on the inclusion of social rights, see E/1371, para. 17. The commission requested the preparation of a survey by the Secretary General on activities of other organs of the United Nations and specialised agencies falling within the scope of Articles 22-27 of the Universal Declaration.

This survey would enable the commission to decide on inclusion of these Articles into the Covenant or in later conventions. The survey (E/CN.4/364 rev. 1) includes a summary of the work of the World Health Organization. In this respect the following was stated: 'The recognition of the right to medical care is implicit in these activities when viewed as a whole' (paras. 130-135).
14. See also Assembly Resolution 303 I (XI) of 9 August 1950.

sideration of the decision of drafting just one text, including both categories of human rights (E/CN.4/619/Rev.1).

This proposal, however, was not accepted. It was in fact felt that the rights were interconnected and interdependent and that they should, therefore, be included in one instrument (E/1992, para. 67).

During the thirteenth session of the Council (30 July to 21 September 1951), however, Resolution 384 (XIII) was drawn up, asking the Assembly to review its decision to draft one 'Convention' covering all the pertinent rights. This resolution was inspired by the same arguments as those which caused the representative of India previously to make such a suggestion to the commission. The difference of nature of the rights, and therefore of a state's obligations in respect thereof and the international implementation in fact was in favour of two separate instruments (A 2929, p. 22-24).

The Assembly, at its sixth session (6 November 1951 to 5 February 1952), decided favourable on the preparation of two distinct Covenants (Assembly Resolution 543 (VI); see also Council Resolution 415 (S - 1)). [15]

The commission finished its work on the Covenants at its tenth session (23 February to 16 April 1954; E/2573). The texts were subsequently submitted to the Council and then to the Assembly (Council Resolution 545 B (XVIII)). On 16th December 1966 the Assembly adopted both Covenants (Assembly Resolution 220 A (XXI)). [16]

Unlike in the case of the civil and political rights, there were many problems to formulate the economic, social and cultural rights. The commission grappled with the difficulty of defining them in precise legal terms. Further, it was unclear whether all or only some of these rights as formulated in Articles 23-27 of the Universal Declaration were to be included in the Covenant. Another problem was the advisability of incorporating a broad, general provision modelled after Article 22 of the Universal Declaration, which would be designed to promote conditions of economic, social and cultural progress and development, and be supplemented by special undertakings. During the discussions in the commission the representative of the International Labour Organisation (ILO) suggested that articles on economic, social and cultural rights should be simply and precisely stated. This was emphasised because much of the detailed work was already being carried out by the competent specialised agencies. (See also the survey of activities of these organizations, E/CN.4/364 rev. 1.)

So as to ensure certain conditions for the enjoyment of these rights by all, he also recommended that specific obligations be placed upon states party to the Covenant. Turning to another aspect, the WHO representative advised for his part that 'provisions on the right to health (care), couched in terms identical to those used in the Constitution of the Organization, should be included by the commission in its draft, especially as they had been recognised by seventy nine countries, and as without them, other rights became almost

15. See also E/2256, Para. 56 for discussions on this subject in the commission.
16. See also A 2929, Ch. I and van Boven, 1968, p. 4 a.f.

meaningless' (E/1992, para. 38). (See also Assembly Resolution 544 (VI) and E/CN.4/650.)

The actual drafting of the substantive articles of both Covenants has been influenced by two 'schools of thought'. One was of the opinion that a brief clause of a general character would be sufficient, while the other insisted that each right, its scope, as well as its substance, its limitations, as well as the obligations of states in respect thereof, should be drafted with the greatest possible precision. As a result of these divergent views, some articles of the Covenants are formulated in a very general manner (for instance Article 6 of the International Covenant on Civil and Political Rights on the right to life, and Article 12 of the International Covenant on Economic, Social and Cultural Rights concerning the right to health care), while others are drawn up in much more elaborate terms (for instance Article 7 of the International Covenant on Civil and Political Rights on maltreatment and experimentation).

The Covenants are in fact a compromise formula of a mere declaration and a compendium of all civil and criminal codes and all social and educational laws (A/2929, pp. 24-27). The same compromise drafting is found in the European Convention on the Protection of Human Rights and Fundamental Freedoms.

2.2.2. Impact of the Covenants

In particular the International Covenant on Civil and Political Rights is more detailed and more precise than the Universal Declaration (E/Conf. 32/5, p. 66). Apart from the binding power of this Covenant on the state party to it, it also contains legislative processes. The provisions of the International Covenant on Civil and Political Rights are to be implemented through appropriate legislative, administrative and other measures (A/2929, p. 28).

With a few exceptions the legally not binding provisions of the Universal Declaration relating to civil and political rights were thus transformed into conventional international law. States party to it have entered into obligations of an international character (Article 2.2. of the Covenant).

However, the rights embodied in the Covenant are not strictly speaking absolute rights in so far as they do not necessarily have direct effect on the national legal system (Article 2.2.). They can furthermore be subject to derogation[17] (Article 4), except some of the rights, among which are the right to life (Article 6) and Article 7 dealing with maltreatment and experimentation (Article 4.2. refers). [18] Unlike the International Covenant on Civil and Political Rights, the International Covenant on Economic, Social and Cultural Rights should be looked upon as a 'Covenant Programme', which should be developed and completed by a series of subsequent measures on international, national and local as well as professional scale.

This Covenant has a distinctively progressive character (see Article 2 of the Covenant). States are committed to the extent of doing everything necessary

17. There is no such derogation clause in the other Covenant.
18. See also E/Conf. 32/5 p. 35.

by their own particular constitutional, legislative, administrative or other methods to ensure that steps are taken which will finally result in the full exercise of social, economic and cultural rights (human rights commission, tenth session, 23 February to 16 April 1954; E/2573).

There is yet another difference between both Covenants. The International Covenant on Economic, Social and Cultural Rights contains a *general, overall* clause of permissible limitations in Article 4, where it is stated that states may subject the rights contained in the Covenant only to such limitations as are determined by law, but only in sofar as this may be compatible with the nature of these rights and solely for the purpose of promoting the general welfare of a democratic society. The International Covenant on Civil and Political Rights on the other hand, defines precisely the permissible limitations for each formulated right, and regulations are clearly outlined for their direct application.

The International Covenant on Economic, Social and Cultural Rights furthermore contains a certain weakness, which comes to light, for instance, in Article 12 (on health), namely that a number of recognized rights have not been defined explicitly enough by means of social criteria and directives, which are their essential components. In respect to Article 12, for instance, it would have been more useful to have retained a definition of health, based on the one incorporated in the Constitution of the World Health Organization. Also, it would have been preferable to formulate the rights more clearly as states obligation.

Many of the rights proclaimed in this Covenant fall into the sphere of specialised agencies of the United Nations, such as the World Health Organization.

The role of these agencies in achieving the observance of these rights is explicitly recognized by the Covenant by way of the reporting system, provided for in Article 18.

2.2.3. Implementation of the Covenants [19]
The measures for implementation of the Covenants are different, due to the different nature of the rights contained in them. Unlike the rights contained in the International Covenant on Civil and Political Rights, which are to be applied immediately, the economic, social and cultural rights are to be achieved progressively and are formulated in general terms, with an overall clause concerning permissible limitations (see para. 2.2.2.).

Unlike the civil and political rights, the economic, social and cultural rights in fact require the supply of adequate resources and the organization of appropriate services by governments (E/CN.4/1213, para. 7).

— *International Covenant on Civil and Political Rights*
To implement on the international level the provisions of the International Covenant on Civil and Political Rights a (permanent) human rights committee

19. See for instance A/5411 and Resolution 9 (XXXIV) of 1978 of the human rights commission.

has been established. This committee may deal only with complaints by one state party, that another state party was not giving effect to a provision of the Covenant (A/2929, p. 29).

Various attempts to enlarge the right to initiate proceedings to include individuals and organizations failed for numerous reasons. [20]

Some of these were that only states were subjects of international law, that the Covenant would be fully safeguarded by a system of state to state complaints, and that international responsibility for the promotion of human rights was relatively a recent development. Though it was felt that the right of petition of individuals and non-governmental organizations ought to be recognized internationally, as it had been done nationally, there were fears of the right being abused.

Others, however, pleaded that the problem of implementation had also to be examined from the point of view of the individual, whose rights were being guaranteed. It was indicated that regional organizations and agreements, such as the European Convention on the Protection of Human Rights and Fundamental Freedoms of 1958 also recognized the position of the individual.

Finally, agreement was reached on a double system of implementation for the International Covenant on Civil and Political Rights. Under this scheme a compulsory reporting system is provided for. States parties report on measures they have adopted to give effect to the rights recognized in the Covenant, and on progress made in the enjoyment of those rights. These reports are submitted to the human rights committee for possible comments to the states and, or transmission to the Council (Article 40 of the Covenant).

There is furthermore an optional system of fact finding and conciliation, which applies to states, which have expressly agreed to this procedure (Article 41 of the Covenant). This system is supplemented by a provision for ad hoc conciliation, if the parties to a dispute agree (Article 42 of the Covenant). Individual petitions or communications to the human rights committee are possible by virtue of a separate 'Optional Protocol to the International Covenant on Civil and Political Rights' (Assembly Resolution 2200 A (XXI) of 16 December 1966; doc. 334, para. 68).

The functions of the human rights committee in respect to inter-state complaints are confined to fact-finding and conciliation. The reports of the committee, to be elaborated on every case, are sent to the states concerned and then to the Secretary General of the United Nations for publication. In cases where no friendly solution could be reached, the committee will state its opinion in the report as to whether the facts found disclose a breach by the state concerned of its obligations under the Covenant (Article 42.7 (c) of the Covenant).

Thus, the work of the committee has no judicial or compulsory character, its functions being of a quasi judicial nature. There was a prevailing opinion, when deciding for this procedure, that the publicity given to any case would be an effective means of enforcement, although it was also expressed that the

20. See A/2929, pp. 233-253 for a description of discussions which took place on this subject.

decisions of the human rights committee should be mandatory and that it should be authorized to make recommendations or to suggest possible solutions (A 2929, p. 260, para. 108 a.f.).

— International Covenant on Economic, Social and Cultural Rights
The implementation of the International Covenant on Economic, Social and Cultural Rights is laid down in Articles 16-25. The system chosen is one of a reporting procedure. States parties are to submit reports to the Secretary General of the United Nations for the attention of the Council on the measures adopted and the progress made in achieving the observance of the rights recognized in the Covenant. These reports are to be submitted in stages in accordance with the programme established by the Council. The Council may transmit to the commission on human rights for study and general recommendations the reports received from states as well as those submitted by specialised agencies in pursuance of Article 18. The Council may also submit reports on progress made in achieving general observance of the rights set forth in the Covenant to the General Assembly. The Council is, in this system, the main organ of implementation (E/CN.4/AC.21/L 1).

The purpose of this reporting system is to ascertain the progress made by states parties in achieving observance of the rights recognized in the Covenant on the one hand, and on the other to be informed about any factors or difficulties affecting the degree of fulfilment of obligations under the Covenant (A 5411, para. 12, p. 8).

The Commission, during its tenth session (23 February to 16 April 1954), considered the desirability of applying the human rights committee procedure of the International Covenant on Civil and Political Rights equally to the International Covenant on Economic, Social and Cultural Rights, but decided against such a provision.

It was, in fact, considered impractical to apply this particular complaint procedure to the International Covenant on Economic, Social and Cultural Rights, where complaints could only concern insufficient programmes for the achievement of the rights set forth in the Covenant (A/2929, pp. 357-359), and where it would be difficult to determine what the stage of progress in any particular case would be.

However, it was also argued that the rights contained in the two Covenants were closely interrelated and that therefore the full implementation of one category of rights would be inconceivable without a full implementation of the other category.

The following arguments prevailed: The economic, social and cultural rights were to be achieved progressively. This justified two distinct methods of implementation. The periodic reporting system, in close co-operation with the specialised agencies of the United Nations concerned, was the best method of implementation for this category of human rights.

The World Health Organization was one of the specialised agencies, which stressed the importance of these agencies for implementing the economic, social and cultural rights because they are technically qualified for this purpose.

The arrangements made for implementation through the specialised agencies of the United Nations, in particular in Articles 16.2 (b) and 18, were based on the concept, that the general obligations contained in the Covenant would be elaborated by the competent specialised agencies into detailed obligations required for the realization of the rights set forth in the Covenant, that these organizations will report on progress made in achieving the observance of the provisions of the Covenant falling within their scope of activities.

In 1951 the WHO suggested to the commission that full use would be made of the reports received by the Director General of the WHO from member states under Articles 61-64 of its Constitution. Reports to the Organization could in fact be prepared in such a way that they would show clearly the progress achieved in implementation of the right to the enjoyment of the highest attainable standard of health (E/CN.4/544 Add. 1).

The states parties to the Covenant agreed that international action for the achievement of the rights set forth in it, may include the conclusion of conventions, the adoption of recommendations, the furnishing of technical assistance, and the holding of regional and technical meetings (Article 23; see also Article 22 for international action by specialised agencies in this respect).

Thus, the implementation system under the International Covenant on Economic, Social and Cultural Rights is not so much a machinery of enforcement, but rather of mutual aid and progressive promotion of human rights.

The proper way of implementation of this Covenant is a constant preoccupation of the commission on human rights, which has placed it as a standing item with high priority on its agenda. In Resolution 1988 (LX) of the Economic and Social Council a programme is established in accordance with which states parties and specialised agencies should furnish reports on the various articles of the Covenant. (Reports relating to Article 12 on the right to health care will become due in 1980.) Representatives of specialised agencies may take part in proceedings of a working group of the Council, which is to assist the Council in the consideration of reports submitted by states and specialised agencies. There is, as yet, no specific procedure for examination of reports by the working group; specific standards or criteria to be applied to various expressions used in the various Articles are still missing (such as in Article 12: 'highest attainable standard of ... health').

2.3. EUROPEAN CONVENTION FOR THE PROTECTION OF HUMAN RIGHTS AND FUNDAMENTAL FREEDOMS (1950)

2.3.1. Brief drafting history

The first international instrument on human rights in the European region was the Council of Europe's Convention for the Protection of Human Rights and Fundamental Freedoms. The instrument was the first achievement of the Council of Europe in the field of international legislation (Collected edition of the travaux préparatoires, 1975, Vol. I, p. XXII).

The roots of the Convention precede the Council of Europe itself, the statutes of which were signed on 5 May 1949. The basis of the Convention was the 'message to Europeans' adopted at the final session of the Congress of Europe, which was convened by the (unofficial) International Committee of Movement for European Unity (the Hague, 8 to 10 May 1948) (Robertson, 1948, p. 6). This message stated inter alea:

'We desire a Charter of Human Rights guaranteeing liberty of thought, assembly and expression as well as the right to form a political opposition; we desire a Court of Justice with adequate sanctions for the implementation of this Charter' (Doc. 3334).

The drafting of a European Convention on Human Rights and of a Statute of the European Court of human rights were subsequently taken up by the International Juridical Section of the Movement in 1949. The drafts prepared by this section were then submitted to the Committee of Ministers [21] of the Council of Europe on 12 July 1949. [22] But it was on the initiative of the Consultative Assembly [23] of the Council of Europe that the matter was, in fact, placed on the agenda of the Assembly.

The Committee of Ministers, who were first to approve this agenda did not favour the inclusion of the subject, as they were at the time of the opinion that the subject was sufficiently covered by, and studied within the United Nations. They therefore decided on 9 August 1949 not to include an item on human rights on the Assembly's agenda. The Assembly then made a formal proposal to the Committee of Ministers to add such an item on its agenda, which was approved on 13 August 1949. That same year the Consultative Assembly reported on this matter to the Committee of Ministers (Recommendation no. 38 of 8 September 1949; doc. 108 of the Consultative Assembly) proposing that the Committee of Ministers should draw up a draft Convention.

On the initiative of the Committee of Ministers the proposals put forward by the Consultative Assembly were subsequently studied by a comittee of governmental experts in February and March of 1950, in the light of the United Nations work in this field.

This committee proceeded with its task to transform the recommendation of the Consultative Assembly into a draft convention and to solve existing problems of methodology (mere reference to relevant articles of the Declaration of Human Rights of the United Nations, as suggested by the Consultative Assembly, or insertion of these articles in the text), on the basis of a report of the secretariat general. This report not only contained the text of the relevant articles of the UN Declaration of Human Rights, but also included a comparison with the then available draft text of the UN International Covenant on Civil and Political Rights. The committee of governmental experts presented its report to the Committee of Ministers on 16 March 1950 (doc. A 925). This

---

21 This body is composed of the ministers of foreign affairs of the Council of Europe member states, or their substitutes.
22. Art. 3 of the Statutes provides that: Every Member of the Council of Europe must accept the principles of the rule of law and the enjoyment by all persons within its jurisdiction of human rights and fundamental freedoms ...
23. This body groups together parliamentarians from Council of Europe member states. In 1974 its name was changed into 'Parliamentary Assembly'.

report contained two alternatives on the method for the drafting of the Convention, leaving it to the Committee of Ministers to take a (political) decision on this matter. The first method consisted in a system similar to the one applied in the UN Declaration, namely a mere enumeration of the rights to be protected. The alternative method parted from the concept that the rights should be clearly defined and that possible limitations to these rights should also be included in a detailed manner.

The Committee of Ministers then decided on the 1st April 1950 to convene a conference of senior officials to put forward a proposal on this matter and to further prepare the draft Convention accordingly (doc. Committee of Ministers, 3rd session, page 13).

The conference, which met on 8 to 17 June 1950, presented its report on 19 June 1950, including the text for a draft convention. This draft was a compromise solution between the two systems and also contained a proposal for the creation of a European Court with optional jurisdiction (doc. A 1431). The final text of the Convention which was largely inspired by the UN Declaration of Human Rights as well as by discussions on the preparation of the UN International Covenant on Civil and Political Rights, was signed by the Committee of Ministers at their 6th Session on 4 November 1950.

When drawing up the Convention, the question of including economic and social rights was also discussed. It was fully recognized that the full and complete legal equality of man could be reached only when the political and civil rights were complemented by economic, social and cultural rights. Yet, it was felt in this respect that these latter rights were too controversial and too difficult to enforce to be appropriate for inclusion in combination with the classical, individual rights in one instrument. It was, therefore, decided to draft two different instruments, the economic and social rights being set forth at a later date (1961) in the European Social Charter (see below, para. 2.4.).

2.3.2. Impact of the Convention

As was seen before, under para. 2.3.1., the European formulation of human rights not only consisted of a general statement of the rights to be guaranteed, as had been the case with the Universal Declaration of Human Rights, but comprised in most cases also a more detailed definition of possible restrictions (Weil, 1963, p. 31). This system was adopted with a view to guarantee fundamental rights and freedoms of the individual in such a way that at the same time those of others would also be fully respected: the limitations to some of the rights contained in the Convention are based on the individual rights of others.

Thus, for instance, 'health' appears in various articles (see Articles 8-11) as one of the conditions which might limit some of the rights in the Convention (such as privacy, religion, expression, assembly). 'Health' in this context is used with a view to maintain the particular state of health, which is protected by the states parties to the Convention in applying democratic principles of state ruling, and not with a view to provide adequate health care, which is covered by the European Social Charter.

24

Application nr. 104/55 is an example where this restriction has been applied by the European commission on human rights. The case was brought before the commission on basis of an alleged breach of Article 8 of the Convention (respect of family life) by the Federal Republic of Germany in its (now obsolete) legislation whereby homosexuality was made punishable. The commission judged legitimate this legislation on grounds of the protection of health (decision of 17 December 1955, Yearbook I, p. 229). (The evolution of morals has caused since the abandonment of this principle in the Federal law. It is thought most likely that the commission, if seized again with such a case, would also come to a contrary decision.'[24]

In applying the combined system of 'enumeration' and 'definition', the Convention transformed fifteen of the principles of the United Nations Declaration into legal obligations for the member states.

Where the Declaration does not contain legal effects for securing the rights and liberties of the individual, the purpose of the Convention was to provide for such legal guarantees at a regional scale.

The Convention lays down minimum requirements for the legal protection of the safety and freedom of the individual, which may not be violated and thus contains the basic requirements of freedom and the rule of law.

In a number of states the normative provisions of the Convention have the force of internal law; many national courts apply the 'European standards'. There is thus a continuing process of interaction between European law and national law; in many cases national law was amended in order to conform with European standards (doc. 334).

The rights contained in the Convention may be subject to derogation in time of war and public emergency. No derogation is allowed from Article 2 (right to life) except in respect of death resulting from lawful acts of war, or from Article 3, dealing with maltreatment and experimentation (Article 15 refers).

2.3.3. Implementation of the Convention

The material contents of the Convention and the UN International Covenant on Civil and Political Rights are very similar. The European Convention however goes much further in its international control of implementation.

For this purpose there are three bodies vested with jurisdictional review powers:
— the European commission of human rights;
— the European Court of human rights;
— the Committee of Ministers of the Council of Europe.

Like the procedure provided for in the International Covenant on Civil and Political Rights, the Convention does not limit the appeal procedure only to inter-state applications, though the complaints procedure is more far reaching than the one under the Covenant.

The main purpose of the Convention being the protection of individuals,

---

24. A similar restriction of the liberty of the individual is in Article 5. 1.e., where detention is considered lawful for the prevention of the spread of infectious diseases or in cases of alcoholics and drug addicts.

and not of states, the elaborators of the Convention wanted to give the individual a right of appeal to an international organ, which is competent to call the offending state party to account. Thus individuals as well as non-governmental organizations may bring a cause of alleged breaches of the rights set forth in the Convention by a state party to it before the European commission of human rights, provided that the state concerned has declared its willingness to submit to such a procedure. Whenever relevant, and here appears the main difference with the Covenant, such a case may be brought to the Court, through the channels of the commission. (Direct appeal to the Court remains reserved to states and the European commission.)

It should, however, be added that, like the optional Protocol to the Covenant whereby communications from individuals may be received by the human rights committee, the right of petition of the individual, as well as the jurisdiction of the European Court were made optional, because various governments had some hesitations to accept this innovation in international law.

A merit of this system is moreover that solutions reached in a case of an individual application are of benefit to those who are affected by similar problems (doc. 3334). The commission of human rights has no power of decision. The report expressing its opinion is transmitted to the Committee of Ministers of the Council of Europe. It is then possible that either the commission or the government concerned refers the matter to the Court of human rights. Contracting parties, who have accepted the Court, have recognized its jurisdiction as compulsory. In those cases, which are not referred to the Court, the Committee of Ministers decides whether there has been violation of the Convention, but it is left to the government concerned to decide what remedial action is necessary. The decision of the Committee of Ministers is binding on the contracting parties. In this respect the control procedure under the European Convention (binding character of decisions) goes further than those under the International Covenant on Civil and Political Rights where the fact finding and the opinion of the human rights committee is limited to a mere reporting system.

It is possible that problems arise from the co-existence of the two supervisory systems under these two distinct human rights instruments. In conformity with Article 33 of the UN Charter and on basis of a study made by the Council of Europe committee of experts on human rights it has been decided to adopt the following policy. Member states of the Council of Europe, in cases of inter-states complaints or 'communications', will use the procedures provided for in the European Convention, but will accept the procedures provided for in the UN International Covenant on Civil and Political Rights for cases which may be brought against them by non-European states (Resolution (70) 17 on the procedure for dealing with inter-states complaints).

Whenever individual complaints or 'communications' are involved, the individual is free to make a choice between the two procedures on grounds that the governing consideration should be the desire to secure the most effective protection of individual rights. An applicant is however not allowed to submit the same case simultaneously or successively to the bodies under both systems. [25]

2.4. EUROPEAN SOCIAL CHARTER (1961)

2.4.1. Brief drafting history
The establishment of the Social Charter was envisaged after the completion of the European Human Rights Convention. It was in fact already explicit from the Preamble of this Convention that such an instrument should be prepared. (See the 6th clause of the Preamble 'to take the first steps for the collective enforcement of certain rights stated in the Universal Declaration'.)

It is clear from this wording that the Human Rights Convention was only a first step and that other instruments should follow to enforce all rights contained in the Universal Declaration on a European level. Discussions on the Social Charter began in 1953, while the Charter itself was signed in Torino (Italy) on 18 October 1961 and entered into force on 26 February 1965. The preparation of the Social Charter was part of the social programme of the Council of Europe, which is based on two major principles: firstly the progressive harmonization (as far as possible) of legislation and practices of member states in the social field and, secondly, the suppression of discrimination, which exists in this field. (The Assembly recommended already in 1951 that study be given to a common policy in social matters (Recommendation no. 14.))

Various kinds of instruments were held as an example for drafting the Charter, such as:
— international declarations and agreements on economic and social rights, drawn up by international organizations (such as the UN Declaration of Human Rights, the UN International Covenant on Economic, Social and Cultural Rights, and the European Human Rights Convention);
— statutes of international organizations, as far as they pertained to these rights (such as those of the United Nations, the International Labour Organisation, the World Health Organization and the Council of Europe);
— conventions of the International Labour Organisation;
— national constitutions and national human rights instruments (such as the American Declaration on Human Rights and Obligations, Bogota, 1948).

(European Social Charter, Collected texts of the travaux préparatoires, Vol. I, p. 186, unpublished; 'What is the Council of Europe doing to protect human rights', Council of Europe, 1977, p. 49.)

The purpose of the Charter was to define the social objectives aimed at by members (a guide in particular for a common European social policy), to establish social principles that correspond to individual rights and to lay down the aims of a European social policy in these specific fields as well as to

25. See for instance Consultative Assembly's doc. 3334 of 13 September 1973, Report on the 25th anniversary of the Universal Declaration and 20th anniversary of the European Convention on Human Rights, paras. 77 and 78.

27

establish binding provisions which would guarantee certain minimum standards in vital social fields (document 312 of the Consultative Assembly, September 1954).

The outline for a Social Charter was first given in a memorandum by the secretariat of the Council of Europe on the role of the Organization in the social field (document 140, 1953). [26] This memorandum was transmitted to the executive body of the Organization, the Committee of Ministers, as well as to the deliberative body, the Consultative Assembly. Having received a positive advice from the latter body, the Committee of Ministers then charged one of its governmental expert committees, namely the social committee, to prepare a draft Social Charter. At the same time the Consultative Assembly instructed one of its committees – the committee on social questions –, to proceed with the drafting of such a Charter.

Various drafts, elaborated on by the latter committee in close co-operation with others, such as particularly the political and economic ones, were presented to the Assembly. The successive drafts were prepared out of consideration to present a text which would make real progress, whilst still remaining acceptable to all. Thus the various texts took account of the discussions in the Assembly.

The first draft, presented to the Assembly in October 1955 (7th session, doc. 403) was considered too far reaching in suggesting that the supervision of the Charter should be the responsibility of a European economic and social council, to be composed of representatives of employers, workers and the general public.

A second draft was then submitted to the Assembly in April 1956 (8th Session, doc. 488), which in every aspect was very similar to the first draft, except for the matter of implementation. In this draft it was suggested to entrust the main supervision of the implementation of the Charter to an intergovernmental social committee, while some control would be entrusted to the Assembly. This proposal was felt to be too weak and a third draft was presented in September 1956 (8th Session, doc. 536) which closely followed the second draft and contained the suggestions to create an organ, 'the European Social Chamber', to be composed of representatives of various sectors of society, which, in a consultative capacity, would be responsible for promoting the fulfilment of the social policy of the Council of Europe and in particular, the implementation of the Charter. This text was adopted by the Assembly in October 1956 (Recommendation 104, 1956).

At the same time the (governmental) social committee proceeded with its work and undertook a survey of the practices of member states of the Organization in the present field, as well as a study of the standards contained in the various international instruments. The committee prepared draft provisions

26. For a clear description on the drafting history of the European Social Charter see for instance F. Tjennford, 1961, the European Social Charter, an instrument of social collaboration in Europe. See also 'Drawing up and implementation of the European Social Charter', doc. AS/Coll/Charte 1, Council of Europe, 1977, pp. 3-8.

concerning some basic social rights to be included in an international instrument. This committee was of the opinion that such an instrument should be a purely declaratory one, of a general nature. The Assembly on the contrary was strongly in favour of a mandatory instrument in the form of a Convention.

Inadequate co-ordination of activities at these two levels at this stage of drafting resulted in a difference of view points on the nature the instrument should have.

To break through this deadlock, the Committee of Ministers instructed its social committee in December 1956 (Resolution (56) 25) inter alea to direct its work in the present field in consultation with European employers and trade union organizations towards the establishment of a European Social Charter and to continue its work on the lines followed sofar by the Assembly.

The final draft of the social committee, which took largely account of the work done by the Assembly, was completed in February 1958 and, in order to enable those concerned to express their opinion, was submitted in December of the same year to a tripartite conference.

This conference was convened by the International Labour Organisation at the request of the Council of Europe and was composed of representatives of governments, employers and workers.

During this conference important amendments were presented with a view to strengthen the text and to define more clearly and in a more far-reaching manner, the obligations of the states party to the Social Charter.

The text was then again submitted to the Assembly and the (governmental) social committee. Its final form is a compromise text between the view-points of these two bodies.

The fact that the European Social Charter contains rights, which are less legal principles than rules of action, and that many of the rights involve expenditure by the contracting parties, may well explain why its drafting was so slow, and why sofar only little more than half of the Council of Europe member states have ratified the Charter ('What is the Council of Europe doing to protect human rights', Council of Europe, 1977, p. 50; see also 'Drawing up and implementation of the European Social Charter', doc. AS/Coll/Charte 1-E, Council of Europe, 1977, pp. 1-3).

2.4.2. Impact of the Social Charter
The Charter can be seen as the counterpart and complement of the European Human Rights Convention.

With the coming into being of the Charter a gap was filled, which existed in the social policy in Europe. Until then, the approach by the Council of Europe had been empirical, dealing with social problems one by one as the need arose. Co-ordination and general planning were missing at that time. The Charter establishes a guide for common social policy; social programmes are given a definite direction and principles of social justice are laid down.

The Charter is a political and legal instrument as it confirms fundamental rules for safeguarding the liberty, dignity and security of human beings in the social field. [27] Minimum standards are drawn up for wide fields of general social policy, including public health.

As with the Human Rights Convention, the Charter is a legal instrument for ensuring the effective enjoyment of recognized rights and not a purely declaratory document. Unlike the Convention, the Charter does not, however, include common legal obligations. The variety in social and economic levels of the member states is such that a system of enforcement of the social rights by the means of international law and judgements would be impracticable: hence, the social rights have not yet reached the full stage of international protection (v. Asbeck, 1964, p. 447). In this respect, the Charter is only the formal complement of the European Convention; it is not a material complement of the European Convention, because it does not create real international legal protection for the rights it contains.

The Charter confirms, in its Preamble, a certain number of individual social rights and principles of common social policy.

The contents of these rights and principles are further elaborated in Part II of the Charter, which includes the measures to be taken by contracting parties for ensuring the effective exercise of each of the rights covered by the Charter, as well as the general conditions governing the exercise of each individual right. Measures to be taken with a view to the realization of the rights are either formulated in the form of concrete obligations (undertakings on the part of states parties) or by way of some examples of measures which could be taken. Action to be taken by states parties in respect of these rights may be either of a legislative or of an administrative nature.

The Charter deals exclusively with obligations on the part of states parties and does not refer to the plights of the individual. This is in contrast with one of the instruments which was held as an example for the elaboration of the Charter, namely the American Declaration of Human Rights and Obligations (Bogota, 1948).

Each right included in the Charter is cited in the heading of the Article dealing with the specific right, without further defining such a right. The reason for this is that the possibility of defining social rights was considered doubtful, especially where some of the rights covered by the Social Charter were thought to be moral, or natural, but not legal rights. Restrictions may be placed on the exercise of the rights contained in the Charter, provided they are laid down by law and necessary in a democratic society in order to safeguard the rights and freedoms of others or protect the public interest, national security, public health or morals (Article 31). This general clause of possible limitations, which is similar to the one used in the International Covenant on Economic, Social and Cultural Rights (Article 4), does not appear in the European Convention.

Derogation from the obligations of the Charter is possible in time of war and public emergency (Article 30). The comparable Covenant does not contain such a derogation clause.

27. European Social Charter, Collected texts of the travaux préparatoires, Vol. I, p. 413; unpublished.

Another point of weakness in the Charter is that there is no obligation for contracting parties to accept all the rights included in Part II (see also below, para. 2.4.3., Implementation of the Charter). It should be emphasised in this respect, that the positive aspect of the Social Charter lies in the fact that it creates a framework for a common social programme, as in the case of the International Covenant on Economic, Social and Cultural Rights. It is also important that at least some of the principles proclaimed by the Charter are binding upon the states party to it. The advantage of the flexibility of the Charter lies moreover in the fact that national commitments may be adjusted according to economic and social conditions and that the evolution of the latter will stimulate the scope of obligations. The Charter meets in this way to a certain extent the needs existing on an international level to harmonize to some degree social conditions and social policy.

2.4.3. Implementation of the Social Charter

The Charter has been drawn up in such a manner, that it constitutes a kind of 'legal framework': the establishment of a series of measures and programmes for a piecemeal implementation as provided for in Parts III and IV of the text. Seven of the articles contained in the Charter are regarded as fundamental and as such form what is generally known as the 'hard core' (nucleus). The right to 'protection of health' (Article 11) does not figure among this 'hard core'. Each contracting party chooses at least five of these seven articles and undertakes to implement them fully and promptly. There are a further twelve articles, from which it must select a certain number of complete articles or *separate paragraphs.* [28]

This system of piecemeal implementation was a compromise solution between the views of the Consultative Assembly to make all rights contained in Part II binding upon contracting parties and the views initially held by members of the Social Committee to be content with a mere declaratory character of the Charter.

The system adopted under the Social Charter is based on the model applied by the International Labour Organisation. The concept of gradual implementation was chosen because it was recognized that the achievement of at least part of the rights contained in the Social Charter depends largely upon the economic and social structures in the states party to the Charter and might, therefore, be of a too high level to be attained immediately.

Therefore, the scope of the undertakings of the contracting parties varies in accordance with the time it takes to fulfil these undertakings (European Social Charter, Collected texts of the travaux préparatoires, Vol. II, p. 96, unpublished). The United Nations International Covenant on Economic, Social and Cultural Rights, which served as a model for the Social Charter, also contains this concept of gradual implementation (Articles 16-18). But the former instrument does not go as far as the Social Charter, which imposes the immediate application of some of its rights. The system of implementation chosen for the Social Charter is realistic, because it enables states to adhere to

28. Ireland has only accepted para. 3 of Article 11: prevention of epidemic, endemic and other diseases.

the Instrument who would otherwise be opposed to the adoption of one or more of the rights contained in the Charter. In this way much is left to the latitude of the contracting parties.

The machinery for supervision of application of the Charter, which is contained in Part IV of its text is confined to a reporting system.

Reports concerning accepted provisions are to be sent to the Secretary General of the Council of Europe two-yearly (Article 21 of the Social Charter) and those concerning provisions which are not accepted at the appropriate intervals (Article 22 of the Social Charter). The latter provision is the only (moral) pressure which can be put on governments to accept the provisions of Part II of the Charter to which Governments did not yet subscribe.

Regarding the application of Article 21 a form has been prepared, the terms of which determine the way in which the Charter's provisions are interpreted. The latter is particularly important in the case that an article of the Charter is worded in such general terms, that it is essential to give it a positive content. This is, for instance, the case with Article 11, dealing with the right to health care. For the purpose of controlling the implementation of this Article a series of questions has been embodied in the form relative to:
— principal medical statistics;
— information on preventive institutions, medical practitioners and auxiliaries, hospitals and treatment organizations;
— health protection of children;
— public health, pollution, health control of food-stuffs;
— fight against social scourges: drugs, alcoholism, tobacco;
— health education;
— methods of financing health measures etc.
('Drawing up and implementation of the European Social Charter; Doc. As/Coll/Charte 1, Council of Europe, 1977, pp. 17-19).

There are two committees charged successively with the examination of reports received in application of Article 21. Firstly, they are examined by a committee, composed of independent experts of recognized competence in international *social* questions (Articles 24 and 25 of the Social Charter). The International Labour Organisation is invited to the meetings of this committee in a consultative capacity (Article 26 of the Social Charter). Secondly, the reports are examined by a subcommittee of the governmental social committee. This subcommittee is composed of one representative from each of the contracting parties, while international organizations of employers and trade unions, as well as international non-governmental organizations may attend meetings in a consultative capacity (Article 27 of the Social Charter). The Committee of Ministers adopts recommendations on the basis of the reports and conclusions of the two committees by a two-third majority, after consultation of the Parliamentary Assembly (Article 29 of the Social Charter). Thus the Assembly has a role to play, as it may express its opinion on reports of the committee of experts (Article 28 of the Social Charter). By this method national parliaments are able to exercise some pressure on governmental bodies. [29]

This system of supervision, unlike the system in force under the European Convention on the Protection of Human Rights and Fundamental Freedoms, is not a control of legality but merely an 'efficacity' control. There is no possibility of insisting states parties to whom a recommendation has been addressed in conformity with Article 29 of the Social Charter, to respect such a recommendation. In this respect the present procedure is more of a nature to assist governments in the realization of the rights set forth in the Charter. The control system of the Charter has not proven very successful for various reasons:

— the workload both of contracting parties and the supervisory organs which is brought about by a strict application of Article 21 of the Charter (reports concerning accepted provisions) is considered too heavy;
— the procedure provided for in Article 22 of the Charter (reports concerning provisions which are not accepted) has not yet been put into practice by the Committee of Ministers.

The Assembly has on various occasions drawn the attention of the Committee of Ministers to this inconvenience, stressing at the same time the need to continue the supervision of the Charter with the requisite thoroughness and to develop the supervision carried out so far (see, for instance, doc. 3592 of 24 March 1975 of the Parliamentary Assembly).

29. It is noteworthy that none of the governmental committees, which are dealing with matters concerning the realization of the right to health care, are somehow involved with the discussions on reports concerning action taken in respect to the right to health care (see Part B, CH. III, para. 4.).

II. Discussion of the relevant articles

Introduction

Two of the rights, contained in the international instruments which include cicil and political rights (see Introduction, para. 2.2.) are relevant for the protection of the individual against violation of his particular level of physical and mental health. They are the right to life (Article 3 of the UN Universal Declaration of Human Rights; Article 6 of the UN International Covenant on Civil and Political Rights; Article 2 of the European Convention for the Protection of Human Rights and Fundamental Freedoms) and the prohibition of maltreatment and experimentation without free consent (Articles 5, 7 and 3 respectively of the three instruments concerned).

The international instruments which include economic, social and cultural rights (see Introduction, para. 2.2.) each contain a right to health care (Article 25 of the UN Universal Declaration of Human Rights; Article 12 of the International Covenant on Economic, Social en Cultural Rights and Article 11 of the European Social Charter).

The development-process of the formulation of these rights during their various drafting stages up until their final wording will now be explored for each of these rights subsequently under the relevant instruments (para. 1-3: individual rights; para. 4-5: social rights).

1. Right to life

1.1. UN UNIVERSAL DECLARATION OF HUMAN RIGHTS (ARTICLE 3)

1.1.1. Brief drafting history
Article 3 of the Universal Declaration reads as follows:

'Everyone has the right to life, liberty and the security of person.'

Initial drafts for this Article were as follows:

— 'Everyone has the right to life. This right can be denied only to persons, who have been convicted under general law of some crime to which the death penalty is attached' (draft outline of an International Bill of Human Rights, secretariat, E/CN.4/AC.1/3, Article 3 and E/CN.4/21 Annex A, Article 3); [30]
— 'The right to life is fundamental and may not be denied to any person except under conviction of the gravest of crimes under general law providing for the penalty of

30. Article 5: 'Everyone has the right to personal liberty' (E/CN.4/AC.1/3; A/CN.4/21 Annex A).

34

death ... .' (United States suggestion to redraft the Article prepared by the secretariat, E/CN.4/21 Annex C, Article 8);
— 'Every human being has the right to life and to respect of his physical inviolability ... .' (Text of temporary working group of the drafting committee of the commission on human rights, prepared by the French representative, E/CN.4/21 Annex D, Article 7). [31]

The drafting committee, when discussing the text for this Article (first session, 9 to 24 June 1947) was opposed to formulating a text in which the United Nations would impliedly approve the death sentence, on the grounds that it was the general tendency to abolish it (Verdoodt, 1964, p. 96).

It was, moreover, pointed out that the word 'life' was intended to mean *physical existence* only and nothing more (E/CN.4/AC 1/SR.3). It was decided to confine the text of the Article to the ideas of liberty and personal security, so that the following text was submitted to the commission:

'Everyone has the right to life, to personal liberty and to personal security' (E/CN.4/21 Annex F, Article 7). Alternative texts, prepared by the representatives of Chile and Lebanon were submitted to the commission at the same time [32], who felt that the idea expressed in the present Article should be expanded:

— Chilean proposal:
'Unborn children and incurables, mentally defectives and lunatics, shall have the right to life.
All persons shall have the right to the enjoyment of conditions of life enabling them to live in dignity and to develop their personality adequately.
Persons unable to maintain themselves by their own efforts shall be entitled to maintenance and assistance.'
— Lebanon proposal:
'Everyone has the right to life and bodily integrity from the moment of conception, regardless of physical or mental condition, to liberty and security of person.'

Discussions in the working group on the Declaration of Human Rights [33] (established by the commission on human rights during its second session, 2 to 17 December 1947) concentrated on various matters, including:
— whether the right to life should also include a specification of the biological moment when life began (vs. Lebanon proposal, protection of life born or concieved). (The Representative of the commission on the status of woman declared in this respect, that, if a notion such as 'from the first moment of his physical development' would be included, this could not be reconciled with the provision of certain advanced legislation providing for the right to abortion);
— whether a statement should be included that the right to life should be protected regardless of physical or mental conditions (vs. Chilean and Lebanon proposals);

31. Article 8: 'Everyone has the right to personal liberty and security' (E/CN.4/21 Annex D).
32. E/CN.4/21 Annex F, Article 7.
33. 6 to 10 December 1947.

— whether it should be expressed that individuals should be able to live their lives in conditions worthy of human race (vs. Chilean proposal).

The majority of the working group were of the opinion that the text as prepared by the drafting committee covered all aspects (E/CN.4/AC.2/SR.3). It was therefore decided to maintain the draft of the drafting committee (E/CN.4/57, Article 7). The representative of France, moreover, insisted that details on this subject should be included in the 'Convention'.

The commission on human rights adopted the draft Declaration at its second session (E/600). [34]

The drafting committee at its second session (13-21 May 1948) confirmed its previous text (E/CN.4/95) [35], which, except for some textual changes, was approved by the General Assembly. Amendments presented to the text of this Article in the committee on social, humanitarian and cultural affairs (third committee) of the Assembly [36] were all rejected on grounds that they had already been dealt with in other Articles of the Declaration. Among these proposals were the following:
— abolishment of the death sentence;
— concrete obligations of the state to protect individuals against any criminal attempts;
— inclusion of 'integrity' after 'security' (A/C.3/259 and A/C.3/259 add. 1). The last suggestion was rejected on grounds that 'security' sufficiently covered the idea of physical integrity (Verdoodt, 1964, p. 100). The 'physical integrity' (medical experimentation) covered by the term 'security of person', is further safeguarded in Article 5 of the Declaration (see below, para. 2.1.).

1.1.2. Some conclusions
The rather vague, overall statement contained in Article 3 is intended to express the idea of 'liberty' (the protection of human life and the right to existence), which is elaborated in the following nine Articles.

These Articles express a progressive extension and growing precision of the concepts introduced in Article 3.

With reference to the preparatory work and in the context of the Declaration as a whole, Verdoodt (1964, pp. 99-100) seems to correctly interpret Article 3 as declaring a right which everyone has to 'physical existence'. The right to 'health protection' is clearly indicated here, provided 'physical existence' is qualified. The Article, however, does not give any indication on the scope of 'physical existence', and, therefore, does not give any guidelines for subjects as abortion (the beginning of existence) and euthanasia (ending of existence, the right to die).

During the various drafting stages attempts were made to qualify 'physical existence' by explicitly stating that the right to life begins at the moment of

---

34. For discussions during the second session of the commission on human rights, see E/CN.4/SR 35. For comments by governments on this text, see E/CN.4/82 and E/CN.4/82 add. 12.
35. See E/CN.4/102 for an amendment proposal from China.
36. Third session, 21 September to 12 December 1948.

conception. However, the opinion of those, who feared difficulties with existing abortion law, if such a notion were included, prevailed (Verdoodt, 1964, p. 100).

1.2. UN INTERNATIONAL COVENANT ON CIVIL AND POLITICAL RIGHTS (ARTICLE 6)

1.2.1. Brief drafting history

Article 6 the International Covenant on Civil and Political Rights reads as follows:

'1. Every human being has the inherent right to life. This right shall be protected by law. No one shall be arbitrarily deprived of his life.

2. In countries which have not abolished the death penalty, sentence of death may be imposed only for the most serious crimes in accordance with law in force at the time of the commission of the crime and not contrary to the provisions of the present Covenant and to the Convention on the Prevention and Punishment of the Crime of Genocide. This penalty can only be carried out pursuant to a final judgement rendered by a competent court.

3. When deprivation of life constitutes the crime of genocide, it is understood that nothing in this article shall authorize any State Party to the present Covenant to derogate in any way from any obligation assumed under the provisions of the Convention on the Prevention and Punishment of the Crime of Genocide.

4. Anyone sentenced to death shall have the right to seek pardon or commutation of the sentence. Amnesty, pardon or commutation of the sentence of death may be granted in all cases.

5. Sentence of death shall not be imposed for crimes committed by persons below eighteen years of age and shall not be carried out on pregnant women.

6. Nothing in this article shall be invoked to delay or to prevent the abolition of capital punishment by any State Party to the present Covenant.'

The commission on human rights, when discussing the text for this Article at its second session (2 to 17 December 1947), had before it various drafts, which were as follows:

— 'It shall be unlawful to deprive any person of his life save in the execution of the sentence of a court following on his conviction of a crime for which this penalty is provided by law' (E/CN.4/37, Article 6; text included in a proposal made by the representative of the United States for a Human Rights Convention);
— 'It shall be unlawful to deprive any person of his life save in the execution of the sentence of a court following on his conviction of a crime for which this penalty is provided by law' (E/CN.4/21, Annex G, Article 1).

This text stemmed from the drafting committee of the commission [37], which followed in this respect the proposals made by the United Kingdom (E/CN.4/AC.1/4, Article 8):

37. First session, 9 to 25 June 1947.

— 'It shall be unlawful to deprive any person, from the moment of conception, of his life or bodily integrity [38], save in the execution of the sentence of a court following on his conviction of a crime for which this penalty is provided by law' (E/CN.4/21, Annex G, Article 1).

This text was an alternative proposal to the text of the drafting committee, presented by the representative of Lebanon, who was of the opinion that the latter was not precise enough in two respects. First the *condemnation of abortion* should be in his view clearly stated by affirming that life began at the moment of conception (i.e. from the development of the embryo), which was not a novelty, but rather a confirmation of already existing national legal rules (E/CN.4/AC.3/SR.1). Second, the term *'bodily integrity'* was introduced as a reaction against the Hitlarian practice of sterilization, which made it necessary to stipulate precisely in the Convention, that it was unlawful to mutilate a person's body (E/CN.4/AC.3/SR.1);

1. 'It shall be unlawful to deprive any person of his life save in the execution of the sentence of a court following on his conviction of a crime for which this penalty is provided by law.
2. It shall be unlawful to procure abortion except in a case in which it is permitted by law and is done in good faith in order to preserve the life of the woman, or on medical advice to prevent the birth of a child of unsound mind to parents suffering from mental disease, or in case where the pregnancy is the result of rape' (E/CN.4/56, Article 4).

This draft stemmed from the working group on an International Convention on Human Rights [39], prepared during its unique session (5-10 December 1947). It was a compromise resulting from the difficulties, centered around the suggestion of the representative of Lebanon. The introduction of the word *'conception'* would prevent abortion on justifiable medical grounds and the legislation of a large number of countries authorised medical abortion in cases of justifiable necessity. The replacement of the words 'from the moment of conception' by 'at any stage of human development' met with similar opposition, because some countries would then find it difficult to ratify the Convention. It was therefore decided to first state the general principle (para. 1 of the Article) to be followed by the exception, namely in the case where abortion was sanctioned by law (para. 2 of the Article) (E/CN.4/AC.3/SR. 1, 2 and 9). The term *'bodily integrity'* was not included, because it was considered to be sufficiently covered by the following Article, dealing with maltreatment (E/CN.4/AC.3/SR.2). [40]

When discussing this Article in plenary session and in particular the question of abortion, the commission also gave due attention to the corresponding Article (7) of the draft Declaration. Arguments, which were raised against the inclusion of the second paragraph of the text of Article 4, prepared by the working group, were:

— the wording sanctified an unscientific principle, which, though some existing laws authorised abortion, did not yet justify an unlawful act as the present one;

38. See para. 2.2. below.
39. Established by the commission on human rights at its second session, to deal with the draft of a Convention.
40. See also para. 2.2. below.

38

- the prediction, that a child would be born mentally unsound was considered impossible at the time; (such an argument would be difficult to accept today in the light of the advances of medical science in general, and genetic counselling in particular);
- in some cases children of mentally deranged parents were very healthy;
- the paragraph was not of general application and states should be free to legislate according to their own needs and prevailing convictions of their people.

Against these views, it was argued, that the laws of many countries permitted abortion in certain well-defined cases, and that, therefore, this situation should be confirmed, especially where otherwise those countries, who had already established this principle by law, would be prevented from ratifying the Convention. On voting, however, the majority was in favour of deleting the second paragraph of the text of the working group (E/CN.4/SR/35). Thus, the commission confirmed the text [41], which had been adopted previously by its drafting committee:

'It shall be unlawful to deprive any person of his life save in the execution of a sentence of a court following his conviction of a crime for which this penalty is provided by law' (E/600 Annex B, Article 5). [42]

When the drafting committee reconsidered this text during its second session (3 to 21 May 1948) it was suggested to draft this Article in such a manner as to take account with various exceptions. The decision to include such exceptions was, however, subject to the decision being taken to insert an overall limitation clause in the Convention. The drafting committee decided to submit the following text to the commission:

'No one shall be deprived of his life save in the execution of the sentence of a court following his conviction of a crime for which this penalty is provided by law.'

To this text a list of possible exceptions was added, which included items such as suppression of rebellion and riots, selfdefence, killing by medical operation, killing through voluntary medical experiments etc. (E/CN.4/AC.1/SR.23; E/CN.4/AC.1/38;E/CN.4/AC.1/SR.29; E/CN.4/95, Annex B, Article 5).

The commission on human rights again discussed the Article at length during its fifth and sixth sessions (9 May to 20 June 1949 and 27 March to 19 May 1950 respectively).

41. To this text an amendment proposal of the representative of Urugay was added, who was opposed to the wording, in particular because he was against the death sentence:
'Every person* has the right to life. It is the duty of the State to protect persons born or conceived, incurables, and persons physically or mentally incapable. The State is obliged to ensure minimum condition enabling all persons to live a dignified and worthy life. The death penalty shall never be applied to political or ordinary offenders merely by decrees issued in virtue of laws previously in force, but only after trial in which all the guarantees necessary for reaching a just verdict are ensured' (E/600, Annex B, p. 38).
   * See E/CN.4/AC.1/SR.22 for the replacement of the words 'any person'.
42. For comments by governments on this text, see E/CN.4/82 add. 4 and 8.

During the fifth session of the commission, various drafts [43] of this Article were presented, but no unanimity could be reached. It was therefore decided to include a provisional text in the report. The wording of this text, which is given below, was based upon the commission's conviction that an instrument to be signed by the largest possible number of states must take into account existing conditions, so that the application of the Covenant should not in any way injure fundamental human rights and freedoms:

'1. No one shall be deprived of his life.
2. In countries where capital punishment exists, sentence of death may be imposed only as a penalty for the most serious of crimes.
3. No one may be executed save in virtue of the sentence of a competent court and in accordance with a law in force and not contrary to the principles expressed in the Universal Declaration of Human Rights.
4. Amnesty, pardon or commutation of the sentence of death may be granted in all cases' (E/1371, Annex I, Article 5). [44]

During its sixth session, the commission had before it various comments[45] submitted by governments, which together with other texts, were presented during the meeting and again discussed at length. It would go far beyond the scope of the present study to reproduce all the discussions during the fifth and sixth sessions of the commission, as well as all the amendments presented in the course of these sessions. Summary records of the discussions may be found in: E/CN.4/SR 90; 91; 93; 94; 97; 98; 101 and 135 (fifth session) and in E/CN.4/SR 139; 144; 149; 152; 153 and 199 (sixth session). Among the main items discussed were the objective of the Covenant (inclusion of measures for protection of the individual against arbitrary action by states only or also against arbitrary action by other citizens (horizontal working of the Convention); inclusion of either the word 'intentionally' or of the word 'arbitrarily' (the former being considered to exclude from the Article such cases as fatal accidents); and the enumeration of possible exceptions (arguments that inclusion would signify a limitative list, which would be necessarily incomplete, were countered by arguments that the prepared list was exhaustive and that by not stating the exceptions too much lattitude would be given to governments in respect of such an important right as the right to life).

From among the proposals[46] submitted during the sixth session, it is worthwhile noting the Lebanon amendment to the wording of the first paragraph of the French proposal[47]:

43. See for instance: E/CN.4/170;E/CN.4/188;E/CN.4/193;E/CN.4/204;E/CN.4/SR.99; E/CN.4/W.21;E/CN.4/W.22;E/CN.4/170/add.5.E/CN.4/W.23;E/CN.4/193 and E/CN.4/241.
44. The report contained also an alternative draft, presented by Australia, Denmark, France, Lebanon, United States and supported by India, on grounds that the present wording of the text did not state precisely enough the right which it conferred, nor the limitations to this right; see E/1371, Annex II, Article 5 for the text.
45. See for instance: E/CN.4/353/add. 1, 2, 8, 10, 11 and E/CN.4/365.
46. See for instance: E/CN.4/387; 393; 413 and 417.
47. E/CN.4/353/add. 8.

'Human life, from the *moment of conception*, is sacred' (E/CN.4/386) (See also E/CN.4/398, where Lebanon subsequently suggests the following wording:
  'Human life is sacred from the moment of conception').

Furthermore, the United States commented that the United Kingdom proposal[48] was in their view impracticable, because it omitted in para. 3. a number of possible exceptions to the right to life (E/CN.4/383).

There was finally agreement on a text, which merged various of the proposals[49] (E/CN.4/SR.153), and was restyled by a special drafting committee (E/CN.4/SR.199):

'1. Everyone's right to life shall be protected by law.
2. To take life shall be a crime, save in the execution of a sentence of a court, or in selfdefence, or in the case of enforcement measures authorized by the Charter.
3. In countries where capital punishment exists, sentence of death may be imposed only as a penalty for the most serious crimes, pursuant to the sentence of a competent court and in accordance with law not contrary to the Universal Declaration of Human Rights.
4. Anyone sentenced to death shall have the right to seek amnesty, or pardon, or commutation of the sentence. Amnesty, pardon or commutation of the sentence of death may be granted in all cases' (E/1681, Annex I, Article 3).

Various comments[50] on this text were also included into the report (Annex II). This text was then discussed by the social committee of the Economic and Social Council[51] and the third committee of the General Assembly.[52]

During these meetings it was considered once more that the right to life was inadequately formulated. It was felt to be too vague a statement, while the matter of 'capital punishment' was discussed again.[53]

The Article was not discussed during the seventh session of the commission (16 April to 19 May 1951). Some amendment proposals to this Article were, however, inserted into the report of that session (E/1992), among which the Yugoslav proposal aimed to insert the following sentence at the end of paragraph 4. of Article 3[54]:

'In no case shall sentence of death be put into effect where the sentence concerns a pregnant woman' (E/CN.4/573).

The Article was then discussed at the eighth session of the commission (14 April to 14 June 1952) where the arguments of the fifth and sixth session

48. E/CN.4/365.
49. E/CN.4/353/add. 8;E/CN.4/365;E/CN.4/393 and E/CN.4/386.
50. Australia, France and the United Kingdom.
51. Eleventh session, 3 July to 16 August, E/AC.7/SR.147-149.
52. Fifth session, 20 September to 11 December 1950, A/C.3/SR.288-291.
53. See the memorandum prepared by the secretariat general for the seventh session of the commission on human rights, which included the various comments made during the session previously mentioned, E/CN.4/528.
54. For amendment proposals from India and the United Kingdom see E/CN.4/563, rev. 1 and E/CN.4/628 respectively.

were more or less repeated [55]. The text which was finally adopted reads as follows:

'1. No one shall be arbitrarily deprived of his life. Everyone's right to life shall be protected by law.
2. In countries where capital punishment exists, sentence of death may be imposed only as a penalty for the most serious crimes pursuant to the sentence of a competent court and in accordance with law not contrary to the principles of the Universal Declaration of Human Rights or the Convention on the Prevention and Punishment of the Crime of Genocide.
3. Any one sentenced to death shall have the right to seek pardon or commutation of the sentence. Amnesty, pardon or commutation of the sentence of death may be granted in all cases.
4. Sentence of death shall not be carried out on a pregnant woman' (E/2256, Annex I, Part III, Article 5).

The commission did not alter this text any more in the course of its subsequent sessions.

The third committee of the Assembly discussed the Article at its twelfth session (12 November 1957 to 12 February 1958).

In an attempt to bring together all the numerous submitted amendments, as well as the suggestions put forward during the discussions, a working party was established, which presented a report [56], containing various suggestions.

In plenary session the third committee discussed again at length the same topics, which had also been raised during discussions in the commission on human rights. [57]

Of the two topics that shall be mentioned here, one is a proposal submitted by the Netherlands (A/C.3/L.651), which was based on Article 2 of the Convention for the Protection of Human Rights and Fundamental Freedoms of the Council of Europe, which specified cases in which deprivation of life would be deemed lawful. The majority did not favour the proposal, as they feared it would be incomplete, and would convey more weight to the exceptions than to the right itself (A/3764, para. 114).

There was also a proposed amendment [58] to insert the following sentence into the first paragraph of the Article:

'From the moment of conception, this right shall be protected by law' (A/C.3/L.654).

Those who were in favour of this text, were of the opinion, that it was logical to protect the right to life from the moment it began. Furthermore, the provisions of paragraph 4. of the Article aimed at protecting the life of the unborn child, whose mother had been sentenced to death and that this protection should be extended to all unborn children. Also legislation of many

55. See E/CN.4/SR.309-311 and E/2256 paras. 167-174 for discussions, and E/CN.4/L.122; 176 and 179 for some of the amendment proposals.
56. A/C.3/L.655/Corr. 1 and 2.
57. See A/3764, paras. 84-120.
58. Put forward by Belgium, Brazil, El Salvador, Mexico and Morocco.

countries accorded protection of life from the moment of conception.

Those who were against this proposal argued that it was impossible for the state to determine the moment of conception and that the insertion of the amendment would involve the question of rights and duties of the medical profession. Legislation on this subject was based on different principles in different countries and it was, therefore, inappropriate to include such a provision in an international instrument (A/3764, para. 112).

The third committee finally decided upon the text as presently formulated in the International Covenant.

1.2.2. Some conclusions

It is interesting to note that although the right referred to in this Article was generally considered to be the most important human right, some important aspects of the right to life, namely those involving medical acts, such as in the cases of abortion and euthanasia, were mentioned only occasionally during the discussions on this Article, particularly in the course of the fifth and sixth sessions of the commission on human rights.

Thus, for instance, the matter of legal abortion was raised, when the list of possible exceptions to the right to life were being discussed. It was in fact mentioned that the list, as presented by the United Kingdom in the course of the fifth session [59], did not include the case in which a doctor, in order to save the life of the mother, intentionally killed the child during or after delivery (E/CN.4/SR.140). Furthermore, when the Lebanon proposed amendment [60] which again introduced the notion of 'from the moment of conception', was discussed at the sixth session of the commission, it was rejected on the ground that this would give rise to legal, medical and moral problems and would compel the commission to mention other exceptions, such as legal abortion. The Lebanese proposal was also rejected because where the commission was trying to ensure that human rights would be respected, the rights of the unborn were not universally recognized. On the other hand, the commission thought that it was recognized everywhere that those rights began with physical birth (E/CN.4/SR.149).

The matter of euthanasia was raised when discussing the question whether or not cases in which the death sentence would be permitted, should be enumerated. The representative of Egypt was opposed to such a listing, on the ground that the consequences would be too far reaching. He thought, for instance, that in this case one could ask oneself, whether euthanasia was permissable. [61]

Thus, the Covenant does not give an indication either on when life begins, nor on when life ends.

59. E/CN.4/W.21.
60. E/CN.4/398.
61. E/CN.4/SR.144.

1.3. EUROPEAN CONVENTION FOR THE PROTECTION OF HUMAN RIGHTS AND FUNDAMENTAL FREEDOMS (ARTICLE 2)

1.3.1. Brief drafting history

Article 2 of the European Convention reads as follows:

'1. Everyone's right to life shall be protected by law. No one shall be deprived of his life intentionally save in the execution of a sentence of a court following his conviction of a crime for which this penalty is provided by law.
2. Deprivation of life shall not be regarded as inflicted in contravention of this Article when it results from the use of force which is no more than absolutely necessary:
   a. in defence of any person from unlawful violence;
   b. in order to effect a lawful arrest or to prevent the escape of a person lawfully detained;
   c. in action lawfully taken for the purpose of quelling a riot or insurrection.'

The text which was presented by the Consultative Assembly to the Committee of Ministers in 1949 merely referred to Article 3 of the Declaration of Human Rights of the United Nations in respect of the right to life.

This text, which had first been drafted by the committee on legal and administrative matters of the Assembly (report Teitgen, doc. 77 of 5 September 1949) and which was subsequently discussed in the Assembly in the course of its first Session (5 to 8 September 1949) reads as follows:

'In this Convention Member States shall undertake to ensure to all persons residing within their territories:
1) security of persons in accordance with articles 3, 5 and 8 of the United Nations Declaration' (Article 2, Recommendation nr. 38 of the Consultative Assembly, adopted on 8 September 1949).

The committee of governmental experts to whom the text was subsequently referred by the Committee of Ministers (doç. A 809 of the Consultative Assembly), replaced at their first session (2 to 8 February 1950) the mere reference to Articles of the UN Declaration of Human Rights by the text of these Articles. The right was then formulated as follows:

'Every person has a right to life, liberty and security of person' (doc. 809, Article 3).

During discussions at the second session of this committee (6 to 10 March 1950) an amendment was presented by the United Kingdom delegate, with the purpose of changing the wording of the Article by defining the right to life precisely by mentioning the exceptions to it:

'1. No one shall be deprived of his life intentionally save in execution of a sentence of a court following his conviction of a crime for which this penalty is provided by law.
2. Deprivation of life shall not be regarded as inflicted in contravention of this Article when it results from the use of force which is no more than absolutely necessary:
   a. in defence of any person from unlawful violence;
   b. in order to effect a lawful arrest or to prevent the escape of a person lawfully detained;

c. in action lawfully taken for the purpose of quelling a riot or insurrection'
(doc. A 915, Article 4).

The committee of experts decided to present both drafts to the Committee of Ministers (doc. A 925).

The conference of high officials (8 to 17 June 1950) studied both alternatives on the request of the Committee of Ministers and decided to combine both suggestions into a text in which the right to life as well as a more detailed description of its content were formulated (doc. A 1445). This text was adopted by the Committee of Ministers on 7 Augustus 1950.

Although the human rights commission of the Council of Europe recognizes the violation by an individual of the right to life as described in Article 2, it so far has not taken a positive stand on this matter. [62]

1.3.2. Some conclusions
The first paragraph of Article 2 of the Convention contains a general statement on the legal protection of life. As a consequence of the application of the 'definition' system (see CH.I, para. 2.3.2.) this general principle is followed by rules (equalling exceptions) valid in particular situations, such as: self-defence, arrest, escape and riots.

The drafting of this Article was inspired largely by the deliberations of the United Nations commission on human rights on Article 6 of the International Covenant on Civil and Political Rights. The first paragraph is lifted literally from the UN draft at the 6th session of the human rights commission (1950, doc. E/1681 and doc. E/CN.4/507; Partsch, 1968, p. 102; Weil, 1963, p. 45). The Article is generally interpreted as applicable in cases of a *States'* unlawful interference in the life of an individual, which is similar to the UN Covenant

62. For states interference, see Application no. 867/60, decision of 29 May 1961, Yearbook IV, p. 270, on compatability with the Convention of the Norwegian law authorising interruption of pregnancy (application declared inadmissable). For individuals violation, see Application no. 1287/61, decision of 4 October 1962 (unpublished), on sterilization (application declared inadmissable) (sterilization can in some circumstances constitute a breach of Article 2 of the Convention).
  The commission considered the following case from the angle of the protection of the right to life: The eviction of an old person with serious heart trouble from the home where he had been living for years. This could, according to his doctors, have endangered his life. (Application no. 5207/71; decision of 1 June 1972; declared inadmissable; European commission of human rights, collection of decisions no. 39 (1972), pp. 99 a.f.; no. 42 (1973), pp. 85 a.f.). In 1977, the commission declared admissable application no. 6959/75, lodged by two woman against the Federal Republic of Germany; in this case objections are made against limitations in the legislation, authorising termination of pregnancy during the first twelve weeks only. The complaints are essentially concerned with Article 8 of the Convention (the right to respect for private life). In its Resolution DH (78)1 of 17 March 1978, the Committee of Ministers agreed with the opinion expressed by the commission of human rights, that 'not every regulation of the termination of unwanted pregnancy constitutes an interference with the right to respect for the private life of the mother; and that therefore ... the legal rules in force in German law ... about which the applicants complain, do not interfere with their right to respect for their private life' (The Brüggeman and Scheuten Case, Council of Europe, 1978).

in its final version, but which last initially also aimed at covering individual's interference with the rights of others.

The interpretation of the Article does not lead to the consequence that it contains a general prohibition of legalized abortion. This matter was in fact left to the states, who in their national laws are free to consider the risk of endangering the life and health of the future mother. Nor does the Article justify any demand to be made concerning the standard of social services in a country (Castberg, 1974, p. 81).

(In the Brüggeman and Scheuten Case, the commission has not decided whether the unborn child is to be considered as 'life' in the sense of Article 2 of the Convention; the commission considers it without doubt that certain interests relating to pregnancy are legally protected.) [63]

2. Maltreatment and experimentation

2.1. UN UNIVERSAL DECLARATION OF HUMAN RIGHTS (ARTICLE 5)

2.1.1. Brief drafting history
Article 5 of the Universal Declaration of Human Rights reads:

'No one shall be subjected to torture or cruel, inhuman or degrading treatment or punishment.'

Initial drafts for this Article were:

— 'No one can be submitted to torture or to any unusual punishment or indignity' (draft outline of an International Bill of Human Rights, secretariat, E/CN.4/AC.1/3, Article 4);
— 'No one, even if found guilty, may be subjected to torture, cruelty or degrading treatment' (text of the French Delegate, prepared for the temporary working group of the drafting committee, E/CN.4/21 Annex D, Article 7, second clause);
— 'No one, even if convicted for a crime, can be subjected to torture' (text of the temporary working group, E/CN.4/AC.1/W.1).

Discussions on this Article during the first session of the drafting committee (9 to 24 June 1947) centered on the meaning of 'torture', which is primarily physical, but possibly includes mental torture as well as torture resulting from involuntary experimentation. There was a consensus of opinion on these points, the final wording being left for a later decision, so that the text prepared by the temporary working group was confirmed at this stage (E/CN.4/AC.1/SR.3 and E/CN.4/21, Annex F, Article 10, second clause).

At the second session of the commission on human rights (2 to 17 December 1947) it was decided to include also a reference to degrading practices other than torture. This resulted in the following draft:

63. The Brüggeman and Scheuten Case (application no. 6959/75), Council of Europe, 1978, para. 60.

'No one shall be subjected to torture or to cruel or inhuman punishment or indignity' (E/600, Article 7, para. 3 and E/CN.4/57, Article 10, second clause).

No substantive remarks were submitted by governments on this text. [64] However, following a proposal made by the Belgium representative, the commission decided during its third session [65] (24 May to 16 June 1948 to rearrange the text in a more logic sequence:

'No one shall be subjected to torture or cruel, inhuman or degrading treatment or punishment' (E/CN.4/SR 54).

This was to be the final wording of the Article on this subject (E/800, Article 4, para. 2).

During discussions at the third commission of the Assembly, it was emphasised that the wording of the Article was ment to indicate that vivisection, if carried out without the free consent of the person concerned, is a violation of one of the most elementary human rights.

2.1.2. Some conclusions

There were no extensive discussions on the text of this Article during the various drafting stages of the Declaration. The Article can be interpreted in the widest possible sense to include not only the prohibition of vivisection without the free consent of the person concerned, but also of (inhuman) medical experiments without free consent, so that physical integrity is safeguarded in the best possible method (Verdoodt, 1964, p. 107).

2.2. UN INTERNATIONAL COVENANT ON CIVIL AND POLITICAL RIGHTS (ARTICLE 7)

2.2.1. Brief drafting history

Article 7 of the International Covenant on Civil and Political Rights reads as follows:

'No one shall be subjected to torture or to cruel, inhuman or degrading treatment or punishment. In particular, no one shall be subjected without his free consent to medical or scientific experimentation.'

This Article is closely related to the preceeding Article (6) on the right to life, because both deal with the physical integrity of man. Article 7 contains two ideas, the first is concerned with human dignity (maltreatment) (first sentence) (see under b) and the second with bodily integrity (see under c). Untill 1950 these two ideas were expressed in two separate Articles (see under a).

---

64. See E/CN.4/82. rev. 1 and E/CN.4/82 add. 9 for comments from the Netherlands and the United Kingdom.
65. For a suggestion made by the representative of China, see E/CN.4/102.

a). one or two Articles

The preliminary decision to draft two separate Articles as the mode for expressing the ideas of bodily integrity and human dignity was taken by the working group on an International Convention on Human Rights [66] during its unique session (5 to 10 December 1949), when in discussing the right to life, it was decided not to include the term 'bodily integrity' in that Article (E/CN.4/AC.3/SR.2) [67]. It was felt that the right to life and the items under discussion covered the three closely related ideas of the right to life, bodily integrity and maltreatment as a physical being, which pleaded in favour of drafting three distinct Articles on physical integrity of man (one on the right to life, one on bodily integrity and one on human dignity).

The question whether to draft one or two articles to cover the ideas of human dignity and bodily integrity was raised again during the fifth session of the commission (9 May to 20 June 1949).

The idea of merging the two articles into one [68] was then opposed on grounds that there were in fact two distinct ideas: one proclaiming the right of the individual to decide whether he would be submitted or not to medical or scientific experimentation (the individual's right to dispose of his body) and the other dealing with human dignity (maltreatment) (E/CN.4/SR.92). The World Health Organization, to whom the proposals [69] of the commission were then submitted for advice, considered a separate Article on the subject of medical experimentation unnecessary. Amongst other arguments, it was thought that the Article (6) dealing with maltreatment sufficiently covered the subject. [70] Discussions on this point during the sixth session of the commission (27 March to 19 May 1950) resulted in the acceptance of a proposal of the French representative to delete the Article and to include its substance in the Article (6) dealing with maltreatment, because the drafting of the Article on experimentation (bodily integrity), as it stood, was considered unsatisfactory. [71]

b). maltreatment (human dignity)

The commission on human rights, when discussing the wording of the text on maltreatment during its second session (2 to 17 December 1947) had before it various drafts which were as follows:

— 'No person shall be subjected to:
 a) torture in any form;
 b) ....
 c) cruel or inhuman punishment' (suggestions made by the drafting committee of the commission [72], E/CN.4/21, Annex G, Article 2);

66. Established by the commission on human rights at its second session to deal with the draft of a Convention.
67. See para. 1.2.
68. Proposal from Lebanon, E/CN.4/193.
69. E/1371, Annex I, article 7.
70. E/CN.4/359.
71. E/CN.4/471.
72. First session, 9 to 25 June 1947.

48

- 'It shall be unlawful to subject any person to torture, or to cruel or inhuman punishment, or to cruel or inhuman indignity' (text submitted by the United States, E/CN.4/37);

  (in this proposal the words 'cruel or inhuman indignity' replace the words 'physical mutilation' in the text of the drafting committee, because sterilization, which is sanctioned by certain national laws, and which as such is considered to be a form of mutilation, would otherwise be forbidden under this Article);

- 'It shall be unlawful to subject any person to torture in any form, or to cruel or inhuman indignity' (text prepared by the working group on an International Convention on Human Rights, E/CN.4/56, Article 6). [73]

In plenary session, the commission considered the wording of the text closely to the corresponding Article (10) of the draft Declaration. The latter was considered preferable, as it contained the essential notion of 'punishment' to take care of criminal cases (E/CN.4/SR.37); therefore the commission decided upon the following wording:

- 'No one shall be subjected to torture or to cruel or inhuman punishment or to cruel or inhuman indignity' (E/600, Annex B, Article 7). [74]

When the drafting committee reconsidered this text during its second session (3 to 21 May 1948), the imprecise nature of the terms 'cruel or inhuman' was discussed. It was, however, argued that inhuman acts, such as those which occurred during the Second World War, should be prevented by a positive and condemnatory formula. Therefore, the text adopted was similar to Article 7 of the commission on human rights (E/CN.4/AC.1/SR.23 and 30; E/CN.4/95, Annex B, Article 7). The commission resumed discussions on the Article's text at its fifth session (9 May to 20 June 1949), when it had before it various proposed amendments. [75] The proposal from the Lebanese representative (E/CN.4/193), expressed the concept of cruel, degrading, or inhuman treatment or punishment, and was adopted by the commission in the following terms:

'No one shall be subjected to torture or to cruel, inhuman or degrading treatment or punishment' (E/CN.4/SR.92 and E/1371, Annex I, Article 6).

73. The term 'indignity' (vs. United States proposal) was maintained despite the fact that some considered it unsufficiently clear; an alternative proposal to replace it by 'any form of physical or mental torture' could not be accepted, as there were many examples of mental suffering, which would hardly be considered unlawful, and therefore 'indignity' was preferable, as it always implied a *physical act* (E/CN.4/AC.3/SR.2).
74. For comments by governments on this text, see E/CN.4/82 add. 4 and 8. Major objections were that the terms 'cruel or inhuman' were too subjective to be included in a legal instrument as the present one, which created international obligations.
75. See E/CN.4/170 for the United States' proposal, which was inspired by the idea that the Covenant should protect individuals against the state only, and not also against other individuals. This proposal was subsequently replaced by another one, because the commission did not favour this limited concept of the Covenant (E/CN.4/SR.91 and 92). See E/CN.4/188 for the United Kingdom proposal, which aimed at abbreviating the original text in the interest of legal clarity.

Despite the fact that during the commission's sixth session (27 March to 19 May 1950) there were lengthy discussions on this proposal, its wording was confirmed and maintained in the final text of the Covenant.

These discussions again concentrated on the imprecise nature of various words (treatment, cruel, inhuman, degrading). Deletion of the word 'treatment' in particular was opposed, because, it was argued, it would restrict the application of the Article to prisoners only, while the Article, as it stood, covered four kinds of 'treatment' (torture, and cruel, inhuman and degrading treatment), which as a whole represented a coherent idea. [76]

c). experimentation (bodily integrity; the right to dispose of ones body)

The commission on human rights, when discussing the text on experimentation during its second session (2 to 17 December 1947), had before it the following drafts:

— 'No one shall be subjected to:
  ....
  b. any form of physical mutilation or medical or scientific experimentation against his will;
  ....' (suggestion made by the drafting committee of the commission [77], E/CN.4/21, Annex G, Article 2);
— 'It shall be unlawful to subject any person to any form of physical mutilation or medical or scientific experimentation against his will' (text from the working group [78], E/CN.4/56, Article 5; the maintenance of the words 'against his will' was strongly emphasised, because otherwise the text would stop all medical or scientific experimentation, E/CN.4/AC.3/SR.2).

The commission confirmed the latter text presented by its working group (E/CN.4/SR. 42; E/600, Annex B, Article 6). [79] When the drafting committee reconsidered the text at its second session (3 to 21 May 1948), it was suggested by the representative of the United States to either include an article of general limitations in the Covenant, or to add a specific list of limitations to the present Article. This proposal was put forward, because there were national laws which, in order to promote health and welfare of the people, provided for compulsory vaccination and treatment of certain infectious diseases, whilst there were also emergency cases in which amputation and surgical

76. The Egyptian proposal (E/CN.4/381) which aimed at the prohibition of the use of a certain drug to extract confessions from an accused person was rejected, because it covered only one product, and did not cover other methods to undermine a person's resistance; his subsequent suggestion to insert the words 'physical and mental' before 'torture' was equally rejected on grounds that 'torture' applied to every form of physical and mental torture, and that, if it were defined, it would limit its scope (E/CN.4/SR.141). For further proposals and discussions, see E/CN.4/353 add. 1 and 10; E/CN.4/359 and 365; E/CN.4/SR. 182 and 183.
77. First session, 9 to 25 June 1947.
78. Established by the commission on human rights at its second session, to deal with the draft of a Convention.
79. For the comment made by the government of Sweden on this text, see E/CN.4/82/ add. 11, in which it was presumed that blood-tests in case of suspicion of driving under influence or for establishing paternity were not inconsistent with the wording.

operation might be carried out without the consent of the patient (E/CN.4/AC.1/SR.23). These acts would be punishable, if there was no provision included to exempt these particular instances, which were acknowledged to be in the interest of humanity. Though it was felt to be difficult to list all exceptions in the Article, the suggestion was felt preferable to that made by the USSR. The latter suggested to add to the Article the words 'as are punishable by the law of the country'. This, however, was considered to leave too much lattitude to states, who would then be the sole judges (E/CN.4/AC.1/SR.30). Eventually the following text was agreed upon:

'No one shall be subjected to any form of physical mutilation or medical or scientific experimentation against his will'.

This text was followed by a list of possible limitations, with the understanding that others might be added:

— compulsory vaccination;
— legitimate medical and scientific experimentation in hospitals for the insane, with the consent of parent or guardian of the patient;
— emergency operations, undertaken to save the life of a patient, where the patient is unable to give his consent or where a person empowered to give consent on behalf of the patient gives such consent (E/CN.4/95, Annex B, Article 6).

It will be noted that all these limitations are in fact intended to give effect to the right to health care, and that, though they have been deleted from the final text, they are all commonly accepted in medical practice.

The commission on human rights resumed its discussions on this text during the fifth session (9 May to 20 June 1949), concentrating on various proposed amendments. [80]

As no agreement could be reached on a text, it was decided to refer it to the World Health Organization for comment because of the many medical technical problems involved [81], with the proviso that the Organization should be precisely informed of the commission's purpose vis-à-vis the list of exceptions, as well as of the reasons underlying the formulation of the present Article. This was thought necessary because of the ideas of physicians and politicians on the question of guaranteeing physical integrity differed greatly. (Some feared, however, that the Organization adopt a too scientific approach to the problem; E/CN.4/SR.91.) (See also E/1371, Annex I, Article 7.) In its

80. See E/CN.4/192 for the proposal from Denmark, in which it was suggested to add to the list of exceptions sterilization or castration on mentally deficient persons, and castration of dangerous sexual offenders, both being authorised by law in Denmark (the first is also authorised in Norway) (E/CN.4/353/add. 11). This proposal was opposed on grounds that it would not prevent criminal offences arising; that there was a possibility of abuse by states and that mental ailments were not proven to be hereditary (E/CN.4/SR.91). See E/CN.4/197 for the proposal from France, with a view to avoid a too narrow interpretation of the word 'experimentation', thus preventing cure of some patients through medical treatment which can be experimental to some extent (E/CN.4/SR.91); see also E/CN.4/SR.92 for the comments of the representative of the USSR on this proposal.
81. See E/CN.4/170 for the United States proposal to this end, as well as E/CN.4/193.

comments, the World Health Organization advised [82] against inclusion of a text on experimentation into the Covenant, because this might lead to complications and hinder genuine medical progress. It was in fact considered to be difficult to draft a text, which, while preventing improper medical intervention and experimentation, would not prejudice legitimate medical and social needs (E/CN.4/359). This point of view was emphasised during the sixth session of the commission (27 March to 19 May 1950), when the representative of the WHO stated that the text of the commission was unsatisfactory, as it might be interpreted to prevent certain activities, such as vaccination without consent and medical experimentation on the insane. There were also difficulties of dealing with dangerous sexual offenders, and also such cases as the removal of a tumor, which, although clearly intended for the preservation of a patient's life, might sometimes be considered as mutilation (E/CN.4/SR.182). Those who were in favour of maintaining a wording related to experimentation considered that the subject was not sufficiently covered by Article 5 of the Universal Declaration of Human Rights. Moreover, the right to bodily integrity was considered to be so fundamental, that deletion of the text might be regarded as a tacit acceptance by the United Nations of illegal mutilation or experimentation. The right was of such importance that it should be guaranteed and respected through positive action and any derogation from it should be permitted only when it was necessary for the saving of life. [83]

It was also pointed out that a distinction should be made between curative medicine and improper medical intervention. The present wording was not intended to prevent physicians and surgeons from exercising their professions for the benefit of the patients, but to prevent unnecessary mutilations and experimentations. On the whole, there was not a divergence of opinion on the principle, but rather on the question whether the Article (6) dealing with maltreatment sufficiently covered the point under discussion. As the suggested text was related to two different matters, namely the protection of human rights on the one hand and the progress of medical science on the other, there was a problem of striking the balance between the legitimate interest of society and those of the individual (E/CN.4/SR.182). The text which was finally adopted[84] at this session was:

82. Prior to establishing its advice, the WHO consulted two organizations, the World Medical Association and the International Council of Nurses. The first suggested the following text on the subject: 'No one shall be subjected without his free consent either to medical or scientific experimentation, or to physical mutilation except, in his own interests, in case of emergency and when unconscious'. The latter submitted the following: 'No one shall be subjected against his will to physical mutilation or medical or scientific experiment not required by his state of health, both physical and mental' (E/CN.4/SR.141 and 142; see also E/CN.4/389).
83. The Yugoslavian delegation even presented an amendment to add a new para. to the text, stipulating that no experimentation even with the consent of the person concerned may be undertaken without the previous consent of an authoritive medical organization, with a view to avoid exploiting poverty for obtaining consent for mutilation from a person in return of payment (E/CN.4/SR.141).
84. For proposed amendments to this text (which were not accepted), see E/CN.4/472 and 473. The text was opposed on grounds that it did not provide for cases where a person might have to be subjected to medical treatment in the interest of the community (inocula-

'..............
In particular, no one shall be subjected against his will to medical or scientific experimenta-
tion involving risk, where such is not required by his state of physical or mental health'
(E/1681, Annex I, Article 4). [85]

Both during discussions at the social committee of the Economic and Social
Council [86] and the third committee of the General Assembly [87] the inclusion
of a provision relating to medical experimentation in the Covenant was again
opposed for the same reasons as those advanced by the WHO. There were,
furthermore, two new arguments opposed to the text. One, put forward in the
social committee, that the words 'medical or scientific experimentation' in
particular were not very clear and might well – in case where a wide interpretation is given to these words – 'open the door to practices like euthanasia'
(E/AC.7/SR.148). The other argument, advanced in the third committee, was
that in its present wording the text implicitly condemned scientific methods
for the investigation of crime (A/C.3/SR.290, para. 64). [88] The commission
on human rights discussed the wording again at its eighth session (14 April to
14 June 1952) [89], when there remained divergence of views on the opportunity of including a text relating to experimentation.

There were in fact two groups of proposed amendments to the text (see
E/CN.4/SR.311 and 312). The first category tended to weaken the wording
among other grounds because the present formulation would delay progress of
medical science and would hinder desirable (experimental) treatment in those
circumstances, where it would be impossible to obtain the consent of the
(sick) person concerned, which would thus prevent saving human lives, and
that the text contained a general prohibition, while it was on the other hand
not possible to properly distinguish between treatment and experimentation.
Finally it should be left to the medical profession to take the decisions regard-

tions, treatment of sex offenders); that 'involving risk' would exclude the possibility to
subject a person to medical or scientific experimentation involving risk, in cases it was not
possible to obtain a person's consent before doing so (WHO); that the proposal referred
only to experimentation for which there was no justification on grounds of health, while
there is a fundamental difference between medical and scientific treatment for purely
experimental purposes and therapeutical treatment (E/CN.4/183).
85.   To this, the remark from the Indian representative was added, who called for careful
consideration of the negative advice of the WHO. (Some felt that the advice of the WHO
was a too negative one, and that the Organization should on the contrary be constructive in
submitting proposals.)
86.   Eleventh session, 3 July to 16 August 1950; E/AC.7/SR. 148 + 149.
87.   Fifth session, 20 September to 11 December 1950; A/C.3/SR.290.
88.   The application of the present text to medical treatment was also considered by the
international group of experts on the prevention of crime and the treatment of offenders,
second session, December 1950, when it was considered essential to include the word
'treatment' in order to emphasis the necessity of prohibiting certain methods of examination during criminal proceedings (E/CN.4/523 and E/CN.4/528, paras. 99-100).
89.   The text was not discussed during the seventh session of the commission (16 April to
19 May 1951). There were, however, two amendment proposals inserted into the report
(E/1992, Annex III, Section A), one in support of the views of the WHO (see also E/CN.4/
628) and one aiming at the requirement to obtain the approval of a higher medical institution, designated by law, before carrying out experimentation (see also E/CN.4/573).

ing the use of new techniques for curing the mentally and physically ill. [90] The second category of amendments aimed at strengthening of the formulation among other grounds because the paragraph under discussion had no application to experimentation nor treatment, provided it was carried out with the free consent of the person concerned.

Second, the medical experimentation referred to did not apply to cases of treatment of sick persons, but on the contrary to the healthy persons and sick persons who need protection from treatment not related to their illness. Moreover, if the Covenant recognized the right to life, it must certainly protect healthy persons from being subjected against their will to medical or scientific experiments dangerous to their health. [91]

During the discussions, considerable importance was attached to the retention of the notion of 'risk' (see second criterium of footnote [91]), which was urged to be applied as one of the criteria for prohibiting medical or scientific experimentation. [92]

As to the free consent of the person concerned there was general agreement that failure to obtain the consent of the sick (sometimes unconscious) person should not make any dangerous experimentation illegal, where such was required by his state of physical or mental health (see E/2256, paras. 175-179).

Agreement was reached on the following text:

'............

In particular, no one shall be subjected without his free consent [93] to medical or scientific experimentation involving risk, where such is not required by his state of physical or mental health' (E/2256, Annex I B, Article 6; see also E/2573, Annex I B).

During discussions in the third committee of the Assembly[94] previous arguments of the commission either in favour, or against maintenance of this text

90. The representative of the United Kingdom suggested to draw up in due course a Convention dealing with problems of the medical profession (E/CN.4/SR.312); this was opposed by the Lebanon representative, who felt that borderline cases (such as complications during an operation when a patient could not be consulted) should be left to professional ethics and law of the country concerned. A similar viewpoint was held by the French representative.
91. The French representative felt that the criteria which applied to medical experiments on sick persons were even more essential in the case of healthy persons. These criteria, which were the terms of reference of 'the Committee on the Public Health of the five countries' (presumably the committee of the Brussels Treaty is referred to here, see below, Part B. CH. III, para. 1) were the following: medical experiment should be of real medical importance; it should be in the patient's interest and not involve any risk of injuring his health; medical experiments could be carried out only with the free consent of the person concerned.
92. The representative of the United States stated in this respect that suppression of this notion would exclude community programmes such as fluoridation of drinking water, spraying of food with DDT and others. 'Prior to the adoption of such programmes, the absence of risk or impossibility of harmful effects were carefully ascertained and the general consent of the community rather than of individuals was given. To safeguard such programmes, the words "involving risk" should therefore be retained' (E/CN.4/SR.312).
93. See E/CN.4/L.159 for the proposed amendment by France to substitute 'against his will' by 'without his free consent', the latter being a positive condition.
94. Thirteenth session, 16 September to 8 December 1958, A/C.3/SR. 848-856.

54

were again advanced. There was also a reference made to the European Convention for the Protection of Human Rights and Fundamental Freedoms of 1950 [95], which did not contain a clause akin to the present one 'because the Convention was a legal document which should remain valid for a long time to come, and that, therefore, its drafting should remain flexible without reference to special cases'. The repetitive character of the present clause in respect to the Article on maltreatment was also underlined.

Favourable comments, similar to those already advanced at earlier drafting stages, included the fact that the clause referred to well defined scientific experiment and met with a real need as it contained ideas of fundamental importance and was therefore independent from the one on maltreatment, which, in its turn, was based on purely humanitarian consideration. Also the value put by legislation upon the right of a person to determine for himself what should be done to him was greater than the value the law puts on his health.

Moreover, emergency, medical or surgical treatment with the purpose of healing the sick was not covered by this clause, which would not prohibit legitimate scientific experimental methods of medical treatment, but would bring a halt to abuses, which are related to scientific progress; criminal experiments are distinct from legitimate experimentations, designed only to further scientific progress or experiments on a sick person in an attempt to improve his health. [96] The amendment proposals [97] aiming at the deletion of all references to normal and legitimate medical practices ('required by his state of physical and mental health') and the deletion of the words 'involving risk', (a criminal experiment violated the dignity of the individual, even without endangering life or health), was acceptable to those who were opposed to the maintenance of the clause and thus the second sentence of the Article could be adopted. [98]

2.2.2. Some conclusions

As is clear from its drafting history, the Article's purpose is to protect both bodily integrity and human dignity. The two sentences of the Article are closely linked to each other. Together with the Article (6) on the right to life the aim is to ensure the right to physical existence.

The first sentence reproduces Article 5 of the Universal Declaration of Human Rights. From the discussions on this sentence it may be concluded that the word 'torture' is intended to cover both mental and physical maltreatment. The drafting of this sentence did not give rise to any particular

---

95. See also below para. 2.3.
96. Medical treatment was considered to be fully covered by Article 13 of the draft Covenant on Economic, Social and Cultural Rights, see also para. 4.2.
97. This (Dutch) amendment proposal was based on the fact that confusion existed about the exact meaning of the sentence, which aimed at the protection of the individual as well as at the possibility for medical science to make progress at the same time. The attempt to combine these two aspects into one short phrase was the cause for its ambiguity.
98. The notion 'free consent' could not hamper scientific progress, but was on the contrary almost the only criterion to determine whether an experiment was legitimate or whether it amounted to torture or cruel, inhuman or degrading treatment.

problem because its content was considered essential in sofar as it covers inhuman acts, committed in the past, and those that might be committed in the future (A/C.3/SR.850, p. 77).

The second sentence, however, met with opposition throughout the drafting of the Article. Its wording, which seems more or less a repetition of the first sentence, was mainly inspired by the atrocities which occurred during the Second World War. The Article intends to express that torture or degrading treatment may also include medical and scientifical experimentation without the free consent of the person concerned. It does, however, not imply that medical investigation for the purpose of tracing illegal acts (such as blood-tests) are forbidden.

The Article, moreover, provides for the protection of the individual against the state as well as against his fellow citizen. There is no clause in the Universal Declaration dealing explicitly with medical experimentation on human beings. Article 5 of the Declaration does not give any indications in this respect, nor does Article 27 [99] attempt to surround scientific progress with guarantees necessary for the health and physical integrity of the human being (Saba, 1968, p. 261).

Yet, apparently there is a need for a built-in system of guarantees, as may be concluded from the inclusion of the second sentence in Article 7 of the Covenant. Various attempts made during the eighth session of the commission to create even further guarantees, requiring in addition to the consent of the person concerned the approval of a higher medical institution designated by law before any experimentation would be carried out (E 1992, Annex III, section A; E/CN.4/SR 312) failed for various reasons. Thus it was felt, especially by the United Kingdom, that such a provision aiming at legal experimentation imposes a professional ethical code at international level, which is of the domain of national legislation and national medical and scientific associations.

The fear was also expressed, especially by the USA, that the amendment might imply that a medical institution authorises an experiment against a person's will. Though the interest of the matter was achnowledged, especially by France, it was felt that there would be problems to realize the idea and therefore was thought preferable to deal with the matter by a seperate recommendation to be sent to governments and to the World Health Organization (E/CN.4/SR.312 and E/2256, para. 117).

99. Article 27:
1. Everyone has the right freely to participate in the cultural life of the community, to enjoy the arts and to share in scientific advancement and its benefits.
2. Everyone has the right to the protection of the moral and material interests resulting from any scientific, literary or artistic production of which he is the author.

2.3. EUROPEAN CONVENTION FOR THE PROTECTION OF HUMAN RIGHTS AND FUNDAMENTAL FREEDOMS (ARTICLE 3)

2.3.1. Brief drafting history

Article 3 of the European Convention on Human Rights and Fundamental Freedoms reads as follows:

'No one shall be subjected to torture or to inhuman or degrading treatment or punishment.'

As was already indicated when discussing Article 2 of the Convention (right to life, see para. 1.3.) the guarantees of states regarding the safety of a person, including torture, were formulated in the text prepared by the committee on legal and administrative matters of the Consultative Assembly (Report Teitgen, doc. 77 of 5 September 1949, Article 2.2.) by a mere reference to the relevant articles of the UN Universal Declaration of Human Rights, which in the case of torture is Article 5.

During discussions in the Consultative Assembly (first session, 5 to 8 September 1949), it was suggested to make a stronger statement on the subject of torture than a mere reference to Article 5 of the Declaration, which was felt to be too casually and hence insufficiently worded.

An amendment was then presented, which read as follows:

'In particular no one shall be subjected to any form of mutilation or sterilization, nor to any form of torture or beating. Nor shall he be forced to take drugs nor shall they be administered to him without his knowledge and consent. Nor shall he be subjected to imprisonment with such an excess of light, darkness, noise or silence as to cause mental suffering' (Doc. 90, amendment of the delegate of the United Kingdom).

At the same time an amendment was put forward to complete Article 1 of the draft text, which contained a general recommendation by the Consultative Assembly to the Committee of Ministers to elaborate as soon as possible a Convention on Human rights:

'The CA takes this opportunity of declaring that all forms of physical torture, whether inflicted by the police, military authorities, members of private organizations or any other persons are inconsistant with civilised society, are offences against heaven and humanity and must be prohibited. They declare that this prohibition must be absolute and that torture cannot be permitted by any purpose whatsoever, neither by extracting evidence for saving life nor even for the safety of the State.
(They believe that it would be better even for Society to perish than for it to permit this relic of barbarism to remain)' (doc. 91, presented by the delegate of the United Kingdom).

These texts were presented with a view to stress the unlawfulness of torture under any circumstance and in particular to forbid bodily infliction and sterilization.

They were, however, opposed on the grounds that if some forms of torture were mentioned in particular, there could be a risk of an 'a contrario' interpretation to permit those forms of torture which were not specifically mentioned, and that when a particular clause was included on one subject only, the whole text would lose its balance.

After a decision to make a special resolution on this particular subject, both amendments were withdrawn [100] and the text as prepared by the committee on legal and administrative matters was adopted (Article 2, Recommendation no. 38 of the Consultative Assembly, adopted on 8 September 1949).

(When discussing the drafting of the special resolution there appeared, however, to exist some further controversies on some items such as sterilization, which was considered lawful by various countries in particular circumstances.)

The text of the draft Convention was then referred by the Committee of Ministers to the committee of governmental experts, who discussed the matter during two sessions (2 to 8 February and 6 to 10 March 1950). The report (doc.B 22) prepared by the secretariat general for the attention of this committee included a comparison of the draft under discussion with the UN Universal Declaration of Human Rights as well as the (draft) UN International Covenant on Civil and Political Rights. It indicated in its comments on the draft Article 7 of the Covenant dealing with medical experimentation, that this subject would in the views of the Consultative Assembly need not be included in the draft Convention, because it would be the subject of a special resolution under preparation by the Assembly. This resolution in fact never materialised.

The representative of the United Kingdom, however, presented to the committee during its first session a proposal for the insertion of various articles after Article 2 as follows:

'article
No one shall be subjected to torture or to cruel, inhuman or degrading treatment or punishment.
article
No one shall be subject without free consent to physical mutilation or any form of medical or scientific experience' (proposed amendments contained in doc. A 798 of 6 February 1950).

The committee of governmental experts then drafted a provisional text on the subject:

'No one shall be subject to torture, or to cruel, inhuman or degrading treatment or punishment' (doc.A 833 of 15 February 1950, Article 2. I. b.).

In this text the second Article suggested by the United Kingdom delegate does not appear any more, presumably because it was decided by the Assembly to make a seperate declaration (Article 6 of the Covenant on Civil and Political Rights, however, does contain such a formula, see para. 2.2.1. under c).

The text of this Article, as well as another amendment proposal made by the delegate of the United Kingdom during the second session of the committee of governmental experts, were submitted to the Committee of Ministers (doc. A 925 of 16 March 1950). The latter proposal read as follows:

100. see also Consultative Assembly, first session, official report, 1949, p. 152 a.f.

'No one shall be subjected to torture or to inhuman treatment or punishment.'

The conference of high officials (8 to 17 June 1950) decided on the final drafting of the Article (doc. A 1445 of 19 June 1950), which was adopted by the Committee of Ministers on 7 August 1950.

In application no. 986/61 medical examination of accused persons has been brought before the European commission of human rights as an alleged breach of Article 3 (as well as of Articles 5 and 6). The commission decided in this respect that 'medical examination of accused persons constitute a normal and often desirable part of a thorough and conscientious investigation of a case' (decision of 7 May 1962, Yearbook V, p. 192).

2.3.2. Some conclusions

The final text is similar to Article 5 of the Universal Declaration, except that it does not mention the word 'cruel' presumably because it was felt to be sufficiently covered by the term 'inhuman'. The Article can be interpreted in such a way that it precludes extreme medical interventions without free consent (Partsch, 1966, p. 107).

Unlike earlier drafts for this Article, its final wording does not give any indication as to what is to be considered to be degrading treatment or punishment. [101] It is unlikely that sterilization with free consent would be considered to fall within the scope of this Article. [102] Despite the fact that the Article does not explicitly mention 'medical experimentation', it is not impossible that such acts might fall under this Article, when carried out without the free consent of the person concerned.

3. Some general remarks on the Articles discussed [103]

3.1. RIGHT TO LIFE

Whereas Article 3 of the UN Universal Declaration merely affirms the right to life, both Article 6 of the UN International Covenant on Civil and Political Rights and Article 2 of the European Convention on the Protection of Human Rights and Fundamental Freedoms are more elaborate on this point. The Covenant includes one possible limitation to the right to life, namely the death penalty. The European Convention also mentions other possible limitations, such as selfdefence and quelling a riot. However, none of the three instruments is explicit on the extent of the protection of life.

Despite the formulation of Article 6, para. 5. of the International Covenant, where it is stated that the death penalty shall not be inflicted on preg-

---

101. In its report of 14 December 1976 on application no. 5856/72, the commission of human rights has considered judicial corporal punishment (birching) as a breach of Article 3.

102. See Application no. 1287/61, decision of 4 October 1962 (unpublished), where the commission recognized that in some specific circumstances sterilization can contribute a breach of Article 2 of the Convention.

103. See also Part B, Ch.I, para. 4, and Ch. III, para. 4.

nant women, none of the instruments indicate clearly whether the right to life also extends to the unborn child (abortion) and, if so, at what time during the pregnancy. It would, however, be difficult to conclude, when reviewing the discussions on the formulation of the right to life with respect to the various instruments, that abortion, if allowed under the relevant Articles, would be permitted up until the time of birth. Another undecided matter in these instruments is the question of the rights of the sick and dying (euthanasia).

Recently, however, international organizations have focused attention on these matters. The Parliamentary Assembly of the Council of Europe, for instance, in 1976 called upon the European office of the World Health Organization to 'examine the criteria for the determination of death existing in the various European countries, in the light of current medical knowledge and techniques, and to make proposals for their harmonisation in a way which will be universally applicable not only in hospitals, but in general medical practice' (Resolution 613, 1976).

In January 1976, the Assembly also adopted a recommendation on the rights of the sick and dying (Recommendation 779, 1976). In this Recommendation it has been stated, amongst other considerations, that doctors shall act in accordance with science and approved medical experience and that no doctor or other member of the medical profession may be compelled to act contrary to the dictates of his own conscience in relation to the rights of the sick so that they do not suffer unduly.

Member states are requested by this Recommendation to establish ethical rules for the treatment of persons approaching the end of their life, and to determine the medical guiding principles for the application of extra-ordinary measures to prolong life. They should thereby consider, inter alia, the situation which may confront members of the medical profession, such as legal sanctions, (whether civil or penal), when they have refrained from effecting artificial measures to prolong the death process in the case of terminal patients, whose lives cannot be saved by presentday medicine, or have taken positive measures whose primary intention was to relieve suffering in such patients and which could have a subsidiary effect on the process of dying. They are also requested to examine the question of written declarations made by legally competent persons, authorising doctors to abstain from lifeprolonging measures, in particular in the case of irreversible cessation of brain function. Already at an earlier time, namely in 1971, the Parliamentary Assembly of the Council of Europe, when holding a conference on human rights (Vienna, 18 to 20 December 1971), recommended a special study on the beginning and end of life. It was in fact regretted that 'abortion legislators in different countries find no guidelines in the European Convention' (page 12 of the Report).

Closely linked to the determination of the moment of death is the right to dispose of the death body. These matters are also of international importance, as, for instance, in respect of transplantation of organs of human origin. The Council of Europe has developed some initial studies in this field with a view to establishing international guidelines. However, having regard to the complexity of this problem, as well as to the divergence of existing legislation in

60

this respect, it is not expected that there will soon be an international agreement to an instrument dealing with this subject. [104]

It is realistic to expect that the boundaries of the Article dealing with the right to life will become more precise as to the concepts of the beginning and the end of life, as in democratic countries they are becoming more specifically defined.

3.2. MEDICAL EXPERIMENTATION; MALTREATMENT; TORTURE

3.2.1. Medical experimentation

Article 5 of the Universal Declaration and Article 3 of the European Convention are almost identical. Article 7 of the International Covenant on Civil and Political Rights on the other hand, in an attempt to further specify the prohibition contained in the first sentence of the Article, explicitly mentions the prohibition of medical experimentation without the free consent of the person concerned. Though the relevant Articles of the other two instruments do not contain such a specification, they can hardly be interpreted not to cover this aspect too.

Fortunately, the fears expressed during the various drafting stages of Article 7 of the Covenant that the inclusion of a specific reference to medical experimentation would hinder genuine medical progress, have not been confirmed so far. On the contrary, medical experimentations are increasing in scope, and have already called for special safeguards at an international level. Whereas medical science, and hence medical experimentation, has become less restricted to the purely domestic level, it is clear that international codes, covering international research as well as 'international treatment' (such as in the field of transplantations), are increasingly required. Another aspect is the matter of approval of medical experimentation other than by the person concerned. It is the practice in various European countries to let an independent committee decide on the permissability of any such medical experimentation. It is likely that, if the Articles on this subject were elaborated at the present time, a positive stand would be taken on the inclusion of a clause relating to the approval by an independent body of any medical experimentation. It is, moreover, the opinion of many, that too often experiments are carried out on people in ill health without explicitly asking for their consent, or without any possibility for a 'medical audit' before (or after) carrying out such an act.

Both the World Health Organization and the Council of Europe have been aware of the problems relating to medical experimentation and research.

The World Health Organization is presently very involved in the development and co-ordination of biomedical research. The Organization played an

104. Council of Europe Resolution (78) 29 of 11 May 1978 on 'harmonisation of legislations of Member States relating to removal, grafting and transplantation of human substances' only contains the following on this subject: 'Article 11.1. Death having occurred a removal may be effected even if the function of some organ other than the brain may be artificially preserved'.

active part in the preparatory work on the revision of the Declaration of Helsinki of 1964 (code of ethics of the World Medical Association).

The revised code of ethics, which was adopted by the World Medical Association in Tokyo in 1975, widens the scope of the provisions of the Helsinki Declaration to include not only clinical research, but also biomedical research involving human beings. It is in this revised code that recommendations are included on the formulation − in an experimental Protocol − of all procedures involved with this kind of research and on the review of such a Protocol from the ethical point of view by an independent body.

Moreover, the role of the World Health Organization in the development and co-ordination of bio-medical research has been the subject of discussions within the Organization from 1975 on. The Organization recognizes the importance of strengthening the relationships with national and international bodies dealing with biomedical research.

In 1976 the WHO regional committee for Europe decided to set up an advisory committee for medical research with a view to shape all European research in the biomedical field in the years ahead. The setting of research priorities and outlining a co-ordinated plan of action are also envisaged.

Since 1976, WHO co-operates closely with UNESCO in the programme of the Council for International Organizations of Medical Sciences (CIOMS) on the role and functions of the ethical review committees for research involving human subjects.

The object of this programme is to:
− collect information about the experiences of the ethical review committees in countries where they have been established;
− study the methods of establishing such committees and their effectiveness in protecting the rights and welfare of human subjects used in research;
− explore the methods used in other countries for the protection of human subjects used in research.

The Council of Europe has not yet been involved with matters arising from medical experimentation and medical ethics related to research involving human subjects, though it does not neglect the topic. Resolution (73) 5 on standard minimum rules for the treatment of prisoners, for instance, refers to this matter. Rule 22 of Part I of the Appendix to the Resolution reads:

'The prisoners may not be submitted to medical or scientific experiments which may result in physical or moral injury to their person.'

Finally, the commission on human rights of the United Nations has also been attentive to the influence medical and biological scientific advances might have on the protection of human rights.

In implementation of paragraph 1b) of Resolution 2450 (XXIII) of the General Assembly of the United Nations, in which a study was requested on 'protection of the human personality and its physical and intellectual integrity, in the light of advances in biology, medicine and biochemistry', the commission discussed a report on this subject during its 31st session (1975). The report covered biological, medical, biochemical developments and experiments on human subjects (E/CN.4/1172; E/CN.4/1172/add. 1-3). The study had been undertaken with a view to explore the possibilities of preparing international instruments designed to strengthen the protection of the human rights as proclaimed in the Universal Declaration. WHO contributed to this study by preparing a report on 'health aspects of human rights in the light of scientific and technological developments' (see Part B, Ch. I, para. 4.).

These activities show that the protection of the individual against violation of his state of physical and mental health, through an active observance of the relevant Articles in the human rights instruments is a matter of constant concern of the relevant international organizations.

3.2.2. Maltreatment; torture

The abolition of torture has been a matter of concern to the UN, the WHO and the Council of Europe.

The UN adopted a Declaration on the protection of all persons from being subjected to torture and other cruel, in-human or degrading treatment or punishment on 9 December 1975 (Resolution 3452 (XXX)). From the same date stemms Resolution 3453 (XXX) in which, among other requests, the WHO was invited to give further attention to the study and elaboration of principles of medical ethics relevant to the protection of persons subjected to any form of detention or imprisonment against torture and other cruel, in-human or degrading treatment or punishment. (Resolution 3059 (XXVIII) of 2 November 1973; Resolutions 3218 (XXIX) of 6 November 1974 and 31/85 of 13 December 1976 also refer to this subject.)

On 8 December 1977 the General Assembly of the UN requested the commission on human rights to draw up a draft Convention on this subject in the light of the principles embodied in the before mentioned Declaration (Resolution 32/62).

In Resolution 32/63 of 8 December 1977 it was decided to draw up and circulate among member states a questionnaire on the steps taken to put into practice the principles of the before mentioned Declaration and in Resolution 32/64 of the same date member states were invited to make unilateral declarations against torture and other cruel, inhuman or degrading treatment or punishment for which purpose a model was designed. The WHO for its part, in pursuance of Assembly Resolution 3453 (XXX) sponsors a joint action by the World Medical Association and CIOMS to elaborate the Declaration of Tokyo for the purpose of drafting a code of medical ethics for the protection of prisoners against torture for eventual submission to the General Assembly.

Already in 1975 the WHO, upon invitation of the General Assembly of the UN (Resolution 3218 (XXIX)), prepared a report on 'the health aspects of avoidable maltreatment of prisoners and detainees' (A/Conf. 56/9). Also the Council of Europe Parliamentary Assembly has frequently debated the problem of torture (see, for instance, Recommendation 768 (1975) on torture in the world).

Another matter which requires increasingly attention is the question of how the prohibition, contained in the Articles discussed, can be more clearly described in order to determine to what point governmental interference should be tolerated and what kind of legal protection is required in this respect. Examples of these circumstances are fluoridation of drinking water, general vaccination and drug-additives. The present wording of the Articles allows for the possibility of interpretation according to national concepts, and the question then arises whether the safeguard, as presently formulated, is sufficient in this respect.

It will be clear form these brief comments that the development of medical science calls for the strengthening of existing formulations and, or establishing additional international rules to better safeguard the life and physical integrity of any human being. Due regard should in this context be paid to the fact that, though it is recognized that scientific medical research is useful and desirable, research on human beings should never be carried out for the sole purpose of research. The informed consent of the person concerned is one of the first prerequisites before any such medical experimentation may be carried out.

This problem requires the full attention of the international organizations, which are operating in the field of health care. Particularly the structure of international health care needs to be adequately organized, with a view to avoid undue overlapping or conflicting opinions, and thereby contrary action on an international scale.

4. Right to health care

4.1. UN UNIVERSAL DECLARATION OF HUMAN RIGHTS (ARTICLE 25)

4.1.1. Brief drafting history
Article 25 of the Universal Declaration of Human Rights reads as follows:

'1. Everyone has the right to a standard of living adequate for the health and well-being of himself and of his family, including food, clothing, housing and medical care and necessary social services, and the right to security in the event of unemployment, sickness, disability, widowhood, old age or other lack of livelihood in circumstances beyond his control.
2. Motherhood and childhood are entitled to special care and assistance. All children, whether born in or out of wedlock, shall enjoy the same social protection.'

During a preliminary discussion on this Article [105] at the first session of the commission on human rights (27 January to 10 February 1947) it was felt

105. Panama, in presenting a statement on the essential human rights on behalf of the Institute of American Law to the General Assembly in 1946, presented the following Article (25):
'SOCIAL SECURITY
.....
The State has a duty to maintain or insure that there are maintained comprehensive arrangements for the promotion of health, for the prevention of sickness and accident, and for the provision of medical care and of compensation for loss and livelihood'.
The comment to this Article included a statement that 'the duties imposed upon the State by this Article are to see that resources of society are organised:
1. to raise standards of health

insufficient to mention only the right to medical care. It was the opinion that one should refer to the 'right to health'[106], which not only includes medical care to be insured by the state, but also preventive measures to protect the health of the individual (E/CN.4/SR.14, p. E 64). The delegate of the USSR insisted moreover that the 'right to health' — a right universally recognized — was too vague. It would be preferable to indicate how this right could be exercised and implemented, which would be by declaring the right to medical care. If needed, this right to medical care could be worded more precisely by mentioning, for instance, the right to subsistence for the elderly and the ill, as well as in the case of the loss of the ability to work. The drafting committee of the commission on human rights, when discussing this particular right at its first session (9 to 25 June 1947) had before it the following drafts:

— 'Everyone has the right to medical care. The State shall promote public health and safety' (draft outline of an International Bill of Human Rights, secretariat, E/CN.4/ AC.1/3, Article 35 and E/CN.4/21, Annex A, Article 35);
— 'Every human being has the right to assistance from the community to protect his health. General measures should, in addition, be taken to promote public hygiene and the betterment of housing conditions and nutrition' (text of the temporary working group of the drafting committee of the commission on human rights, prepared by the French representative (E/CN.4/21, Annex D, Article 39).

The drafting committee itself was of the opinion that the Article should closely follow the Constitution of the World Health Organization, and that attention should be paid to the role of the community in fulfilling this right.[107] The then prepared text was taken from the Constitution of the WHO:

'Everyone, without distinction as to economic or social conditions, has a right to the highest attainable standard of health. The responsibility of the State and Community for the health and safety of its people can be fulfilled only by provision of adequate health and social measures' (E/CN.4/21, Annex F, Article 33).

The drafting committee suggested that this and other relevant economic and social rights should be referred to the appropriate specialised agencies of the UN for their consideration and comment. The working group on the Declaration of Human Rights[108] (established by the commission on human rights at its second session, 2 to 7 December 1947) was of the opinion that this text was too general, so that the following wording was suggested by the French representative:

2. to prevent sickness and accident
3. to provide medical care whenever needed, including maternity cases
4. .....
The wording of this Article leaves full scope to private initiative in countries where this is considered desirable, to accept as much of the responsibility as it can and will. The Article is reasonably secured' (A/148).
106. For a discussion on this term, see Part B, Ch. II para. 3.1.
107. See, also E/CN.4/21, p. 51; E/CN.4/AC.1/11 and E/CN.4/AC.1/SR 14.
108. 6 to 10 December 1947.

'Everyone has the right to protection of his health, by means of good housing, adequate food and medical care.'

The representative from the USSR, however, still felt that the text needed further clarification. He insisted that the most important object of this Article was the provision of adequate medical assistance to the poorer classes. Therefore, he was of the opinion that the right of the individual to proper protection of his health should be expressly formulated in this Article. Thereupon, the representative of the Philipiness suggested a new text for the first para. of the Article, which was acceptable to the working group (E/CN.4/AC.2/SR.8).
The full text of the Article adopted by the working group read as follows:

'Everyone, without distinction as to economic and social conditions, has the right to the preservation of his health by means of adequate food, clothing, housing and medical care. The responsibility of the State and Community for the health and safety of its people can be fulfilled only by provision of adequate health and social measures' (E/CN.4/57, Article 33).

The commission, when discussing this text in plenary session, was of the opinion that details should be defined in the Covenant and that the Declaration should only contain a synthesis. It was moreover suggested to specify in the Article, that the availability of national resources predetermine the services the state and community are able to render.
A suggestion made by the representative of Uruguay to insert 'everyone has the duty to preserve his health', however, was rejected. This amendment had been based on the idea that the imposition of this duty justified a states' intervention in matters of health (E/600, p. 24). [109]
The discussion on the insertion of this idea has two aspects. One is a matter of interpretation, that is, whether a human rights instrument places duties and obligations solely on the state or whether it also implies an individual's self-discipline. [110] Secondly, it may be argued that a person has the freedom to deal as he chooses with his own body. Certain questions arise from this concept. First, may a protection be imposed upon an individual for the sake of his own health and thus can he be prevented from certain dangerous behaviour? Further, can this sort of protection be imposed for his 'environment's' sake? The answer to the latter question seems clearly positive. The first question relates to and requires determination of the amount of responsibility a person is capable of carrying; in some cases (children or the mental ill for instance), the answer would probably be positive, at least in situations of emergency. However, there still remains the question whether treatment may be imposed on persons, who clearly refuse to accept such treatment, whenever there is only risk for his own safety, and the person concerned is supposed to

109. The same idea is found in the European Human Rights Convention; Articles 8 through 11, there state that interference in the personal life and freedom of the individual is justifiable as based upon — inter alia — the protection of health in general.
110. A somewhat similar notion is introduced in Article 11, para. b, of the European Social Charter (see para. 4.3.).

be able to express his will. The answer to this last question should in the author's opinion be a negative one.

The commission agreed on the following draft at its second session:

— 'Everyone, without distinction as to economic and social conditions, has the right to the preservation of his health through the highest standard of food, clothing, housing and medical care which the resources of the State or the Community can provide. The responsibility of the State and the Community for the health and safety of its people can be fulfilled only by provision of adequate health and social measures' (E/600, Article 25 and ESC (VI) suppl. 1, Annex A). [111]

One may note from this drafting that a qualification was introduced. By aiming at the *highest* standard, the duties and responsibilities of the state and community are clearly laid out in the light of prevalent economic and social conditions.

The drafting committee of the commission on human rights, when holding its second session (3 to 21 May 1948), did not consider the wording of the Article as adopted by the commission during its second session. [112]

During its third session (24 May to 16 June 1948), the Commission on Human Rights had moreover before it an amendment proposal from India and the United Kingdom, to substitute Articles 24-26 of the draft by the following:

— 'Everyone has the right to a standard of living adequate for health and well-being, including security in the event of unemployment, disability, old age or other lack of livelihood in circumstances beyond his control' (E/CN.4/99).

111. For comments submitted by governments, see:
E/CN.4/82 — Netherlands: delete the second sentence (too obscure);
E/CN.4/82 add. 9 — United Kingdom: delete in the first sentence the words 'without distinction as to economic and social conditions' (already covered by Article 3 of the draft); state obligations of the State more concise;
E/CN.4/82/add. 4 — South Africa: the Article describes in general terms the duties of states, rather than specific rights and freedoms of the individual. The Article goes beyond the scope of what would legitimately be regarded as rights and freedoms so fundamental as to call for international protection;
E/CN.4/82/add. 8 — France: replace the text by the following:
'Everyone without distinction as to economic or social conditions has the right to protection of his health by all the appropriate means relating to food, clothing, housing and medical care to as great an extent as the resources of the State or Community permit.
It is the duty of the State and the Community to take all adequate health and social measures to meet the responsibilities incumbent upon them'.
E/CN.4/82/add. 12 — New Zealand: replace the text by the following:
'Everyone has the right to health, and, therefore, to the benefits of the highest standard of food, clothing, housing and medical care which the resources of the State or Community can provide'.
112.` In the report of the drafting committee two alternatives were also included:
a. alternative text as presented by France, see previous footnote.
b. alternative text suggested by the United States for Articles 25 and 26:
'Everyone has the right to a standard of living necessary for health and general well-being, including social security and the opportunity to obtain adequate food, clothing, housing and medical care' (E/CN.4/95, Article 25).

The delegation of China furthermore proposed to amalgamate Articles 23-29 of the draft:

'Everyone has the right to a decent living; to work and leisure, to health, education, economic and social security' (E/CN.4/102).

During the discussions various other drafting proposals [113] were made, which were referred to a drafting subcommittee. [114] This subcommittee drafted the following text:

'1. Everyone has the right to social security. This includes the right to a standard of living and social services adequate for the health and well-being of himself and his family and to security in the event of (against the consequences of) unemployment, sickness, disability, old age or other lack of livelihood in circumstances beyond his control;
2. Mother and child have the right to special care and assistance' (E/CN.4/SR.70). [115]

It was pointed out during the discussions that the term 'social security' signified in this context the right everyone has to a standard of living and social services adequate for the health and well-being of himself and his family. In order, however, to avoid confusion with the usual definition and scope of this term, the representative of the International Labour Organisation (ILO), suggested the following redraft for para. 1.:

'Everyone has the right to a standard of living, and to social services adequate for the health and well-being of himself and his family (and to social security), including protection in the event of unemployment, sickness, old age or other lack of livelihood in circumstances beyond his control' (E/CN.4/SR.71; see also E/CN.4/SR.70).

The representative of the USSR, who considered that the Article should include the right to medical care as well as a guarantee of this right through legislative measure, presented the following text:

'1. Everyone has the right to social security and to a standard of living sufficient for the maintenance of his own welfare and health as well as those of his family, and in particular the right to material security in case of unemployment, sickness, disability,

113. These were for instance:
— India: include a new paragraph into the joint India/United Kingdom proposal: 'Mothers and children shall be granted special care and assistance'.
— U.S.A.: insert into the joint India/United Kingdom proposal before 'security' the words 'necessary social services and' in order to make clear that 'social security' included the right to services as well as to economic protection.
— United Kingdom: replace the second part of the joint India/United Kingdom proposal by: 'including social security in the event of unemployment, disability, old age or other lack of livelihood in circumstances beyond his control, and special care and assistance for mothers and children'.
— USSR: include a reference to the right of man to medical care (E/CN.4/SR.66).
114. This subcommittee was assigned the task to draft Article 22 (on social security) in a general manner as a type of 'umbrella article', and to include the essence of the earlier draft of Article 22 into the present Article on health (see para. 2.1.1.).
115. The mention of states' obligations was deleted from the Article, further to the decision to delete any such mention from the entire text (see also CH. I, para. 2.1.1.).

old age or the loss of means of existence for reasons beyond his control, and in case of unemployment, the right to social insurance at the expense of the State or of employers, in accordance with the legislation of each country.

2. Everyone has the right to medical care and physician's help in case of sickness.
3. Everyone has the right to housing worthy of the dignity of the human being. The State and community should take all necessary measures, including legislative ones, to insure for every person *real* possibilities of enjoying all these rights' (E/CN.4/ SR.71).

The ILO draft covered in general terms the principles set forth in the USSR proposal and was considered preferable to the USSR text on the grounds that it was considered impossible to issue rigid directives to individual states, as required by the latter text. The ILO text was then adopted with some amendments [116] :

'1. Everyone has the right to a standard of living, including food, clothing, housing and medical care, and to social services adequate for the health and well-being of himself and his family and to security in the event of unemployment, sickness, disability, old age or other lack of livelihood in circumstances beyond his control.
2. Mother and child have the right to special care and assistance' (E/800, Article 22 and ASC (VII), suppl. 2, Annex A). [117]

The words 'medical care' were inserted into the text, because otherwise the Article would lack any indication as to what the individual's right would be in the case of loss of health or endangered health.

The committee on social, humanitarian and cultural affairs of the Assembly [118] (third committee) to which the text of the commission has been transmitted by the Economic and Social Council, completed the Article with the inclusion of the term 'widowhood' and the sentence 'All children, whether born in or out of wedlock, shall enjoy the same social protection'. [119]

4.1.2. Some conclusions

Article 26 proclaims the right of everyone, without discrimination, to a standard of living, sufficient for his health and well-being. It thus states the fundamental right everyone has to health care. However, mere recognition of this right is not sufficient, as this right cannot be claimed as long as its content is not qualified. As this right is not well-defined, it must be interpreted according to some common rules. An attempt to qualify the right to health care was made during the various drafting stages of the Article by mentioning the

116. Chinese proposal: include 'housing and medical care, food and clothing'. United Kingdom proposal: delete 'and to social security'; replace 'including protection' by 'security' (E/CN.4/SR.71). The latter proposal was made with a view to avoid difficulties of interpretation of the words 'social security' used in the ILO text. The words were later on inserted into the 'covering' Article (22) (see also para. 2.1.1.).
117. One of the USSR proposals, which were included into the report of the third session of the commission was the following: add to the Article: 'Everyone has the right to medical care and assistance in case of illness'.
118. Third session, 21 September to 12 December 1948.
119. See, for instance, A/C.3/233 and 267. Records of the third session of the third committee, 1948; A/777.

highest standard of health and by delegating responsibility to the state and community. The present wording, however, leaves the interpretation of the word 'health' open, as well as the responsibility of those who are willing to recognize the right to health care and to act accordingly (implementation, or means for achieving the standard of living adequate for ones health). Some attention is given to this in the 'umbrella' (covering) Article 22 of the Universal Declaration, which refers to 'national efforts' and 'international co-operation'. [120] (See also Verdoodt, 1964, pp. 240-241.)

4.2. UN INTERNATIONAL COVENANT ON ECONOMIC, SOCIAL AND CULTURAL RIGHTS (ARTICLE 12)

4.2.1. Brief drafting history

Article 12 of the International Covenant on Economic, Social and Cultural Rights reads as follows:

'1. The States Parties to the present Covenant recognize the right of everyone to the enjoyment of the highest attainable standard of physical and mental health.
2. The steps to be taken by the States Parties to the present Covenant to achieve the full realization of this right shall include those necessary for:
    a. The provision for the reduction of the stillbirth-rate and of infant mortality and for the healthy development of the child;
    b. The improvement of all aspects of environmental and industrial hygiene;
    c. The prevention, treatment and control of epidemic, endemic, occupational and other diseases;
    d. The creation of conditions which would assure to all medical service and medical attention in the event of sickness.'

The special provisions concerning the right to health care were first discussed [121] during the seventh session of the commission on human rights (16 April to 19 May 1951). Various proposals [122] for an Article on this subject were submitted to the commission, including a text [123] submitted by the Director General of the World Health Organization (WHO). The latter was of the opinion that 'enjoyment of the highest obtainable standard of health should be included among the fundamental rights of every human being', and, further, that it was desirable to make provisions 'for an undertaking by Governments that adequate health and social measures be taken to that end, with due allowance for their resources, their traditions and for local conditions'.

The clauses suggested by the WHO were:

---

120. See also Ch. I, para. 2.1.1. ·
121. For previous general discussions see for instance the report of the fifth session of the commission (9 May to 20 June 1949); E/1371, para. 17; E/CN.4/353/add. 10 and discussions in the Economic and Social Council's social committee (eleventh session, 3 July to 16 August 1950; E/AC.7/SR.147).
122. E/CN.4/582, 583, 589; E/CN.4/AC.14/2/add. 4.
123. E/CN.4/544 and add. 1.

'Every human being shall have the right to the enjoyment of the highest standard of health obtainable, health being defined as a state of complete physical, mental and social well-being. Governments, having a responsibility for the health of their peoples, undertake to fulfil that responsibility by providing adequate health and social measures.

Every Party to the present Covenant shall therefore, so far as its means allow and with due allowance for its traditions and for local conditions, provide measures to promote and protect the health of its nationals, and in particular:

to reduce infant mortality and provide for healthy development of the child;

to improve nutrition, housing, sanitation, recreation, economic and working conditions and other aspects of environmental hygiene;

to control epidemic, endemic and other diseases;

to improve standards of medical teaching and training in the health, medical and related professions;

to enlighten public opinion on problems of health;

to foster activities in the field of mental health, especially those affecting the harmony of human relations.'

This text was, according to its proposor, inspired by a 'dual principle'. The first is that 'some governments, with immense financial resources can concentrate on highly specialised problems and provide measures which only benefit a very small number of people'. The second is that 'other have still to create a medical profession and health services before they can contemplate action of any kind' (E/CN.4/544).

It should be noted that the WHO, which proclaimed this 'dual principle' in 1951, on which the Organization based the fundamental right to the enjoyment of the highest attainable standard of health, has orientated its activities during the early seventies more than before towards developing countries, thus concentrating on the second part of its own principle. This adaptation of the Organization's basic philosophy is more akin to the general principle, underlying the right to health care, namely the idea of 'social justice' (equitable distribution of health care to all). There is, however, a certain risk in focusing in particular on this second part of the principle proclaimed in 1951, to lose side of the fact that the first principle is likewise of much importance (provided it does not aim at selective medicine) and equally needs international support and attention. [124]

During the discussions in the commission, the representative of the WHO also emphasized the importance of the fact that the Organization had abandoned the to some extent negative concept of health as denoted by the freedom from disease and replaced it by the notion of 'a state of complete physical, mental and social well-being' (E/CN.4/SR. 223). The proposal submitted in the course of the seventh session of the commission by the Egyptian representative served as a basis for the text of the Article, which was adopted by the commission at that session.

This proposal, which was largely inspired both by the Constitution of the WHO and by the suggestions made by the Director General of that Organization, was as follows:

124.   See also Part C, Ch. II, para. 1.2.

'.....................
Everyone shall have the right to the enjoyment of the highest standard of health obtainable. With a view to implementing and safeguarding this right [125] :
Each State party hereto undertakes to provide legislative measures to promote and protect the health of its nationals [126] and in particular:
1. to reduce infant mortality and provide for healthy development of the child;
2. to improve nutrition, housing, sanitation, economic and working conditions and other aspects of environmental hygiene;
3. to control epidemic, endemic and other diseases;
4. to improve standards of medical teaching and training in the health, medical and related professions;
5. to enlighten the public opinion on problems of health;
6. to foster activities in the field of mental health, especially those affecting the harmony of human relationships' (E/CN.4/AC.14/2/add. 4, Article 18(c)). [127]

In view of the decision taken by the commission to draft the Covenant in more general terms, this proposal, as well as the Chilean amendment to it was, however, felt by some to be too detailed. It was considered that the Constitution of the WHO made it unnecessary to detail the concept of health, of which it was recognized that social welfare formed an essential element, especially since the purpose of the Covenant was to define the position of the individual in society as a whole. Moreover, methods of providing individual medical care did not all emanate from the state, but also from health organizations, voluntary initiatives and other such bodies. The representative of the USSR in contrast, insisted that definite obligations on the part of governments should be formulated where the present Article was concerned. His views were supported by the representative of Chile, who underlined the responsibility of the state in respect to taking preventive action against disease and combating it through public health services. In his view the Article should clearly indicate the relationship between health and the standard of living (E/CN.4/SR. 223).

The majority supported these latter views, so that the Egyptian proposal, as amended by the United States and Chile, was adopted [128] :

'The States Parties to the Covenant recognize the right of everyone to the enjoyment of the highest standard of health obtainable. With a view to implementing and safeguarding this right, each State Party hereto undertakes to provide legislative measures to promote health and in particular:
a. to reduce infant mortality and provide for healthy development of the child;
b. to improve nutrition, housing, sanitation, recreation, economic and working conditions and other aspects of environmental hygiene;
c. to control epidemic, endemic and other diseases;

125. Amendment proposed by United States: replace this sentence by: 'The States Parties to this Covenant recognize the right of everyone to the enjoyment of the highest standard of health attainable' (E/CN.4/SR.233).
126. Amendment proposed by Chile: delete the words 'of its national' (E/CN.4/SR.223).
127. Amendment proposed by Chile: delete paras. 4, 5 and 6 and replace by: '4. To provide conditions which would ensure the right of all to a medical service and medical attention in the event of sickness' (E/CN.4/SR.223).
128. See also E/1992, para. 45.

d. to provide conditions which would assure the right of all to medical service and medical attention in the event of sickness' (E/1992, Annex I, Article 25). [129]

The text of the Article was discussed again during the eighth session of the commission (14 April to 14 June 1952) upon the decision whether to elaborate the two Covenants (see para. 2.2.1.). Various amendments [130] to the previous draft were presented, among which the following two are the most significant:

— United States of America:
    'The States Parties to the Covenant recognize the right of everyone to the enjoyment of the highest standard of health obtainable.
    The steps to be taken by the States Parties to the Covenant to achieve the full realization of this right shall include those necessary for:
    a. The reduction of infant mortality and the provision for healthy development of the child;
    b. The improvement of nutrition, housing, sanitation, recreation, economic and working conditions and other aspects of environmental hygiene;
    c. The prevention, treatment and control of epidemic, endemic and other dideases;
    d. The creation of conditions which would assure to all medical service and medical attention in the event of sickness' (E/CN.4/L.79/rev. 1.)
    Replace in the second paragraph of the previous proposal the words 'The steps to be taken by the Parties .... those necessary for' by the words: 'Each State Party hereto undertakes to provide legislative or other measures to promote and protect health and, in particular:' (E/CN.4/L.109).
— Uruguay:
    Add at the end of the first paragraph of the previous proposal:
    'realising that health is a state of complete physical, mental and social well-being, and not merely the absence of disease or infirmity'.

This amendment proposal contains two aspects, one being the inclusion of a definition of health and the second being the formulation of states' obligations in respect of the realization of the right to health care. Discussions in the commission centered on both these aspects. [131]
    — definition of health

129. Discussions in the Economic and Social Council (thirteenth session, 30 July to 21 September 1951) and in the third committee of the General Assembly (6th session, 6 November 1951 to 5 February 1952) did not give rise to any particular remarks; see A/2112 and E/CN.4/650. One of the comments presented by non-governmental organizations was from the World Medical Organization, which did not agree to refer to legislation only as the method for accomplishing the desired aim (E/CN.4/660).
130. See for instance E/CN.4/L.84 and 86.
131. There were also discussions on the word 'obtainable' in the USA proposal, which seemed to give consideration not only to the *individual's* inherent *limitations* to the realization of the right to health care, which were included into the word 'attainable', used in the Constitution of the WHO, but also to *social limitations*. There was general agreement that the word 'obtainable' (which was due to a translation error) implied a restriction to the obligation of a state in respect to the realization of the right under discussion, by the physiological characteristics of the individual which, at the current stage of scientific development, might prove an unsurmountable obstacle. Therefore it was decided to use the word 'attainable' (E/CN.4/SR.295).

The addition to the first paragraph of the USA proposal which was inspired by 'its origin and its intrinsic worth as representing a new and valuable idea' in stating that health was not merely the absence of disease or infirmity, but a state of complete physical, mental and social well-being (E/CN.4/SR.296 and E/2256, para. 132), was opposed on grounds that it was unnecessary to define this specific right any more than other rights. Moreover, the definition which was considered excellent in the context of the Constitution of the WHO, seemed out of place in the present context because it referred not only to complete physical and moral well-being, but also to complete social well-being. The concept of the latter was given sufficient attention in other Articles (E/CN.4/SR.295 and 296). It was, however, concluded that this part of the amendment proposal of Uraguay to the USA text was a genuine one and so it was adopted.

— states obligations

The idea to emphasize the obligation of a state to assure the right to health care to everyone was strongly supported by some delegates. The Russian representative felt that the arguments put forward by others that it was unnecessary to formulate obligations on the part of states in this Article as relevant provisions had been laid down in the general Article (2) [132] governing all the subsequent Articles, did not cover his point. The general Article (2) only laid down the obligation for states to undertake to take certain measures for the progressive realization of the rights recognized in the Covenant, which did not necessary lead to the desired results. The USSR representative emphasised in particular the need for clear and definite obligations on the part of the state to assure the right of all to medical service and medical attention in the event of sickness. The representative of Poland, moreover, considered the wording suggested by the USA to vague, so that the obligations of the state were only minor ones in that formulation.

It was also felt that the reference to the undertaking of legislative measures was preferable, as it represented a strong statement. It was in fact considered, that the Covenant on Human Rights defined obligations of states to assure rights for everyone, which therefore pleaded for a precise formulation, in order that anyone would know what their rights were and would thus be able to protest in case of violation of these rights. However, arguments of those, who were of the opinion that the general Article (2) laid down the obligations of states clearly and that a repetition of the obligations in the present Article would only weaken the meaning of the general one, prevailed (E/CN.4/ SR.296 and E/2256, para. 132), so that the following text was adopted:

'1. The States Parties to the Covenant, realizing that health is a state of complete physical, mental and social well-being, and not merely the absence of disease or infirmity, recognize the right of everyone to the enjoyment of the highest attainable standard of health.

2. The steps to be taken by the States Parties to the Covenant to achieve the full realization of this right shall include those necessary for:

132. The inclusion of this Article was decided at the seventh session of the commission (16 April to 19 May 1951, E/1992, para. 52).

a. The reduction of infant mortality and the provision for healthy development of the child;

b. The improvement of nutrition, housing, sanitation, recreation, economic and working conditions and other aspects of environmental hygiene;

c. The prevention, treatment and control of epidemic, endemic and other diseases;

d. The creation of conditions which would assure to all medical service and medical attention in the event of sickness' (E/2256, Annex I A, Article 13).

In the third committee of the General Assembly, which met from 12 November 1956 to 12 February 1957, during the eleventh session of the Assembly, the following major issues were raised (see A/3525, paras. 145-157 and A/C.3/SR.743, 744, 747 and 748).

— definition of health

Its maintenance was pleaded for on grounds that it would remove obscurity from the word 'health'; that it would stress the positive approach (health as a state of complete well-being) and that it defined the relationship between disease and social environment. The representative of the WHO was of the opinion that not only this definition had been accepted by all member states of the WHO, but that the definition also represented a summary of the health implications of the other Articles of the Covenant, because it recognized the close relationship between social factors and some specific diseases (leprosy, venereal diseases, mental and occupational diseases and others).

The arguments of those who considered the definition unnecessary and unsatisfactory, because it was likely to be incomplete and also unnecessary 'verbose', however, prevailed. A suggestion was then made to delete the definition in the first clause of Article 13 of the draft text of the commission on human rights and to replace it by the following: 'The States Parties to the Covenant recognize the rights of everyone to the highest attainable standards of physical, mental, moral and social well-being' (A/C.3/L.589).

Though there was agreement on the deletion of the definition of health, it was considered to be essential to somehow retain the word 'health', as it was the subject of the Article. 'Moral' in this concept was thought to be inappropriate and out of place. The word 'social', which was suggested to replace the words 'social well-being' as the latter was opposed to on grounds that health — being the subject of the Article — and well-being are two different concepts, which vary widely in scope, was not found clear enough, so that agreement was reached on the wording 'the highest attainable standard of physical and mental health'.

— inclusion of the word 'stillbirth'

It was decided to include the word 'stillbirth' (A/C.3/L/593) on the ground that it would complete the words 'infant mortality', which referred only to death after birth, and not to death previous to, or at the time of delivery.

— treatment and prevention of occupational diseases

The inclusion of these words were favoured on grounds that it would stress the duty of the State to protect workers from occupational diseases. A minority of the Committee, however, was of the opinion, that the words 'and other

75

diseases' in para. 2(c) of the Article under discussion made such an inclusion superfluous, and that the protection of workers against occupational diseases was sufficiently covered by the provisions of Articles 7 and 8 of the Covenant.

  — compulsory medical treatment (freedom of the individual)

There was considerable discussion on the question whether the Article should provide some safeguard against compulsory medical treatment. It was felt that this Article, which was concerned with the protection of the health of the individual, should specify the limits beyond which the individual could not be compelled to accept medical treatment, in order that the provisions drawn up would not infringe the personal freedom. The need for a proper balance between the interests of the community and those of the individual was stressed. It was, for instance, felt that the individual had the right to choose his own doctor or to select the type of treatment he preferred. An amendment to this end was suggested by Italy and Uruguay which aimed at adding a third paragraph to the Article:

'3. Everyone is under a duty to care for his health and to undergo appropriate medical treatment.
Nothing in this article may be interpreted as authorizing the compulsory imposition of particular medical treatment, except as provided by law for reasons of public health. The law may not go beyond the limits imposed by respect for the human person' (A/C.3/L.590/Rev. 1).

The main purpose of this proposal was to protect the freedom of the individual against certain abuses, such as compulsory sterilization. The representative of Uruguay stated in this respect '... . The question was by no means one of justifying suicide or ignorance, but avoiding abuses that might arise, for example, from the enthousiasm of the medical profession for certain kinds of treatment which, in the long run, might not achieve the expected results. Science was not infallible. The law should therefore proceed with caution and should accordingly provide explicitly that it could not go beyond the limits imposed by respect of the human person ...' (A/C.3/SR.746 par. 28).

It was felt that Article 4 of the draft Covenant, which defined the circumstances in which the rights set forth in the Covenant could be subjected to limitations by the state, did not cover this point. When discussing this amendment proposal, there was a divergence of views on the question whether or not the point at issue was sufficiently covered by Article 7 of the Covenant on Civil and Political Rights, which dealt with torture, degrading punishment and medical experimentation without the free consent of the person involved.

The inclusion of the proposed paragraph was, however, rejected on various grounds. These included that such a provision would be out of place in the Covenant under discussion; that it would interfere with the doctor-patient relationship; that it would raise practical difficulties; that legislative measures obliging the individual to care for his health, which logically followed from the first sentence seemed inappropriate; that there was a great variety of measures which were regarded normal in some countries and violations of respect for the human person in other; that there were many situations in which it was impossible to obtain consent; and that the matter was preferably dealt with in the Covenant on Civil and Political Rights.

The text, as amended by the third committee, was then adopted by the General Assembly.

4.2.2. Some conclusions

The second paragraph of the Article dealing with the right to health care should not be looked upon as an exhaustive enumeration of the fields in which states party to the Covenant are to take action to ensure the realization of this right. They are merely some examples of the fields in which at the time of drafting the Article action was found to be most urgently needed.

The first draft of the Article was much stronger in its formulation of obligations to be undertaken by states; it included, for instance, the provision of legislative measures. However, the consequence of the inclusion of a general (covering) Article, was that in this Article undertakings on the part of states for the realization of all rights covered by the Covenant are formulated in general terms and that it indicates the progressive character of the Covenant, so that the Article on the right to health care has become much less stringent. Any indication as to how states are to fulfil their obligations is missing from the text, nor does it contain an indication as to the level of provisions to be taken. The Article now is a mere statement of those conditions, which are considered essential for the protection and promotion of health of the individual. Any claim by individuals on the state to fulfil its obligations in this respect can hardly be based on the wording.

It should further be noted, that unlike the Universal Declaration where an 'adequate standard of living' is closely linked to the level of 'health' which should be attained, the International Covenant on Economic, Social and Cultural Rights has separated the 'standard of living' from the Article on the right to health care.

Finally, mention should be made of the fact that though the Covenant does not contain a definition of health, which would necessarily be incomplete, an attempt has been made to qualify the notion of health in making a distinction between *physical* and *mental* health. It is to be noted that the first clause of the Preamble of the Constitution of the WHO of 1946 contains a definition of health. In this clause a distinction is made between *physical* and *mental* health and *social wel-being*.

4.3. EUROPEAN SOCIAL CHARTER (ARTICLE 11)

4.3.1. Brief drafting history

Article 11 of the European Social Charter reads as follows:

'The right to protection of health
With a view to ensuring the effective exercise of the right to protection of health, the Contracting Parties undertake, either directly or in co-operation with public or private organizations, to take appropriate measures designed inter alia:
1. to remove as far as possible the cause of ill-health

2. to provide advisory and educational facilities for the promotion of health and the encouragement of individual responsibility in matters of health
3. to prevent as far as possible epidemic, endemic and other diseases.' [133]

The memorandum by the secretariat general of the Council of Europe on the role of the Council in the social field was the first document relating to the drafting of a Charter. It contained 'general health protection' as one of the principles which might be included in the Charter (document 140, 1953, para. 16).

— proceedings in the Consultative Assembly [134]

The aforementioned suggestion was reflected in the following preliminary draft [135] of the Charter, prepared by the secretariat of the committee on social questions of the Consultative Assembly in April 1955, and discussed by a working party of that committee.

'Every person should have access to facilities for ensuring a high standard of health.
The measures to be taken by the signatory Governments to secure the enjoyment of this right, in cases where the private resources and initiatives of individuals or communities are inadequate, will include:
(a) the reduction of infant mortality and provision for the healthy physical and moral development of the child; assistance to mentally defective children and those deserted or in distress; re-education of maladjusted children;
(b) the improvement of nutrition, housing, education, recreation and other health factors connected with his surroundings;
(c) the prevention, treatment and control of epidemic, endemic and other diseases;
(d) the organisation of services and facilities to ensure for all effective medical attention in the event of sickness;
(e) free basic medical care and treatment.'
(European Social Charter, Collected texts of the travaux préparatoires, Vol. I, p. 42, Article 3; unpublished.)

The working party of the committee on social questions adopted this text in June 1955 with a minor amendment to the first sentence, where *'access to'* was replaced by 'the benefit of'. [136]

The committee on social questions of the Assembly decided at its meeting on 10 September 1955 to submit this text to the Consultative Assembly with a minor amendment to the second paragraph, in which the words *'to be taken by the signatory Governments'* were replaced by the words *'by which the High Contracting Parties undertake'*. [137]

---

133. Clause eleven of the Preamble of the Social Charter states in respect to the right to health care, that 'everyone has the right to benefit from any measures enabling him to enjoy the highest possible standard of health attainable'.
134. See para. 2.4.1. for the simultaneous discussions in the Consultative Assembly and the social committee (governmental experts).
135. This text was first included in a memorandum of the secretariat of the committee on social questions of 19 March 1955 (AS/SOC (6) 25; unpublished).
136. European Social Charter, Collected texts of the travaux préparatoires, Vol. I, p. 81; unpublished.
137. Consultative Assembly, second ordinary session, September 1955, doc. 403 of 26 October 1955, Article 12.

During discussions, which were held at the Consultative Assembly (seventh session, September/October 1955) on the draft Charter, the necessity for providing free basic medical care and treatment to everyone, as included in paragraph (e) of the Article on the right to health care, was questioned by some. It was argued in this respect that every individual should bear his own responsibility (self help). There was a feeling that a system of free medical care for everyone could be the solution in some countries, but not necessary in all. The meaning of the notion 'free medical care' was equally questioned. At the request of the committees on economic questions and social questions of the Consultative Assembly, the Office of the Clerk then prepared a revised draft, in which the challenged notion of 'free basic medical care and treatment' was weakened to the level that effective medical attention should be available for everyone, irrespective of their circumstances. In this way states would be free in their choice of the system of either free medical care or any other solution. This draft, presented to the committees on social questions and economic questions of the Consultative Assembly in January 1956, reads as follows:

'The right to a high standard of health
In order to ensure the enjoyment of this right, the High Contracting Parties *will take all* appropriate measures:
(a) to ensure the reduction of infant mortality and provision for the healthy physical, mental and moral development of the child;
(b) to improve nutrition, housing, sanitation, health education, recreation and other environmental health factors;
(c) to prevent epidemic, endemic and other diseases;
(d) to organise services and facilities so that all may receive effective medical attention in the event of sickness, irrespective of their economic circumstances.' (European Social Charter, Collected texts of the travaux préparatoires, Vol. I, p. 181, Article 9; unpublished.)

It will be noted that the reference to private resources, initiatives of individuals or communities, which was contained in the draft of the secretariat was deleted from this text.

The committee on economic questions adopted the draft for this Article at its meeting of 24 January 1956 with the following amendments:

— Deletion of the words '*In order to ensure the enjoyment of this right*' in the first line;
— replacement of the word '*receive*' by the words '*be assured*' in paragraph (d);
— deletion of the words '*irrespective of their economic circumstances*' in paragraph (d). (Doc. AS/EC (7) PV 11; unpublished.)[138]

In this text, which was equally adopted by the committee on social questions[139] on 9th March 1956 and then presented to the Consultative Assembly

138. This amendment tallied with some proposals presented to the committee on social questions by the chairman of the committee on economic questions, during a joint meeting of both committees, equally held on 24th January 1956.
139. There is a synoptic table of the draft Social Charter which is in doc. 403, the

(eighth session, first part, April 1956, doc. 488, Article 10; European Social Charter, Collected texts of the travaux préparatoires, Vol. I, p. 293; unpublished), the consideration of economic circumstances had disappeared entirely.

In the Assembly the close co-operation with the World Health Organization in respect of the realization of this right was insisted upon, while it was also remarked that states should not have too great an influence on public health measures. This latter remark tallied with the previous draft of the secretariat (April 1955), where a reference was made to private resources, initiatives of individuals or communities. [140]

A new text was then prepared by the rapporteur of the committee on general affairs of the Assembly (11 July 1956), in which the following words were added to the first sentence of the Article:

'With a view to ensuring the exercise of this right, ...' (European Social Charter, Collected texts of the travaux préparatoires, Vol. I, p. 351, Article 9; unpublished).

The committee on general affairs was itself of the opinion, that though 'health' was one of the fields of collective responsibility, more emphasis should be placed upon private organizations and the role of the state to encourage such organizations in their activities in the field of health, and that the state should intervene only if these organizations were absent or inadequate.[141]

This point was incorporated into the text which was then presented to the Consultative Assembly and adopted by the latter at its eighth session (second part) in October 1956:

'*The right to a high standard of health*
With a view to ensuring the effective exercise of this right, the High Contracting Parties will take all appropriate measures directly or in co-operation with local authorities and competent private organisations:
(a) to ensure the reduction of infant mortality and provision for the healthy physical, mental and moral development of the child;
(b) to improve nutrition, housing, sanitation, health education, recreation and other environmental health factors;
(c) to prevent epidemic, endemic and other diseases;
(d) to organise services and facilities so that all may receive effective medical attention in the event of sickness'. (European Social Charter, Collected texts of the travaux préparatoires, Vol. I, pp. 380, 389 and 392; unpublished.)[142]

amendments of the committee on economic questions, and the observations by the rapporteurs of both committees in: European Social Charter, Collected texts of the travaux préparatoires, Vol. I, pp. 278-279; unpublished.
140. European Social Charter, Collected texts of the travaux préparatoires, Vol. I, p. 309; unpublished.
141. European Social Charter, Collected texts of the travaux préparatoires, Vol. I, p. 366; unpublished.
142. Doc. 536. Submitted to the Committee of Ministers by Recommendation 104, in which the Consultative Assembly recommended to that Committee to establish a European Convention on Social and Economic Rights, taking into consideration the Assembly's draft.

Thus, in this text the previous notion of 'private resources, initiatives of individuals or communities', included in a negative manner in the draft of the secretariat (April 1955), was re-inserted, but this time in a more positive sense. The formulation of the undertakings from the part of contracting parties in respect to the realization of the right to health care is very similar to the one used in the (then still draft) International Covenant on Economic, Social and Cultural Rights (at that time Article 13). [143]

The Committee of Ministers then instructed the social committee (of governmental experts) to proceed with the drafting of a European Social Charter (and not, as previously envisaged by the social committee, of a text of a purely delaratory nature), taking into account the text prepared by the Consultative Assembly. [144]

— proceedings in the social committee (governmental experts)

The social committee also worked on a text for social rights, while the Assembly discussed this matter. At its third session, held in January 1956, the social committee already envisaged 'health' to be one of the subjects for inclusion into the text. With a view to prepare the contents of such an Article a questionaire[145] prepared by the committee of experts in public health (the body competent to deal with matters in the field of health) was sent to member governments in February 1957. This questionaire was largely inspired by the Constitution of the World Health Organization. It contained some basic principles: the definition of health in para. 1; the rights of individuals in para. 2; the responsibility of governments and measures to be taken by the latter in paras. 3 and 4; three questions and a note from the committee of experts on public health. The questions were of the following nature:
— whether the principles formulated in the four paragraphs of the text were acceptable;
— whether these principles should be formulated as a declaration of principles or whether they should take the form of obligations;
— other possible remarks governments might wish to make.

The description of the kind of measures to be taken by governments to ensure the realization of the right to health care as included in the questionaire parted considerably from the draft prepared by the Consultative Assembly. In the latter undertakings were precisely formulated, while the first was confined to a general statement of appropriate measures in the social and health field to be taken by governments in implementing their responsibility for the health of their people (para. 3), which was followed (para. 4) by three kinds of measures to be taken to that effect (removal as far as possible of causes of ill health; adequate medical care in case of illness, or for readaptation purposes and advisory and educational facilities for the promotion of health and the encouragement of individual responsibility). [146] The commit-

143. See para. 4.2.
144. Resolution (56) 25 of 15 December 1956.
145. European Social Charter, Collected texts of the travaux préparatoires, Vol. II, pp. 76-85; unpublished.
146. From paragraph 4 the clauses dealing with the removal of causes of ill-health (para. 4 (a)) and with the provision of educational facilities (para. 4 (c)) were included in the final text of the Article (paras. 1 and 2).
⟶

tee of experts in public health in fact thought this formulation preferable, as it appeared more prudent and realistic. [147]

The note of the committee of experts in public health which was included in the text sent to governments included a statement that the committee was of the opinion that countries might contribute effectively to progress in the field of health through co-operation, in particular within the framework of international organizations.

The replies received to the questionaire showed a divergence of opinion, in particular on the desirability to include a definition on the notion of 'health' and on the form the right should be presented in (declaration of principles or a precise statement on undertakings from the part of contracting parties). [148]

The secretariat then prepared two alternatives for the text of this Article on basis of the wording prepared by the Consultative Assembly, the questionaire and the replies received to the questionaire. The first proposal was drafted in the form of a declaration, and the second was formulated as an obligation on the part of contracting parties. Both proposals contained possible variations based upon the replies to the questionaire (European Social Charter, Collected texts of the travaux préparatoires, Vol. II, pp. 77-79; unpublished).

The legal department of the Council of Europe then prepared a revised text which was similar to the second proposal. This text did not, however, contain a definition of 'health':

'*Right to health*
With a view to ensuring the effective exercise of this right, the High Contracting Parties undertake, either directly or in co-operation with public or private organisations, to take appropriate measures designed inter alia:
a)   to remove as far as possible the cause of ill-health;
b)   to provide advisory and educational facilities for the promotion of health and the encouragement of individual responsibility in matters of health;
c)   to prevent as far as possible epedemic, endemic and other diseases'. (European Social Charter, Collected texts of the travaux préparatoires, Vol. II, p. 161; unpublished.) [149]

During discussions at the sixth session of the social committee (25 to 29 November 1957) the Swedish representative was opposed to the obligatory character of the formulation of this Article because only those undertakings on the part of the contracting parties which can be controlled effectively, could in his views be formulated as obligations (European Social Charter, Collected texts of the travaux préparatoires, Vol. II, pp. 165 and 201; unpublished).

The clause dealing with provisions for adequate medical care in case of illness and adequate measures for readaptation (para. 4 (b)) was not maintained in the final text because it was felt that this matter was sufficiently covered by other articles of the Charter.
147.   European Social Charter, Collected texts of the travaux préparatoires, Vol. II, p. 77; unpublished.
148.   European Social Charter, Collected texts of the travaux préparatoires, Vol. II, pp. 76-85; unpublished.
149.   This Article was slightly amended at the seventh session of the social committee (17 to 21 February 1958): the leading of the Article: 'the right to protection of health' and the first sentence: 'With a view to ensuring the effective exercise of the right to protection of health ...' (CE/Soc/Tr.Pr. (70) 13, p. 26; unpublished).

— further proceedings

This text was then discussed at the tripartite conference of governmental experts, and representatives of organizations of employers and workers, convened by the International Labour Organisation in December 1958. [150]

At the conference, the divergence of views between those who preferred the Article relating to the right to health care to be formulated as a mere declaration and those who wanted to maintain the obligatory character, persisted.

The draft of the Article [151] was then considered in a subcommittee of the committee of social questions of the Consultative Assembly (June 1959), which suggested to read the first sentence as follows:

'with a view to ensuring the effective exercise of the right to protection of *physical* and *mental* health, the High Contracting Parties ...' (Doc. AS/Soc (11) PV 2; unpublished).

It was furthermore suggested to include at the end of clause a) *'including slums'* [152]. This text was confirmed by the committee on social questions in September 1959, and by the Consultative Assembly in January 1960 (opinion no. 32).

The social committee (governmental experts) examined once more the draft in April 1960, when it had also before it the opinion (no. 32) of the Consultative Assembly of January 1960. The committee decided not to include the words 'physical and mental' in the first sentence, as recommended by the Consultative Assembly, because this expression was thought to be too vague. (This is in contrast with both the Preamble of the Constitution of the WHO and the International Covenant on Economic, Social and Cultural Rights, in which texts this qualification has been introduced.) The amendment proposal of the Consultative Assembly to insert at the end of clause a) 'including slums' was also not maintained, as it was felt that it was preferable not to cite one cause of ill-health if they were not all to be included. [153]

The Committee of Ministers finally adopted the text of the Article on 6 July 1961 as prepared by the legal department in November 1957, with the amendment made to it in 1958 by the social committee to read the heading of the Article as 'the right to protection of health' and to read the first sentence: 'with a view to ensuring the effective exercise of the right to protection of health ...'.

---

150. A table comparing the draft European Social Charter and corresponding standards of the International Labour Organisation was presented at the conference (European Social Charter, Collected texts of the travaux préparatoires, Vol. II, pp. 261 and 262; unpublished).

151. The text was also subject of a study of the Charter in relation to activities in various countries by a commission of the 'European Symposium of the International Conference of Social Service' (July 1959). In its conclusions the commission remarked that the Article was too generally formulated. The need for a stronger formulation of requirements for public health, of the importance of public health for mothers, children and elderly people was also stressed (CE/Soc/Tr.Pr. (70) 13, p. 31; unpublished).

152. Doc. AS/Soc (11) PV 2 and CE/Soc/Tr.Pr. (70) 13, p. 30; both unpublished.

153. CE/Soc/Tr.Pr. (70) 13, p. 36; unpublished.

4.3.2. Some conclusions

The Consultative Assembly's draft of Article 11, which closely followed the text of the International Covenant on Economic, Social and Cultural Rights, was more far reaching in the measures to be taken by contracting parties, than the final wording. Thus, for instance, the notion of the right on access to facilities etc. has been replaced by simply stating 'ensuring the effective exercise of the right to protection of health'. The right to free medical care and treatment has also disappeared.

The only clauses adopted from the draft of the text of the Consultative Assembly are the one pertaining to the tasks of public and private organizations, and the clause which is in para. 3 (prevention of epidemic, endemic and other diseases). The Constitution of the World Health Organization (one of the texts on which the drafting of the Article was based) contains an identical clause on prevention, namely in Chapter II, Article 2 (g).

It is also worthwhile noting that the 'heading' of the Article has changed in the course of its drafting from 'right to a high standard of health' and 'right to health'[154] into 'right to protection of health', which has a narrower sense.

The whole of Article 11 gives the impression to have been written with a very cautious pen and does not seem to give full justice to the right to health care. No attempt has been made to qualify the right to 'protection of health' as has been the case both with the Constitution of the WHO and the International Covenant on Economic, Social and Cultural Rights. Furthermore, the only direct, concrete obligation of governments without the reservation 'as far as possible' is to provide advisory and educational facilities. The Article also does not indicate limitatively what should be undertaken by contracting parties with a view to realize the right to 'protection of health'. It only gives examples of general governmental tasks and possible measures in this respect.

Thus great lattitude is given to contracting parties and there is no precise guarantee for the individual who wishes to claim his right.

The realization of the right to 'health protection' depends entirely on the readiness of the governments to undertake formally obligations. The measures recommended for the realization of the right contained in Article 11 of the Charter lack undertakings on the part of states, whilst also the non-immediate binding character of the relevant right will fail to stimulate its realization.

Therefore, not much is to be expected from the influence of the Social Charter in respect of the realization of the right to health care.

It is of course inevitable that the system of flexibility has been chosen because much depends on the development of national economy and social structures. The availability of medical facilities and the possibility to develop them will inevitable influence the application of this right.

There are, however, some interesting points in the Article, in that it expressly formulates the task of public and private organizations in respect of the realization of the right to health care and that it draws attention to the individual's responsibility.

154. For a discussion on this term, see Part B, Ch. II, para 3.1. on the World Health Organization.

5. *Some general remarks on the Articles discussed* [155]

The right to health care is formulated differently in the three instruments which were discussed (Article 25 of the Universal Declaration of Human Rights; Article 12 of the International Covenant on Economic, Social and Cultural Rights and Article 11 of the European Social Charter). In none of these instruments is the term 'right to health care' used. The relevant right appears as 'a right to a standard of living adequate for the health' (Universal Declaration), 'a right to the enjoyment of the highest attainable standard of health' (International Covenant, reflecting the definition of health used in the Constitution of the WHO), and as 'a right to health protection' (Social Charter). [156] Despite this difference in approach, there can be no difference of opinion on the fact that the three Articles aim at 'the right to health care'.

The difficulty which was encountered when drafting the various Articles was to define this right as clearly as possible, which may be one of the reasons for the various formulations. Article 25 of the Universal Declaration does not contain any indication on the measures to be taken by the states to realize the right to health care. In the Social Charter, the formulation of undertakings by contracting parties is a general and prudent one; see, for instance, paras 1 and 3, where the measures to be taken by contracting parties are subject to the reservation 'as far as possible'. Also the Social Charter does not make a distinction between *physical* and *mental* health, as in the case of the International Covenant [157] , because its significance was considered to be unclear. It does in fact contain no 'qualification' of the notion of 'adequate health care' or 'standard of health' as is the case in the two other instruments.

In order to ensure the most effective guarantee of this right its formulation should be as precise as possible. An attempt to achieve this has been made in the formulation of the right to health care in the International Covenant. This instrument clearly reflects the growing tendency to pay more attention to the social human rights. In respect of the right to health care it is more mandatory than the Social Charter in the formulation of some of the obligatory measures which are to be taken by states parties. They also cover more fields than those included in the Social Charter, including, for instance, the creation of conditions for medical services available to all, as well as child health care. On the other hand, unlike the International Covenant, the Social Charter puts a certain responsibility regarding the fulfilment of the right under discussion on public and, or private organizations. [158] It also stresses the individual's responsibility in matters of health (para 2).

However, though these may be the general guidelines which are given to

155. See also Part B, Ch. I, para. 4. and Ch. III, para. 4.
156. For a discussion on these terms, see Part B, Ch. II, para. 3.1. on the World Health Organization.
157. The Preamble of the Constitution of the WHO, which served as an example for both texts includes, moreover, the notion of 'social well-being'.
158. During discussions on Article 25 of the Universal Declaration the issue of community involvement was also raised (see para. 4.1.). The role of health organizations, voluntary initiatives and other such bodies was also hinted at during discussions on the International Covenant (see para. 4.2.).

states concerning the realization of the right to health care, the respective instruments do not exclude the possibility that states may adopt a divergent policy without denying the existence of this right in a particular case. There remains the difficulty that this right, as well as the other rights covered by the respective instruments, are not enforceable before a court.

The periodic reporting system which applies to both the Covenant and the European Social Charter has its obvious weaknesses. Moreover, in the case remarks and comments are made as to the implementation of this particular right, they will mostly not have a wider audience than the national health departments.

Still the programme of reporting on the implementation of the Covenant includes various arrangements for securing co-operation of the specialised agencies (see Resolution 1988 (LX)). Reports under Article 12 of the Covenant will be due in 1980 only; therefore it is still too early to pass judgment on the role of the WHO in this context.

Regarding the European Social Charter, the implementation procedure does not provide for a specific task of one or the other governmental experts committees which deal with matters relating to the realization of the right to health care. On the other hand the Parliamentary Assembly has been assigned a specific task in the supervisory system of the European Social Charter. Thus, for instance, the report of the Parliamentary Assembly (doc. 3949 of 1977) on the fourth period of supervision of the Charter, calls attention to the fact that the provisions of Article 11 are considered to be ineffective in respect of the problems of pollution and the environment. The need for particular attention to prophylactic measures is also underlined in this report, in particular as regards the recrudescence of epidemic and venereal diseases. It moreover draws attention to iatrogenic diseases and new risks to consumers resulting from, for instance, food processing.

Through discussions in the Parliamentary Assembly, there is a possibility to raise subsequently particular matters in national parliaments, but it is rather doubtful that this will happen in practice regarding the right to health care. In general those who are directly concerned with the realization of the right to health care and to whom, therefore, specific recommendations should be addressed, will hardly be aware of the fact that attention has been called to some specific aspects of the realization of this right. The involvement of mass media and, or specialised magazines could make a useful contribution to the spreading of such knowledge.

It would be of interest to hold an enquiry within states parties to the International Covenant and to the Charter to find out their opinion on the urgency, necessity and methods for application of the right.

In view of the above it seems logical to study the ways and means in which the right to health care could be better guaranteed, preferably by elaborating legal instruments with a view to develop an effective control system. During the Council of Europe parliamentary conference on human rights, which was held in Vienna in October 1971, it was stated that at least some of the economic and social rights should be developed into full 'individual' rights, similar to the 'classical' human rights, by giving them more substance and by submitting their observance to a more effective control system. (See the report of the conference, 1972, p. 25.) Such a control system should contain a complaints procedure for individuals in respect of the presumed non-observance of the right to health care.

It is recognized that a more effective control system is all the more difficult to set up when more states are called to make choices of priority as to the organization of health care systems on the national level. Also, the fact that due to the relative scarcity of particularly advanced treatment methods, decisions have to be made on who will benefit the most from a specific treatment, complicates an effective system of control, whereby an individual might claim optimal measures for his own health.

Despite these difficulties in ensuring the optimal realization of the right to health care, it is encouraging that states have realized that international cooperation is indispensable in this respect. The need for international co-operation through international organizations was stressed both during discussions on the Article pertaining to the right to health care in the International Covenant and in the European Social Charter, and is also given attention in Article 22 of the Universal Declaration. In particular the task of the World Health Organization in this field was underlined during the discussions.

It should be noted, moreover, that the United Nations through its commission on human rights continues to deploy its efforts for the further elaboration of the right to health care in drawing up additional and more detailed standards on various aspects of this right:

Examples of achievements are: [159]

— the Standard Minimum rules for the Treatment of Prisoners (Resolution 663 C (XXIV) of 31 July 1957);
— the Declaration on the Rights of the Child (Resolution 1386 (XIV) of 20 November 1959); [160]
— the Declaration on the Rights of the Mentally Retarded Persons (Resolution 2856 (XXVI) of 20 December 1971);
— the Declaration on the Rights of the Disabled Persons (Resolution 3447 (XXX) of 9 December 1975).

Yet another formal declaration deserves to be mentioned. This is the Declaration on Social Progress and Development of 11 December 1969 (Resolution 2542 (XXIV)). This Declaration was prepared by the commission for social development. Article 19 of the Declaration advocates the provision for health, social security and social welfare services to all as well as the institution of appropriate measures for the rehabilitation of the mentally and physically handicapped.

Furthermore, various aspects of the right to health care in relation to scientific and technological developments have been the subject of reports prepared in the United Nations division of human rights, such as: The protec-

159. The WHO contributes to these activities, see Part B, Ch. I, para. 4.
160. In 1978 the Commission has taken the initiative with a view to the conclusion of a convention on the rights of the child and the adoption of this Convention by the General Assembly during the International Year of the Child (1979); Resolution 29 (XXVIV).

tion of the human personality and its physical and intellectual integrity in the light of advances in biology, medicine and biochemistry; the balance which should be established between scientific and technological progress and the intellectual, spiritual, cultural and moral advancement of humanity; the right to a standard of living adequate for health and well-being; the impact of scientific and technological developments on economic, social and cultural rights; the protection of the individual against threats arising from the use of computerised personal data systems; the human rights implications of the genetic manipulation of microbes. Finally, principles for the protection of prisoners or detainees which are in the process of being formulated will include relevant clauses on medical supervision and care, the recording of results of physical examination and suitable medical attention. Also the possibility for formulating guidelines on the protection of those, detained on the grounds of mental ill-health, against treatment that may adversely affect the human personality and its physical and intellectual integrity, is under study.

The Council of Europe also deploys various activities in this field, which mostly result in the adoption of a resolution. Council of Ministers Resolution (73) 5 on standard minimum rules for the treatment of prisoners is one example. In this Resolution rules are laid down for hygiene measures, medical services, individualization of treatment and special rules for insane or mentally abnormal prisoners. Another example is Resolution (78) 29 on harmonization of the legislation of member states relating to removal, grafting and transplantation of human substances; a resolution on the international exchange and transport of substances of human origin and a resolution on human artificial insemination are under preparation. The possibility of drawing up an instrument for the protection of the rights of the patient is under consideration. [161]

161. See also Part. B, Ch. III, para. 3.3.

Part B- International organizations

I. The World Health Organization

1. Brief historical review

1.1. HISTORICAL DEVELOPMENT OF INTERNATIONAL HEALTH WORK

The creation of the World Health Organization (WHO), which is the single world-wide Organization for directing and co-ordinating intergovernmental health services was not a spontaneous act. On the contrary, it represented the culmination of some 120 years of effort (at first on a very limited scale, with restricted objectives) for international co-operation in solving health problems. The roots of international co-operation for the improvement of health conditions lay in Europe where the first international health gatherings took place in Paris in 1851 on sanitary regulations and in Brussels in 1853 on the use of a uniform classification of the causes of death.

The basis for the initial, concerted governmental action in the health field lay not, as might have been expected, in the human consideration for the protection of the health of individuals. It was the growing concern for the removal of hindrances to trade and export and the defence of Europe against 'exotic pestilencies'. It was in particular the quarantine regulations of various nations to combat the spread of infectious diseases such as cholera, yellow fever and plague, which brought − in first instance European − governments together. Therefore, the international health congresses, of which ten were held during the 19th century, were only concerned with the eradication of communicable diseases.

In 1851, when the first international health meeting was held, quarantine and pilgrimages were the major topics of discussion. Unlike other international gatherings held during this period, this one brought together not only, as usual, diplomats, but also technical (medical) experts.

Gradually, the concerted action of governments in the health field was extended; attention became focused on larger fields. Certain ideas touched on during consequent international health conferences held in the 19th century, which were realized during the 20th Century, included:
− bringing about a single general quarantine convention;
− organizing an epidemiological intelligence service;
− focusing attention not only upon quarantine, but also upon the active combat of these diseases (preventive action);
− developing specific measures for pilgrimages, and
− setting up a permanent organization for the realization of the above (v.d. Berg, 1973, p. 3).

Thus, concerted governmental efforts for the improvement of health evolved gradually towards the attainment of the ideal of unity and universality and of its present broad humanitarian objectives. Activities were gradually undertaken to include the establishment of international standards as well as international assistance in the amelioration of health services in less advanced countries. Presently, the scope of international health work covers practically the entire range of health concerns, among which an important place is given to the international exchange of knowledge and combined research.

In 1851, the first International Sanitary Convention was drawn up on Quarantine Regulations (Goodman, 1971, p. 46). It dealt with plague, yellow fever and cholera. Despite the fact that the Convention never came into force, it still may be seen as the root of the present International Sanitary Regulations. One of the reasons that the Convention remained a dead letter was that some provisions of the Convention dealt with matters of strictly national concern and could therefore interfere with national sovereignty (Arbab — Zadeh, 1963, p. 2543). Furthermore, the knowledge of the nature and mode of propagation of the three diseases concerned was not yet well enough advanced.

1.2. FORMER INTERNATIONAL HEALTH ORGANIZATIONS

1.2.1. Office International d'Hygiène Publique (OIHP)

The idea for the creation of a permanent non-regional health organization was first launched at the fourth international health meeting, held in Paris in 1874. This meeting recommended the establishment of a permanent commission on epidemics. The recommendation was, however, not implemented, presumably because a number of governments expressed doubts as to the practicability and feasibility of this type of institution (Goodman, 1971, pp. 59-60).

This concept was elaborated at the eleventh international health meeting, held in Paris in 1903, when the French government put forward proposals for the establishment of an International Sanitary Office in Paris (Fraser Brockington, 1975, p. 153; Goodman, 1971, p. 70). At the same meeting, four separate international sanitary conventions (of 1892, 1893, 1894 and 1897) were consolidated into a single Convention. It included up to date international quarantine requirements as well as specific measures on cholera and plague and to a lesser extent on yellow fever.

The very existence of this Convention made it indispensable that its application be placed in the hands of an international body. Article 181 of the Convention contained provision for the possible creation of such an office.

Therefore the 1903 proposal was bound to become reality, and in 1907 an international agreement was signed in Rome setting up the first worldwide body to deal with health: l'Office International d'Hygiène Publique (OIHP), with headquarters in Paris.

The functions of the Office were given in Article 4 of its Statutes:

'The principal object of the Office is to collect and bring to the knowledge of the participating states the facts of a general character which relate to public health, and especially as regards infectious diseases, notably cholera, plague and yellow fever, as well as the measures taken to combat these diseases'.

92

Thus the two primary objectives of the Organization were the preparation and control of the application of the International Sanitary Convention as well as the exchange of information.

Epidemic intelligence, principally concerning the five conventional diseases (the three enumerated in Article 4 of the Statutes plus smallpox and typhus), was the major activity of the Office during the 40 years it remained operative. Attention was also focused on other subjects such as the use of drugs, the transfer of corpses[1], foodhygiene, construction and management of hospitals and biological standardization. These activities were, however, not carried out through field work, but remained on the level of exchanges of information on an international scale: the Office constituted a useful forum for discussion on scientific and practical problems.

One of the outstanding features of the Office in this respect was that, in its multidisciplinary composition, it constituted a link between scientific research and its application on the international level (v.d. Berg, 1973, p. 6). The Office maintained, furthermore, in accordance with Article 2 of its Statute, direct contact with the national health authorities, without using the customary diplomatic channels. It did not, on the other hand, have constitutional power to undertake direct action in individual countries: it could in no way interfere with the national administration. The strength of the OIHP was in its complete separation from political considerations (Art. 2), and in its accessibility to all countries (WHO, Off. Rec., no. 1, 1947, p. 18).

During the time the Office was functioning, new international sanitary conventions were elaborated in 1912, 1926 (dealing essentially with maritime traffic), and 1933 (air traffic), in close cooperation with the OIHP. These conventions remained limited to sanitary regulations: international health legislation was still limited to infectious diseases. Nevertheless, with the development of international health activities, legislative action was also simultaneously extended. (It should be noted that in its monthly bulletin the Office published a summary of laws and regulations on public health in force in various countries. This activity is still carried out by the WHO.)

Though at the moment of its inception the OIHP was predominantly European in its orientation, its character became more truly international through the adherence of a large number of non-European states.

1.2.2. Health Organization of the League of Nations
The progressive development of international activities was strengthened through the activities of the Health Organization of the League of Nations. The combination of epidemics and the westward migration of liberated prisoners in Europe were at the root of the need for strong international co-operation. The League of Red Cross Societies, created in 1919, had been endowed with insufficient power for action to assume this task, and therefore provision for the necessary measures had to be made by the League of Nations (WHO, Off. Rec., no. 1, 1947, p. 54).

1 See Ch. III, para. 3.2.2. under a. for achievements in the latter field on a European level.

The Covenant of the League of Nations which came into force in 1920, contained the basis for the establishment of this health organization in Article XXIII (f):

'to endeavour to take steps in matters of international concern for the prevention and control of disease' (Fraser Brockington, 1957, p. 134).

Thus, the scope of international health work was extended from quarantine to include other fields of health as well, although it was still disease-oriented in its wording. The concern for the realization of the individual's right to health care was not yet the basis for international action. The Health Organization of the League, which became operative in 1923 was in fact born out of the consciousness that, besides quarantine, other health questions also needed consideration in the then new international structures (Goodman, 1971, p. 107 a.f.).

When the League of Nations was formed in 1919 it was the intention to integrate existing international organizations with the League. Article XXIV of the Covenant states in the first paragraph that all international Bureaus already established by general treaties shall be placed under the direction of the League if the Parties to such treaties consent. (Furthermore through Article XXV of the Covenant the co-operation with the Red Cross was to be ensured: 'The members of the League agree to encourage and promote the establishment and co-operation of duly authorized voluntary national Red Cross associations having as purpose the improvement of health, the prevention of disease and the mitigation of suffering throughout the world' (Howard-Jones, 1977, p. 396)).

At the time that the Health Organization of the League of Nations was created, it seemed therefore logical to make the OIHP an integral part of this Organization. Indeed a proposal to this effect was advanced by the International Health Conference, which was to make suggestions on a permanent body to advise the Council of the League of Nations on action to be taken in respect of Articles XXIII (f) and XXV of the Covenant of the League.

This Conference, which met from 13 to 17 April 1920 in London, recommended to the Council of the League of Nations to propose to its first Assembly the adoption of a resolution:

'That a permanent International Health Organization be established as part of the organization of the League of Nations.'

The functions of such a health organization would be:
— to advise the League on health matters;
— to promote relations between national health administrations;
— to organize rapid interchange of information, especially on epidemics;
— to provide a machinery for securing or revising international agreements on health questions;
— to co-operate with the International Labour Office[2] in the health protection of workers;

2. Secretariat of the International Labour Organisation, founded in 1919.

94

- to confer and co-operate with the League of Red Cross Societies;
- to advise authorized voluntary organizations on health matters of international concern;
- to organize health missions on the request of the League or any member country.

The OIHP would, in the view of the Conference, become part of the International Health Organization as its 'General Committee' (Howard-Jones, 1977, pp. 401 and 402). This was, in fact, a logical consequence of the inclusion into the Covenant of the League of Nations of Article XXIII (f), which clause would limit the further development of the OIHP. The inclusion into the Covenant of the League of this latter Article might be explained by the reason that there was a general desire for co-ordination of all international activities in the League and by the fact that the state of world health after the Second World War was such that the OIHP's staff and budgetary possibilities were too limited (WHO, the first ten years of the World Health Organization, 1958, p. 22). Political arguments, however, impeded the establishment of a single health organization (The United States of America, not a member of the League of Nations and France were the major opponents of the merger).

Thus, two independent international health organizations coexisted in Europe during the interval between two world wars. Some co-operation between the two Organizations was initially based upon an agreement in 1923, later extended by further agreements. Though the character of their activities was similar, their respective fields of activity were more or less distinct. The OIHP remained charged with the responsibility of administering and revising the International Sanitary Conventions, while the Health Office of the League of Nations operated within the broader terms of Article XXIII (f) of the Covenant: its functions were those proposed by the International Health Conference held in London, except that the Health Office would not co-operate with the League of Red Cross Societies alone, but with 'international Red Cross Societies' (Howard-Jones, 1977, p. 450). Thus, the first official basis was laid down for co-operation (and co-ordination) in the field of health activities between international organizations: the International Labour Organisation and international Red Cross Societies, as well as the OIHP (on the basis of a separate agreement).

The main activities of the Health Office were those concerned with combating epidemics. The epidemic work performed by the Organization was meant to complement the activities of the OIHP, which latter were mainly limited to the five 'conventional' diseases, and which were devoid of any concrete action in giving direct international help. The occupations of the Health Office in this field included epidemiological intelligence and technical help and advice to international health administrations. For the latter purpose technical committees were set up, which dealt not only with communicable diseases, but also with 'social' diseases, medical and public health teaching, standardization of drugs and so forth. Not only the negative aspects of public health (means of combating infectious diseases through preventive and other actions based on Article XXIII (f) of the Covenant of the League), but also its positive aspects (improvement of public health by physical education, medical care and so forth) became part of the activities (WHO, Off, Rec., no. 1, 1947, p. 55). For the latter purpose the Health Office effectively deployed international expert committees. One of their important activities was biological standardization, which is a subject of continuing international concern. For the first time, direct communication was established with the biomedical community through their work, and this has been kept up since that time. In the field of nutrition minimum diet standards were drawn up, and dietary and nutrition surveys of population groups were published. Still another major field of activities was that concerned with narcotics. Apart from technical advice on the matter (substances to be brought under control for instance) the Office prepared an 'international method', a standard method for determining the morphine content of raw opium. After the second world war, narcotics were taken over by the United Nations.

Progress was made in the development of the concept that international conferences could be an effective tool for the development of a broader approach to public health. Thus, a number of regional conferences were organized on various topics.

During the Second World War, the Health Organization of the League continued — though on a limited scale — its epidemiological work. The epidemiological intelligence service concentrated attention on Europe. Biological standardization was ensured through the co-operation of the two international organizations in Europe.

Advantages of the League of Nations' Health Organization were the flexibility of its activities, ist continuous access to specialised knowledge, and its direct contact with statesmen responsible for broad government policies (WHO, Off, Rec., no. 2, 1948, p. 56). On the other hand, the functions of the Health Organization were entirely dependent on the League of Nations, while the OIHP was far more independent in carrying out its activities.

1.2.3. United Nations Relief and Rehabilitation Administration (UNRRA)
During the Second World War, the work in international public health was also performed in another setting.

The Inter-Allied Post-War Relief Committee, set up in 1941, created a technical advisory committee on medical problems. It prepared a standard list of essential medical supplies. Eventually, the work of the committee was taken over by the United Nations Relief and Rehabilitation Administration. This was established as a temporary Organization in 1943. The agreement with which the UNRRA came into being was founded on a proposal by the U.S.A. for the creation of an organization to provide aid and relief for the liberated populations ... 'aid in the prevention of pestilence, and in the recovery of the health of people' (Goodman, 1971, p. 140).

At the first session of the Council of UNRRA certain directives, covering the scope of the health work to be undertaken, were adopted. These directives also contained rules on the relationships with other international agencies, and provided for regionalization. Functions for the Health Division — an important Division of the UNRRA — were concentrated upon: assistance to national health service; revision and administration of international sanitary conventions for maritime and aerial quarantine; provision and technical supervision of medical and sanitary personnel for the care and health protection of persons displaced by war; and the training of professional health and medical personnel in the assisted countries. Furthermore, the Health Division took over the work of the OIHP as an administering body, responsible for epidemiological notification. Considering the rather detailed directives on the health work of the Organization, a new dimension was given to international health work: not only relations with international agencies and regionalization (a regional office for Europe was set up in London) were particularly stressed, but also an extension of previous activities to include direct support to less developed countries. So far international health work had been limited to health problems met by countries with well-developed health care systems. In this way, these directives were the basis for the subsequent work of the World Health Organization. International co-operation and regionalization were further amplified with the establishment of the World Health Organization.

The achievements of the UNRRA were limited by the fact that it operated only in 15 countries and represented primarily a donor/recipient function in concentrating its work on relief and rehabilitation and in acting as a stopgap for epidemiological intelligence in the framework of the international sanitary conventions. Furthermore, both the Health Organization of the UNRRA and the Organization of the League were hampered in their efforts and growth by the lack of political support from national governments (Arbab − Zadeh, 1963, p. 2543). The concept of national sovereignty still prevailed over international interest. Yet the Health Organization of the UNRRA, set up as a temporary organ to deal with an emergency situation, constituted the link between continuing intergovernmental health activities before and after the Second World War.

Thus, there were three international organizations involved with health when the United Nations were created in 1945:
− the OIHP, an Organization devoted to a specific aspect of health (quarantine, epidemiological intelligence). Advantages of this Organization were, for instance, freedom from political influence of a non-technical nature, its powers to distribute the technical know-how it acquired on a large scale and to publish legislative acts and regulations concerning public health in the various countries and of obtaining information concerning pestilential diseases[3];
− the Health Organization of the League of Nations, with major activities in the technical and epidemiological field. Advantages of this Organization were its broad and flexible nature, its ability to make extensive use of specialists in ali branches of health science and its direct relationship and contact with those responsible for any broad governmental policies which have a bearing on health issues;
− the UNRRA, acting as a temporary Organization, with limited tasks in the field of health. Advantages of this Organization were more limited than

3. W.H.O., Off. Rec., no. 1, 1946, pp. 56 and 57.

those of the other two Organizations, though it had some of their constitutional assets such as the composition of its health committees (representatives of the national health administrations).

2. Creation of the World Health Organization (WHO)

2.1. CHARTER OF THE UNITED NATIONS

Despite the fact that international attention was keenly focused on health in
the early fourties, the draft Charter of the United Nations, based upon the
Moscow Declaration (1943) and the Dumbarton Oaks Conference (1944), did
not include health issues when presented at the United Nations Conference on
International Organization in San Francisco (April to June, 1945). The Charter which resulted from this drafting conference for the United Nations gave
to the United Nations' General Assembly an exclusive, ultimate authority in
all fields other than peace and security (the Security Council), while two
specialised councils (one of which was the Economic and Social Council) were
established with authority in their own spheres.

It is due to the delegations of Brazil and China that the notion of 'health'
was included in this Charter (see Articles 13, 55, 57 and 62). They considered
health to be of such importance that it should be mentioned separately and
not simply be covered by the phrase 'social matters'. They therefore expressed
the wish for ECOSOC to deal specifically with health matters (WHO, Off.
Rec., no. 2, 1948, p. 32). By making this proposal, it was recognized that
'health' was one of the significant factors in the promotion of conditions of
stability and well-being, which was characterised by the idea of respect and
protection of human rights (Berkov, 1957, p. 25; Goodman, 1971, p. 152).
The articles which make some provision for 'health' are scattered around the
text of the Charter and they are rather uniquely worded.

Of these articles, Article 55 in particular, is important, as it established
'health' as a matter with which the United Nations should be concerned:

'With a view to the creation of conditions of stability and well-being which are necessary
for peaceful and friendly relations among nations based upon respect for the principle of
equal rights and self-determination of peoples, the United Nations shall promote:
a. ....
b. solutions of international economic, social, *health* and related problems; ... .'

Article 55 stands out because of its lack of precision, both structurally and
procedurally (Nicholas, 1962, p. 22). Little can be expected from this and the
other articles as far as health is concerned, beyond the recognition that it is a
field meriting international promotion. This vagueness can be explained partially by the fact that it was a relative novelty to consider economic and social
human rights as subjects requiring concerted international activity.

Moreover, the expansion of international activities in these fields escaped
the control of the United Nations through the creation of specialised agencies,

in conformity with Article 57, with considerable independence.[4] The wording of Article 55 does not give legislative power to the United Nations in economic and social matters, and limits its powers to study relevant problems and have them widely discussed and to invite members to reach agreement on proposed courses of action.

Article 57 stipulates the creation of a specialised health agency:

'1. The various specialised agencies, established by intergovernmental agreement and having wide international responsibilities, as defined in their basic instruments, in economic, ... in *health*, and related fields, shall be brought into relationship with the United Nations in accordance with the provisions of Article 63.
2. Such agencies thus brought into relationship with the United Nations are hereinafter referred to as specialised agencies.'

Functions in the health field are also given to the Economic and Social Council (ECOSOC), which in accordance with Article 62, may make or initiate studies and reports on international economic ..., *health* and related matters. The ECOSOC, the co-ordinating body for the activities of specialised agencies, can make recommendations on these matters to the General Assembly, the members of the United Nations and the specialised agencies concerned.

Those delegates responsible for the inclusion of 'health' in the Charter also succeeded in having a declaration adopted at the San Francisco Conference, urgently calling for an international conference to establish an independent (politically as well as economically) international health organization, to work in collaboration with the Economic and Social Council:

'The Delegations of Brazil and China recommended that a General Conference be convened within the next few months for the purpose of establishing an international health organization. They intend to consult further with the representatives of other Delegations with a view to the early convening of such a General Conference to which each of the Governments here represented will be invited to send representatives.

They recommend that, in the preparation of a plan for the international health organization, full consideration should be given to the relationship of such an organization and methods of associating it with other institutions, national as well as international, which may hereafter be established in the field of health. They recommend that the proposed international health organization be brought into relationship with the Economic and Social Council' (WHO, Off. Rec., no. 1, 1947, p. 39; Fraser Brockington, 1957, p. 135; Berkov, 1957, p. 25).

Although the governments of Brazil and China followed up the declaration by suggesting that a conference be held before the end of 1945, the resolution relating to this proposal was only adopted by the Economic and Social Council on 15 February 1946.

Under the terms of this resolution, the ECOSOC was '... to call an international conference to consider the scope of, and the appropriate machinery for, international action in the field of public health and proposals for the estab-

4. For the reasons underlying the concept of creating functional (specialised) organizations with great independency of the UN see Schermers, 1957, pp. 14 and 15.

lishment of a single international health organization of the United Nations'. (Resolution 1 (I) of the Economic and Social Council of 15 February 1946; UN document E/9 and E/9 rev. 1; WHO, Off. Rec., no. 1, 1947, p. 39.)

In accordance with the terms of para. 3 of the Resolution, the Economic and Social Council established a Technical Preparatory Committee and directed that it should meet in Paris not later than 15 March 1946 to prepare a draft annotated agenda and proposals for the consideration of the conference, to be held not later than 20 June 1946 (WHO, Off. Rec., no. 1,1947, p. 39).

Recognition of the need to develop international action in the field of public health in the interests of both security and peace facilitated rapid progress. Thus the negotiations for the creation of the World Health Organization, initiated by ECOSOC, were in fact negotiations for the promotion of the right to health care, which was to be formulated in 1948 under Article 25 of the United Nations Declaration of Human Rights.

2.2. TECHNICAL PREPARATORY COMMITTEE

At the Technical Preparatory Committee meeting in Paris[5] (18 March to 5 April 1946), four proposals for an international health organization were advanced (by France, the United Kingdom, the U.S.A. and Yugoslavia).[6] These drafts were very similar in substance (except with regard to the establishment of regional organizations) but rather divergent in their form (WHO, Off. Rec., no. 1, 1947, p. 16). There was general agreement that there must be a *new* organization to deal with health in its broadest sense, that is, without any restrictions; thus the traditional concept of medical science in international relations, involving freedom from diseases, was discarded and replaced by an international cognisance of the concepts of both positive health and mental health.

There was also consensus that the international health organization should work in close co-operation with national health services, and that this sole world health organization should have a proper degree of autonomy and should work in close relation with other organizations operating in related fields. The character of this body, which was to be a universal one, was to be non-political. There was also consensus of opinion that the OIHP should be abolished.

There was, however, divergence of opinion on the degree of independency to be owned by the organization. Some wanted to strengthen the role of the United Nations, by making the new organization an integral (though autonomous) unit of the United Nations. To others the term 'specialised agency' as used in Article 57 of the Charter meant an organization independently established and subsequently brought into relationship with the United Nations.

5. See WHO, Off. Rec., no. 1, 1947, for the Minutes of the Technical Preparatory Committee for the International Health Conference.
6. See Annexes 6-9 of WHO, Off. Rec., no. 1, 1947.

Advantages of the latter form — which was chosen by the Technical Preparatory Committee — are, for instance, the power to dispose over its own budget and staff, direct access to national health administrations and greater political independence (Calderwood, 1975, pp. 435-437).

As to the form of the Constitution, the Technical Preparatory Committee decided to include a Preamble (in which the right to health (care) was formulated as one of the fundamental rights of each human being), the aims, objectives and functions of the organization. It was furthermore decided to submit to the International Health Conference two alternative proposals on the matter of regional organizations (WHO, Off. Rec., no. 1, 1947, Annex 23).

The ECOSOC considered the report of the Technical Preparatory Committee[7] in May/June 1946, and adopted a resolution on 11 June, approving the majority of recommendations of the Committee, and transmitting to the International Health Conference various observations made on the draft constitutional proposals by various members of the Council.

2.3. INTERNATIONAL HEALTH CONFERENCE

The International Health Conference met in New York from 19 June to 22 July 1946, to discuss the proposals for the Constitution of the World Health Organization as submitted to the ECOSOC, as well as the proposals put forward by the latter.

Three developments emerged from the Conference[8], viz.:

i.   The Constitution of the World Health Organization was signed on 22 July, 1946, by representatives from 61 states (WHO, Off. Rec., no. 2, 1948, p. 100);

ii. The Conference drew up a schedule for the termination of the Rome Agreement of 9 December, 1907, and laid down plans to have the duties and functions of the Office International d'Hygiène Publique transferred to the WHO[9];

iii. Pending the coming into force of the Constitution of the World Health Organization [10], an Interim Commission was set up by the Conference. [11] The arrangement establishing the Interim Commission set out its functions, which fell into three categories:
     — preparation for the permanent organization;

7. Journal of the Economic and Social Council no. 13, 22 May 1946, pp. 138-225.
8. See WHO, Off. Rec., no. 2, 1948, for the Proceedings and Final Acts of the International Health Conference. See also E/155 for the Final Acts of the Conference.
9. The transfer took place before the end of 1946.
10. The WHO came into existence through ratification by the 26th state on 7 April 1948 (Article 80 of the Constitution), and the first World Health Assembly was held subsequently from 24 June — 24 July 1948 (on 31 December 1978 there were 157 members and 2 associate members).
11. The first World Health Assembly decided that the Interim Commission would cease work on 1 September 1948, the date that the Organization was to start functioning (Resolution WHA 1.87, WHO, Off. Rec., no. 13, 1948, p. 317).

— carrying out the statutory functions of the previous health organizations;
— emergency international health work.

2.4. INTERIM COMMISSION

Despite the fact that the Interim Commission had been established to function for only a limited time, it in fact operated for two years. This delay was due to the slow ratification process of the Organization's Statute in obtaining a sufficient number of signatory countries. But it did enable the Commission to conclude the international Lists of Diseases and to revise the existing International Lists of Causes of Death. This was the first time that an international classification of diseases and injuries was agreed upon [12], and the first single classification permitting the parallel presentation of morbidity and mortality statistics.

The Interim Commission also produced significant work on the unification of pharmacopoeias. By the time the World Health Assembly met for the first time, the publication of an international pharmacopoeia became a real possibility (Goodman, 1971, p. 171).

These and other activities, resulting in international health legislation, were endorsed by the World Health Organization. The Executive Board, considering that the World Health Organization was the authority for international health legislation and that there was a need for continuity of action in this field, 'express(ed) the opinion that all technical decisions taken in regard to the International Sanitary Conventions and their application, biological standards and habit-forming drugs, by the Permanent Committee of the Office International d'Hygiène Publique, the Health Organization of the League of Nations, the Quarantine Commission of UNRRA, and the Interim Commission of the World Health Organization, (should) remain in force unless rescinded or modified in an appropriate manner' (EB 2 R 30 of November 1948). Since then the World Health Organization has not added much to these substantive international legislative achievements (except for regular revisions of existing ones; see below para. 3.5.).

Among the other activities of the Interim Commission was the implementation of measures which called for immediate international action (cholera epidemic, Egypt, 1947). The Commission was also to prepare the agenda for the first World Health Assembly. This agenda was to include studies regarding the definition of geographical areas with a view to the eventual establishment of a regional organization in conformity with Chapter XI of the Constitution. The Commission was also to take all necessary steps to effect the transfer of activities of the existing international health organizations and to negotiate with the Pan American Sanitary Organization as well as with other intergovernmental regional health organizations (such as the Pan Arab Health Bureau,

12. For previous classifications of causes of death, see WHO, International Classification of Diseases, 1965 revision, Vol. 1, pp. IX-XIII.

which had been projected by the League of Arab States, but not yet established) which were in existence prior to the date of signature of the WHO Constitution (WHO, Off. Rec., no. 2, 1948, p. 24). [13]

The preparatory work carried out by the Interim Commission for the permanent organization included the recommendation for four fields of priority for the new organization: malaria, tuberculosis, venereal diseases and maternal and child health care. The Assembly itself added two other fields to be emphasised in international health work: nutrition and environmental sanitation (Berkov, 1957, p. 67; WHO, Off. Rec., no. 13, 1948, pp. 308 and 344).

3. Constitution of the World Health Organization

3.1. GENERAL CONSIDERATIONS

The World Health Organization was the first specialised agency created by the United Nations. [14] When it started functioning in 1948, it was the first worldwide intergovernmental organization which was empowered to deal with all aspects of human health. It was distinct from its predecessors in so far as it was endowed with legislative power in this field. It was only with the coming of the WHO that some of the national sovereignty was given up in favour of international co-operation, though this was still done on a rather limited scale and only concerned subjects of a technical nature.

The Constitution as the basic charter of the Organization sets forth its overall objective, enumerates its functions, establishes its central and regional structure, defines its legal status, and provides for co-operative relationships between the United Nations and other organizations, both governmental and private, concerned with health matters (WHO, Off. Rec., no. 2, 1948, p. 16).

The work of the Organization was based on a rather revolutionary Constitution. Revolutionary at least for that time, because in the first of the 9 principles of the Preamble is a definition of the term 'health' which had never been used hitherto.

Previously the concept of health had been presented in a negative, and hence limited way, as being concerned only with 'the absence of disease or infirmity'. The Preamble took cognisance of the term 'health' in its broadest sense in defining it positively in the first clause as 'a state of complete physical, mental, and social well-being, and not merely the absence of disease or infirmity'. This implies promotion of health, prevention of disease and 'practical social medicine' before, during and after sickness (Fraser Brockington, 1957, p. 130).

Emphasis was thus put in the Preamble on *mental* health and *social well-being*. The healthy development of the child was equally stressed (sixth clause).

13. See also Ch. II, para. 1.1.
14. Other specialised agencies were already functioning before the creation of the UN, such as the International Labour Organisation ans the Food and Agriculture Organization.

It was, in fact, recognized by the International Health Conference that the environment of man is the whole world and that it is essential to the health of every individual to be able to live with all kinds of people all over the world (WHO, Off. Rec., no. 2, 1948, p. 45). Therefore the growing responsibility of Governments everywhere for 'the provision of adequate health and social measures' for their peoples was expressed in the Preamble.

The Preamble's basic principles emphasise the importance of health in the social development of the world in the sense of the inter dependence of states in the development of higher levels of national health. They also recognize the importance of an informed public opinion in matters of health and the need for an extension of the benefits of medical, psychological and related knowledge to all people (Report of the United States Delegation on the International Health Conference, 1946, p.9).

In pursuance of the optimal physical and mental health of every individual, the Constitution covers both the somatic and psychosomatic aspects of health. Further, it lays the groundwork for activities in the preventive as well as curative health efforts. While the predecessor of the World Health Organization mainly concentrated on fighting disease and epidemics, the new Organization, having to deal with health in a general, and not a restrictive sense, is much more far-reaching in its goals. It concentrates not only on the fight against the dangers, which threaten the health of peoples, but also on the general aspects of well-being and health. The tools for this goal were twofold: to make available medical knowledge to everybody, and to carry out research.

Not only the first principle of the Preamble (definition of 'health') made the text of the Constitution outstanding, the second principle was of no less importance.

In the second clause of the Preamble the right to health care was formulated for the first time in the constitution of an international organization: 'The enjoyment of the highest attainable standard of health is one of the fundamental rights of every human being ...'.

This wording is more prudent than the one advanced by the Technical Preparatory Committee, which stated the following in its concept for the Preamble: 'The right to health is one of the fundamental rights to which every human being is entitled ...' (WHO, Off. Rec., no. 1, 1947, p. 69).

It is remarkable that the insertion of such an important notion into the Constitution did not give rise to any particular discussion. In fact the formulation adopted by the Technical Preparatory Committee was advanced by a subcommittee of that Committee.

None of the draft proposals for the Constitution of the Organization which were presented by several delegates to the Committee contained the notion of this specific human right.

At the Conference itself no discussion was devoted to this item and the text suggested by a special committee of the Conference was adopted unanimously.

— definition of health and right to health (care)

When one examines both clauses of the Preamble (definition of 'health' and 'right to health') the wording used is open to criticism. The definition given

104

by the Constitution of the term 'health' is unacceptable for various reasons.

Health is a very subjective concept and attempts to define it can never be successful, because a definition is intended to give an objective description of a given idea.

The notion of 'health' can, however, never be judged objectively, as it is a purely subjective individual judgement of what a person understands to be his (level of) health. Criteria varying from person to person and from society to society will determine the judgement of what exactly may be considered to be 'good health'. The very level of health in a given society is on the other hand largely dependent on other factors, such as socio-cultural and economic conditions.

(When drafting Article 12 of the International Covenant on Economic, Social and Cultural Rights and Article 11 of the European Social Charter discussions equally took place on the opportunity of including a definition of 'health'. [15] In both cases it was considered unsatisfactory to attempt to define this term, though in the International Covenant an attempt was made to qualify the term 'health' in mentioning both 'physical' and 'mental' (health). 'Social well-being' was not included, because this notion was considered to be an entirely different concept.)

It is noteworthy that attempts to indicate the relativeness of the objective laid down in the second clause of the Preamble, which resulted in an amendment by the International Health Conference to the wording suggested by the Technical Preparatory Committee did not also lead to an indication of the relativeness of the word 'health'. Despite this amendment which resulted in the present formulation, the wording is still not very precise.

A 'right to health' can never be obtained as it implies a right of everybody to a given good which cannot be formulated objectively. The realization of the right as presently formulated could only be obtained at that moment in time when there would be a cure for every disease: complete health is, however, outside the reach of man (Leenen in v. Zonneveld e.a., 1974, p. 101).

It would then have been more realistic to formulate the right as a right to health *care*. Health care can be at the disposal of man as far as this is realistic, which implies that the undertakings should be within the normal possibilities. A right to health care — other than a 'right to health' — can be legally invoked by man: there is a legal duty to provide such care. It is unlikely that the WHO used the present terminology with the intention of expressing a very restricted right in the sense that no one may be deprived of his health by the action of another. The terminology used should mainly be placed in its (historical) drafting context. [16]

It is likely, and at least realistic, to conclude that given the time at which the draft was prepared, the objective was no more and no less than to express the need for adequate health measures to ensure man a liveable life, and to clearly underline the social responsibility of governments to undertake every effort in this respect, as far as this would be within their power. It was at the

15. See Part A, Ch. II, paras 4.2. and 4.3.
16. None of the international human rights instruments which contain an Article on the right to health care employ this wording (See Part A, Ch. II, para. 5.).

time recognized that given this purpose international co-operation was indispensable to give the fullest effect to these responsibilities. [17]

Despite the fact that Resolution WHA 23.41 (WHO, Off. Rec., no. 184, 1970, p. 21) reformulates the original wording of the Technical Preparatory Committee of the Health Conference in declaring that 'the right to health is a fundamental human right', it seems logical to qualify this terminology in such a manner that it is formulated with the intention to secure adequate health care. This view is supported by, for instance, Resolution WHA 23.61 (WHO, Off. Rec., no. 184, 1970, p. 34) which states that 'the attainment by all peoples of the highest possible *level* of health' is the main long-term objective of the WHO, for which achievement various recommendations are formulated, all pointing at adequate health care provisions.

— implementation of the principles

Both the broad definition of the word 'health' and the formulation of the 'right to health care' should have been guarantees for the attribution of major legislative facilities to the WHO. Unfortunately, however, the Organization is only bestowed with limited, though not insignificant, legislative power. This is presumably due to such factors as political arguments concerning the prevailing national sovereignty. The WHO has no real supranational power [18] and has only limited political strength. Furthermore, despite the fact that the Constitution creates possibilities for the fulfilment of the right to health care, limitations to the availability of health care were introduced from the onset for a variety of reasons.

Firstly, financial restrictions have obliged the Organization from the moment of its creation to concentrate on priorities at the expense of other (no less important) activities.

WHO's present policies, for instance, which are guided by the principle of social justice, are directed towards the reduction of the gap between the health level of the developed and developing countries. By 1980 at least 60 per cent of the regular budget will be allocated to programmes of technical co-operation and provision of services to developing countries. With this emphasis less attention is given to programmes in developed regions.

Secondly, the Organization can only tackle such activities which are internationally feasible and hence acceptable on a world wide scale. Differences in the standard of living which exist in various countries have a significant influence on decision-making. Due to its worldwide scope the WHO is, like its predecessors, hampered by a certain degree of ineffectiveness with regard to optimalising the prerequisites for successful international health work.

A third limitation is caused by the very level of technology itself. The combined effect of these various limitations is that priority decisions are inevitable, whereby the costs have to be balanced against the increase of effectiveness which is aimed at and where an equitable distribution of health resources at an international level is of major concern.

17. See also Article 1 of the Constitution of the WHO, in which it is stated that its objective shall be 'the attainment by all peoples of the highest possible level of health'.
18. In the sense that it can directly bind member governments, as in the case of the European Community.

It cannot be emphasised strongly enough that in practice social, political and economical aspects will all be determinants for the level of health of the population.

Developments in the international health field should therefore be viewed in the light of social goals and economic realities.

3.2. OBJECTIVE

The Technical Preparatory Committee suggested in its draft for the Constitution under chapter II — 'Aims and Objectives' — seven items. The International Health Conference, however, following the suggestion of Canada, opted for one general statement to cover the overall objective of the Organization (Article 1 of the Constitution): 'The objective of the World Health Organization shall be the attainment by all peoples of the highest possible level of health'. This was decided on the grounds that the suggestions made by the Technical Preparatory Committee were more appropriately placed under the functions of the Organization (WHO, Off. Rec., no. 1, 1947, p. 44).

3.3. FUNCTIONS

To implement the overall objective in Article 1 of the Constitution, the Organization may exercise numerous functions. There are 22 of these functions enumerated in Article 2 of the Constitution, which established the WHO as the directing and co-ordinating authority in international health work.

The International Health Conference separated these functions into six closely interrelated categories:
— general and co-ordinative tasks;
— co-operation with other organizations;
— research and technical services;
— promotional and educational activities;
— field operations;
— regulatory measures
(WHO, Off. Rec., no. 2, 1948, pp. 17 and 18).

It would be preferable to make a slightly different distinction by combining the first category (co-ordination) and the second (co-operation), since both functions are closely interrelated: co-operation will not be successful if it does not include co-ordination of activities. Furthermore, with a view to the new orientation of the work of the WHO (see below under d) it would seem preferable that the category 'field operations' be replaced by 'technical co-operation and field services'. Finally, another category could be added, namely 'other functions'; representing all other action necessary to attain the objective of the Organization (Article 2 (v) of the Constitution). The majority of the 22 functions in Article 2 were already performed by the predecessors of the WHO. Quarantine, epidemic intelligence, statistics, biologicals and drugs, and nomenclatures are examples of these. The tasks of co-operation were already partially performed by the Health Organization of the League of Nations. Others, such as prevention of accidents, public health and medical care research activities, were entirely new ones in the field of international health work.

Two of the most important tasks of the WHO are to act as the directing and co-ordinating authority on international health work and to assist governments upon request in strengthening their health services.

a. co-ordination and co-operation [19]

As the leading authority in all matters relating to international health work, the WHO occupies a paramount position in relation to all other intergovernmental organizations which are concerned with any aspects of health (WHO, Off. Rec., no. 2, 1948, p. 17). In its co-operative activities, the Organization does not only aim at collaboration with international organizations, but also with national health administrations, private scientific and professional groups and others. Both functions (co-operation and co-ordination) primarily depend on the initiative of the WHO itself, in contrast with other functions, such as technical assistance, which depend largely on the initiative (request) of governments.

Van den Berg (1973, pp. 23 and 24) is of the opinion that Article 2 (a) of the Constitution on co-ordination does not give a formal competence to the WHO in the sense that in his view it cannot derive an exclusive right to co-ordination from it. It is evident of course, that other organizations, which are active in the field of health may take the initiative to bring about necessary co-ordination (and co-operation), for which they will evidently turn to the WHO. Furthermore, as stated by Van den Berg, it is logical that if states decide to create a world health organization, they will confine to this organization the task of acting as a co-ordinator whenever such is required in the field of international health work. The WHO remains the directing and co-ordinating authority in all matters relating to health work and should, as such, approach any project aimed at the improvement of health with scrupulous regard to its broader repercussions in the context of health development as a whole (WHO, Off. Rec., no. 181, 1970, p. 98). It is therefore the responsibility of the Organization to see that co-ordination is brought about whenever necessary.

Van den Berg makes this task of the WHO subject to two restrictions:
— the function of co-ordination only relates to the health field and not to such activities as social, cultural or economic ones;
— the co-ordination of international health work as implied in the Constitution of the Organization must have a global character.

The first restriction, provided it is one of a general nature, appears to be relevant.

It should, however, not be lost sight of that public health activities are closely related to social, economic or cultural fields; they are in fact interrelated and interdependent.

19. See also below, para. 5.

108

Co-ordination with related fields, e.g. the economic and social, is of equal importance because they have their bearing on human health and their close relationship should not be disturbed.

Social policies, for instance, should guarantee the access to the best possible medical care, while health policies should aim at protecting man in his living and environmental conditions.

Economic policies will guide decision-making on priorities for undertakings in the health field, while health policies on the other hand will have an influence on economic decision-making. The growth of the social sector (including health) has to be synchronised with general economic growth: they will be of mutual influence and support.

The International Health Conference noted on the function of co-operation with other organizations, that 'active and sustained co-operation with such specialised agencies as the International Labour Organization, the Food and Agriculture Organization and the United Nations Educational, Scientific and Cultural Organization would be essential in connexion with the promotion of measures for the improvement of economic and social conditions affecting health and for the advancement of general health education' (WHO, Off. Rec., no. 2, 1948, p. 17).

The second restriction, however, seems less acceptable. It seems contradictory to the concept of regionalization, which is one of the prerequisites for successful work in the health field.

In fact the regional offices have among their tasks the co-ordination with other organizations in their region, the co-ordination with universal organizations regarding their activities in the specific region and the intercountry co-ordinative role.

It would seem more correct to consider the task of co-ordination as an overall one, incumbent on the world body, to bring into line the general policies of world organizations, leaving it to the regional bodies to take care of the more specific regional aspects.

b. Research and technical services

Activities under this heading are broadly aimed at prevention, control and eradication of diseases.

In performing its tasks in the field of research four methods are applied: support of national research (either internationally collaborative or through grants to individual research workers); the provision of services for research (establishment of reference centres, publication of reports of expert groups); research training grants and improvement of communication (Goodman, 1971, p. 308).

Resolution WHA 2.19 (WHO, Off. Rec., no. 21, 1949, p. 23) sets out the first research policies of the WHO: research and co-ordination of research being considered as essential functions of the WHO, first priority should be given to research directly relating to the programme of the World Health Organization; research should be supported in existing institutions; the WHO should not consider (at the present time) the establishment, under its own auspices, of international research institutions. This implies that the tasks of the WHO in respect to research are primarily the co-ordination and promotion of research as well as assistance to national research programmes; the WHO is not so much to organize research at an international scale through its own institutions, but rather to offer health challenges, to stimulate ideas and to co-ordinate work especially in multidisciplinary and intercultural settings (WHO, Off. Rec., no. 220, 1947, p. 12).

The research programme of the WHO was intensified in 1959, when it was decided to set up an advisory committee on medical research in order to provide the Director General with the necessary scientific advice in relation to the research programme (Resolution WHA 12.17; WHO, Off. Rec., no. 95, 1959, p. 27).

Since 1972 in particular the co-ordination of biomedical research and its application to health services development has been focused upon. Criteria for biomedical and medicosocial research were established in 1973 as follows: its application to the development of health services; its contribution to the improvement of the health status of the mass population in member states; its impact on the best use of available resources; the promotion of national capability for research (Resolution WHA 26.34; WHO, Off. Rec., no. 209, 1973, p. 24).

In 1967 a division of research in epidemiology and communications science was established with the aim of 'proposing new methods or alternative solutions, their development in the field, and their adaptation to situations useful to the Organization and to the Governments of its Members and Associate Members, using techniques of a variety of disciplines' WHO Chronicle, 32, 1978, p. 436). Besides the co-ordination of biomedical medicine, present research programmes of the Organization include items such as reproduction and family planning with a view to improving reproductive health, regional health manpower development problems, standardization of diagnostic procedures, improvement of public health practices and tropical diseases. Technical services in respect to research include the establishment and administration of epidemiological and statistical services, the development of international standards and the organization of blood transfusion services. Research is mostly carried out through a network of collaborating research centres.

Despite the fact that the research programme of the WHO has been intensified, the aforementioned original guiding principles to be applied in the organization of research under the auspices of the WHO are still prevalent, in that the Organization primarily focuses upon stimulation, promotion and assistance rather then upon organizing and carrying out research itself.

An attempt to establish a world health research centre with a view to contribute towards the resolution of major world health problems that could not be readily achieved otherwise (primarily in the field of epidemiology and the analysis and handling of health and biomedical information) failed in 1965, mainly because of the financial and organizational implications. [20]

The conception of the Organization's role in the field of research appears to

20. Moreover, the long-established policy of the WHO is not to consider the establishment, under its own auspices, of such institutions.

be in line with Article 2 (j) of the Constitution, in which the function of the Organization in this respect is given: 'to promote co-operation among scientific and professional groups which contribute to the advancement of health'. However, bearing in mind the general objective of the Organization, and considering one of the functions of the World Health Assembly, as outlined in Article 18 (k)[21], one might well query whether this concept of the Organization is not too narrow. It is recognized that regional offices are becoming more involved in research activities than the global Organization, in such a manner that first research priorities are defined in each region and a longterm programme for the development and co-ordination of biomedical and health services research will reflect the aggregate priorities of the entire Organization (WHO, Off. Rec., no. 246, 1978, p. 258; see also Resolution WHA 31.35 of May 1978). Research has moreover become decentralized through the setting up of advisory committees in medical research in every region. Members of these committees are increasingly acting as focal point for contact and co-ordination with national medical research councils, academies and so forth (WHO, Off. Rec., no. 243, 1978, p. 28). However, initiating and conducting special research activities through institutions of the WHO itself is still lagging behind. [22]

Even if this would not be feasible or desirable at a global level, it seems commendable that such institutions be set up under the auspices of regional offices of the WHO in regions where the level of technology makes such an initiative essential.

In addition to furthering medical research, the Organization is empowered to study and report on the administrative and social aspects of public health and medical care from the preventive as well as curative standpoint, including hospital services and social security (WHO, Off. Rec., no. 2, 1948, p. 17).

c. promotional and educational activities

Maternal health and child welfare as well as mental health are explicitly classified as promotional activities.

The Organization has an expanded programme on mental health and is also entering the field of promotion of environmental hygiene, nutrition, sanitation, housing etc.

Educational activities are of various kinds.

On the one hand, standards of teaching and training are improved through training courses and fellowship programmes. On the other hand, the Organization co-operates with other organizations, which pursue the mutual recognition of health diplomas and degrees. As a first step, the efforts have aimed at reaching agreement at a regional level. Several legal instruments for mutual recognition of diplomas have been adopted or are being drawn up in the

21. 18 ( ): 'To promote and conduct research in the field of health by the personnel of the Organization, by the establishment of its own institutions or by co-operation with official institutions of any Member with the consent of its Government.'
22. The International Agency for Research on Cancer, established in 1965 as an autonomous body within the framework of the WHO to promote international collaboration in cancer research is the only example of such an institution. This Agency established (regional) research centres for field studies on local cancer problems in 1967.

European Region (through, for instance, the Council of Europe and the European Community). In addition, a multinational study on international migration of physicians and nurses is being carried out.

Finally, the public is constantly being approached and educated through the mass media and WHO publications. In respect to publications, it may be mentioned that the Organization publishes quarterly the International Digest of Health Legislation.

This publication, which is the only one on health legislation of international significance to date, contains a selection of (national) health legislation. Moreover, comparative studies of legislation on special subjects are published occasionally.

Examples of these are: legislation on vaccination in the member states of the European Economic Community, abortion laws, treatment of drug addicts and use of human tissues and organs for therapeutic purposes. Presently the Organization is re-examining the criteria for the International Digest of Health Legislation (Resolution WHA 30.44; WHO, Off. Rec., no. 240, 1977, p. 25).

In pursuance of the same Resolution the WHO's programme in the field of health legislation will be strengthened with a view to assisting member states in the development of appropriate health legislation adapted to their needs. The collaboration with other specialised agencies concerned with the development of guidelines on health legislation will also receive more attention. So far, the nature of the International Digest of Health Legislation is purely informative. It is regrettable that it has not yet been used as a medium through which discussions at an international level could take place regarding legislative aspects of various health subjects. It could well be used to stimulate international opinion-forming in this respect, in which way it would usefully complement the small number of national magazines on public health law existing at present.

d.   technical co-operation and field services
One of the major functions of the WHO is to assist governments (upon request) in the strengthening of their health services. This function receives major attention and is mainly directed towards developing countries.

The Organization is also expected to furnish appropriate technical assistance in emergencies (epidemics) with the approval of the government concerned. This particular function of the WHO has gained in importance since Resolutions WHA 28.75; 28.76 and 29.48 [23] on technical co-operation with developing countries.

By using the term 'technical co-operation' the Organization has in fact turned away from the traditional approach of 'technical assistance' (donor-recipient relationship) towards a new approach of technical co-operation with countries and among countries themselves (partnership).

In this way the technical co-operation becomes supportive of the first function of the WHO, namely co-ordination. It is based upon the high degree of social relevance for member states and on the principle of developing

23.   WHO, Off. Rec., no. 226, 1975, pp. 42 and 43; no. 233, 1976, p. 30.

112

national self-reliance in matters of health. Since 1977 the Organization's main target is that by 2000 all citizens of the world should have attained a level of health that will permit them to lead socially and economically productive lives. In this respect the following are regarded as essential elements for health:

adequate food and housing, with protection of houses against insects and rodents; clean and safe drinking water; suitable waste disposal; services for the provision of ante-natal, natal and post-natal care; infant and childhood care; immunization against major infectious diseases; prevention and control of locally endemic diseases; elementary care for injury and diseases; easy access to sound and useful information on prevailing health problems and the methods of preventing and controlling them (Mahler, 1977, p. 492).

This new concept of one of its functions confirms the constitutional role of the WHO as the international co-ordinating authority on international health work, with a technical leadership role to play in international health activities (WHO, Off. Rec., no. 238, 1976, pp. 115-118). The work of the Organization is thus reoriented towards increasing the effectiveness of technical co-operation and services to governments.

e. regulatory measures
This category of functions attributes to the Organization explicit legislative power with respect to international health matters and may therefore be seen as one of the most powerful tools of the Organization to achieve its objective.
The proposal advanced by the Technical Preparatory Committee in this respect was much weaker. The draft mentioned the *promotion* of conventions, regulations and agreements with respect to international health and sanitary matters (WHO, Off. Rec., no. 1, 1947, p. 70). The text adopted by the Conference reads: 'to *propose* conventions, agreements and regulations, and make *recommendations* with respect to international health matters' (Article 2 (k) of the Constitution). The procedures and conditions for exercising these functions are described in Chapter V of the Constitution and will be dealt with when discussing this section (para. 3.5.).

f. other functions
The activities of the Organization are not limited to the functions which are explicitly enumerated in Article 2 of the Constitution. The last clause of this Article gives the Organization the authority to deal with any health subject relevant for the attainment of the overall objective of the Organization.
Some of the criteria used in determining whether an activity other than those falling outside the explicitly mentioned functions can be taken up are:
— international feasibility and acceptability;
— the universal nature of the problem;
— the possibility of assessing progress and results;
— financial feasibility (WHO, Off. Rec., no. 25, 1950, Annex 5, p. 30 and EB 41/24).

The general programme of work of the WHO for the period 1978-1983 in-

cludes six major areas of concern, which fall within almost all of the categories of functions mentioned before, although there is a primary emphasis on a specific category indicated between brackets:
- development of comprehensive health service (category d);
- disease prevention and control (category b);
- promotion of environmental hygiene (category c);
- health manpower development (category d);
- promotion and development of biomedical and health services research (category b);
- programme development and support (category d).

The programme is primarily directed towards efforts to diminish the gap between the health status of populations in various parts of the world.

To implement this programme, various activities are deployed, such as tendering advice to member states, giving direct assistance, organizing expert meetings, granting fellowships, carrying out research, elaborating international guidelines and recommendations, organizing special 'development' programmes etc., etc.

Generally speaking the results of some of the programmes carried out at a global level, in particular those concerned with research, will have direct influence on national activities. Often national (legal) measures taken in these particular fields will be reported back to the Organization so that other countries can profit from them.

3.4. ORGANS OF THE WHO

All specialised agencies of the United Nations perform their work through three organs. In accordance with Article 9 of the WHO Constitution, the central institutional structure for the Organization is such that the work is performed by
- the World Health Assembly (WHA):
- the Executive Board (EB);
- the secretariat.

a. World Health Assembly (Articles 10-23 of the Constitution)
The WHA is the general policy body of the Organization. Its name as suggested by the Technical Preparatory Committee was the 'World Health Conference'.

Members of the International Health Conference, however, thought that the name 'World Health Assembly' would be more suitable as it emphasises more appropriately the representative functions of the WHO's deliberative organ (WHO, Off. Rec., no. 2, 1948, p. 19).

The WHA is the sovereign deliberative body of the Organization and is as such entrusted with general responsibilities for approving the programme of work of the Organization, as well as with the supervision of its financial policies. It is also responsible for relationships with governments and other organizations. One of the most significant powers is the authority to establish institutions for research and other purposes (Article 18 of the Constitution). Another important role of the Organ is carrying out the quasi-legislative and regulatory functions conferred upon the Organization. This specific role of the WHA is not mentioned in Article 18, but subject to the Articles 19-23. The Technical Preparatory Committee had suggested to include them equally in the Article establishing the functions of the WHA (WHO, Off. Rec., no. 1, 1947, p. 71). The Conference on the other hand wished to underline the importance of the role of the WHA in carrying out the quasi-legislative and regulatory functions conferred upon the Organization and therefore decided to cover these functions by separate Articles (WHO, Off. Rec., no. 2, 1948, p. 20).

At the fourth session of the WHA, the examination of special topics of common interest, the so-called 'technical discussions', held during its annual meetings, was added to its functions. Since then, these have become a regular agenda item.

The WHA, which in principle meets annually (Article 13 of the constitution), is composed of a maximum of 3 delegates per member state, 'chosen from among persons most qualified by their technical competence in the field of health, preferably representing the national health administration of the member' (Article 11 of the Constitution). This composition was felt preferable to the suggestion of the Technical Preparatory Committee of one delegate per member state, as it would allow member states to include also non-governmental experts in their delegation (WHO, Off. Rec., no. 2, 1948, p. 19). In practice, however, delegations to the WHA are mostly composed of governmental officials, which is regrettable for two reasons. First, highly specialised skill is in general not found among governmental officials, who have to cover a too broad field. Second, discussions and exchange of information remain thus mostly limited to the governmental circuit.

The Technical Preparatory Committee could not reach agreement on the qualification delegates to the WHA should have, so two alternatives were submitted:

- 'In selecting their delegates due regard should be paid by the Member States to the technical nature of the work of the Organization;
- The delegate should be chosen from among persons qualified by their technical competence in the health field, preferably representing the national health administration of the Member State' (WHO, Off. Rec., no. 1, 1947, p. 71).

The second qualification was suggested in order to avoid as far as possible that not only problems in the field of health would be discussed but that also other, in particular political, issues would be raised (Schermers, 1957, p. 86).

Both qualifications are inserted into Article 11 of the Constitution as a desirability and not as an obligation.

According to Article 12 of the Constitution alternates and advisers may accompany delegates. The right to vote is given to alternates and not to advisers (Rule 19 of the rules of procedure of the World Health Assembly).

b. the Executive Board (Articles 24-29 of the Constitution)

The Board is the secondary policy body of the WHO. Its functions include provisions that the Board acts primarily as the executive organ of the WHA; it gives effect to the decisions and policies of the latter, advises on matters referred to it by the WHA and performs the powers delegated to it on behalf of the WHA (Articles 28 and 29). Included amongst its duties is the examination of WHO programmes and budget estimates as prepared by the Director General for eventual submission to the WHA. (The approval or modification of the budget proposals by the Director General is restricted to the WHA; Berkov, 1957, p. 28.) Furthermore, the Board not only oversees other administrative matters, but also functions as a first 'clearing house' for reports prepared by expert committees. It may start action on these reports and decide whether or not they should be published. It is also allowed to take emergency measures whenever needed (Article 28 (i). The role of the EB as seen by some delegates at the Conference was that it would primarily be that of a standing committee of the WHA for matters of programme and policy, leaving executive functions almost entirely in the hands of the Director General.

The opinion of the majority, however, who preferred that the Director General was made responsible to the WHA through the Board prevailed (Article 31 of the Constitution: in his capacity as the chief technical and administrative officer, the Director General is subject to the authority of the Board). Thus, as suggested by the Technical Preparatory Committee, the Board became the executive organ of the Organization (WHO, Off. Rec., no. 1, 1947, p. 72; WHO, Off. Rec., no. 2, 1948, p. 21; Report of the United States Delegation to the International Health Conference, 1946, pp. 18 and 19).

Board membership as proposed by the Technical Preparatory Committee involved between 12 and 18 positions, which were to be filled by persons 'technically qualified in the field of health'. These persons would theoretically not represent governments but were understood to serve in an individual capacity: members were 'to exercise the powers delegated to them by the Conference on behalf of the whole Conference (=WHA) and not as a representative of their respective governments' (WHO, Off. Rec., no. 1, 1947, p. 72). This recommendation of the Technical Preparatory Committee was based on proposals submitted by the United States (WHO, Off. Rec., no. 1, 1947, p. 47). The Conference, though recognising the importance of independent membership of the Board did, however, not insert this proposal into the Constitution, presumably because this point was felt to be sufficiently covered by 'a person technically qualified in the field of health' (Article 24 of the Constitution).

Despite the fact that the Organization, unlike the International Labour Organization and the United Nations Educational, Scientific and Cultural Organization, where members of the Board are governmental representatives, has maintained the principle of the independent position of members of the Board, this construction is in practice not followed by the majority of the member states (Van den Berg, 1973, pp. 54-57; see also Schermers, 1957, pp. 115-121). This fact is regrettable because it hinders the development of the

116

Board as a truly independent body, which as such could form a useful counterpart and, or complement to the WHA, which works entirely according to national policy lines.

In confirmity with one of the alternate proposals of the United States (WHO, Off. Rec., no. 1, 1947, p. 47), the WHA elects members entitled to designate a person to serve on the Board; the WHA moreover gives due regard to an equitable geographical distribution in selecting these states (WHO, Off. Rec., no. 2, 1948, p. 21).

The Board, which meets twice a year (Article 26 of the Constitution), is presently composed of 30 persons (Article 24 of the Constitution) who are elected for three years and may be re-elected (Article 25 of the Constitution).

c. the secretariat (Articles 30-37 of the Constitution)

The secretariat is the main administrative unit of the World Health Organization. It comprises the Director General and technical as well as administrative personnel.

The Director General is the chief technical and administrative officer of the Organization. He is responsible to the WHA through the Executive Board. The Director General has the right to establish 'by agreement with members', direct access to governmental departments, especially the national health administration, to governmental or non-governmental health organizations. He may also establish direct contact with international organizations (Article 33 of the Constitution).

The Technical Preparatory Committee, which did not recommend such a strong position of the Director General as included in the Constitution, only referred to direct contact with national health administrations (WHO, Off. Rec., no. 1, 1947, p. 72).

The Director General furthermore prepares for the attention of the Board the financial and budget estimates of the WHO (Article 34 of the Constitution).

Staff are recruited from numerous countries, and generally include the following categories:
- technical specialists (advisory services to governments, medical and dental advisors, scientific officers, public health agents, nurses, technicians, etc.);
- administrative officers (language and library staff, information and liaison officers, legal personnel etc.);
- locally recruited secretariat and general staff;
- short term specialist consultants;
- temporary ad hoc staff.

3.5. INSTRUMENTS

As was indicated earlier, the attainment of the Organization's objective is limited for a variety of reasons. The legislative power allotted to the Organization by its Constitution is likewise limited in its application. Few really significant legislative achievements have in practice been obtained so far, and most of these found their roots in the work performed by the predecessors of the Organization, by whom they were drafted to a great extent.

Yet the Constitution provides for enough legislative possibilities in its Articles 19-22.

The limitations which have made the legal results so minimal are due to the fact that the Organization operates on a world-wide level and is not vested with legislative possibilities which are directly binding upon member states.

Prevalent discrepancies in economic and sociological circumstances in various parts of the world are a natural obstruction to the optimal functioning of the Organization.

A possible means of overcoming this difficulty would be to proceed with far-reaching decentralization by endowing the organizational regional branches with their own legislative functions. This would result in legal rules adapted to regional circumstances; a most beneficial situation provided that other regions could profit of these legal achievements.

The international quasi-legislative and regulatory functions of the Organization which are formulted in Article 2 under k) of the Constitution are to be carried out by the WHA in accordance with Articles 19-23 of the Constitution.

a. conventions and agreements (Articles 19 and 20 of the Constitution)
  — constitutional provisions
The Technical Preparatory Committee recommended that the functions of the World Health Conference (=World Health Assembly) in respect to international legislative (health) measures should be as follows:

(It should) 'have the authority to recommend new conventions or amendments of existing conventions with respect to any appropriate matter within the scope of the Organization, which would become operative as to each Member State when accepted by it in accordance with its constitutional procedures' (WHO, Off. Rec., no. 1, 1947, p. 71).

The majority of a drafting committee of the Economic and Social Council, when examining the report of the Technical Preparatory Committee, recommended that 'the World Health Conference should be empowered to prepare and sign international Conventions without recourse to special diplomatic conferences'. (The minority was of the opinion that this function of the WHA should be presented as an observation, rather than as a recommendation; WHO, Off. Rec., no. 2, 1948, p. 120.)

The final wording adopted by the International Health Conference strengthened the original proposal in giving the Health Assembly the authority 'to adopt (and not to recommend) conventions or agreements with respect to any matter within the competence of the Organization' (Article 19 of the Constitution).

The Health Conference did not envisage to endow the Assembly with full legislative power enabling delegates to sign conventions on behalf of their governments without reservations as to acceptance. It was decided that the instruments were only to come into force when accepted in accordance with constitutional procedures of a member state. It was in fact felt at the time that the stage of international law made such a procedure impracticable (WHO, Off. Rec., no. 2, 1948, p. 20). It cannot be denied that the procedure provided for in the Constitution was a considerable improvement when compared with earlier attempts for unification and improvement of international sanitary conventions, when special conferences resulting in undue delay had to be convened (WHO, Off. Rec., no. 2, 1948, p. 20).

The procedure opted for by the Conference aimed in particular at timely unification and modernization of existing sanitary conventions, so as to follow scientific developments closely (Report of the United States Delegation to the International Health Conference, 1946, p. 16).

    — subject matter

Any matter falling within the competence of the Organization may be the subject of agreements or conventions (Article 19 of the Constitution).

    — effect of conventions and agreements

In accordance with Article 19 of the Constitution conventions and agreements are to be adopted by a two-thirds majority and will come into force when accepted in accordance with any member's own constitutional procedure.

Member states are bound to report within 18 months after adoption of such an instrument by the WHA on the respective action taken by their governments (Article 20 of the Constitution). This provision also meant a further strengthening of the convention process applied hitherto: conventions and agreements are considered to be binding rules, which are to be accepted by each member (Schermers, 1957, p. 146).

    — application of Articles 19 and 20

Despite these legislative powers of the Organization aiming at an effective system of binding rules in the field of health no sanitary arrangements have yet been concluded in this fashion. Instead, the more flexible procedure of regulations is applied (see below under b.). The reason for this may be found in the difficulties inherent in the treaty-making process when dealing with a large number of states (Gutteridge, 1971, p. 294).

In this respect we may speak of a certain weakness of the Organization when compared with other intergovernmental organizations, which, despite the long difficult process involved in international treaty-making, nonetheless succeed in drawing up such instruments. This holds in particular for international organizations, operating on a regional scale, where the geografic restriction makes the process of drawing up conventions relatively easy compared to organizations operating on a world-wide scale.

b. regulations (Article 21-22 of the Constitution)

    — constitutional provisions

The introduction of these kinds of instruments into the Constitution was an innovation, especially in respect to the procedure for the entry into force of these instruments (Article 22 of the Constitution). This procedure provides for a 'contracting out' (principle of tacit approach) of obligation by members, and not, as usual, for the 'contracting in' by act of formal acceptance: it places the burden on each member state of declaring its refusal to accept a regulation. The present method conveniently sidesteps the complicated and lengthy procedure for the adoption and ratification of conventions and agreements and confers to the Assembly a certain quasi-legislative power, which facilitates the acceptance by governments of certain international health arrangements with a minimum of delay.

In this manner yet another disadvantage inherent in the more common procedure of drawing up conventions is avoided. This disadvantage lies in the fact that often states, though recognizing the principles contained in a convention, hesitate to ratify such a convention in view of the (mostly economic) consequences and thus delay its entry into force (see Schermers, 1972, pp. 516-518 for the advantages and disadvantages of applying the 'negative ratification procedure'). The concept underlying this regulatory power of the WHO was to create a mechanism in the international field, which would permit rapid general application of new scientific techniques in the international control of the spread of disease without requiring competent national organs to consider highly specialised technical matters (Report of United States Delegation on the International Health Conference, 1946, p. 17). The international health measures proposed in the form of regulations thus have direct impact on those member states who did not expressly reject them.

A drafting committee of the Economic and Social Council of the UN, when discussing the proposals of the Technical Preparatory Committee to give the WHA authority to apply this regulation procedure in five given areas (see below) could not reach agreement on this procedure. Some members, instead, opted for the official (traditional) acceptance procedure, while one member was in favour of the proposed procedure because of its expediency.

The International Health Conference, after some discussion, was in favour of the stand taken by the Technical Preparatory Committee and considered that the proposal did not constitute an infringement of sovereignty. [24] (WHO, Off. Rec., no. 2, 1948, p. 20; Report of the United States Delegation on the International Health Conference, 1946, pp. 16-18; Van den Berg, 1973, pp. 47-50.)

A special provision on the number of votes required for the adoption of regulations is not contained in the Constitution, so that Article 60 of the Constitution, providing for a simple majority (Article 60 under (b)), applies.

Reservations in respect to regulations must be made by member states within the period indicated in the notification of adoption by the Health Assembly (Article 22).

This latter provision makes it possible to avoid another disadvantage of the regulation procedure, lying in the fact that member states will not have

24. This conclusion was reached by a special subcommittee, which considered the Provision of the International Sanitary Convention for Aerial Navigation of 1933 as a precedent; some also found a precedent in the agreement establishing the Provisional International Civil Aviation Organization. Several proposals involving complicated safeguards were presented by the subcommittee as alternatives to the original proposals. These were, however, ultimately rejected.

enough time to consider the consequences of the proposed measures and to put forward reservations, and will thus be bound by the regulations (Schermers, 1972, p. 517).

The regulations come into force for the states concerned except for the parts on which reservations are made in good time (WHO, Off. Rec., no. 13, 1948, pp. 99 and 335).

The Health Assembly may, however, refuse such reservations when they are not compatible with the character and, or purpose of the regulations adopted (Yemin, 1969, p. 196; A/2119, p. 84). If, in such a case, the reservations, which have a unilateral character, are not withdrawn, the regulation will not enter into force for the state who has proposed these reservations.

   — subject matter

The subject matter to be covered by regulations is limitatively enumerated in Article 21 of the Constitution. The Technical Preparatory Committee proposed the following five areas in which the WHA would have authority to adopt regulations:

- sanitary and quarantine requirements and other procedures designed to prevent the international spread of disease;
- nomenclature with respect to diseases, causes of death, public health practice and standards with regard to diagnostic procedures for international use;
- standards with respect to the safety, purity and potency of drugs moving in international commerce under names in official pharmacopoeia;
- standards with respect to the safety, purity and potency of biological products moving in international commerce;
- conditions with respect to labelling pharmaceutical products moving in international commerce (WHO, Off. Rec., no. 1, 1947, p. 71). [25]

The Conference expanded slightly on these divisions as follows:

- 'Standards with respect to the safety, purity and potency of drugs ... under names in official pharmacopoeia' and 'standards with respect to the safety ... potency of biological products moving in international commerce' (third and fourth area) was altered in:
'Standards with respect to the safety ... of biological, pharmaceutical and *similar* products moving in international commerce'.
- The suggestion concerning 'labelling of pharmaceutical' products (fifth area) was amplified to include 'advertising' of these products and to cover also 'biological' and 'similar' products. (WHO, Off. Rec., no. 2, 1948, p. 21; Article 21 of the Constitution.)

The suggestion [26] made by some of the members of the Economic and Social Council that rules regarding medical standards and biological remedies for international trade should not be obligatory but rather dealt with by way of recommendations was thus not followed by the Conference (WHO, Off. Rec., no. 2, 1948, p. 21).

25. In the drafting committee of ECOSOC, when considering these proposals, it was felt that regulations regarding medical standards and biological remedies for international trade should not be obligatory but should be submitted as recommendations (WHO, Off. Rec., no. 2, 1948, p. 120).
26. See previous footnote.

On the other hand, a proposal made at the Health Conference to include also the prevention of importation by members of biological, pharmaceutical and similar products not confirming to standards adopted by the Assembly was rejected. It was argued in this respect that this was a matter of commercial policy, not properly falling within the jurisdiction of a health organization (WHO, Off. Rec., no. 2, 1948, p. 21 and pp. 60-61).

Underlying this argument was the wish to reassure member states that the subject matter of regulations as in Article 21 of the Constitution is of a purely international nature (Yemin, 1969, p. 184). The areas in which regulations may be adopted are those in which for preventive reasons international measures are required, without for that reason impinging upon national policies. To carry out its constitutional functions, the Organization needs to regulate a number of activities which can only be determined at the international level (Gutteridge, 1971, p. 281).

It seems in any case rather unlikely that once regulations on the afore mentioned subject are accepted by members the question of the importation of non-conforming products will be a matter of importance. Furthermore, Article 21 under (d) provides for sufficient guarantee that products moving in international commerce comply with the standards drawn up by the Assembly, assuming, of course, that every member has accepted the regulations concerned.

   —   effect of regulations

The regulations adopted by the Assembly under Article 21 'produce intended effects not as a result of any immediate acceptance of such regulations by member states which is not required by the Constitution but as a result of the operation of Article 22 which provides for their entry into force for all members not rejecting them in a given period. The effect of these provisions is to grant competence to the Assembly to bring such regulations into force for all members not rejecting them: regulations are imputtable to an international organ distinct from the member states represented in it'. They thus represent a unilateral form of action (Yemin, 1969, p. 201).

Including Articles 21 and 22 in the Constitution clearly reflected the intention to create legal norms through the WHA. This intention also became clear through the actual terms of the regulations, which specify the rights and obligations of their addressees in respect of the subject matter dealt with (Yemin, 1969, p. 203).

Certain provisions of the two regulations presently in force were reduced to the status of recommendations mainly with a view to simplify necessary adaptation procedures (see below). They are, however, different from those adopted by the Assembly under Article 23 of the Constitution insofar as they are intended to grant a certain discretion to member states as to their execution (Article 3 of the Nomenclature Regulations and Article 14.2 of the International Health Regulations).

These provisions lay down qualified legal obligations. The competence of the Health Assembly 'to adopt regulations having full legal force may be considered to include the competence to adopt provisions having a legal status intermediate between binding rules and recommendations' (Yemin, 1969, p.

204). The regulations adopted by the Assembly under Article 21 of the Constitution comply with the prerequisites for an act to be legislative with full legal force. Their form is unilateral, they contain a legal norm and they are of a general nature. The Health Assembly has in this respect the power to adopt provisions in the nature of legal norms (Yemin, 1969, p. 204). [27]

— application of Articles 21-22

The Organization has to date used its authority to adopt regulations by virtue of Article 21 of its Constitution only twice. These regulations, which concern the first two subject matters indicated in the relevant Article, were moreover prepared at an early stage of the existence of the Organization. Although many other fields seem as though they might have been indicated to be subject to regulations, they were instead dealt with by recommendations.

International Nomenclature Regulations (ICD)[28]

The regulations regarding the nomenclature with respect to diseases and causes of death include the compilation and publication of statistics, their major concern being the international classification of diseases.

The general statistical conference, which was held in 1853, recommended that an international nomenclature of causes of death should be established (WHO, the first ten years of the World Health Organization, 1958). The first international list of causes of death was adopted in 1893. The first revision took place in 1900, followed by regular 'decennial' revisions. The lists were first prepared under the responsibility of the International Institute of Statistics; the revisions of 1929 and 1938 were made under the joint responsibility of that Institute and the Health Organization of the League of Nations. After 1946, the WHO assumed responsibility for subsequent revisions (Kupka, 1978, p. 219). The first World Health Assembly in 1948 adopted the Nomenclature Regulations to guide national administrations in the elaboration and publication of statistics in conformity with the International Classification.

The seventh revision (1955) grouped for the first time in a single system the causes of morbidity and mortality.

The Nineteenth World Health Assembly in 1966 adopted a proposal to review the Nomenclature Regulations in such a way that they would be restricted to a minimum of requirements considered to be indispensable as a

27. Van Pannenborg (1978, pp. 332 a.f., see also footnote (2) on page 321) attributes supranational power to the WHO on the basis of its Constitution, in particular Articles 21 and 22 of the Constitution. I would not stress this point of view, because, as seen, WHO member states have in no way transferred sovereignty to the WHO and its various organs as in the case of the sole real supranational organization, the European Community. It is, moreover, doubtful, whether all or some of the WHO member states would be prepared to attribute supranational power to the Organization. This is supported by the very fact that already in respect of the European Community some of the member states are hesitant to entrust the Organization with powers in the public health field.

28. See: International Classification of Diseases: Manual of the International Statistical Classification of Diseases, Injuries, and Causes of Death, based on the Recommendation of the eighth revision Conference, 1965, and adopted by the nineteenth World Health Assembly, World Health Organization, Geneva, 1967. See also the ninth revision of 1975, which will come into force on 1 January 1979.

basis for international comparability. Other matters would have to be adopted under Article 23 of the Constitution (see below under c.). It was also requested by the WHA that a compendium of *recommendations*, definitions and standards relating to health statistics would be prepared for adoption by the Health Assembly (Resolution WHA 19.45 of May 1966; see also Resolution WHA 20.19 of May 1967). These decisions were of considerable significance, not only with regard to the classification system but also concerning the form given to the regulations. The greater part of the clauses of the nomenclature regulations (the actual lists) was removed from the regulations and issued in the form of recommendations. [29]

The reason for this significant change was twofold. Firstly, it enabled governments to make small adaptions if necessary, which would have been impossible under a too rigid system of regulatory procedure. Secondly, it simplified periodical revisions of the ICD by the Health Assembly since they did not have to go through the normal regulatory process (Gutteridge, 1971, p. 281).

The ninth revision (1975, to come into force on January 1st, 1979), though basically maintaining the structure of the classification, is directed towards the inclusion of more details and also reflects changes in medical knowledge. (Thus, for instance, a new rule for the classification of mortality has been added that will permit the coding of cases of death attributable to errors and accidents in medical care.)

In accordance with Article 2 of the Regulations, the ICD is obligatory for the compilation of morbidity and mortality data. The classifications represent a valuable system for international classification procedures of diagnosis, treatment and prevention. They promote the international comparability of data and are also the basis for the diagnostic indexing of clinical hospital records. Despite the efforts of the Organization to promote an international statistical system of this kind, they still fail at an international level of application.

Efficiency in acquiring reliable data at a national level is often inhibited by lack of organization. The system is also not yet applied by every country so that it is difficult to obtain fully reliable comparable data at an international level. The WHO publishes annual statistics on morbidity and mortality compiled in accordance with the ICD.

International Health Regulations (IHR) [30]

These regulations – originally called International Sanitary Regulations – were the result of many sanitary conferences held from 1851 onwards. They replace the provisions of the international sanitary conventions, regulations and similar agreements (Article 99 of the regulations). The 1951 edition represented an up-to-date version of the rules contained in previous conventions

---

29. The International Classification of Procedures in Medicine (1978) is similar in structure to the ICD and in fact supplements the ICD (WHA 29.35 of May 1976).
30. See: WHO, International Health Regulations (1969); second annoted edition, 1974. See also N. Howard-Jones in various editions of the *WHO Chronicle* of 1974 for an extensive description of the scientific background of the international sanitary conferences.

from 1903 onwards. [31] They have been regularly revised since. The current IHR were adopted in 1969 (in force since January 1st, 1971). [32] With this latest revision it was intended 'to strengthen the use of epidemiological principles as applied internationally, to detect, reduce or eliminate the source from which infection spreads, to improve sanitation in and around ports and airports, to prevent the dissemination of vectors and, in general, to encourage epidemiological activities at the national level so that there is little risk of outside infection establishing itself' (Foreword to the IHR of 1969).

The regulations include threefold obligations for participating states as follows:
– an elaborated notification system (Articles 2-10 and Article 13);
– a health organization system at frontiers (airports and ports included) (Articles 14-23);
– health measures (Articles 24-50) and special provisions relating to each of the diseases subject to the regulations (smallpox, plague, cholera, yellow fever) (Articles 51-83).

For the purpose of health and sanitary measures the health organization system at ports and airports shall comply as far as practicable to the principles and recommendations set forth in publications of the WHO on this subject (Article 14.2 of the IHR). As in the case of the Nomenclature Regulations and for the same reasons as set out above these relevant clauses are not issued as regulations but merely as recommendations. [33]

There is a committee on international surveillance of communicable diseases [34] (Article 106 of the IHR) for the purpose of reviewing the Regulations and other relevant legislation, of preparing recommendations on amendments to the IHR, on additional regulations on diseases not covered by the IHR and on practices, methods and procedures in connexion with the subjects included in the recommendations (WHA 6.20; WHO, Off. Rec., 1953, no. 48, p. 23).

Any state may ultimately refer disputes concerning the interpretation or application of the Regulations to the International Court of Justice (Article 100 of the IHR).

The purpose of the IHR is to ensure a maximum of security against the international spread of diseases with a minimum of interference to world traffic. They are meant to provide an adequate system of epidemiological surveillance at an international level (notification of diseases).

Readiness to notify on the part of national governments, and in particular rapidity of notification when major problems arise and the taking of adequate measures, are indispensable conditions for making the regulations effective.

---

31. See before, paras. 1.1. and 1.2.1.
32. The IHR were amended in 1973, particularly as regards the provisions for cholera.
33. Diseases which are not covered by the IHR and which may yet pose a considerable threat to public health as the risk of occurrence of an epidemic is always present, the so-called diseases under surveillance such as malaria and poliomyelitis, have also been subject to recommendations. These recommendations aim at appropriate collection and analysis of epidemiological information and co-ordination of activities with regard to such epidemic diseases.
34. Up until 1969 the committee was called 'committee on international quarantine'.

Adequate national facilities for rapid diagnosis are also indispensable for the success of the regulations (Delon, 1975, p. 23).

Information received by the WHO in accordance with the regulations is disseminated to all member states in various ways (weekly epidemiological record, daily epidemiological radio-telegraphic bulletin). While the IHR work acceptably under normal conditions, there is some risk that notifications obligatory under these regulations become insufficient in periods when major health problems arise. Delon (1975, p. 24) gives three reasons for this relative failure:
— the time needed for a health administration to identify the disease;
— the concern for 'national honour' felt by some health administrations;
— the fear of excessive reactions by neighbouring countries (economic losses in trade and tourism).

Despite these possible unfavourable side-effects, the co-ordinated programmes of disease control which were developed in recent years, have been rather successful, particularly as regards the eradication of smallpox Yellow fever and plague are today of little significance in international travel. In 1973 all references to cholera vaccination were eliminated from the IHR, it being accepted that vaccination does not prevent transmission of this disease (Resolution WHA 26.55; WHO, Off. Rec., no. 209, 1973, p. 29).

'Today effective methods of immunization, vector control and therapy have minimized the need for border surveillance, and have even led to the suggestion that the International Health Regulations be abandoned' (*WHO Chronicle*, 32, 1978, p. 440). Abandonment of the regulations is, however, opposed to on the grounds that the IHR have an important role to play in the international control of communicable diseases (prevention of international spread of disease; protection of the international traveller from preventable disease and inconvenience; improvement of the control of preventable disease). The question whether the IHR should be changed at all and if so, how, is presently pending before the World Health Assembly. In the meantime new regulations were proposed, which are administrative in nature and attempt to define general principles. (See 'The long-term future of the International Health Regulations', *WHO Chronicle*, 32, 1978, pp. 439-447 for the proposed regulations.)

d.   recommendations (Article 23 of the Constitution)
    — constitutional provisions
The Technical Preparatory Committee did not refer to this function of the Health Assembly in its draft. The matter was advanced by the working committee of the International Health Conference on scope and functions of the World Health Organization. The only discussion which took place during the Conference on this subject was related to a matter of procedure for the adoption by member states of recommendations. The proposal made by the Belgian delegate consisted of a procedure by which member states were asked to present within 18 months each recommendation to the authority or authorities competent to enact legislation or to take other appropriate action. This proposal, which was based upon the practice of the International Labour

Organisation, was weakened by the Conference on grounds that enough authority was given to the Health Assembly relative to conventions and regulations. Thus, member states are now merely required to submit annual reports on the action taken with respect to recommendations (Article 62 of the Constitution; WHO, Off. Rec., no. 2, 1948, p. 21).

— subject matter

The subject matter of recommendations is not limited. Matters which may be covered by agreements, conventions, and, or regulations can thus also be subject to less binding rules. The regulations regarding nomenclature (including the compilation and publication of statistics with respect to diseases and causes of death), for instance, refer to *recommendations* made by the WHA on classification, coding procedure, age grouping, definition of territorial areas and other relevant definitions and standards (Article 3 of the Regulations). Members for whom regulations are in force must comply as far as possible with these recommendations in compiling and publishing mortality and morbidity statistics (see also above under *b.*).

— effect of recommendations

The recommendations of the Organization have no legal force: member states are not bound to their contents; compliance is sought through persuasion rather than through direct procedures.

The value of the yearly reporting system, which applies also to action taken in respect to regulations and conventions, is that attention is regularly drawn to the objectives laid down in these instruments. Although in practice very few members live up to this obligation, the recommendations still form a valuable tool for influencing member states in their national policies. The texts are not easily ignored or disregarded (Gutteridge, 1971, p. 283). They form in fact one of the methods for constant stimulation to thought and action.

— application of Article 23

Due to the difficulties in drawing up binding regulations on a world-wide scale, technical considerations (rapid technical development quickly makes fixed rules obsolete), the historical background of international organizations in the public health field ('official science' should not be adopted by an international health organization), the Organization prefers to turn to recommendations which are not binding instruments (Gutteridge, 1971, p. 282). They have the apparent advantage of being flexible, simple and adaptable.

Moreover, as long as the recommendations deal with very technical matters, prepared by highly qualified experts, it is most likely that member states will conform to them. So far no major difficulties in following these types of recommendations have become evident. It is hardly likely that countries would apply other international standards than those laid down in the recommendations of the Health Assembly. An additional factor in opting for the formula of recommendations may be found in the fact that often various activities which are proposed for international action are not yet fully regulated at a national level (as, for instance, in the case of the purity and potency of pharmaceutical preparations destined for export).

Problems may arise, however, when factors other than technical considerations are involved, such as commercial interests (international non-proprietary names for pharmaceutical products are an example of these). Important recommendations are those concerning the development of international non-proprietary names for drugs, the establishment of an early warning scheme for drugs and the development of an international pharmacopoeia. All these matters could have been the subject of regulations. Originally it was envisaged (in 1951) to prepare regulations embodying the International Pharmacopoeia and replacing the Agreements of 1906 and 1929 on the Unification of Pharmacopoeial Formulas for Potent Drugs (WHO, Off. Rec., no. 36, 1951, p. 12).

In 1952, however, it was decided to terminate the former agreements without replacing them by regulations and to retain for the International Pharmacopoeia the status of a recommendation. (The International Pharmacopoeia was already recommended for inclusion into national texts by the Resolution of the WHA 3.10 of May 1950; WHO, Off. Rec., no. 28, 1950, p. 19.)[35]

At the moment a revision of the International Pharmacopoeia is under study to suggest the inclusion of a list of pharmaceutical substances and general guidelines for selection.

Recommendations on the manufacture and quality control of drugs and certification schemes governing the quality of pharmaceutical products moving in international commerce are also regularly revised (lastly by the 28th WHA in 1975, Resolution WHA 28.65).

Another set of recommendations which could have been the subject of regulations, and which despite thier non-obligatory character are effective, are the international standards and units for biological substances, which were the subject of Assembly Resolution WHA 18.7 of May 1965.

Finally, it is worthwhile mentioning a specific field in which the WHO has to issue recommendations, though it is admitted that, because of the Organization's obligations to do so under the terms of an international convention it might be argued that these recommendations fall under its general function of co-operation (Article 2 (b) of the Constitution) rather than under its own free authority to issue recommendations under Article 23 of the Constitution.

The recommendations in question are those which the Organization has to issue on the basis of its responsibilities under the 1971 UN Convention on Psychotropic Substances (in force since 1976).

This Convention requires WHO to recommend to the United Nations Commission on Narcotic Drugs whether a psychotropic substance is to be controlled nationally and internationally and if so, in what manner.

The recommendations of the WHA in this respect, which concern the scheduling of a new substance, the transfer of an already controlled substance from one schedule to another or the removal of a controlled substance from control, are of decisive influence on the medical and scientific sectors.

Abuse liability, public health and social problems stemming from abuse and therapeutic usefulness are all factors determining these recommendations.

It is, however, the UN Commission itself which has final authority in approving the

35. At a European level there are presently two pharmacopoeia conventions in force, one drawn up by the Council of Europe and one in the framework of the European Free Trade Association (see below, Ch. III, para. 3.4.2. and Ch. IV, para. 5.).

scheduling of individual drugs (*WHO chronicle*, 32, 1978, pp. 3-8). This Convention, under the terms of which the WHO has an important role to play, is an outstanding example of a combined effort on a world-wide scale to promote public health in a specific field.

Despite the existence of considerable constitutional powers to regulate activities in the international public health sphere, one is struck by the limited use made by the Organization of its legislative possibilities (conventions, agreements and regulations). Admittedly it is difficult to develop uniform international instruments on a world-wide scale. Difficulties encountered with such a system (lengthy procedures, rigidity of fixed rules) underline all the more the need (already mentioned in para. 3.5.) for a system whereby the same legislative possibilities would be given to regional organizations, although it is recognized that non-obligatory measures (recommendations) have not failed to achieve results in certain fields. Such a system of far-reaching decentralization would require a complete re-assessment of the functioning and structure of the Organization. Until then the Organization must try to use the most appropriate instruments at its disposal in a given situation.

4. World Health Organization and human rights

The creation of specialised agencies is one of the methods for promoting human rights laid down in the various human rights instruments of the UN, because these agencies are technically well equipped for special subjects.

The WHO, created as a specialised agency to deal with health, is obviously designed to contribute to the realization of the right to health care. Its formal tasks in respect of Article 12 (on health) of the International Covenant on Economic, Social and Cultural Rights are to elaborate the obligations formulated in that Article at an international level with a view to implementing the right to health care internationally (Articles 21 and 22 of the Covenant refer in particular to this, see also Articles 16.2 (b), 18-20 of the Covenant). [36]

In accordance with the procedure of reporting on the implementation of the International Covenant on Economic, Social and Cultural Rights the reports relating to Article 12 will become due in 1980 (Resolution 1988 (LX) of ECOSOC). Reports submitted will be examined by a working group of ECOSOC in the proceedings of which the WHO may participate. Though the exact role of the specialised agencies on matters falling within their competence is not yet clear, this procedure presents theoratically a possibility for urging the WHO to take further international action, including the drawing up of international legislative instruments, for the purpose of giving further content to the various aspects of the right to health care. It is, however, likely that when examining reports under Article 12 of the Covenant, the work will be hindered by the lack of criteria on basis of which the standards under that Article may be qualified.

36. See part A, Ch. I, para. 2.2.3. The formulation of Article 12 of the Covenant was largely based on the concept of the Organization of the notion of health, see Part A, Ch. II, para. 4.2.

The formal tasks in respect of the implementation of the Articles of the International Covenant on Civil and Political Rights, which deal with those human rights having a direct bearing on the realization of the right to health care (Article 6: right to life; Article 7: torture and experimentation) are much less obvious. The only reference to specialised agencies in the Covenant is in Article 40, para. 3, namely that the Secretary General of the UN may transmit to the agencies concerned copies of such parts of the reports of states parties as may fall within their field of competence.

This difference with the International Covenant on Economic, Social and Cultural Rights stems from the difference in the nature of the rights covered by the respective Covenants (see Introduction). Moreover, under the provision of Articles 61-65 of the Constitution of the WHO, members of the Organization are to report annually on action and progress achieved in improving the health of its people *as well as on other relevant matters*. By applying these Articles information may also be obtained on the implementation of the respective Articles of the Covenant. Relevant information is passed on by the WHO to the competent organs of the UN (See also Article 18 (g) of the Constitution for the functions of the WHA in this respect).

Though the Covenant does not confer any direct obligation upon the WHO to furthering the realization of the individual rights contained in Articles 6 and 7 of the Covenant, the Organization has formally recognized its duties for promoting these rights, whenever aspects of health are involved (see, for instance, Resolution 23.41; WHO, Off. Rec., no. 184, 1970, p. 21).

In practice, the contribution of the WHO to the realization of the right to health care mainly consists of operational activities and studies which are intended to influence national and international attitudes. The Organization, through its activities, strives to ameliorate the health situation of all people by improving existing health services. The most appropriate tool in this respect, i.e. legislative action, tends to be rejected in favour of less binding recommendations. [37] The constitutional tasks of the WHO in respect to the realization of this particular right was already discussed in previous paragraphs.

Through recognizing the importance of appropriate (national) health legislation for the realization of the right to health care (see, for instance, Resolution WHA 30.44; WHO, Off. Rec., no. 240, 1977, p. 25) the Organization's scope of action in this respect still remains limited. It concentrates on assistance to member states (upon request), on strengthening the collaboration with other specialised agencies of the United Nations concerned with the development of guidelines for health legislation and on implementing optimal means for the dissemination of legislative information.

This rather limited approach may partly be explained by the fact that existing differences in legislative provisions dealing with health care are due not only to variations in the level of scientific knowledge and economic development, but also to other factors, such as religious, moral, ethical and traditional attitudes. In cases where the latter factors have a paramount influence on national policies regarding legislative measures, the Organization con-

37. See para. 3.5.

siders its role very limited, and restricts its influence mainly to organizing scientific conferences, discussions and other such methods. [38]

This applies not only when the right to health care is involved, but also when the right to life and, or medical experimentation have a profound influence on legislative measures (examples are problems such as abortion, contraception, sterilization, euthanasia and medical experimentation on human beings).

Obviously these factors also influence the practical contribution of the WHO towards the implementation of the right to life and towards the safeguarding of human beings against torture and unacceptable forms of experimentation. With regard to the right to life activities are concentrated on promotion of research, organization or support of international scientific discussions and dissemination of information. These are activities of an indirect nature, because the aspects of this particular human right in which the WHO is most interested are regarded as too controversial to achieve international consensus. The efforts deployed by the Organization in relation to medical experimentation are, however, increasing. At the time of drafting the International Covenant on Civil and Political Rights there was still much discussion on the inclusion of a reference to medical experimentation. The WHO was at that time strongly opposed to the idea of including such a reference, because it feared that it would hinder genuine medical progress. [39] But it was this very concern which in the late sixtieth encouraged the Organization to seek for means of protecting human life against unwarranted excesses perpetrated by medical science, and in particular by biomedical research. Thus the twenty-third WHA affirmed in May 1970, that the protection of the human personality and its physical and intellectual integrity, as part of the health aspects of human rights are within the competence of the Organization (Resolution WHA 23.41; WHO, Off. Rec., no. 184, 1970, p. 21). [40]

Thus, for instance, the Organization works closely with the (non-governmental) World Medical Association (WMA) in respect to the drawing up of its international declarations and codes of medical ethics. Although the WMA is a professional organization, its instruments [41] are widely applied and put into practice.

38. E/CN.4/1173, p. 6.
39. See Part A, Ch. II. para. 2.2.2.
40. See WHO, Health aspects of human rights with special reference to developments in biology and medicine (1976). This study is based on Resolution 2450 (XXIII) of the UN General Assembly of 19 December 1968. In the preface of this study, which was prepared in pursuance of Resolution WHA 23.41, consideration is given to the responsibilities (and limitations) of the WHO in attempting to arrive at international consensus on the point at which certain medical investigations and procedures may offer a threat to human rights. There is no consideration in the report on entering the domain of drawing up international principles nor is there an indication of fields which are suitable for intergovernmental action through the WHO.
41. Declaration of Geneva (1948, revised in 1968), which contains a modified form of the Hippocratic Oath; International Code of Medical Ethics (1949); Declaration of Helsinki (1964) containing recommendations guiding doctors in clinical research, revised and extended by the WMA in 1975 (Tokyo) to include not only clinical research, but also biomedical research involving human subjects; Declaration of Sidney (1968) relating to the determination of the time of death; Declaration of Oslo (1970) relating to therapeutic abortion (see Part. A, Ch. II, Para. 3.2.1.).

The WHO moreover co-operates closely with the (non-governmental) Council for International Organizations of Medical Sciences (CIOMS)[42], set up jointly by the WHO and the United Nations Educational, Scientific and Cultural Organization in 1949. This co-operation is mainly for the purpose of developing codes of medical ethics, including those related to the protection of persons subjected to any form of detention or imprisonment against torture and other cruel, inhuman or degrading treatment or punishment (Resolution EB 55. R. 64; WHO, Off. Rec., no. 223, 1975, p. 40 and Resolution EB 57, R. 47; WHO, Off. Rec., no. 231, 1976, p. 34; see also Resolution WHA 30.32; WHO, Off. Rec., no. 240, 1977, p. 17). Through Resolution EB 61/R.37 (WHO, Off. Rec., no. 244, 1978, p. 25), the CIOMS and the WMA are requested to further develop under the sponsorship of the WHO the Declaration of Tokyo (1975), which contains guidelines for medical doctors concerning torture and other cruel, inhuman or degrading treatment or punishment in relation to detention and imprisonment as a basis for a draft code of medical ethics for the protection of prisoners against torture.

The elaboration of such a code is in conformity with the repeated invitations of the UN General Assembly to the WHO to draft an outline of principles of medical ethics which might be relevant to the protection of prisoners or detainees against torture and other cruel, inhuman or degrading treatment or punishment. [43]

The WHO also assists CIOMS in matters concerning the ethical aspects of biomedical research involving human subjects. [44] Presently, for instance, a joint survey is being carried out on ethical review committees or other mechanisms which are used in various countries for the protection of human subjects in clinical research. This is done for the purpose of the development by CIOMS of a programme on the role and function of ethical review committees for research involving human subjects.

Furthermore the advisory committee on medical research, which was established in 1959 (Resolution WHA 12.17; WHO, Off. Rec., no. 95, 1959, p. 27; see above, para. 3.3. under b.) has intensified its activities on this subject of medical research.

Resolution WHA 29.64 (WHO, Off. Rec., No. 233, 1976, p. 41) confirms the need for drawing up a comprehensive long-term programme for the development and co-ordination of biomedical and health research (including policies for priority definitions) and calls for an analysis and evaluation of WHO's research co-ordination activities including a formulation of possible ethical and other recommendations. This Resolution underlines, though in a careful manner, the need for establishing at an international level ethical rules which should guide biomedical research.[45]

42. Former title: Council for the Co-ordination of International Congresses of Medical Sciences.
43. See Part A, Ch. II, para. 3.2.2.
44. See Part A, Ch. II, para. 3.2.1.
45. See also for instance Resolution WHA 25.60; WHO, Off. Rec., no. 201, 1972, p. 32; Resolution WHA 30.40; WHO, Off. Rec., no. 240, 1977, p. 23; Resolution EB 61. R.36; WHO, Off. Rec., no. 244, 1978, p. 24 and Resolution WHA 31.35; WHO, Off. Rec., no. 247, 1978, p. 23.

Though all activities undertaken in the framework of the Organization's programme of research have to be cleared by the secretariat committee on research whenever there is a question of medical experiments involving human beings, the WHO itself has not yet been engaged in the elaboration of principles for safeguarding human rights in the case medical research projects involving human subjects.

But in view of the growing potential of medical science in promoting health and preventing disease, the need for international principles of this kind has never been so pressing. Considering the absence of any attempt to elaborate such international principles, it would seem that the Organization tends to regard its role in respect of medical experimentation involving human subjects as being of a somewhat 'promotional' nature.

Finally, WHO's contribution to the drafting of various UN human rights declarations was already mentioned in Part. A, Ch. II, para. 5. Worth memorising particularly are the Declaration on the Rights of the Child (adopted by the UN General Assembly on 20 November 1959, Resolution 1386 (XIV), in which the right to adequate health care occupies a predominant place; the Declaration on the Rights of the Mentally Retarded Persons (adopted by the UN General Assembly on 20 December 1971, Resolution 2856 (XXVI), which reflects the opinions of the WHO on health aspects of mental retardation (doc. E/CN. 5/472) and the Declaration on the Rights of Disabled Persons, which provides that disabled persons have the right to medical, psychological and functional treatment, including prosthetic and orthetic appliances and to medical and social rehabilitation (Resolution 3447 (XXX) of 9 December 1975).

When reviewing the specific contribution of the WHO to these aspects of human rights discussed above, it should be borne in mind that increasing demands will be made on the Organization to contribute more effectively still to the realization of the right to health care and other rights, since the more people become conscious of the significance of these rights, the more their demands will grow.

5. World Health Organization and its tasks in the field of co-ordination and co-operation

5.1. SOME GENERAL REMARKS

The realization of the right to health care also implies taking action to avoid diversion of scarce resources to unproductive activities as well as unnecessary utilization of financial resources for duplicating activities.

Constitutionally, the Organization has a predominant role to play in co-ordinating health activities.

Being the co-ordinating authority in international health work [46], it not only aims at a rational organization of the whole field of health activities, but

46. See para. 3.3. under a.

also has to focus attention on closely related fields, such as the social and economic ones, which interact on health.

With growing awareness of the importance of the health aspects of a number of organized human rights activities, co-ordination has become increasingly vital.

The legal basis for the co-ordinating task of the WHO lies in:
— its Constitution: Article 2 (functions of the Organization), Articles 69-72 (on relations with other organizations), (Article 50 (d) is the basis for regional co-operation);
— the agreements between the WHO and other international organizations (WHO, Off. Rec., no. 181, 1970, p. 40).

In accordance with Article 2 (b) of its Constitution, the WHO has furthermore the obligation to establish and maintain effective collaboration with the UN, specialised agencies and other institutions. The primary aim of combining these two functions (co-ordination and co-operation), is to prevent unnecessary overlapping of public health activities by international organizations: special relationship agreements, for instance, indicate respective areas of competence. This negative aim is complemented by a positive objective, to achieve a maximum of effectiveness in attaining common goals through a common approach, while utilizing technical and scientific resources in the most productive way.

This positive objective also finds its expression in special relationship agreements, specifying when areas of common interest render co-operation necessary and when this co-operation is a mean of achieving common ends.

The co-ordination policy of the WHO is guided by two main principles:
— the responsibility of the Organization to act as the directory and co-ordinating authority on international health work;
— the inseparability of social, economic and health factors.
This policy is indispensable in the field of health — as in any other field — with a view to achieving unified efforts and at the same time reducing expenses and duplication of work.

The tasks of the WHO in the fields of co-ordination and co-operation are not restricted to the UN system but apply also to other bilateral and multilateral organizations (WHO, Off. Rec., no. 227, 1975, p. 340). It is of importance that one single organization has been assigned the task of co-ordinating activities in the field of health at a global as well as regional level. Were this not the case, there would doubtless be a considerable amount of unsound competition between the various international organizations which are active in this field. Even so, this competitive element is still quite prevalent, making one wonder whether the co-ordinating role of the WHO is yet strong enough.

Obviously, the Organization has to apply certain criteria with regard to co-ordination. Some of the technical considerations are:
— the problem must be of major public health importance;
— the solution to a given problem must depend on international collaboration;

134

- the involvement of the Organization will have a significant impact on the solution of a given problem.

The following organizational criteria can be mentioned:
- the programme areas should be reflected in the Constitution of the WHO;
- the activities should be based on the general programme of work of the Organization, on recommendations, or on specific request form governments.

The WHO considers co-operation to be one of the best possible means towards exploiting to the full its own and others' resources in carrying out a given task.

Co-ordination and co-operation are pursued either by using formal methods (agreements on areas of competence and co-operation; exchange of programmes; prior consultation on practical co-operation; maintenance of liaison offices etc.), or by less formal procedures (such as preparation of joint studies and reports, participation in concerted programmes, interagency-programmes, reciprocal participation in meetings; WHO, Off. Rec., no. 181, 1970, p. 110).

Prior consultation on matters of concern to more than one agency is considered as basic to effective co-operation among the organizations (Resolution WHA 14.29 of February 1961). Obviously, prior consultation on programmes of work is one of the most important tools for successful co-ordination and co-operation.

5.2. FORMAL RELATIONSHIP AGREEMENTS (WITHIN THE UNITED NATIONS SYSTEM)[47]

Co-ordination and co-operation are crucial aspects of the relationship between the WHO and other specialised agencies of the United Nations: aims and objectives should not only respond to the Organization's own obligations, but should at the same time tie in with the aims and objectives of the United Nations' system as a whole. There is not only an official relationship agreement with the United Nations, but also with those organizations, whose constitutional aims haven planes tangent with the functions of the WHO. Thus, agreements have been concluded with the specialised agencies of the UN: the International Labour Organisation (ILO), the United Nations Educational, Scientific and Cultural Organization (UNESCO), the Food and Agriculture Organization (FAO), as well as with the International Atomic Energy Agency (IAEA).

The Interim Commission, which had initiated co-operation of the WHO with the various specialised agencies of the United Nations, had prepared a report on agreements between the WHO and other specialised agencies which existed at that time (see for instance WHO, Off. Rec., no. 7, 10 and 12, 1948). This report served as a basis for discussions in the first World Health Assembly, when the conclusion of such agreements was discussed. In the view of the Interim Commission there should not be a distinction in the type of agreements made with specialised agencies.

47. Formal relationship agreements on a regional basis will be dealt with in Ch. II, para. 2.5.

The formal relationship agreements (see below) contain provisions for the exchange of information and documents, reciprocal representation at meetings and co-operation in the field of statistical information. The agreements between the WHO and the other specialised agencies also contain provisions on joint committees, to which matters of common interest may be referred.[48]

A provision is also included in these agreements on consultation regarding the establishment of regional offices. These consultations are, however, limited to the questions concerning common use of premises, staffing and common services.

   — United Nations (UN) (1945)

The agreement between the UN and the WHO, which is based on Article 63 of the UN Charter and on Article 57 of the WHO Constitution, was adopted by the first World Health Assembly on 10 July 1948 (Resolution WHA 1. 102; WHO, Off. Rec., no. 10, 1948, p. 59). Full recognition is given in this agreement to the WHO as the responsible body for taking action within the scope of its Constitution (Article II of the agreement).

Under the terms of the agreement, the UN may propose items for inclusion on the agenda of the Health Assembly or the Executive Board (Article III).

Furthermore, the organs of the UN may make recommendations to organs of the WHO concerning health matters, as well as for the co-ordination of policies and activities of specialised agencies (Articles 55, 58, 62 and 63 of the UN Charter and Article 18 (i) of the WHO Constitution). Human rights have, for instance, been the subject of recommendations aiming at co-ordination of this kind. Thus, the UN General Assembly in its Resolution 2450 (XXIII) (1968) requested the Secretary General of the UN to prepare a study of problems in connection with human rights arising from developments in science and technology, to be prepared in co-operation with the competent specialised agencies. [49]

Regarding human rights, the WHO has also been consulted on the drafting of the relevant parts of the International Covenants on Civil and Political Rights and on Economic, Social and Cultural Rights. [50] The Organization furthermore supplies the commission on human rights with regular information in the form of periodic reports. The WHO has, too, prepared reports on various subjects, with a view to the preparation of human rights declarations.

The WHO also has to report to the UN on action taken by the Organization on any recommendations it might have received from the UN (Article IV). This Article furthermore provides the WHO with the legal basis to participate in the co-ordination machinery set up by the UN. The UN is recognized as the central agency for the collection, analysis, publication, standardization and improvement of statistics, serving the general purpose of international organizations. Certain forms of statistical information fall within the special sphere of competence of the WHO. UN programmes which are of interest to the WHO include economic and social development planning, water and natu-

---

48. This is not the case with the agreement between the WHO and the IAEA.
49. See also above, para. 4.
50. See also Part A, Ch. I, para. 2.2.3. and Ch. II, paras, 2.2.2. and 4.2.

ral resources, rehabilitation, social aspects of economic development, narcotic drugs and human rights. The last two subjects are of particular importance. The WHO undertakes, for instance, activities in the field of drug dependence (both at a global and a regional level) in close co-operation with the UN.

The relationship agreement between the WHO and the UN in fact reaffirms the great independence of the WHO in the field of health, in line with the principle of functional decentralization favoured by the UN. In this way international co-operation in the technical field, removed as far as possible from political influences, is given a maximum chance of success (Jenks, 1951, p. 47).

— International Labour Organisation (ILO) (1919)

The ILO has competence in social matters, particularly with a view to the progressive elaboration of standards for world-wide social legislation. One of the fu ctions of the Organization in this respect is the promotion of workers' occupational health and safety. In this framework numerous agreements [51] and recommendations have been drawn up on items such as social insurance, occupational health services and prevention of industrial accidents.

Not only occupational health but also workers' health in general — its preservation and improvement — receives full attention.
The relationship agreement between the WHO and the ILO was adopted by the first World Health Assembly on 10 July 1948 (Resolution WHA. 1.125; WHO, Off. Rec., no. 13, 1948, p. 322). It frequently serves as a basis for guidance to the Director General of the WHO, because there are several areas in which the work of both Organizations overlap. They are, for instance, both involved with occupational health, medical care aspects of social security, child welfare, maternity protection etc.

Though the emphasis and approach of both Organizations is different (the ILO, for instance, puts emphasis on working conditions which might have adverse effects on health, while the WHO emphasizes not only the working conditions, but also living conditions and therefore the total health of the worker), there remains the common interest in specific fields of health, which calls for close collaboration (WHO, Off. Rec., no. 181, 1970, p. 82). [52] There is, for instance, a standing joint ILO/WHO Committee on occupational health.

— Food and Agriculture Organization (FAO) (1945)

The agreement between the WHO and the FAO was adopted by the first World Health Assembly on 17 July 1948 (Resolution WHA 1.123; WHO, Off. Rec., no. 13, 1948, pp. 323 and 324). Fields of common interest are, for instance, nutrition, insecticides and pesticides, food standards, food additives, veterinary public health and rural development projects.

An important joint programme is the preparation of a 'Codex Alimentarius' (global programme of standardization of foodstuffs). Between these two Orga-

51. See in particular the Medical Care and Sickness Benefits Convention of 1969 (no. 130).
52. Much of the information on the relationship of the WHO with UN specialized agencies is based on the review of the organizational study on co-ordination with the United Nations and the specialized agencies', which is contained in Annex 4 of Part I of WHO, Off. Rec., no. 181, 1970, pp. 39-153.

nizations, too, there is a difference in approach. The FAO puts emphasis on nutrition in relation to production, distribution and consumption of food. The WHO on the other hand, emphasizes on nutrition in relation to the maintenance of health and the prevention of disease.

— United Nations Educational, Scientific and Cultural Organization (UNESCO) (1946)

Unlike the agreements with the ILO and the FAO, the agreement between the WHO and UNESCO clearly delineates the responsibilities of both Organizations. Article I of the agreement, which was adopted by the first World Health Assembly on 17 July 1948 (Resolutions WHA 1.126 and WHA 1.127; WHO, Off. Rec., no. 13, 1948, p. 323) states in this respect in para. 2:

'In particular, it is recognized by UNESCO that WHO shall have the primary responsibility for the encouragement of research, education and the organization of science in the fields of health and medicine, without prejudice to the right of UNESCO to concern itself with the relations between the pure and applied sciences in all fields, including the sciences basic to health.'

Whenever there is any doubt about the division of responsibilities between both Organizations on any activity, the Organization which initiates the activity in question has the obligation, in accordance with Article I, para. 3 of the agreement, to consult the other Organization with a view to adjust the matter.

The comparable text of the agreements with the ILO and the FAO limits co-operation and co-ordination to a general statement that the respective Organizations will 'act in close co-operation with each other and will consult each other regularly in regard to matters of common concern'.

Both the UNESCO and the WHO are constitutionally involved with (health) education and (health) sciences, although the WHO undoubtedly has the primary responsibility in these fields. Both Organizations aim at optimal use of each others' resources and capabilities in respect to these matters.

Some examples of activities of UNESCO in the field of health are studies on the impact of science from the angle of (medical) ethics and biomedical research. Research on artificial recombination of genes is also considered as a possible activity.

As a result of a joint UNESCO/WHO action the 'Council of Medical Sciences' (CIOMS)[53] was set up in 1949 (see, for instance, Resolution WHA 2.5.; WHO, Off. Rec., no. 21, 1949, p. 19).[54]

— International Atomic Energy Agency (IAEA)[55] (1957)

The co-ordination between the WHO and the IAEA is rather complex, because their respective Constitutions overlap in some respect. The IAEA has

53. Former title: 'Council for the co-ordination of International Congresses of Medical Sciences'.
54. See above, para. 4.
55. The IAEA is not strictly speaking a specialised agency because there is no relationship agreement with ECOSOC. It is, however, very similar to it, where it has concluded an agreement with the UN General Assembly providing for mutual co-operation. Its status represents a compromise between ttose who desired full autonomy for it and those who wanted it to be brought under UN control (Nicholas, 1962, p. 143; see also Goodman, 1971, p. 358).

the statutory task to accelerate and enlarge the contribution of atomic energy to peace, *health* and prosperity throughout the world and is authorized

'to establish or adopt, in consultation and, where appropriate, in collaboration with the competent organs of the United Nations and with the specialized agencies concerned, standards of safety for protection of health and minimization of danger to life and property (including such standards for labour conditions), and to provide for the application of these standards to its own operations as well as to the operations making use of materials, services, equipment, facilities, and information made available by the Agency or at its request under its control or supervision ...'

WHO on the other hand has constitutional functions which also apply to the field of ionizing radiation as related to health. This was moreover stressed by the seventh World Health Assembly which, in 1964, reaffirmed

'the responsibility of WHO at the international level for activities in the field of health involving ionizing radiation, including protection from radiation hazards and the medical uses of radiation and radioactive isotopes' (Resolution WHA 17.47; WHO, Off. Rec., no. 135, 1964, p. 21).

Naturally, these overlapping provisions can give rise to difficulties, which will be aggravated by the fact that in various countries different ministries are competent for matters relating to these two Organizations.

The agreement between the WHO and the IAEA was adopted by the 12th World Health Assembly on 28 May 1959 (Resolution WHA 12.40; WHO, Off. Rec., no. 95, 1959, p. 37).

Unlike the relationship agreement with the UNESCO, the agreement with the IAEA does not recognize the WHO as the primarily responsible Organization in the field of health implications of the use of ionizing radiation.

Article I, para. 2 and 3 states in this respect the following:

2. 'In particular, and in accordance with the Constitution of the World Health Organization and the Statute of the International Atomic Energy Agency and its agreement with the United Nations together with the exchange of letters related thereto, and taking into account the respective co-ordinating responsibilities of both organizations, it is recognized by the World Health Organization that the International Atomic Energy Agency has the primary responsibility for encouraging, assisting and co-ordinating research on, and development and practical application of, atomic energy for peaceful uses throughout the world without prejudice to the right of the World Health Organization to concern itself with promoting, developing, assisting, and co-ordinating international health work, including research, in all its aspects.
3. Whenever either organization proposes to initiate a programme or activity on a subject in which the other organization has or may have a substantial interest, the first party shall consult the other with a view to adjusting the matter by mutual agreement.'

Leaving the question of overlapping aside, it is clear that the WHO's involvement in the field of radiation is somewhat limited, while the IAEA's activities obviously respond to urgent needs. Co-operation in this particular situation has been of a pragmatic nature. Prior consultation has gained in importance since 1966 through an unofficial intersecretariat arrangement, and special stress is laid on joint meetings and joint research projects as well as on linking national programmes.

Permanent liaison officers, moreover, represent a practical contribution to finding solutions when difficulties arise from overlapping in the basic mandates.

5.3. OTHER FORMS OF RELATIONSHIP (WITHIN THE UNITED NATIONS SYSTEM)

Besides the official relationship agreements mentioned under para. 5.2. there are also arrangements for co-ordination between the WHO and other specialised agencies and bodies which have an official relationship with the UN. The most important of these are the relationship arrangements with the UN specialised agencies: the International Civil Aviation Organization and the World Bank and those with the United Nations International Children's Emergency Fund. Others include the following specialised agencies: the Inter-governmental Maritime Consultative Organization, the International Monetary Fund and the World Metereological Organization. [56]

– International Civil Aviation Organization (ICAO) (1947)

Collaboration with the ICAO is based on earlier arrangements made between the CINA (Comité International pour la Navigation Aérienne) and the Office International d'Hygiène Publique when the International Sanitary Convention for Aerial Navigation was drafted in 1933. The duties and responsibilities of these Organizations having been taken over by the ICAO and the WHO respectively, the first World Health Assembly in 1948 considered the question of drawing up a relationship agreement between both Organizations. The Interim Commission had in fact prepared a draft agreement to this end (WHO, Off. Rec., no. 10, 1948, p. 71). Contacts between both Organizations consisted mainly of mutual consultation on technical matters particularly for the purpose of drafting international standards and recommended practices of international air transport. For the latter purpose ICAO had established a Quarantine Working Group, which recognized the WHO as the sole body responsible for regulations governing the sanitary control of international traffic (WHO, Off. Rec., no. 12, 1948, p. 47).

During discussions in the Health Assembly on the advisability of establishing a formal relationship agreement with the ICAO, it became apparent that the latter preferred co-operation to continue through informal working arrangements.

The reason for this was the inflexibility inherent in formal agreements in general, and the successful nature of the co-operation between both organizations up till then despite the absence of a formal agreement. The will to co-operate alone was considered more than sufficient. (See WHO, Off. Rec., no. 13, 1948, pp. 231 and 232.)

56. Resolution WHA 2.89; WHO, Off. Rec., no. 21, 1949, p. 51; Resolution EB 8.R43; WHO, Off. Rec., no. 36, 1951, p. 14 and Resolution WHA 5.74; WHO, Off. Rec., no. 42, 1952, p. 43 respectively.

The first World Health Assembly decided, therefore, to merely adopt a resolution that the course which was being followed by both Organizations and which was directed simply by informal arrangements, should continue to be pursued (Resolution WHA 1.124; WHO, Off. Rec., no. 13, 1948, p. 322).

    – United Nations Children's Fund (UNICEF)[57] (1946)

UNICEF was first set up on a temporary basis to provide vital assistance to children, assistance which became imperative as a result of the Second World War (General Assembly Resolution 57 (I) of 1946). Under the terms of this Resolution UNICEF has been established 'for the benefit of children and adolescents of countries which were victims of aggression ... (and) for child health purposes generally'. Though the Organization is an integral part of the UN, it is not a specialised agency, but rather a specialised body. It is financed independently by donations from, for instance, governments (Goodman, 1971, p. 360 and Nicholas, 1962, p. 131).

At that time any spare UNRRA funds were used for carrying out activities in the field of child health.

Early programmes of UNICEF included the BCG immunization programme carried out under the auspices of the Organization, anti-syphylis campaigns and the granting of fellowships for training in child care. The Interim Commission established collaboration in these fields with UNICEF (WHO, Off. Rec., no. 10, 1948, p. 66). The Interim Commission, when preparing discussions on relations between the WHO and UNICEF for the first World Health Assembly, recommended that the Assembly 'consider principles involved, in the conduct of international projects in the field of health, with particular reference to the relations existing between UNICEF and the Interim Commission'. It prepared for this purpose a draft resolution, in which the Assembly was to decide that all international health projects, including those of UNICEF, fall within the competence of the WHO, and that the WHO be prepared to negotiate on means of handling these projects (WHO, Off. Rec., no. 12, 1948, pp. 41 and 42).

During discussions at the first World Health Assembly delineation of responsibilities between both Organizations was questioned. Some members feared that despite its temporary character, UNICEF would expand activities in the medical sphere, which activities would not be confined to the 'medical supply' aspect but would enter into fields, which were the responsibility of the WHO. It was in fact emphasized that it was an unsound principle to transfer health care for children to a body separate from the one responsible for all international health care. Hence it was felt that the role of UNICEF should be confined to the general relief aspects only (WHO, Off. Rec., no. 13, 1948, pp. 240-244). The World Health Assembly then recommended – pending the assumption of responsibility by the WHO – that the health projects financed by UNICEF should be established by mutual agreement between that Organization and the WHO, for which purpose a joint committee on health policy was to be set up (Resolution WHA 1.120; WHO, Off. Rec., no. 13, 1948, p. 327).

57. Previously called: UN International Children's Emergency Fund.

This joint committee was to operate on a temporary basis only, until all health activities of UNICEF were taken over by the WHO. The committee was established as an advisory committee on the understanding that its advice would be respected by UNICEF. Despite the temporary basis both of UNICEF and the joint committee, their respective positions were consolidated since.

In 1953 UNICEF became a permanent part of the UN by Resolution of the General Assembly 802 (VIII). The World Health Assembly in turn confirmed the position of the joint commitee in its Resolution WHA 7.50 (WHO, Off. Rec., no. 55, 1954, p. 40).

In this Resolution the WHA reaffirmed that the projects jointly assisted by UNICEF and the WHO were of major importance and that the co-operation between both Organizations should be strengthened. Gradually the concept of UNICEF has been broadened to cover not only its immediate task of providing children with medical assistance but also a broader context of assistance to basic health services with emphasis on maternal and child health (including education and training).

In 1960, following these developments, the WHO Executive Board confirmed the new terms of reference of the joint committee on health policy (Resolution EB 25.R30; WHO, Off. Rec., no. 99, 1960, p. 15). Under these terms the joint committee is, among other tasks, to review regularly the overall needs of mothers and children in the health field and to recommend to the UNICEF Executive Board the types of health programmes having as their objective the improvement of the health of mothers and children which could appropriately receive UNICEF support (para. 1 of the terms of reference). UNICEF assistance to WHO activities include eradication programmes for contagious diseases, community health programmes and family planning programmes. Mutual consultation takes place whenever one Organization is confronted with a subject falling within the other's field of interest (WHO, Off. Rec., no. 181, 1970, pp. 77-79). An international conference on primary health care was organized by WHO and UNICEF in September 1978.

One of the first resolutions of the World Health Assembly with a bearing on the activities of UNICEF was Resolution WHA 1.108 (WHO, Off. Rec., no. 13, 1948, p. 322) in which it was decided that the WHO should co-operate in the preparation of documentation on the Declaration of the Rights of the Child. [58] (This Declaration was adopted on 20 October 1959, United Nations General Assembly Resolution 1386 (XIV).) In its resolution WHA 13.63 (WHO, Off. Rec., no. 102, 1960, p. 29) the World Health Assembly endorsed the policy of the Organization to collaborate within the UN family in activities for the implementation of the objectives laid down in the Declaration.

Co-ordination between both Organizations is sometimes hindered by the fact that their terms of reference are fundamentally different. UNICEF's approach is a comprehensive and integrated one revolving around the 'whole child' and programmes of assistance are made subject to this objective. Thus, for instance, UNICEF is reluctant to assist WHO in its eradication pro-

58. See above, para. 4.

grammes, unless these are not complementary to, but part of the development of basic health services and are limited to well defined situations (WHO, Off. Rec., no. 181, 1970, pp. 78 and 79).

— International Bank for Reconstruction and Development (IBRD; World Bank) (1945)

The WHO also maintains close contacts with the IBRD, another specialised agency of the UN in terms of its Charter, though it has by reason of the nature of its international responsibilities, its operations, its structure and its financial procedures a somewhat special position in that it is and functions as an independent organization. [59]

The co-operation between the WHO and the IBRD consisted first of the latter's consulting WHO on the references to public health contained in the reports drawn up by the Bank's economic survey missions to developing countries. Since 1962 co-operation was expanded to include water supply and sanitation projects. Consultation is now being increasingly replaced by association in various projects (WHO, Off. Rec., no. 181, 1970, pp. 98 and 99).

This growing co-operation is a consequence of the philosophy that health development both contributes to and benefits from social and economic development.

The World Bank became gradually more involved in the health sector, adding health and environmental components to many projects designed to increase the productivity, and hence the standards of living, of the poorest groups of people living in the developing world. Consequently, co-operation with the WHO increased too, as, for instance, in 1970, when the Bank established a joint co-operation programme on water supply projects together with the WHO. Other areas of co-operation include rural development, primary health care, communicable diseases, health economic research, psychosocial aspects of health etc.

The relationship between both Organizations is of a complementary character: the WHO provides mainly technical skill and the World Bank finances principally large capital expenditures and contributes its experience for conducting economic analyses (*WHO Chronicle*, 31, 1977, pp. 94-97).

The co-operation between the World Bank and the WHO is not set down in a formal agreement, but the scope of their collaboration, which goes back for many years, has been confirmed at consultations since 1975. To date neither the WHO nor the Bank have felt the need for an official relationship agreement. Co-operation has evolved out of a joint desire to achieve maximum efficiency in specific activities through close consultation and mutual help (WHO, Off. Rec., no. 181, 1970, p. 99).

---

59. Article 1 of the relationship agreement with the Economic and Social Council of the UN of 15 November 1947.

5.4. RELATIONSHIP ARRANGEMENTS WITH NON-GOVERNMENTAL ORGANIZATIONS

The WHO maintains close working relations with non-governmental organizations in so far as these are professional bodies working in fields touching on medicine and public health.

Criteria for this kind of relationship were established in 1948 by the first World Health Assembly (WHA 1.130; WHO, Off. Rec., no. 13, 1948, p. 326 as amended by the third, eleventh and twenty first World Health Assembly (Resolutions WHA 3.113 of May 1950, WHA 11.14 of June 1958 and WHA 21.28 of May 1968. [60]

These criteria include, for instance, the relevance of the organization's activities for the WHO, the requirement that it be international in structure and scope (although in exceptional cases a national organization may be added to the list of non-governmental organizations forming a relationship with the WHO). The working principles governing the admission of non-governmental organizations with the WHO also include the 'procedure for admittance' and 'privileges conferred by the relationship', such as representation at meetings (without the right to vote), and access to (non confidential) information.

Co-operation with non-governmental organizations is not restricted to exchange of information and attendance at meetings, but also includes the identification of areas of possible joint action and measures to initiate such action (Flacha, 1977, pp. 127-130). The first non-governmental organization to enter into such a relationship with the WHO was the League of Red Cross Societies. Co-operation with, for instance, the World Medical Association, the Council for International Organizations of Medical Science and the International Council of Nurses is of importance too. [61]

6. Some conclusions

The WHO is the sole Organization endowed with world-wide responsibility regarding the realization of the right to health care. Its functions in this respect are almost unlimited; the only restrictions which are set to it are that it may not enter domains outside the health field although closely related issues, in particular economic and social conditions, are fully taken into consideration. The Organization has deployed many efforts towards raising the level of health throughout the world during the thirty years of its existence. It has assured the continuation of the work of its predecessors, and has expanded the scope of these activities both functionally and geographically. Over the years the Organization has extended its tasks from prevention and cure of disease to a broader and more long term approach in the endeavour of reaching the social target set by the Organization in 1977 'the attainment by

60. WHO, Off. Rec., no. 28, 1950, p. 67; no. 87, 1958, p. 23; no. 168, 1968, p. 13.
61. See para. 4. above.

144

all the citizens of the world by the year 2000 of a level of health that will permit them to lead a socially and economically productive life'.

All the prerequisites for reaching this objective are available, although it is recognized that the Organization, being a non-political body, has no constitutional power to impose its policies on member governments. Indirectly, however, there will always be a certain element of political influence.

Important functions are those of ensuring co-operation and co-ordination, especially between other international organizations active in the field of health. There are various formal arrangements for co-operation with specialised agencies of the UN as well as with other international regional organizations, though in practice this co-operation is not yet optimal and there is still too much unnecessary overlapping and duplication of work.

Intensified adaption of programmes and co-ordination between the various organizations active in the field of public health might well be envisaged.

The Organization has usefully contributed to stimulating and co-ordinating biomedical, sociomedical and health services research. It could, however, make more use of its constitutional powers in this respect by initiating and conducting research through institutions functioning under its auspices, either on a global or regional scale.

Furthermore, the Organization has made too little use of its legislative powers. Despite the fact that in given areas it is in a position to draw up regulations and thus sidestep the complicated procedure inherent to the signing of conventions and agreements, it has used this power only twice so far.

In areas where regulations would seem to be the most appropriate, the Organization tends to prefer recommendations.

Reasons for this are the global scope of the Organization, which makes it difficult to reach general consensus, as well as the fact that much depends on the extent to which national governments are prepared to transfer national responsibilities to an international organization. This latter will only be the case when international legislation is indispensable for preventive reasons, and when national consequences are only limited.

The attitude of the Organization with regard to the realization of the right to health care whenever other human rights are involved, in particular those relating to the right to life and to prevention from torture and medical experimentation, is not so much to take initiatives itself, by, for example, drawing up international guiding principles, but rather to promote and stimulate activities undertaken in other settings, though often sponsored by the WHO.

Though there are still many fields in which the WHO could expand or strengthen its activities, it cannot be denied that the necessity for and usefulness of having one Organization with world-wide responsibilities in respect to the realization of the right to health care has been fully proven. Without such an organization the international contribution to health care would mainly be limited to ad hoc operations involving one or more countries, or to regional efforts, so that the right to health care would never be achieved on a broad scale, despite its present world-wide recognition.

II. The World Health Organization and Europe

1. Regional arrangements [62]

1.1. CREATION OF REGIONAL BRANCHES OF THE WORLD HEALTH ORGANIZATION (ARTICLES 44-54 OF THE CONSTITUTION)

The Charter of the United Nations does not preclude the existence of regional agencies. Express provision to this effect has been made in Chapter VIII of the Charter, with respect to political security (Articles 52-54). Article 57 of the Charter on the relation between specialised agencies in the social (including health) and economic fields and the UN is also interpreted as meaning that regional agencies shall exist in these fields and should be brought into relationship with the UN (WHO, Off. Rec., no. 1, 1947, p. 68).

The Charter does not, however, give a juridical definition of these regional arrangements. Variations in size, configuration, population and the number of countries make it particularly difficult to reach a definition of this kind (Padelford, 1955, pages 23-42).

The World Health Organization is the only specialised agency of the United Nations to have adopted a policy of full regionalization based on constitutional provisions. International regional activities in the field of public health have grown out of the past. The repeated outbreak of pestilental diseases and the increase of international transport in the 19th century have stimulated the indispensable co-operation in this field. Thus the Paris Office, the League of Nations and the UNRRA all had their own system of regionalization (Berkov, 1957, p. 35). These did not, however, represent the same form of regionalization as the one which came into being during the functioning of the WHO.

The Technical Preparatory Committee examined the matter in connection with the discussions on the role the Pan American Sanitary Bureau (originally established in 1902 by the first Pan American Sanitary Conference and acting as a regional agency for several international organizations with world-wide responsibilities in the health field since 1926) should play once the new Organization started functioning. The very existence of this Bureau obliged the Committee to consider provisions on regional arrangements.

The continuation of existing, independent organizations [63] was questioned in view of the terms of reference of the Technical Preparatory Committee, set up to prepare the creation of 'one single international health organization'.

---

62. An organizational study on regionalization is in WHO, Off. Rec., no. 46, 1953, pp. 157-173.
63. Another autonomous regional agency was the Egyptian Sanitary Maritime and Quarantine Board, which was expanded into the Pan Arab Health Bureau in 1946. The functions of this Bureau were integrated within those of the WHO Regional Organization for the Eastern Mediterranean area (WHO, Off. Rec., no. 17, 1949, p. 16).

146

The Delegation of the United States took the viewpoint that this did not necessarily imply the abolition or the absorption of the Pan American Sanitary Bureau (WHO, Off. Rec., no. 1, 1947, p. 68). The Committee was well aware of the fact that any solution chosen would set a precedent for other (existing or envisaged) regional organizations (Berkov, 1957, p. 52).

The Technical Preparatory Committee did not, however, arrive at an agreed formula for the regionalization of the Organization. During the discussions which took place on this subject, two main lines were developed.

One favoured a system of regional organizations established by multi-lateral intergovernmental agreement which would be brought into relationship with the central organization as contemplated in Article 57 of the UN Charter, and which would have more or less expanded autonomous functions (co-ordination with the World Health Organization). The other pleaded for dependent regional organizations (to be placed under the direct authority of the central organization) (Berkov, 1957, p. 55). It was generally recognized that some of the functions of the Organization were not appropriate for regionalization. (One example is the establishment of a system of standardized universal application such as in the field of biological products.) Epidemiological information on the other hand was felt to be a matter of concern for the regional organizations (WHO, Off. Rec., no. 1, 1947, pp. 10 and 44).

Some of the delegates were of the opinion that regional organizations should be flexible in character, so as to be adaptable to local needs. Others however were hesitant to adopt a system which would be too flexible, as it would give regional offices the opportunity to uphold sectional interest within the central organization to the detriment of the general interest (WHO, Off. Rec., no. 1, 1947, p. 29). Despite the fact that there was general consensus on the value of establishing new regional branches of the Organization (the establishment of regional committees by the Health Assembly as regional policy bodies, with functions delegated by the Health Assembly, and of regional offices as administrative branches of the Organization), there was no agreement on how to apply this to existing offices. It was argued not to take important decisions on regionalization and decentralization until the Organization started functioning and to set up the WHO in such a way as to make it easily adaptable to all situations. In the light of the discussions the Technical Preparatory Committee decided to transmit two alternatives to the International Health Conference.

One proposed that the functions of the regional offices which were to be created, be dependent of the Health Assembly, while special arrangements be made for the regional organizations, which were already in existence.

The other proposed that regional offices be entrusted with the carrying out of decisions of the Conference, the Board, the Director-General and the regional committees by the creation of new and the integration of existing regional organizations (WHO, Off. Rec., no. 1, 1947, pp. 73 and 74).

It was, in other words, envisaged that activities of existing regional organizations would be absorbed in the new universal organization, or that the services and facilities of existing ones would be utilized by the universal organization through special arrangements. A choice also had to be made between the setting up of regional organs under the direct authority of the central organization (centralization) or the maintainance of autonomy for these regional organizations (decentralization).

Some members of the Economic and Social Council of the UN favoured placing existing regional health organizations under the authority of the central health organization. Others, however, were of the opinion that existing international (regional) health organizations should be co-ordinated with the World Health Organization. Some of those who favoured the latter viewpoint considered that the role of the Health Organization was to co-ordinate and recommend, rather than to direct the regional health work. It was finally decided to submit both alternatives to the Health Conference leaving it up to the Conference to decide what relationship should exist between the WHO and the already existing regional health agencies (WHO, Off. Rec., no. 2, 1948, pp. 119-121; Report of the United States Delegation on the International Health Conference, 1946, p. 20). The Conference was also left to clarify the position of new regional branches of the Organization (either fully dependent or with independence consistent with the overriding supervisory power necessary to the international health organization).

The International Health Conference consequently faced two problems:
— the establishment, functions, and organization of new regional branches of the Organization;
— the relationship of existing regional health agencies to the central Organization.

As to the first problem, the Conference opted for the following. Regional organizations consisting of regional committees and offices would be established by the Health Assembly, with the consent of the majority of the members situated within the region concerned. The composition of the regional committees was also delineated. [64] With regard to the second problem the International Health Conference unanimously approved a text providing for full integration of existing regional organs with the central health Organization (WHO, Off. Rec., no. 2, 1948, p. 24). [65]

Thus, the formula chosen in the Constitution of the World Health Organization is a fairly flexible one. It allows the Health Assembly a great deal of latitude in decisions as to how far decentralization should go (see Articles 44-54 of the Constitution). The Articles of the Constitution dealing with regional arrangements were based on the major assumption that policy-making committees and administrative offices were necessary for the effective discharge of responsibilities of the Organization.

Each regional branch so constituted would be an integral part of the international system.

The solution opted for by the Health Conference paid full tribute to the centralized character of the Organization, while at the same time giving regional organizations considerable freedom of action on regional matters. In

64. See below para 1.2.
65. The results of the negotiations for the integration of the Pan American Sanitary Bureau with the WHO arc embodied in an agreement which was approved by the second WHA (WHO, Off. Rec., no. 21, 1949, p. 52).

adopting this formula full consideration was given to the valuable contribution of a regional agency to the central organization and the impact of the latter on regional agencies in respect to international health activities of world-wide interest. (WHO, Off. Rec., no. 2, 1948, p. 24; WHO, Off. Rec., no. 46, 1953, pp. 160 and 161; Report of the United States Delegation on the International Health Conference, 1946, p. 24).

1.2. DELINEATION OF, AND ASSIGNMENT TO REGIONS

The Health Assembly is given the authority to define geographical areas for the establishment of regional organizations to meet the special needs of such areas (Article 44 of the Constitution). Thus, the process of decentralization was first put into operation by regionalization.

However, despite the fact that all elements necessary for the realization of a complete decentralization policy of the World Health Organization – apart from some essential tasks to be kept on a world-wide scale which are left to the central Institution – are included in the Constitution, the criteria applied for the delineation of geographical areas have hindered the process somewhat.

Socio-economic and cultural conditions which are important factors in activities designed to increase efficiency and effectiveness and to promote co-operation with national health departments, were not given high priority.

The major impetus for the creation of regional offices was the (negative) desire to prevent the establishment of other, independent, regional health organizations.

Only limited attention was paid to factors such as 'standards of health' in certain areas, the efficiency of existing health administrations and so on.

At the first Health Assembly the delineation of geographical areas in which regional offices should be established was laid down as follows:

– Eastern Mediterranean area [66];
– Western Pacific Area;
– South East Asian Area;
– European Area;
– African Area;
– American Area. (Resolution WHA 1.72; WHO, Off. Rec., no. 13, 1948, pp. 330 and 344.)

The same resolution indicated of which countries the geographical areas should be composed. For the European area this was to be the whole of Europe.

It was not until 1952 that the Health Assembly, at its 5th Session, decided to take action based on Articles 44 (a) and 47 of the Constitution in requesting the Executive Board to study rules and criteria for determining the assignment of territory to a geographical area (Resolution WHA 5.43; WHO, Off. Rec., no. 42, 1952, p. 31).

66. It lies outside the scope of this study to deal with problems which existed on the creation of this regional office.

The Executive Board, however, failed to reach agreement as to what methods should be used and therefore decided in 1953 to submit two alternatives to the 6th World Health Assembly.

The first alternative gave paramount weight to the wishes of the appropriate sovereign authority of the state or territory concerned, to be based on the following criteria:
— geographical position;
— similarity of health problems;
— economic aspects;
— administrative considerations;
— relations between the various regions of WHO and regional arrangements made by other international organizations.

The second alternative added another criterion to this list as criterion no. 1, viz. the wishes of the appropriate sovereign authority of the state or territory concerned. Since the authority's wishes featured as a criterion, they received less priority in this alternative than in the first one, where the authority's wishes were regarded as paramount (Resolution EB 11, R 51; WHO, Off. Rec., no. 46, 1953, p. 21). At its sixth session the World Health Assembly adopted a resolution on an organizational study on regionalization. In this resolution the principles which prompted the establishment of regionalization were reaffirmed. At the same time it was recognized that the advantages of regionalization could only be fully achieved by 'continued mutual confidence and co-operation among all those to whom the Constitution and the Health Assembly have delegated responsibility and authority'. The Executive Board was requested to review periodically the problems of regionalization and progress made. Wide differences in the nature and extent of decentralization in the United Nations, the World Health Organization and other specialised agencies were seen to be due to variations in constitution, objectives and organization. These differences often impeded effective co-operation in field programmes (Resolution WHA 6.44; WHO, Off. Rec., no. 48, 1953, p. 33).

Further consideration on this matter was deferred until completion of a study carried out by the United Nations, in co-operation with other specialised agencies on these problems (WHO, Off. Rec., no. 48, 1953, p. 34).

So far the organizational study on regionalization has not resulted in any definition of criteria for a rational basis of assignment to regions.

In practice criteria which are applied at the present time are of a political nature and not primarily based upon arguments concerned with the promotion of world health.

1.3. FUNCTIONS OF REGIONAL BRANCHES

The functions of the regional committees include the formulation of policies on matters of exclusively regional character (guidelines), supervision of activities of the regional offices, tendering of advice on matters of a broader than purely regional significance, co-operation with regional branches of other organizations and advice to the regional offices on the convening of technical conferences for promoting the WHO's objectives in the region (Article 50 of the Constitution) (Berkov, 1957, p. 29).

The central set-up assures unity of action in matters of world-wide impact while still providing flexibility in handling special regional needs.

The functions of the regional committee are, however, subject to the general authority of the Health Assembly, which limits its autonomous powers.

Constitutionally, however, their role could well be expanded by making use of the possibility of delegation of functions to the regional committee by the Health Assembly, the Board or the Director-General, as provided for in Article 50 (g) of the Constitution. It is thus left to the discretion of the Health Assembly, the Board or the Director-General whether they want to extend the process of decentralization further by allotting more or less important functions to the regional committee.

The Executive Board, for instance, in its report on the proposed programme budget for 1978-1979, emphasized the increasingly important role regional committees are expected to play in developing regional programmes (See WHO, Off. Rec., no. 238, 1977, part II).

In its biennial report of the work of the WHO in 1976-1977, the Director-General considered the regional structure of the Organization essential for promoting, accelerating and facilitating national and regional self-reliance in health matters. As some of the tools to attain this end, reference was made to the need to strengthen the role of regional committees, the establishment of regional panels of experts to ensure proper exchange of experience and expertise and to the setting up of regional centres for operational research, development and training in specific areas (WHO, Off. Rec., no. 243, 1978, p. 5). Regional offices are also assuming increasing responsibility for administrative functions as well as programme direction and co-ordination.

These regional offices, functioning under the authority of the Director-General, are the administrative organs of the regional committees and in addition implement within the region the decisions of the Health Assembly and the Executive Board (Article 51 of the Constitution).

Their first and foremost role is to realize effective contacts between national governments and the Organization's headquarters. Programmes of technical co-operation are carried out through the regional offices. They include, for instance, regional panels of experts, regional advisory committees on biomedical and health services research and training (see WHO, Off. Rec., no. 238, 1977, part II). Another role is the collection and dissemination of epidemiological intelligence. In this respect the regional offices have, for instance, effectively dealt with problems which have arisen in the administration of sanitary and quarantine procedures (Gutteridge, 1971, p. 284). (The regional director – in charge of the regional office – is administratively responsible to the Director-General and the regional committees, while the regional staff is administratively responsible to the regional director.) The structure of the regional offices varies greatly from one region to another and is subject to a continuous process of change.

Global responsibility for programmes will gradually be transferred to the regional offices in order to exploit existing recources better. This has already happened in the European region, where global responsibility has been assigned to the European Office for the Organization's programmes on road-accident prevention and care for the elderly (WHO, Off. Rec., 238, 1977, p. 188). [67] The information which is in this manner derived from a given programme will be made available at global level.

1.4. POWERS OF REGIONAL BRANCHES

As was seen before under para. 1.3. the World Health Organization has gradually moved from regionalization to decentralization by giving more real power to the regional branches of the Organization. Regional organizations have thus been deliberately delegated decision-making powers regarding the development of the WHO's programme in their own region: regional committees determine to a large extent how the money alloted to their region shall be spent. [68] In this way the programme can be adapted to regional needs. (The programme and budget estimates are submitted to the Director-General, with the comments and recommendations of the regional committees, to the Executive Board and finally to the WHA; the latter thus possesses an effective control mechanism with regard to the policy of the Organization.)

The central Organization has furthermore delegated an important part of its responsibilities regarding staff matters, management, supervision and control of administrative operations.

Since the WHO became operative genuine evolution has resulted from regions acquiring a certain degree of decentralization and more real power.

It is apparent that current trends favour the effective realization of decentralization, and there is a growing realization that the function of the central Organization is not so much to conduct programmes but to advise, to stimulate regional organizations, to supply information, to co-ordinate WHO's programme with those of other organizations and to review its own programme regularly. Berkov (1957, p. 122) attributes overall co-ordinating power and supervision to the central Organization, leaving the main responsibility for regional activities to the region. This evolution in the concept of the functions of regional branches confirms in fact the opinion expressed by some of the members of the Economic and Social Council of the UN when discussing the report of the Technical Preparatory Committee of the World Health Conference (see para. 1.1. above).

When presenting his annual report for 1974 to the 28th World Health Assembly, the Director-General on his part insisted on the great importance regional offices represent for the central Organization:
— regional offices should become the supreme co-ordinating forum for all regional health matters;
— regional mechanisms should be developed for adapting expensive health

67. See para. 2.2.
68. The Director-General sends to the regional director instructions, which include programme policy guidance and tentative allocations.

technologies to the needs and financial capacities of the countries in the different regions;
— regional offices should attain self-reliance as early as possible (*WHO Chronicle*, 29, 1975, pp. 253-256).

This idea was emphasized again in 1977 when the Director-General stated that greater use should be made of WHO's regional structure, decentralizing the practical day-to-day implementation of WHO's co-ordinating task being the only efficient way to expand the central Organization's efforts at global co-ordination (*WHO Chronicle*, 31, 1977, pp. 8-13).

A clear delineation of the responsibilities of the central and the regional organizations is necessary in order to avoid any conflicts of interests; it is, however, still lacking (see Berkov, 1957, p. 85 for a possible repartition of responsibilities).

2. European region

2.1. ESTABLISHMENT OF THE REGIONAL OFFICE FOR EUROPE

Resolution WHA 1.72, adopted at the first World Health Assembly, indicated Europe as one of the geographical areas of which the WHO should be composed of (WHO, Off. Rec., no. 13, 1948, pp. 330 and 344). At the same session it was decided that a temporary special administrative office should be established as soon as possible. This temporary office was primarily set up for the purpose of dealing with the rehabilitation of war-devastated countries in that area, preceeding the official establishment of a regional office for Europe. (WHA 2.74; WHO, Off. Rec., no. 21, 1949, p. 44). Initially there was some doubt about the usefulness of setting up a regional office in an area containing numbers of highly industrialized countries, and the office was not in fact set up until January 1st, 1952, located first in Geneva and since 1957 in Copenhagen. The European region comprises at present the following countries:

Albania, Algeria, Austria, Belgium, Bulgaria, Czechoslovakia, Denmark, Finland, France, German Democratic Republic, Germany (Federal Republic of), Greece, Hungary, Iceland, Ireland, Italy, Luxembourg, Malta, Monaco, Morocco, Netherlands, Norway, Poland, Portugal, Romania, Spain, Sweden, Switzerland, Turkey, Union of Soviet Socialist Republics, United Kingdom of Great Britain and Northern Ireland, and Yugoslavia.

The preliminary criteria for assignment of territories to a geographical area as formulated by the Executive Board in 1953 (see above, para. 1.3.) are hardly applicable to this region due to its singular composition (both developed and developing countries) and the fact that it also encompasses countries situated geographically in Africa.

Nevertheless, co-operation within this region is in fact relatively easy, at least between the majority of countries, which have undergone similar crises (economic, social and military), and which have developed along more or less parallel lines. The contacts which existed among most of these countries prior to the establishment of the Organization have, too, greatly facilitated work in this region. International activities in the field of health were in fact primarily a European matter, with the purpose of protecting Europe against the importation of contagious diseases (Howard-Jones, 1974, pp. 455-470).

The orientation of the 'Office International d'Hygiène Publique' was also primarily European.

The European region has, moreover, a rather unique position compared with the other regions of the WHO in that the countries it is composed of — the majority at least — are generally speaking not afflicted with the same health problems as those in other regions, in particular the developing countries. Furthermore, the health problems facing the European region have proved to be analogous in most of the countries concerned, and are not similar to those in the developing countries.

2.2. FUNCTIONS OF THE REGIONAL OFFICE FOR EUROPE

Despite the doubts about the usefulness of setting up a regional office for Europe, this office has since its creation contributed most effectively towards the two broad interrelated goals of the Organization, based on the concept of social justice, which underlies the (constitutional) right to health care: the WHO strives, therefore, to attain an acceptable level of health and thus of health care, uniformly distributed among all members of society.

The first goal necessitates a programme directed towards the developing countries, and including the promotion of health development through the complementary efforts of national self-reliance and international collaboration.

The European region, as a 'resource region', can offer an important contribution to the task of balancing health resources throughout the world. The contribution of the European region towards the programme for developing countries is of two kinds, one being of a direct, the other of an indirect nature.

The direct contribution consists mainly of an education and training programme put at the disposal of developing countries, as well as through fieldwork in these countries.

The second, indirect, contribution ties in logically with the Organization's second broad goal, namely the promotion and maintenance of permanent co-operation among medically developed countries, which can concentrate on very specific problems and provide measures which only benefit relatively few people.

This second contribution towards the developing countries consists of carrying out basic and applied research. The results and experience thus obtained can also usefully be employed for the assistance of developing countries.

Co-operation in the European region is of importance in another way too with respect to the target of attaining an acceptable level of health uniformly distributed throughout the world. An effective co-operation system enables the European office to act as the focal point for the development of world-wide programmes, as is the case with the programme on road traffic accidents and health care of the elderly; collection of information and implementation of the programme is done under the responsibility of the European office, while information derived from the programme is made available on a global basis. These schemes are of an interregional nature, while the European office carries world-wide responsibility for the co-ordination.

Due to its present level of development the region also acts as a pilot area in undertaking activities in the field of health of a type that would not yield immediate results, and where the problems are not primarily of a financial nature but rather of a conceptual one. Even in cases where the outcome of such activities proves to be negative, the consequences are not adverse as they would be in the case of regions already facing extremely grave problems in developing their health system (examples are cardiovascular diseases and mental illness; WHO, Off. Rec., no. 224, 1975, p. 138).

The present trend in the region is to develop intensive programmes on subjects in Europe, from which other regions might benefit as appropriate. The region also maintains an active surveillance programme for certain diseases prevalent in other parts of the world.

On the other hand co-operation within the region is naturally also of importance for the region itself (the second goal). Whereas technical co-operation is not regarded as essential for the development of the large majority of national health services in the region, activities are mainly concentrated on the specific problems of countries which have virtually become victims of their high level of technological developments. Co-operation is vital, not only in order to cope with the specific problems the region is facing, due mainly to its advanced level of socio-economic development, but also in order to pool precious and scarce knowledge and resources with a view to making optimal use of them.

At the same time, however, the European office has a 'guardian' task in ensuring that rapid technological development does not undermine the social aim of attaining the highest possible level of physical, mental and social well-being for everyone.

However vast the future scope of disease-oriented medical technology may be, the human factor must be right in sight. Humanization of existing medical services is clearly a matter of great urgency in the European region.

A number of European countries lead the world in terms of impressive infant and maternal mortality rates, morbidity and overall mortality rates as well as longevity records. This position has both positive and negative implications, however. Positive in the sense that these countries can contribute more (intellectually and financially) to the improvement of health conditions in the world. Negative, because new health hazards arise (mostly environmentally related) while many remain unsolved, complicated, problems related to the prevention of disease and elimination of dangerous human habits. Another implicit negative effect is that health benefits often no longer increase to the extent that the rising costs of health care would suggest, so that these benefits will have to be weighed against the costs of the imput of highly advanced technology and know-how.

2.3. SCOPE OF HEALTH ACTIVITIES IN EUROPE

In general, the European office carries out the world-wide functions of the Organization on a regional scale whenever relevant and to the extent necessary in the region. Thus, the international activities in the field of health undertaken by the European office were gradually extended in scope, while the approach towards public health problems changed at the same time.

Initially, during the first ten years of its existence, the European office restricted its activities mainly to traditional curative tasks, to developing schemes for healing the sick. The approach was primarily disease oriented. Communicable disease, with children as the main target group, ranked high in priority.

Subsequently the tasks of the European office were amplified and the approach towards public health problems was modified. The regional programme gradually turned from a disease oriented approach towards an institution oriented and, later on during the third decade of the existence of the European office, towards a community oriented approach (strengthening of health services).

Rising industrialization, new production processes, developments in means of transport, ionizing radiation — these were some of the factors which caused specific risks to health and therefore completely changed the overall pattern of international (European) health problems and hence the structure of health care systems.

It is, however, not only the change in the pattern of diseases which brought about a different approach to public health problems. Other factors like changing demographic structures, the awakening of health consciousness, resulting in more, and more specific, demands for health care, plus the rise in the standard of living as well as continuing advances in medical science, both of which have increased the availability of regional health care, have been of considerable influence, so that great changes in Europe's health services have taken place over the last 25 years. This evolution brought about a shift of emphasis during the mid-sixties towards planning and co-ordination of public health services, evaluation, statistical methodology and epidemiology as well as prevention of chronic degenerative diseases.

When reviewing the programme of work of the European office during the past 25 years, almost all the items which were included in the first years of its existence still appear on the list. The priorities, and the scope and content of these subjects, however, have undergone significant changes. Evolution continued during the Seventies and resulted primarily in the recognition that the approach to public health problems in Europe should henceforth be a multi-dimensional, multi-disciplinary and inter-sectorial one in the frame-work of a long-term programme. Today it is recognized that all aspects of public health (such as education, training, organization, administration) have to be considered as closely inter-related parts of a total system. The present approach of the European office is therefore a broadly based one. Activities include measures to improve the quality of life.

The European region has its own particular problems, such as chronic degenerative disease, mental illness, road accidents and the ageing of the population. These particular problems call for a new approach by the regional office and for a rethinking of psychological and social aspects of health care systems. Priorities are geared towards prevention of disease and promotion of physical and mental well-being in all sectors of the population (WHO, Off. Rec., no. 227, 1975, p. 475). [69] Important tools for this end are the development of information systems and promotion of (biomedical) research.

Regarding the first, the international exchange of information and experience is essential for the European region, not only because of highly developed communications, but also because every country will be faced by the same health problems at one stage or another. Regular and accurate information on health occurrences, on measures taken and on methods used as well as on results obtained is of primary importance. The region has, moreover, a vast technical potential and therefore exceptional possibilities for co-ordinating information. Co-operation in this field is therefore being vigorously pursued at present. The health information unit of the European office has been designated as a regional operational focus for the WHO's information development system. As regards research, in particular development and co-ordination in the field of biomedical research, collaboration between countries is increasing within the region in areas of high social relevance, with a view to increasing the involvement of clinical and scientific institutions in research and development of activities on a regional scale and exchanging information for launching fundamental health technologies.

With the establishment of advisory committees on medical research in every region, research has become more decentralized. In the European region problems in this particular field were reviewed in 1977 with a view to re-assessing priorities in those fields where co-ordination and information would be mutually benificial. The establishment of planning groups on selected research areas and on information systems for medical research was recommended (WHO, Off. Rec., no. 243, 1978, p. 28; see also EUR/RC 26/2, 1976, p. 6).

Complementary to the biomedical research, research is moreover presently being carried out into the various aspects of health care delivery systems, of which very varied types exist in Europe (health services research). For this purpose, pilot areas for research are being established and institutions are encouraged to collaborate with the WHO in carrying out international research.

Since 1977 programme development is taken care of by a consultative group, which reviews trends and policies in the European region as a basis for the development of the future programme of activities and which suggests criteria for setting priorities. Medium term programmes include items such as

69. Major areas of concern of the Regional Office include presently:
— cardiovascular diseases   — health care for the eldery
— cancer control   — road accident prevention
— mental health   — biomedical research
— longterm health manpower development programmes
— public health research (particularly with regard to prevention)
— planning, cost/effectiveness analysis and managerial problems.

appropriate technology for health, national drug policies and management and urgent and unpredictable health problems.

Collaborative medium-term programmes which also include nursing, midwifery and health manpower development are an important tool for seeking common solutions to certain serious problems in the region.

2.4. EUROPEAN OFFICE AND HUMAN RIGHTS

In pursuing its aim of the realization of the right to health care, the orientation of the programme of work of the WHO in the European region is influenced by the specific problems of this region. It is fully recognized that on the one hand the public's expectations regarding the availability of health care claimed as a right to be fulfilled by governmental instances, and the medical and technical possibilities on the other, have now far exceeded what is economically feasible, even for the industrial countries of Europe. Intellectual limits have not yet been reached, financial limitations and limits to the availability of qualified manpower have, however, become a reality we cannot ignore.

Here we face the paradox that present developments guarantee a better realization of the right to health care and at the same time limit the fulfilment of this right. In Europe in particular, where expectations are very high and therefore sometimes unjustified (with excessive demands for expensive and exclusive measures) a balanced choice should be made through a sound priority programme.

The major concern, therefore, is not so much an expansion of services as a critical analysis of existing services and management system methodologies: the promotion of planning, research, evaluation and educational activities (WHO, Off. Rec., no. 227, 1975, p. 447). The growing demand from limited health care resources requires more efficient and realistic health planning and programming processes; the rising costs of health services require new approaches in use and distribution of highly sophisticated health technology (WHO, Off. Rec., no. 221, 1975, p. X; WHO, Off. Rec., no. 245, 1978, p. 15). Therefore, within the European region of the WHO the setting of priorities implies thorough examination of the cost of health care in relation to the expected benefits in terms of human prosperity and happiness.

The European situation, however, calls not only for the setting of priorities with a view to the practical limitations and for establishing rules for the selection of benificiaries as part of the realization of the right to health care.

Protective measures with a view to the increasing possibilities in medical scientific research have become an urgent matter of concern, too. Current European research, especially in the biomedical field, may involve risks to physical and mental health when experimentation on human beings is involved, requiring hard guarantees.

The 'internationalization' of this particular kind of research stresses the need for the Organization to develop, at least for the European region, a legal instrument aiming at the protection of the individual on the one hand and at

158

the pursuance of relevant research under stringent conditions on the other. It should be realized in this respect that the chances of reaching common agreement of principles governing medical experimentation involving human subjects on the one hand and on the other those aiming at the promotion of the full realization of the right to life (in particular when problems such as abortion or euthanasia are concerned) are greater on a European level than when attempting to attain consensus on a global level.

A first step in this direction was made by the Parliamentary Assembly of the Council of Europe, which through its Resolution 613 (1976) on the rights of the sick and dying, invited the European office of the WHO to 'examine criteria for the determination of death existing in the various European countries, in the light of current medical knowledge and techniques, and to make proposals for their harmonization in a way which will be universally applicable not only in hospitals, but in general medical practice'. [70]

2.5. CO-ORDINATION WITH OTHER ORGANIZATIONS

As was indicated in Ch. I, para. 5.1., co-ordination is an useful instrument for achieving common goals in the best possible way through common efforts and better use of resources. Duplication and undue overlapping can be prevented through co-ordination with other organizations, while a maximum of effectiveness can be obtained in confronting common problems. To be successful, there should be a sound system of prior consultation and early mutual information, as well as an equal degree of initiative in the co-ordination process. The task of the central Organization in this respect should be of a general nature, mainly consisting of giving guidance and general advice in those cases where global interests are not directly involved. It should be left to the regional offices to put the co-ordinating machinery into effect in such a way that its operation is adapted to specific regional circumstances.

Besides the horizontal co-ordination which exists within the WHO headquarters, there is therefore also a vertical co-ordination with the regions. The regional offices are continuously kept informed of activities of other organizations which affect health. This system enables the regional office to take suitable action whenever necessary (WHO, Off. Rec., no. 181, 1970, p. 113).

The regional offices are responsible for co-ordination at a regional level through employing procedures which are regularly adapted to regional circumstances.

Careful consideration must thus be given to the most suitable methods to apply in specific circumstances, be it through consultation, the holding of joint meetings, reciprocal attendance at meetings, documentation, joint studies, personal contacts etc.

The modern approach to management and the increased co-operation with other specialised agencies of the UN and with other intergovernmental organizations with the intention of promoting uniformity of action and of avoid-

70. See Part A, Ch. II, para. 3, and below, Ch. III, para. 4.

ing duplication of effort are of particular importance for the work of the WHO in the European region, where increased efficiency in planning, implementation of joint programmes, common approaches to particular problems etc. are much needed. Co-ordination at an inter-country level in the European region is not sufficient: there should also be an effective inter-organizational co-operation system and this all the more in view of the particular situation in the region as briefly described under para. 2.3.

Though there are also of course other means available for attaining a common approach to health problems in Europe, such as bilateral and intergovernmental arrangements, the regional office in Europe has so far proven to be a useful tool for international co-operation (Eur/RC 26/2, 1976), despite the fact that its functions to this end could still be better used. Co-operation with specialised agencies at a regional level as well as with other international regional organizations is based upon Article 50 (d) of the Constitution of the WHO. There are no special rules governing these relationships as in the case of the relations of the central Organization with other organizations, which fall under Articles 69 — 72 of the Constitution. [71]

The co-ordination at a European level takes place with a number of organizations created by the United Nations including the Economic Commission for Europe (ECE), mostly on health statistics and the economic aspects of environmental problems, the United Nations Development Programme (UNDP) on specific projects, and the United Nations Children's Fund, mainly on nutrition, maternal and child health and the control of communicable diseases.

Among the specialised agencies of the UN there is close co-operation at a European regional level with the ILO, which has regional committees and holds regional conferences; with the FAO, which organizes regional committee sessions on specific subjects, and disposes of a regional representative for Europe; and with UNESCO and IAEA.

Co-ordination between the WHO regional office for Europe and the other specialised agencies depends largely on the extent of their decentralization. Differences in delegation of authority, in the location of regional offices and in geographical areas covered by the respective organizations often hamper effective co-operation.

Thus differences in structure can cause operational problems, especially when the delineation of responsibilities has not been clearly made. The extensive decentralization favoured by the WHO through its regional structure on the one hand, and the less decentralized structure of the other specialised agencies on the other necessitate co-ordination for any given activity both at central and regional levels.

The growth of regional activities and the increasing number of organizations working in the region are also complicating factors, especially where fields of competence are not well defined.

71. Principles governing relationships with regional non-governmental organizations were adopted by the third World Assembly (Resolution WHA 3. 114 of May 1950; WHO, Off. Rec., no. 28, 1950, p. 67). They are based on the principles governing the relationship of non-governmental organizations with the central Organization.

In Europe there are several other forms of intergovernmental organizations which are active one way or the other in the field of health and with which the WHO regional office for Europe maintains close contacts, either formally on the basis of a relationship agreement, or informally. There is, for instance, a formal agreement between the Secretary General of the Council of Europe and the Director of the regional office for Europe of the WHO which dates from September 1952. Apart from the Constitutional provision of the WHO itself, this relationship agreement is also based on Article 1 (c) of the Statute of the Council of Europe, where it is stated that 'participation in the Council of Europe shall not affect the collaboration of its members in the work of the United Nations and of other international organizations or unions to which they are parties'.

The agreement provides for exchange of information relating to activities of mutual interest, as well as of statistical and legislative information on subjects in which the organizations have particular interest; mutual consultation, reciprocal attendance at meetings and technical co-operation for the purpose of studying questions of common interest and the execution of certain projects.

Mutual consultation takes place between both organizations on respective work-programmes, which enables each to complement and, or continue any activity taken up previously by the other, and also enables activities to be carried out as joint ventures.

Another particularity of this kind of co-operation is the fact that WHO as a non-political, technical organization can be usefully supported in its activities by the Council of Europe as a political organization, which through its parliamentary forum can contribute to the attainment of the required results.

Relations between the regional office and the European Community comprise mutual attendance at meetings, exchange of documentation and information and regular consultations based upon an exchange of letters of 29 May and 19 June 1972.

There is, for instance, co-operation in the preparation of a report on medical manpower forecasts.

Possibilities for a formal relationship agreement with the Council for Mutual Economic Assistance is presently under study. This Council, which groups together the socialist countries of Eastern Europe as well as Cuba and Mongolia is concerned with, among other things, economic aspects of environmental resources and water resources.

The regional office and the Organisation for Economic Co-operation and Development (OECD) share common interest in, for instance, a regional health university and information systems in public health. Finally, the regional office maintains close contacts with the Nordic Council.

Though the above review shows that co-ordination is energetically pursued by the Regional office, it cannot yet be said that it has reached its optimal form. Too often unnecessary duplication and overlapping of activities occur, related programmes of work are often poorly co-ordinated and little or no attention is paid to the fact that various international organizations could usefully complement each other in their respective activities in the field of health.

3. Some conclusions

It is recognized by the WHO that in view of the prevailing differences in socio-economic conditions throughout the world, there is a need to strengthen the process of regionalization. This has, however, not yet resulted in full decentralization. Moreover, being guided by the principle of the attainment of health care for all by the year 2000, the organization is tempted to focus primarily on the less prosperous countries while those of a more advanced level facing problems caused by their very stage of development need equal attention for the realization of the right to health care, adapted to their own specific problems. Thus, in Europe, the very level of technology and industrialization requires rethinking of priorities in the field of health, oriented towards humanization of health care. In this region the stage has been reached that often the cost involved through advanced medical technology outweigh the benefits of health care, while moreover only relatively few will profit from the most sophisticated medical techniques. Only through a real process of decentralization can an optimal realization of the right to health care be obtained.

Other regions would in due course profit from the results thus yielded in a regional setting, so that eventually the maximum benefits would be obtained from the possibilities existing in the European region. There are already some examples of activities undertaken in the European region for the purpose of developing global programmes, which might well be expanded by using other means too.

In order to increase the effectiveness of efforts to attain the WHO's objective within the European region, it will also be necessary to rethink the structure of the Organization as a whole with a view to giving the European region greater possibilities. Moreover, while uniformity and agreement on guiding rules and principles for the full realization of the right to health care are hard to obtain at a global level, the European region is in an excellent position to establish such principles at a regional level. Thus, for instance, the Organization plays a primarily supportive role at a global level with regard to those aspects of the right to health care which are closely interrelated with other human rights (right to life, prohibition of medical experimentation on human subjects without free consent), while the European region would seem to be ideally suited to focusing upon the possibility of the Organization's acquiring more direct involvement in this respect.

The existing co-ordination and co-operation in the region with other international organizations is also a subject of concern for the European office. Efforts to avoid duplication and overlapping of activities could well be intensified through regular consultation on respective programmes of work and through effective working arrangements. In the European region in particular international co-operation in the field of public health is of paramount importance in order to tackle the specific problems this region is facing.

III. The Council of Europe

1. Creation of the Council of Europe

Historically the idea for a united Europe was launched at various times.

We shall refer here to the plan presented by Sully in 1638, suggesting the creation of a Council of Europe which would supervise the European Confederation of States. The composition and legal powers of such an organization always formed a central theme in discussions on the unification of Europe. After the Second World War, the need for unification became particularly urgent.

In a speech delivered on September 19th, 1946, Sir Winston Churchill, referring to Sully's plan, suggested the creation of the Council of Europe as a regional organization for the purpose of the building up and strenghthening the United Nations. In December 1947 various organizations working for European unity were united in the International Committee of the Movements for European Unity. It was this 'European Movement', which took the initiative for the organizing of a conference (the so-called 'Congress of Europe') which met in The Hague from 8 to 10 May 1948 with the purpose of promoting European unity.

The 'message for Europeans' as well as the various resolutions adopted at this conference show that the creation of the Council of Europe is a direct result of this gathering. The texts adopted by the conference stressed the need for the promotion of an economical and political union or federation, the creation of a multilateral European organization, the elaboration of a human rights charter and the creation of a European Court to supervise the implementation of the latter.

These suggestions were the subject of discussions by the ministers of foreign affairs of the five countries participating in the Brussels Treaty. This Treaty, which was signed on 17 March 1948 by Belgium, Luxemburg, France, the Netherlands and the United Kingdom and entered into force on 25 August 1948, was the first multilateral European treaty after the Second World War. It was concluded primarily for defensive purposes, but it was also the intention of the countries party to it, as expressed in Article 11 of the Treaty, to concert their efforts (by direct consultation) to promote the attainment of a higher standard of living of their peoples, to ensure progress in the social sphere and to tackle questions where immediate practical results might be achieved, especially in the social field.

In October 1948, the Consultative Council of the Brussels Treaty (composed of the five ministers of foreign affairs), charged a committee of 18 experts, appointed by the respective governments, to study possible measures for the greater unity of European countries.

This committee of experts drew up various recommendations, which were

163

subsequently discussed by the Consultative Council of the Brussels Treaty in January 1949.

At that meeting the five ministers of foreign affairs reached agreement on the creation of the Council of Europe, which was to be composed of a committee of ministers, to meet in private sessions, and a consultative body, to meet in public sessions. The latter body would only have deliberative functions. This particular structure was chosen as a compromise solution between the views of those (Belgium, France) favouring a European Assembly possessing considerable authority including legislative and constitutional powers, and functioning independently from the Committee of Ministers, and those (United Kingdom) who wanted an assembly dependent on governments, composed of government delegates, and to be elected and directed by governments. The latter accepted that the assembly would consist of representatives of each member appointed by its country's parliament or appointed in such a manner as that parliament should decide, and that the organ would have a mere deliberative status. (Members of the Consultative Assembly, once nominated, act in an independent capacity.)

In this way, despite the federalistic ideas of the Congress of The Hague favouring an organization to which members would delegate sovereignty, the Council of Europe became a classic international organization based on intergovernmental co-operation.

The Statute of the Council of Europe was signed in London on May 5th, 1949 during a diplomatic conference, convened by the five members of the Brussels Treaty, and to which Denmark, Ireland, Italy, Norway and Sweden were also invited.

The Council of Europe presently has 21 member states: Austria, Belgium, Cyprus, Denmark, France, Federal Republic of Germany, Greece, Iceland, Ireland, Italy, Liechtenstein, Luxemburg, Malta, the Netherlands, Norway, Portugal, Spain, Sweden, Switzerland, Turkey and the United Kingdom.

2. Statute of the Council of Europe

2.1. OBJECTIVE

The aim of the Organization is primarily to achieve greater unity between its members with a view, among other things, to facilitating their economic and social progress (Article 1 (a) of the Statute).

The instruments used to this end are discussions on questions of common concern, agreements and common action in economic, social, cultural, scientific, legal and administrative matters, as well as the maintenance and furtherance of human rights and fundamental freedoms (Article 1 (b) of the Statute).

The aim of the Council of Europe is very broad and almost all matters fall within its scope, except questions relating to national defence, which fall within the scope of other organizations.

164

Despite this almost universal competence the Council of Europe in practice deals only in a limited way with political and economic problems, which are dealt with primarily in the framework of other international settings.

Its attention is focused first and foremost on social, cultural, legal, environmental and human rights questions.

Although health care as such is not mentioned as a field of concern, it was nonetheless intended from the beginning to fall within the scope of the Organization.

The Council of Europe is in fact the only international Organization operating at a regional European level with a fairly broad public health programme.

2.2. ORGANS OF THE COUNCIL OF EUROPE

The Statute of the Council of Europe provides for two organs which are to implement the Organization's objectives: the Committee of Ministers and the Parliamentary Assembly. Both organs are assisted by a secretariat (Article 10 of the Statute).

a. the Committee of Ministers (Articles 13-21 of the Statute)

As a classical political organ, the Committee of Ministers is composed of the ministers of foreign affairs of member countries.

It meets twice a year. Since 1952 the permanent representatives meet about once a month. They are authorised to take decisions on almost every matter, except those with important political consequences. The Committee acts on behalf of the Organization (Article 13 of the Statute) and its task is to consider what action is necessary to further the aim of the Organization, action which includes the conclusion of conventions or agreements, and the adoption by governments of a common policy with regard to particular matters (Article 15 (a) of the Statute). The conclusions of the Committee of Ministers may also be presented in the form of recommendations (Article 15 (b) of the Statute). (See also: Resolution of May 1951 – 8th session of the Committee of Ministers under 'Powers of the Committee of Ministers'.)[72]

The only direct decision-making power of the Committee of Ministers is in matters of minor importance and in internal affairs (Article 16 of the Statute).

The Committee of Ministers furthermore decides on the priority of activities of the Organization in approving its budget, which is based on the Organization's programme of work (Article 20 (d) of the Statute).

This programme of work takes into account, recommendations made by the Parliamentary Assembly and the committees of experts appointed by the Committee of Ministers under Article 17 of the Statute, suggestions

---

72. Text of a statutory nature, adopted by the Committee of Ministers with a view to its ultimate inclusion in a revised Statute.

from other international organizations and other outside services as well as secretarial proposals.

The programme of work attributes to each activity a definite and practical purpose in order to fulfil the objective. It lays down starting and finishing dates for each activity. The framework of the programme [73] enables the Council of Europe to select those problems which most urgently require international co-operation for their solution (Council of Europe, The Consultative Assembly, procedure and practice, 1973, p. 151).

In 1974, for instance, when the future role of the Council of Europe was discussed, the Committee of Ministers decided that the intergovernmental co-operation within the framework of the Council of Europe should concentrate on the following subjects:
— human rights and fundamental freedoms;
— social and social/economical problems, in particular those connected with migrants;
— education and culture;
— youth;
— public health;
— environment, regionalization;
— legal co-operation including prevention of delicts and sentencing. (Resolution (74) 4.)

Important decision-making powers may, however, be bestowed on the Committee of Ministers by virtue of individual conventions. The European Human Rights Convention is an outstanding example. The Committee plays a role in enforcing this Convention in cases where an affair which has been investigated by the European commission of human rights is not referred to the European Court of human rights. (Both organs were set up to ensure the observance of engagements undertaken by the contracting parties.)

The Committee of Ministers decides in such cases, provided there is a two third majority, whether the Convention has been violated. [74]

Another procedure is followed in the European Social Charter where the Committee of Ministers is given the power to address recommendations to governments, on basis of reports from the competent committees, with a view

73. The current programme of intergovernmental activities covers eight fields of activities:
— protection and development of human rights and fundamental freedoms;
— social and socio-economic problems, such as those concerning migrant workers;
— co-operation in the field of education, culture and sport;
— youth affairs;
— protection and promotion of public health;
— protection of nature and the management of natural resources, the man-made environment and regional planning;
— local authorities: matters relating to regional and municipal co-operation;
— co-operation in the legal field, including the harmonization of national legislation and practice in specific legal sectors; the prevention of crime and the treatment of offenders.
74. See Part A, Ch. I, para. 2.3.3.

166

to getting them to adapt their social legislation to the norms laid down in the Social Charter. [75]

The functions of the Committee of Ministers as a political forum are restricted in the sense that it concentrates its attention only on items that are politically feasible, and only furthers proposals which can be accepted by the majority of member governments, although it is recognized that quite a number of resolutions or conventions have been adopted which were in advance of national developments in a particular field.

The Committee of Ministers is assisted in its work by advisory and technical committees (Article 17 of the Statute). These committees, which are composed of experts from the member countries, do the specialised preparatory work on which the Committee of Ministers bases its decisions. One of these committees is the European public health committee.

b. Parliamentary Assembly (Articles 22-35 of the Statute)

This body, composed of parliamentarians of member countries, constituted a novelty in international relations, although it has since been followed by other organizations such as the European Community.

Originally it was called 'Consultative Assembly', but in 1974 its name was changed to 'Parliamentary Assembly', with a view to underlining its importance as a European parliamentary body.

The Parliamentary Assembly is the deliberative organ of the Council of Europe and may discuss any matter falling within the aim and scope of the Organization (Article 23 of the Statute). As a purely deliberative organ its task is limited to influencing public opinion and promoting action. It has not been given any decision making power.

Items are included on its agenda on its own initiative further to a request for opinion from the Committee of Ministers. Any recommendations which result from these discussions are presented to the Committee of Ministers which has no formal, but solely a moral, obligation to take them into account.

Nonetheless, these recommendations often prove to trigger off action which initially was not foreseen by the Committee of Ministers.

The Parliamentary Assembly can, too, exercise important influence in that it acts as a forum of discussion for public opinion of the member states. Another important tool is the organization of conferences for the purpose of gathering information and obtaining a more precise idea of problems the Assembly is dealing with.

The Assembly holds one ordinary session (divided in two parts) a year; extraordinary sessions, which are rare, are held on the initiative of the Committee of Ministers or the President of the Parliamentary Assembly (Article 34 of the Statute).

The Assembly has formed various committees out of its midst, each of them charged with the preparation of work in special fields. The basis for the creation of such committees is in Article 24 of the Statute. One of these committees is the committee on social and public health questions.

75. See Part. A, Ch. I, para. 2.4.3.

Relations between the Parliamentary Assembly and the Committee of Ministers are fostered in various ways. There is, for instance, a system of annual reporting by the Committee of Ministers to the Assembly; the mixed committee set up in 1951 to co-ordinate the activities of both organs and to improve relations between them, as well as periodical symposia on general political matters which have been taking place from 1961 onwards.

c. the secretariat (Articles 36-37 of the Statute)

The secretariat is composed of a Secretary-General, a Deputy Secretary-General (both appointed by the Parliamentary Assembly on the recommendation of the Committee of Ministers), and other staff. The staff members act independently of their country of origin and may not receive instructions from any government or any authority external to the Council. They are, as international officials, responsible only to the Council. In practice, however, ties with the country of origin often remain, so that some national influences can still pass through the channels of the secretariat.

2.3. INSTRUMENTS

The means which are at the disposal of the Council of Europe to attain its aim as defined in Article 1 of the Statute have either a legal nature or are of an operative character:
— the conclusion of conventions or agreements between member states;
— the adoption by governments of a common policy in particular matters.

These functions are to be performed by the organs of the Council of Europe, without affecting the collaboration of its members in the work of other international organizations (co-ordinative task) (Article 1 of the Statute).

a. legislative powers

'Legislative power' (conclusion of agreements and conventions) is confined to the Committee of Ministers (Article 15 of the Statute and Resolution of May 1951 under 'Powers of the Committee of Ministers') [76], but the Parliamentary Assembly may also recommend their conclusion.

These agreements however are concluded between states, members of the Council of Europe and are therefore to be signed and ratified by individual states, so there is never a certainty that a given agreement will enter into force, and if it does enter into force, that it will bind all member states. Thus they are not legal instruments of the Council of Europe itself. European conventions and agreements are open to all members of the Council of Europe, and also to non-members, provided this has been formally stipulated.

These instruments are drawn up with active participation of the Parliamentary Assembly throughout the entire process of preparation, signature and

76. Text of a statutory character, adopted by the Committee of Ministers, eighth session, with a view to its ultimate inclusion in a revised statute.

ratification, and are in this respect different from other international instruments, which are usely concluded by governments only. (Golsong, 1965, pp. 140-147, speaks in this respect of 'interstates treaties'.) Another characteristic of these European conventions and agreements which are binding for all contracting parties is their standardizing nature, which is of great significance when matters of interpretation arise and which enables the common interest to prevail over national interests. Because of the fact that many of the European instruments contain norms of a relatively high level, a system of gradual and, or facultative application has in some cases been introduced (as, for instance, in the case of the European Social Charter).

The system for the control of implementation of agreements and conventions is laid down in Resolution 61 (1) by virtue of which the Committee of Ministers annually examines reports on:
— steps taken towards conventions and agreements or protocols which have been ratified;
— steps taken for ratification of such instruments;
— reasons why instruments for ratification have not been submitted within 18 month after signature.

The Parliamentary Assembly also plays a certain role in this respect by discussing progress reports as well as through the intervention of its representatives in their national parliaments.

Furthermore, specific systems are provided for in other special instruments, varying from the special complaint procedure under the European Convention on the Protection of Human Rights and Fundamental Freedoms, to the special reporting procedure under the European Social Charter.

In the field of public health eleven agreements were concluded as of 1978, of which nine were elaborated at the level of all member states and two in the framework of the so-called 'Partial Agreement'.

b. other powers

Other methods applied to promote a common policy as described in Article 1 of the Statute are:
— resolutions (viz. recommendations)

Conclusions forwarded by the Committee of Ministers may take the form of recommendations, in which case they are called 'resolutions'.

These recommendations, which do not have direct legal binding force on member states, contain general guiding principles for these states.

They are formulated either on the initiative of the Committee of Ministers itself (through its committees of governmental experts) (Article 15 (b) of the Statute) or following an initiative taken by the Parliamentary Assembly (Articles 22 and 23 of the Statute).

Despite the fact that the recommendations impose only a moral obligation on member states, who are expected to implement them voluntarily, the adoption procedure involved is rather laborious presumably because they are intended to be applicable to member states. In general, recommendations on important matters are passed by a unanimous vote from the representatives casting a vote and a majority vote from the representatives entitled to sit on the Committee of Ministers (Article 20 (a) of the Statute).

This procedure implies that the content of the recommendations (mostly presented as a resolution of the Committee of Ministers) will always represent a compromise between different opinions. Other recommendations of lesser importance are taken with a two/third majority (see, for instance, Article 20 (c) of the Statute).

The very nature of these recommendations hampers the establishment of a stringent implementation system. Article 15 (b) of the Statute provides for the possibility of periodical examination of action taken on recommendations by member states, and since 1958 the Committee of Ministers in principle examines the situation ones every three years.

Some recommendations moreover, contain a specific provision for periodical furnishing of information. It is general policy to include such a provision into recommendations pertaining to public health subjects.

Finally, the Parliamentary Assembly discusses progress reports on action taken by member states.

The only direct effect of a regular evaluation of action taken on Council of Europe recommendations is that attention is drawn once more to these recommendations.

— setting up of technical committees

Through committees or commissions which may be set up for specific purposes (Article 17 of the Statute) studies on specific subjects can be carried out. The results of these studies are generally published in reports, which include recommendations or general guidelines. Their contribution to policy development in member states is less important than that of resolutions relating to recommendations, which are supported by all or at least the majority of the member states. They can, however, in view of their specific nature, be useful to those who are working at a policy-paving level, as well as to field-workers, especially when technical subjects are involved, provided the results of these studies are distributed on a large scale.

— attribution of fellowships (individual or collective)

Though not mentioned as such in the Statute, the Council of Europe offers the possibility of attributing individual fellowships or organizing and financing special courses or combined studies. Participants in such schemes are able to apply experience gained in their own working surroundings. Collective fellowships (combined studies) are moreover used for studies on a specific subject of common interest, the results of which are often published by way of reports.

— financing of special projects

Another possibility for promoting the common policy of the Council of Europe is the financing of special projects. Though this, too, is not mentioned in the Statute, the Council of Europe can subsidise projects, enabling activities of a specific nature to be carried out, the results of which are of benefit to all members.

The above review demonstrates that methods for pursuing the aim of the Organization are outlined in a very general manner in its Statute.

This vagueness and lack of precision gives the Organization a great deal of flexibility with regard to the means it may deploy for implementing its objective.

2.4. PARTIAL AGREEMENTS

The adoption of resolutions relating to recommendations (Article 20 (a) of the Statute) involves a common agreement between the majority of the member states (unanimous vote of the representatives casting a vote, and of a majority of the representatives entitled to sit on the Committee of Ministers), whenever these resolutions relate to matters under Article 15 (b) of the Statute.

It furthermore imposes a more or less moral obligation on most member states to follow the general policies laid down in these instruments.

The Committee of Ministers, however, was conscious of the fact that in certain circumstances individual member states would not wish to participate in some activities and that this should not hamper other member states in proceeding with common action in a certain field.

In order not to bind states unwilling to participate in certain activities recommended under Article 20 (a) of the Statute, at the request of the Assembly the Committee of Ministers adopted a special Resolution in August 1951 [77] providing for the possibility of creating Partial Agreements in these circumstances, it being understood that any expenditure incurred by the Council of Europe for activities carried out under such agreements would be borne only by those participating in these special agreements (Resolution (51) 62 on Partial Agreements).

In this way a certain number of states who wish to engage in some specific action are able to conclude a 'Partial Agreement'.

The Committee of Ministers, when transmitting in its special message to the Consultative Assembly the programme of work of the Organization (doc. 238 of May 20th 1954), emphasized the utility of using the procedure instituted by this resolution in appropriate cases, 'provided that none of the Member Governments regards this procedure as likely to prejudice its interests and on the understanding that any partial agreement thus concluded shall be open to accession at any time by any member of the Council of Europe which was not party thereto at the outset' (para. 4 of the Special Message).

One of the results of this resolution was the conclusion of the Partial Agreement in the social and public health field between seven of the member states of the Council of Europe (Belgium, Federal Republic of Germany, France, Italy, Luxembourg, Netherlands and the United Kingdom of Great Britain and northern Ireland) [78]. (Resolution (59) 23, adopted by the Committee of Ministers meeting at deputy level on 16 November 1959.)

77. Text of a statutory character adopted by the Committee of Ministers (ninth session) with a view to its ultimate inclusion in a revised Statute.
78. Since then, other Council of Europe member states have either joined in some or all the activities falling under the Partial Agreement in the field of public health, namely Austria, Denmark, Greece, Ireland, Norway, Sweden and Switzerland.

2.5.1. Co-ordination policy in general

Both the Committee of Ministers and the Parliamentary Assembly maintain relations with other international organizations, relations which, as part of the co-ordination policy of the Council of Europe, are a constant preoccupation of this body.

Article 1 (c) of the Statute states that 'participation in the Council of Europe shall not affect the collaboration of its members in the work of the United Nations and of other international organizations or unions to which they are parties'.

The Assembly is furthermore required when drawing up its agenda to have regard to the work of other European intergovernmental organizations to which some or all of the members of the Council are parties (Article 23 (b) of the Statute).

The co-ordination policy of the Council of Europe, which was formally defined in a special message of the Committee of Ministers to the Parliamentary Assembly in 1954 (doc. 238, 1954, paras. 16-21), is based upon four main principles:

— one of its functions being to form a general framework for European policy, the Council of Europe aims to keep informed about all activities of the main European organizations and to express an opinion on the policy these organizations should pursue in the interest of Europe;

— the Council of Europe attempts to get common solutions for European problems, adopted by the most appropriate international body;

— the Council of Europe constitutes a permanent framework within which international agreements can be negotiated for common action in the fields covered by Article 1 of the Statute, the framework being more effective than when negotiations are undertaken at a purely intergovernmental level;

— the Parliamentary Assembly can at a European political and parliamentary level further, or criticise activities of all international bodies which do not dispose of such a parliamentary forum.

Within the framework of its broad objective the Council of Europe may examine at a European level any matters which are of interest to other international institutions, the latter usually being more specialised, and hence may take the initiative in promoting intergovernmental action which would not otherwise be possible (Council of Europe, the Consultative Assembly, procedure and practice, Strasbourg, 1973, p. 293).

In this manner the Council of Europe can usefully contribute to the co-ordination of activities, by avoiding duplication as well as by promoting the undertaking of activities by the most appropriate body and by stimulating action of a complementary nature as well as material assistance. Moreover, through Resolution 13 (1953) the Committee of Ministers recommended member states to submit every proposal for the creation of new organizations to the Council of Europe in order to be able to establish effective co-ordination in due course. The Secretary General of the Council of Europe in 1965 summarised before the Assembly the aim of the Organization in respect to co-ordination by stating that the promotion of greater unity should be pursued in consultation with other international organizations by means of a comprehensive programme of work drawn up in the light of that of the European Community.

Furthermore, the process of co-operation in technical matters, which are of immediate concern to the Council of Europe member countries and not yet to a world organization such as the United Nations, will promote greater unity in Europe and contribute at the same time towards the work of the world organization.

2.5.2. Co-ordination policy of the Committee of Ministers

The co-ordination policy pursued by the Committee of Ministers is based either upon formal relationship agreements or upon informal arrangements (exchange of letters). The formal authority of the Committee of Ministers to conclude, on behalf of the Council of Europe, agreements with other international bodies is based upon a Resolution which was adopted by the Committee of Ministers in May 1951. [79]

These formal agreements provide in particular for the regular exchange of information, consultation on subjects of common interest and for attendance at meetings as representative or observer.

Such agreements have been concluded with a number of organizations (see below, para. 2.5.4.).

Another major contribution of the Council of Europe to the process of co-ordination with other international organizations is that the Council's programme of work is sent for comment to all interested intergovernmental organizations and non-governmental bodies, so that consultation can take place. Unfortunately, this practice has not been followed by other international organizations (Council of Europe, the Consultative Assembly, procedure and practice, 1973, pp. 295 and 296).

2.5.3. Co-ordination policy of the Parliamentary Assembly

The Parliamentary Assembly in its turn pursues the aim of effective co-ordination on the basis of its position as a general forum for European policy.

The Assembly once again reaffirmed in 1950 the need for close co-ordination between existing European organizations, stressing the need for effective parliamentarian supervision of their activities.

Moreover in 1967, when seeking a further definition of the Council's functions within the system of European international co-operation the Assembly saw its role as that of interlocutor of the great variety of technical agencies, while the Committee of Ministers would ensure political control of the experts' work, 'the whole Council serving as a forum for major political debate in Europe' (Council of Europe, the Consultative Assembly, procedure and practice, 1973, pp. 296-297).

79. Text of a statutory character, adopted by the Committee of Ministers, eighth session, with a view to its ultimate inclusion in a revised statute.

In order to be kept to date on the activities of other intergovernmental organizations and to be in a position to promote the adoption of common solutions to European problems, to be implemented by the most suitable international body, the Assembly discusses annual reports which are presented by international organizations (see also para. 2.5.2.).

Debates may result in the adoption of a resolution containing the views of the Assembly on the various activities and suggested guidelines for the future or in recommendations addressed to the Committee of Ministers.

The Assembly has of course no powers to control the activities of other organizations, but it forms a suitable parliamentary forum, where all activities can be reviewed regularly. In this way organizations which do not have such a forum are enabled to bring their work to the attention of national parliaments represented in the Assembly and to obtain their political support.

Other methods of co-ordination applied by the Assembly are, for instance, inviting other organizations to attend its meetings as well as those of its special committees and charging the Secretary General of the Council of Europe to establish and maintain official contacts with other organizations.

2.5.4. Some examples of relationships with other international organizations

There are various relationship agreements concluded with the United Nations family. They include those with the International Labour Organisation, the Food and Agriculture Organization and the UN Educational, Scientific and Cultural Organization. The relationship agreement with the WHO's regional office for Europe dates from 1952. As was seen before (Ch. II, para. 2.5.) this agreement provides for

- exchange of information (exchange of documents, periodical contacts between members of the respective secretariats for the purpose of consultation as well as making available any relevant statistical and legislative information);
- mutual consultation (at all stages of preparatory work and in the execution of programmes);
- attendance at meetings (Parliamentary Assembly and governmental committees);
- technical co-operation (for the purpose of studying questions of common interest and the execution of certain projects).

The Council's relationship with the European Community has several facets.

Relations with the European Coal and Steel Community (ECSC) are formally based upon Article 94 of its Treaty as well as on a Protocol to the Treaty of April 18th, 1951, providing among other things for annual presentation of reports to the Committee of Ministers of the Council of Europe and to the Parliamentary Assembly. Those with the European Economic Community (EEC) and the European Atomic Energy Agency (Euratom) are based upon Article 230 and Article 200 of the respective Treaties on the one hand, and on Resolution (57) 27 of the Committee of Ministers of the Council of Europe and Recommendation 146 (1957) and Resolution 130 (1957) of the Parliamentary Assembly on the other.

Since the merger of the Commissions of the EEC and Euratom and the High Authority no new formal instrument of co-operation has been made: the previous arrangements for collaboration have been continued with the (single) Commission of the European Community.

At present the European Community participates in the discussions of the Committee of Ministers with regards to problems of a general nature and in the work of committees of experts, subcommittees and working groups. Furthermore, there is an exchange of documentation and information as well as mutual consultation (Resolution (58) 11 and exchange of letters of August 18th 1959). Since 1953 there have been joint meetings between both Parliamentary bodies. Finally, through Resolution (74) 13, the Committee of Ministers of the Council of Europe created a liaison office in Brussels.

The relationship with the European Community is very important for the Council of Europe, because there is always a certain danger that differences of interests within the Committee of Ministers through 'bloc forming' by the nine members of the Community may hamper the work of the Council of Europe. Whenever the nine members of the Community unanimously oppose certain activities of the Council of Europe on the grounds that the latter is not the competent body to deal with these matters, the activity in question will not take place.

It is necessary, therefore, that there be no competetive attitude, but rather an awareness that the roles of both organizations should be complementary to each other. The emphasis should be on co-ordination of activities and mutual assistance, through a pragmatic approach, rather than on the assignment of work to each organization separately.

Other relations of the Council of Europe include those with the North Atlantic Treaty Organization since 1952, when it was decided through an exchange of letters to exchange information on items such as social matters; with the Organisation for Economic Co-operation and Development on basis of a formal Arrangement of 1962 (mutual attendance of observers and liaison committees as well as annual presentation of reports to the Parliamentary Assembly); and with the European Free Trade Association, through consultations, the informal exchange of informations, and, since 1961, the submission of formal reports to the Parliamentary Assembly.

The Council of Europe has also made suitable arrangements for consultation with international non-governmental organizations on basis of a Resolution adopted by the Committee of Ministers in May 1951. [80] Possibilities for such consultations were elaborated in 1960 in regulations which define the conditions for obtaining consultative status and the procedures to be followed.

International non-governmental organizations which have obtained consultative status may attend meetings both of the governmental expert committees and the Parliamentary Assembly as well as submit papers to these meetings. There are, for instance, close relations with the League of Red Cross Societies and the European League for Mental Health.

80. Text of a statutory character, adopted by the Committee of Ministers (eighth session) with a view to its ultimate inclusion in a revised Statute.

2.5.5. Specialised Authority

When discussing the co-ordinative tasks of the Council of Europe and its powers in that field another special power which should be mentioned is its authority to take 'the initiative of instituting negotiations between members with a view to the creation of European Specialised Authorities, each with its own competence in the economic, social, cultural, legal, administrative or other related fields' (Resolution adopted by the Committee of Ministers at its eighth session in May 1951). [81] Members are free to adhere to such European Specialised Authorities, which may also be set up by member states upon their own initiative. There are special conditions for bringing such specialised authorities in relationship with the Council of Europe, including reciprocal representation and, if the question arises, appropriate forms of integration between the organs of the Council of Europe and those of the Specialised Authority; the exchange of information; the presentation of recommendations of the Council of Europe to the Specialised Authority; arrangements concerning staff and administrative, technical and other services.

The Council of Europe may co-ordinate the work of the Specialised Authorities brought into relationship with the Council of Europe by holding joint sessions, and by submitting recommendations to them as well as to member governments. The fact that the Council of Europe has the authority to initiate the creation of European Specialised Authorities which are competent in specific fields gives it ample opportunities for pursuing effective co-operation and co-ordination at a European level.

The only restriction to this broad competence is its dependance on the willingness of member states to join such a Specialised Authority, so that the Organization's powers of conviction are of major influence in this respect.

3. Public health activities

3.1. GENERAL REMARKS

Activities in the field of public health are carried out at a governmental and a parliamentary level.

At the governmental level they basically take place in two different settings.

Firstly, within a programme on public health set up in 1954 which falls under the competence of the European Public Health Committee and in which all member states of the Council of Europe as well as Finland (as an observer) participate. Secondly there are activities carried out by a certain number of member states since 1959 under the so-called Partial Agreement in the social and public health field. The public health committee of the Partial Agreement is the competent body for this particular form of co-operation.

Other activities of a more legal nature are carried out under the auspices of the European committees on legal co-operation and on crime problems, which

---

81. Text of a statutory character, adopted by the Committee of Ministers, eighth session, with a view to its ultimate inclusion in a revised Statute.

in this respect work in close co-operation with the European public health committee.

Secretarial services for these various activities are rendered respectively by the public health division, the public health division of the Partial Agreement and the division of legal affairs.

At the parliamentary level discussions in the Assembly are prepared by its committee on social and health questions.

3.2. GOVERNMENTAL ACTIVITIES AFFECTING ALL MEMBER STATES
European public health committee

3.2.1. Introduction
The first attempts at achieving European co-operation in the field of health date from 1953, when the French Government presented a project for such a form of co-operation to the Organization for European Economic Co-operation.

This project, the so-called 'white pool', included the following suggestions:
— setting up of a common market in medicines, medical equipment and treatment centres;
— co-ordination of medical research;
— exchange of medical knowledge;
— exchange of medical and paramedical personnel as well as public health officers;
— simplification of production and distribution of medicines;
— provision of first-aid in cases of catastrophies or epidemics.

It was the intention that these activities would complement the work carried out by the World Health Organization in the European region, which during the decolonization process of 1950-60 focused its attention primarily upon the needs of the developing countries. This priority assignment resulted in that period in insufficient attention for the health problems in the European region. Negotiations for the realization of the French project, however, never led to positive results.

Therefore, when the Committee of Ministers of the Council of Europe invited member states to submit proposals for action in the field of public health, some of the principles contained in the French project were advanced again in 1954.

These and similar proposals submitted by other governments aimed in general at closer European co-operation in the field of health through exchange of information, co-ordination of research, standardization of methods and pooling of human and material resources. The Committee of Ministers submitted the suggestions to the European office of the World Health Organization, and subsequently, together with the opinion of the latter, to the Parliamentary Assembly (Special Message of the Committee of Ministers transmitting to the Assembly the programme of work of the Council of Europe — doc. 238 of May 20th, 1954).

The Assembly in turn, in its opinion no. 9, adopted at its sixth ordinary session (first part) in May 1954, welcomed the proposals made and expressed agreement with the Committee of Ministers' suggestion to convene without delay a committee of governmental experts to study the recommendations of the governments, the opinion of the World Health Organization and of the Parliamentary Assembly. The Assembly furthermore asked for further proposals from governments for wider collaboration in the health field and referred in this connection to its own study on a system for the exchange of war cripples for the purpose of medical treatment in other countries.

The committee of governmental experts which was convened at that time has been in existence since 1954. It was transformed into the European public health committee in 1966 and into a 'steering committee' with larger competence than before in 1977.

The mandate of this committee may be found in the aforementioned Special Message of the Committee of Ministers (paras. 64-66), in opinion no. 9 (para. 15) of the Parliamentary Assembly and (more recently) in section V of the annex to Resolution (77) 51. It includes at present:
— the development of optimal conditions for the promotion of public health by means of studies, exchange of information on the organizational and operational aspects of health services, as well as on the prevention of illness and the humanization of medicine;
— the improvement of international co-operation in the field of combating drug abuse;
— examination of the achievements reached within the framework of the 'Partial Agreement' on handicapped persons with a view to medical rehabilitation;
— examination of the application of the Council of Europe's conventions and agreements in the field of public health, to assess their effectiveness and, where necessary, to consider means of increasing their effectiveness.

The committee is assisted in its work by the 'committee of experts on blood transfusion and immunohaematology', the 'medical fellowships selection and assessment committee' and various ad hoc 'select committees of experts'.

Steering committees with closely related activities are the European Committee on crime problems (legal aspects of drug abuse), the European committee on legal co-operation and the public health committee and committee for the handicapped, both falling under the Partial Agreement.

The work of the European public health committee is characterised by a pragmatic approach, so that the most efficient use is made of the resources of knowledge, research, experience and equipment available in the member states.

The committee uses a variety of methods. First, it is assisted in its work by so-called 'select expert committees', which prepare studies on specific subjects, the results of which are transmitted to the committee by way of reports and, or recommendations. To assist these ad hoc committees, consultants are generally appointed. These consultants, who are highly specialised persons,

178

prepare a preliminary study on the subject under consideration. Then there are the so-called 'co-ordinated medical research schemes', of which there are two. One is held yearly, when a small number of experts meet to study a special subject in the field of public health of common European interest, and the other on a biennial basis, for the purpose of studying specific aspects of blood transfusion. These schemes are characterised by the fact that they are primarily oriented towards field studies, while the 'select expert committees' mainly perform their work on the basis of the specialised knowledge of the participants and of information received through questionnaires.

Research funds are furthermore made available for laboratory research in blood transfusion, with a view to developing European standards of reference. Planning of activities takes place in close co-operation with the regional office for Europe of the World Health Organization, so that both organizations complement one other's activities in this way. There are also regular contacts with other organizations such as the European Community and the League of Red Cross Societies in order to prevent unnecessary duplication of work.

3.2.2. Programme of work

The activities of the European public health committee are mainly directed towards the development of common standards of hygiene and medical treatment and the adoption of uniform rules in the field of health. It is also the policy of the committee to promote common use of treatment facilities whenever this is required by social or economic circumstances. These general policy lines are pursued with a view to attaining the overall aim of the Council of Europe in the field of health care:
— promotion of uniformity of health care on a European level through development of norms and standards;
— improvement of standards of health and health care in member states.

The instruments through which the Organization implements its aims (legislative measures and development of general policy) are fully applied by the committee.

There are at present 8 European agreements and over 30 resolutions stemming from the Committee and many studies have been published. The European public health committee also establishes priorities for future activities. In planning its long-term programme of work the Committee focuses attention on subjects appropriate for joint studies at an international level on limited questions which are similar in many countries and therefore would generally contribute to national achievements. Attention is also paid to the possibility of promoting co-ordination of national action through the furtherance of harmonization of certain measures on a European level.

The programme of work consists of three main branches, which are closely connected, interrelated and sometimes interdependent:
a. general public health activities;
b. matters related to the use of blood and blood products;
c. education and training.

To implement the general aim of the Organization in the health field, activities in these branches concentrate principally on three objectives:

- mutual assistance (promotion of free circulation of sick persons and material);
- prevention (at a national and international level);
- organization of medical care services (within and outside health institutions at a local, regional, national and international level).

The three branches of the programme of work are briefly reviewed below in the light of these three objectives. [82]

a. general public health activities
   - mutual assistance

Activities directed towards facilitating mutual assistance originate from the Second World War and were therefore initially concentrated upon assistance to war victims. The Parliamentary Assembly adopted a recommendation on this subject in 1954, which resulted in the adoption of the first European agreement in the field of health, elaborated by the European public health committee.

This Agreement (1955, no. 20) on 'the exchange of war cripples with a view to medical treatment' was followed by another Agreement (1962, no. 40) on 'the issue to military and civilian war-disabled of an international book of vouchers for the repair of prosthetic and orthopaedic appliances'. So far attempts to extend the latter agreement to other groups of disabled persons have failed.

Gradually the scope of activities designed to promote mutual assistance was extended. In 1960 European Agreement no. 33 on 'the temporary importation, free of duty, of medical, surgical and laboratory equipment for use free of loan in hospitals and other medical institutions for purposes of diagnosis or treatment' was concluded.

European Agreement no. 38 on 'mutual assistance in the matter of special medical treatments and climatic facilities' was concluded in 1962. Discussions on this subject had already taken place in 1956 and 1957 within the framework of the Western European Union and underlined not only the need for such an agreement, but also the importance of a European social security system.
   - prevention

As was the case within the World Health Organization, the European public health committee became equally aware of the need to strengthen and develop preventive measures in various fields, both on the national and the international level.

All aspects of prevention are, today, of major concern to the committee. Some of the most relevant examples of studies which have been carried out with a view to developing preventive systems on a national level are those on 'the prevention of road accidents', 'accidents in childhood as a public health problem', 'hygiene of hospitals', 'abuse of medicines', 'mass screening', 'the role of the environment among the causes of senescence' and 'the organization of preventive services in mental illness'. 'Prevention of hospital infections',

82. See also under 3.3. below.

180

and 'identification and motivation of population groups disregarding preventive aspects of the health field' are some of the subjects which are included in the current programme of work.

Increasing migration and rapidly improving methods of transport forced the committee to focus attention on the gaps in national and international regulations concerning the transfer of corpses. The existing international agreement – the so-called Berlin Agreement – had become out dated, and the problem – which had already been the subject of a resolution of the Council of Europe in 1958 – was finally dealt with in European Agreement no. 80 on 'the transfer of corpses' (1973). Under this agreement transport is facilitated while at the same time the safety measures required by public health considerations are respected.

The problem of sexually transmittable diseases and drug addiction have also been the subject of studies, particularly because of their international repercussions.

Drug addiction has always been and still is a major subject of concern to many international organizations. In addition to other studies which are currently carried out by the Council of Europe in this field, the Organization has also promoted the co-ordination of activities at an international level as well as co-operation between international organizations. The alcoholic drinking patterns of young people is also the subject of studies.

– organization of medical care services

As far as the organization of medical care is concerned, studies have been conducted on the structure, planning and spread of hospitals as part of an integrated health care system, taking into account also the possible budgetary implications.

These studies resulted among other things in a model of hospital services required in a given region. Health care outside the hospital has also been reviewed, but diversity between member states in this respect made it impossible to come any further than the drawing up of a number of general guidelines for developing this sector. The internal structure of hospitals is the subject of Resolution (77) 3.

Current activities in this field include studies on subjects such as 'study of the comparative cost of health care given inside and outside hospitals' and 'role of school health services within the general health services'.

b. Matters related to the use of blood and blood products
– mutual assistance

The need for mutual assistance in this sector formed the basis for current activities, which include subjects like freedom of movement, standardization methods, improvement of blood transfusion techniques and introduction of automated methods. Considering the importance of this sector the European public health comittee decided in 1961 to create a permanent subcommittee of specialists on blood problems[83], which is responsible for all activities relating to the subject.

83. Since 1977: committee of experts on blood transfusion and immunohaematology.

The floods in the Netherlands in 1952 were a tragic illustration of lack of international regulations, the absence of standardized safety norms resulting in foreign material being wasted. Standardization of blood collecting methods, package, storage and dispatch has since been realized by virtue of European Agreement no. 26, of 1958 on 'the exchange of therapeutic substances of human origin'. The agreement also covered the need for rapid delivery of blood products for non-commercial use, which was made possible by the establishment of a network of national blood transfusion centres.

The technical protocol to the agreement, which includes preventive measures too, is regularly kept up to date.

European Agreement no. 39 of 1962 provides for the standardization and rapid delivery of blood-grouping reagents.

A third agreement in this sector is European Agreement no. 84 of 1974 on 'the exchange of tissue typing reagents'. This agreement will eventually lead to the setting up of large pools of donors and recipients in the field of transplantation of organs. A network of national and regional tissue typing reference laboratories in member states is co-operating to this end.

Another development in the field of mutual assistance was the creation in 1969 of the European frozen blood bank of rare groups in Amsterdam.

This bank, which operates under a co-operative arrangement between the central laboratory of the blood transfusion service of the Netherlands Red Cross and the Council of Europe makes it possible to supply countries rapidly with special types of blood unavailable there.

Leaving aside other apparent advantages of this bank, there is also an important economic aspect to this type of international co-operation.

– prevention

The need for prevention of accidents through blood transfusion or handling of blood by medical personnel is a constant pre-occupation of the subcommittee.

The Agreements no. 26 and 39 contain general norms in this respect, while also special regulations to ensure freedom form toxicity of plastics blood transfusion equipment and on the preparation of blood products used in the treatment of haemophilia are included in the Protocol to Agreement no. 26. Other examples of studies in this field are those on the control of post-transfusion hepatitis and safety factors in transfusion.

– organization of medical care services

Studies on organizational and legal structures of blood transfusion services throughout the whole process of collecting and transfusing blood with a view to protecting the donor and recipient and the development of standardization methods for the measurement of blood components have contributed to an optimal organization of blood services. Automated blood grouping and international exchange of blood and blood products between non profit-making organizations also fall under this objective.

c. Education and training

The promotion of free movement of medical and paramedical personnel largely depends form the extent to which common European standards are developed.

Here again the objective of mutual assistance plays an important role, although also preventive and organizational aspects are involved. The Council of Europe has made in various ways a contribution to the level of instruction and knowledge throughout Europe.

Thus the instruction and education of nurses is the subject of European Agreement no. 59 of 1967. Also recommendations and, or resolutions have been drawn up on various subjects as training and equivalence of qualifications of, respectively, medical laboratory technicians and midwives; instruction in blood transfusion; training of medical students in public health and the regrouping and upgrading in paramedical professions.

Resolution (77) 30 deals with 'the general practitioner, his training, and ways of stimulating interest in his vocation'. This resolution is of particular interest, because whereas, though the free movement of doctors has become a reality within the European Community, the Community has not yet succeeded in harmonizing specific professional education requirements for the general practitioners. The Council of Europe resolution on the other hand contains requirements for basic, professional, and postgraduate training as well as for other items such as means for quality control and improvement.

An individual medical fellowships programme enables members of the medical and related professions as well as public health officials to keep abreast of the latest developments in their respective fields. This programme is closely linked with the fellowships schemes of the World Health Organization.

European blood transfusion courses and courses on histocompatability are organized for the same purpose.

3.2.3. Evaluation of the public health activities of the European public health committee

When reviewing the evolution of activities of the European public health committee since their beginning one may conclude that activities related to the use of blood and blood products have become the most outstanding ones. They are in line with the latest developments in this field. Relevant progress is closely followed and tested on the possible application in member states. Every aspect in this field which is suitable for international co-operation is taken up by the responsible expert committee. The Council of Europe usefully complements in this respect the work performed by the World Health Organization. The latter has only few occupations connected with blood and could not, even if these were extended, easily yield the same results.

Education and training activities are performed as part of the present national and international trends in this field; they follow their normal course.

In the field of the other activities, however, one may note a considerable change of approach since the last few years. Attention is increasingly focused upon the social aspects of health care: the place of the patient in the whole system of health care and the harmful, physical and mental effects from society on the individual are gaining in importance, along with developments of national philosophies in this respect. Prevention of illness, prevention of excessive use of medical resources and humanization of medical care have a high priority.[84]

It might be concluded that here the international action, though slow, is not, as often assumed, lagging behind.

3.3. GOVERNMENTAL ACTIVITIES AFFECTING ALL MEMBER STATES
European committee on legal co-operation; European committee on crime problems

Not only the more general aspects of public health, directed towards the development of international policy, receive attention. The purely legal aspects of health care are also receiving increasingly attention primarily under the responsibility of the European committee on legal co-operation, which for this purpose works in close co-operation with the European public health committee.

Among these legal activities, the legal aspects of drugs and the right to treatment and the right to refuse treatment (in the framework of studies on treatment methods for alcoholism) have been studied. Another example is Resolution (78) 29 which deals with the harmonization of legislation of member states relating to removal, grafting and transplantation of human substances. Other activities of the European committee on legal co-operation are those on the international exchange and transport of human substances, artificial insemination of human beings and data protection (a study on regulations for medical data banks) is being carried out. The 1979 programme will include the subject legal problems in the field of medicine; it is suggested to set up a committee of experts (legal and medical) to draw up standard legislation on several of these legal problems among which the physicians' liability, as well as on problems relating to various aspects of the human rights under review (see below para. 4.).

Yet other activities are carried out under the responsibility of the European committee on crime problems, particularly in the field of drug dependence (see, for instance, Resolution (73) 6, (76) 38, (78) 11 and (78) 12).

3.4. GOVERNMENTAL ACTIVITIES AFFECTING PART OF THE MEMBER STATES
Partial Agreement in the field of public health

3.4.1. Introduction
The creation of the Partial Agreement in the field of public health was a historical result of the Brussels Treaty of 1948. With a view to give effect to article II of this Treaty (as far as the public health field was concerned) a

---

84. Examples are the studies on 'the problems related to death'; 'the patient as an active participant in his own treatment' and 'review of self-treatment habits'.

committee of experts had been set up in July 1948 to discuss legislation on public health, to organize exchange of medical personnel, to implement recommendations from the World Health Organization and to decide the best means of combating epidemics and disease.

The Brussels Treaty was revised and extended on 23 October 1954 to include the Federal Republic of Germany and Italy. These countries then formed together with the members of the former Brussels Treaty (Belgium, France, Luxemburg, the Netherlands and the United Kingdom) the Western European Union.

The latter organization continued the activities in the field of public health of the Brussels Treaty.

Following a recommendation contained in a report on the rationalization of European institutions, which had been prepared by a special committee, certain activities (including those on social matters) were transferred from the Western European Union to the Council of Europe. This decision was taken in common agreement between both organizations (decision of 21 October 1959 of the Western European Union and Resolution (59) 23 adopted by the Committee of Ministers of the Council of Europe on 16 November 1959) with a view to avoiding duplication of activities and to simplifying work.

Already in 1949 the Consultative Assembly of the Council of Europe had insisted, during its second session, on such a decision. The members of the Brussels Treaty, however, did not at that time favour a transfer of activities.

This transfer of social activities implied the transfer of a number of highly specialised committees whose work covered many questions on which the members of the Western European Union had reached an exactly comparable degree of development which only a few other member states of the Council of Europe were at the time in a position to approach, or on which other studies were proceeding at regional level, as was the case in the Scandinavian countries.

Two fields of activities of the Western European Union in the health field were not transferred to the Council of Europe, namely those on the health aspects of the peaceful use of atomic energy (these were sufficiently covered by other organizations), and those on health aspects of civil defence, which were transferred to NATO. The other activities (health control of foodstuffs, pharmaceutical questions, poisonous substances in agriculture, essential drugs, cancer statistics, industrial safety and health as well as rehabilitation and resettlement of the disabled) were all transferred to the Partial Agreement of the Council of Europe.

The committee responsible for the public health activities under the Partial Agreement is the public health committee of the Partial Agreement.

The working methods applied under the Brussels Treaty and later on the Western European Union were continued under the Partial Agreement. One of these special methods was the undertaking by the contracting parties to promote progress in social matters by 'direct consultation'. This method of 'direct consultation' was put into effect by creating 'liaison sections' in the national ministries, to arrange exchange of doctors, of legal and statistical information, of information on epidemics and to work together on tuberculosis, venereal diseases, readaptation of the handicapped and on drug traffic.

This procedure departs from the traditional way of relations through the channels of foreign ministries. In this way delegates themselves — and not their secretariat — were enabled to plan research, to publish reports, etc. for presentation to governments.

The advantage of such a system lies in the fact that in a simplified way without the need to sign an international instrument similar sets of rules are adopted and methods of work and regulations are harmonized often by way of written 'administrative arrangements'.

This in fact contributes to the efficacy of the attempt to develop on corresponding lines the social and related services.

An example of such an 'administrative arrangement', which does not require the signatures of the states adhering to it, is the 'administrative arrangements for the health control of sea, air and land traffic' (1950).

It creates moreover the possibility of swift and continuing contact between the liaison sections of the respective ministries, which is essential in the joint compaign against epidemics and disease. Furthermore, relevant national documents are continuously communicated to each other, which contributes to international co-ordination of national procedures.

Besides these 'administrative arrangements' the traditional method of intergovernmental co-operation through conventions and agreements is also applied by the members of the Partial Agreement.

3.4.2. Programme of work
a. pharmaceutical field

Activities on pharmaceutical questions are by far the most significant ones of the public health committee of the Partial Agreement. The most important achievement in this field is the Convention on the elaboration of a European Pharmacopoeia from 22 July 1964 which will be made up of international monographs. The specifications laid down in these texts are mandatory for the states which are parties to the Convention.

The parties to this Convention are, to date, Belgium, Cyprus, Denmark, France, the Federal Republic of Germany, Iceland, Italy, Luxemburg, Netherlands, Norway, Sweden, Switzerland and the United Kingdom; Austria, Finland and Ireland participate as observers, pending the promulgation of national legislation enabling them to become signatories.

So far three volumes of the Pharmacopoeia have been published. The establishment of the European Pharmacopoeia is a valuable safeguard for public health in matters concerning the use of medicines, facilitating at the same time the circulation of medicines between countries, which in the absence of any international standard was rather complicated.

Technical and procedural matters arising from the elaboration of the European Pharmacopoeia fall within the competence of the European pharmacopoeia commission, which was established by virtue of the Convention.

The detailed work of elaborating the standards is carried out by over fifteen groups of experts. All other decisions which are taken by the commission in this respect (such as the date at which the monographs shall become legally

186

enforceable within member states) are subject to approval by those members of the public health committee of the Partial Agreement who are representatives of the contracting parties to the Convention.

Beside these activities aiming at the international harmonization of specification, various other activities have been deployed in this field. There are, for instance, various resolutions on items such as quality of drugs; control of public drug advertising; marketing of new drugs of the type of barbiturates, tranquillisers, hypnotics and neuroplegics; adverse reactions to drugs and the classification of medicines which are obtainable only on medical prescription. Furthermore a report on adverse reactions to drugs and two pharmaceutical reference books have been published (the Lexicum Pharmaceuticum and a yearly revised booklet on addiction-producing substances currently on the market).

b. health protection

The activities include the already mentioned administrative arrangements for the health control of sea, air and land traffic. Under these arrangements the participating countries are considered to form one geographical area (the so-called excepted area) for the application of the directions under the arrangements. These arrangements facilitate in fact the application of the World Health Organization's International Health Regulations in applying article 92 of these Regulations. A yearly handbook of sea and airports in the excepted areas is published.

The European Agreement on 'the restriction of the use of certain detergents in washing and cleaning products' (1968) is another example of achievements in this field.

c. health control of foodstuffs

Activities in this area are, for example, those on agricultural pesticides, food additives and plastics packaging material. Studies on these problems resulted in various publications and recommendations, including a resolution on antibiotics which could be included in animal feedingstuffs to stimulate growth and antibiotics which should only be used for therapeutic purposes.

d. epidemiology

Demographic studies and immunization programmes are receiving full attention in this field. Hereditary diseases, congenital anomalies and malformation and numerous fatal and, or contagious diseases are included in this part of the programme.

The available medical statistics and other information pertaining to these problems are used by Governments for prevention purposes. Also the practice followed by the members of the Western European Union, whereby current exchange of information on laws, regulations and other texts relating to the public health took place, is continued under the Partial Agreement.

3.4.3. Evaluation of the public health activities under the Partial Agreement
When comparing the activities of the public health committee of the Partial

Agreement with those at the level of all member states one notes that the programme of work of the first is primarily focused upon a limited number of scientific, technical and practical matters for which the countries participating in the Partial Agreement need to find immediate solutions at more or less the same time. The procedure of direct consultation and the possibilities of swift action are very advantageous in this respect.

The European public health committee on the other hand covers a much wider field and focuses also much attention on problems of a more general, policy development and structure oriented nature. Another noticable evolution is that, since its creation, the scope of the Partial Agreement has expanded to include the great majority of member states of the Council of Europe so that gradually the original basis for this Partial Agreement has become less relevant.

3.5. PARLIAMENTARY ACTIVITIES

The description of activities of the Council of Europe in the field of public health would be incomplete without mentioning the activities of the Parliamentary Assembly.

The general role of this body was already discussed in para. 2.2.b. It was indicated there that the Assembly has formed various committees. These committees, charged with the preparation of work in special fields, do not have a precise mandate.

They examine — within their subject field — documents forwarded by the Office of the Clerk (mostly documents originating from the Committee of Ministers and from other international organizations). The committees have also to examine every item delegated to them by the Parliamentary Assembly in preparation for the discussions in that body (mostly by preparing documents on specific subjects) and to supervise the follow-up of recommendations and resolutions of that body.

As far as the activities in the field of health are concerned, various subjects have been studied by the competent committee, the committee on social and health questions, leading very often to recommendations and, or further action by the Committee of Ministers, as, for instance, on subjects such as noise abatement, food protection, public health problems affecting the free movement of workers in Europe, the protection of workers against the risk of atomic radiation, preventive medicine and the European Pharmacopoeia.

Other activities include those on dental health (see Recommendation 837 of July 1978 and doc. 4180) and on cancer control (see Recommendation 836 of July 1978 and doc. 4133). The committee has also appointed a special subcommittee to deal with drug addiction.[85]

Moreover, on the initiative of the committee several symposia were convened including one on public health in 1971 and one on drug dependence in 1972.

85. There is close co-operation with the Assembly's legal affairs committee which also deals with this subject (see, for instance, docs. 4202 and 4203 of September 1978).

In para. 4. the contribution of the Parliamentary Assembly to the rights under review will be dealt with.

4. Council of Europe and human rights

The formulation on the right to health care in Article 11 of the European Social Charter[86] is the most direct contribution of the Organization to the realization of this right.

The implementation of the relevant Article falls, however, entirely outside the scope of the European public health committee. The reporting system is limited to a special committee of experts, composed of members of recognised competence in international *social* questions (Articles 24 and 25 of the Charter) and to a subcommittee of the governmental *social* committee of the Council of Europe (Article 27 of the Charter).[87] No member of the European public health committee is associated (in his capacity as expert in health questions) with these committees. The only direct manner in which attention may be drawn to particular health problems in relation to Article 11 of the Social Charter is through the Parliamentary Assembly, which also receives reports on the implementation of the Charter (Article 28 of the Charter). (The parliamentary committee on social and health questions has appointed a special subcommittee on the European Social Charter.)

The European public health committee seems, however, to be in a position to make a useful contribution to stimulating the application of the said Article.

The committee could well study periodic national reports on the follow-up given to Article 11 and, where appropriate, draw up recommendations on basis of such a study. In addition, the committee could usefully apply information derived from national reports to its own programme of work. It is recognized that the success of such a system depends entirely on the extent to which parties to the Charter live up to their obligation of reporting, but there seems still no reason not to associate the most competent committee with the implementation of Article 11 of the Social Charter.

There are adequate procedures created by the Council of Europe to safeguard those human rights which have a direct bearing on the realization of the right to health care (right to life and prohibition of torture and experimentation without free consent of the person concerned).[88] The European Convention on the Protection of Human Rights and Fundamental Freedoms as well as the legal methods of control of this Convention, are the most significant direct contribution of the Organization to the safeguarding of these rights.[89]

It is to be regretted that also in this respect there is no link with the European public health committee.

86. See Part A, Ch. II, para. 4.3.
87. See Part A, Ch. I, para. 2.4.3.
88. See Part A, Ch. II, para. 1.3. and 2.3.
89. See Part A, Ch. I, para. 2.3.3.

However, as the committee on legal co-operation is recently becoming more involved in fields related to these rights and has for this purpose established close working relations with the European public health committee, it might be expected, that the multi-disciplinary approach necessary for the optimal implementation and further elaboration of the human rights discussed here, will evolve with the years to come. [90] Some of the activities of the European committee on legal co-operation in respect of legal problems in the medical field were indicated in para. 3.3. In addition we should mention the project to tackle items such as:
— intervention or non-intervention in the process of death;
— experiments on man;
— genetic engineering.

Another subject which might possibly be dealt with in a standard setting instrument is the protection of the patients' rights. This subject has been proposed both by the Parliamentary Assembly (Recommendation 779 (1976) on the rights of the sick and dying) and the fifth colloquy on European law held in 1975 under the auspices of the Council of Europe on the subject of 'civil liability of physicians'.

Some of the rights which might be considered in this context are:
— the right to information;
— the right that no medical action should be carried out without the consent of the person concerned;
— free choice of physician;
— the right to obtain treatment and, in particular, to benefit from new forms of treatment;
— the right to professional secrecy.

Moreover, yet another intergovernmental committee of the Council of Europe, the European Committee on Crime Problems, has drawn up minimum rules for the treatment of prisoners (Resolution (73) 5). One of the principles on which these rules are founded is that conditions of detention must be compatible with human dignity. In these rules hygiene standards are laid down; a special section deals with insane prisoners. The implementation of this resolution is being examined with a view to make proposals for the revision of the rules to bring them into line with the requirements of present-day penal policy.

Further to ECOSOC Resolution 1159 (XLI) of 5 August 1966, the Council of Europe also regularly provides the commission on human rights of the UN with the information on the activities of the Council of Europe in the field of human rights, so that also in this respect necessary relations are safeguarded.

(The co-existence of the UN international covenants and the Council of Europe human rights instruments and possible difficulties arising therefrom also receive full attention in this framework.)

Finally, the Parliamentary Assembly plays an active role in the field of these human rights as was already mentioned in para. 3.5. [91] Co-operation

90. See also Part A, Ch. II, para. 5.
91. See also Part A, Ch. II, para. 3.

with the World Health Organizations regional office for Europe is pursued in this respect as may be seen from Assembly Resolution 613 (1976) on the rights of the sick and dying.

Though Recommendation 779 (1976), which deals with the subject, calls upon member states to establish ethical rules for the treatment of persons approaching the end of life and to establish national commissions of enquiry, neither the Recommendation nor the Resolution contains a recommendation for establishing international criteria on this subject through the Council of Europe or the WHO regional office for Europe. On the other hand, it remains significant that, despite the fact that the various recommendations were only a weak extract of the report they were based upon (doc. 3699), in dealing among other items with such a controversial subject as euthanasia, these recommendations could be voted by an international forum. This emphasizes the point that where global agreement on specific subjects seems to be out of reach, regional efforts may well succeed. Another example of the activities of the Assembly is Recommendation 818 (1977) on the situation of the mentally ill.

This Recommendation is based on a report from the committee on social and health questions which deals with questions relating to the medical, social and legal situation of the mentally ill with a special emphasis on the question of internment (doc. 4014).[92]

The Recommendation is destined for national governments only, and no use has been made of the opportunity to recommend either the Committee of Ministers of the Council of Europe or the WHO regional office for Europe, to draw up an international instrument containing principles and guidelines on this specific aspect of human rights.

It cannot be denied, however, that both the resolution and the recommendation of the Parliamentary Assembly are an important contribution to necessary international action in respect of setting up internationl codes for various aspects of the human rights under discussion.

Yet another Parliamentary contribution to the present subject is Recommendation 768 (1975) which deals with torture in the world. [93]

92. One of the items dealt with in the document is that the patient's consent is the legal basis for hospitalization and for his medical treatment. In the case of mental patients there is a limitation to the principle of consent in that their ability to consent freely to hospitalization is doubtful. In this particular situation the medical doctor has to 'notify the judicial authorities of any restrictions of freedom ordered by him for therapeutic purposes, without reference to the criterion of the patient's consent' (p. 5). The recommendation itself not only calls for better medical provisions for the mentally ill but also for furtherance of the human rights which apply to all citizens and to which no exceptions are allowed in cases of mental patients (revision of legislation and administrative rules on the confinement of the mentally ill for the purpose of, for instance, reducing to the minimum the practice of compulsory detention, right to be heard, right to vote, and so on).
93. See also Part A, Ch. II, para. 3.2.2.

5. Some conclusions

It will be clear form the brief review of activities at the level of all member states that the European public health committee is alert to the particular problems which European countries at present are facing in the field of health. Its broad scope of past and present activities underlines the interest of international activities in this field, and also the need which still exists to complement the work of the World Health Organization in the European region.

The co-operation between both organizations has proved to be successful and the complementary aspect of the activities performed within the Council of Europe clearly meets an existing need. Whereas the World Health Organization operates on a purely technical level, the political aspect of the Council of Europe, through its possible influence in national parliaments, can usefully stimulate international decision making.

Also the worldwide character of the WHO, with its inherent weakness, restrains the Organization in its legislative possibilities, so that despite the far-reaching decentralization of the Organization, much work is more usefully undertaken within a regional organization. Moreover, because of the present tendency of the WHO to focus attention primarily outside the European region, the Council of Europe can usefully fill a possible gap.

The complementarity of various activities in the field of public health is also relevant within the Organization itself: the co-operation between the purely legally orientated expert committee and the committee which is more generally orientated has proved to be a very useful element in intergovernmental co-operation.

Furthermore, there are the obvious advantages of the system of 'direct consultation' applied under the Partial Agreement in the field of public health, as was already emphasized.

The efficiency of this system, which can only be successful if applied between countries which are at very much the same level of social progress and technical organization, guarantees benefits to the individual countries, as well as optimal co-ordination between the participating states. Activities under this scheme are, however, limited to a certain number of technical subjects only.

It remains questionable whether the co-operation in the field of public health on two different levels within one organization, as is the case in the Council of Europe, is still sufficiently justified.

It might well be that it is now time to integrate both kinds of co-operation in the health field into one. Besides the intricacy inherent to the functioning of two systems operating on different lines within one organization, which makes it difficult for an outsider to grasp its contents, it is a fact that the development in social and economical level of the member states of the Council of Europe has, since its creation, been such that differences, though still not to be neglected, are much less than when the Organization was created.

The gradual extension of activities of the Partial Agreement either in full or in part to more member countries of the Organization since its creation is a significant indication in this direction. The reasons which brought the Committee of Ministers in 1951 to their resolution on the institution of Partial Agreements in order to avoid the possible deadlock of Article 20 (a) of the Statute seems to be overtaken by this extension.

The integration of both kinds of activities naturally implies the acceptance of the system of direct consultation by all member countries. The efficacy of this method of work, which has been clearly proven along the years, justifies such an acceptance and will prevail over possible political contrary arguments.

Integration under these conditions will, moreover, have the advantage that the positive aspects of the co-operation under the Partial Agreement, as, for instance, in the case of administrative arrangements, will more or less counterbalance the aspect of relative weakness inherent in intergovernmental co-operation in the nature of the Council of Europe.

The contribution of the Parliamentary Assembly to international public health has gained in importance over the past years in particular regarding the establishment of guiding principles for specific aspects of the human rights, which are under review.

Subjects of actual interest are discussed in this forum, so that the interest of the national parliamentarians is raised and the public opinion stimulated. Moreover, the Assembly has taken important initiatives, which have often been followed by the Committee of Ministers.

The simultaneous undertaking of activities in the public health field at governmental and at parliamentary level is in principle an effective system within an international organization. Not only will this have a stimulating effect, but a useful complementary factor is also brought about by such a system because, though the aim is similar, the approach is, however, rather different.

Whenever relevant, initiatives may be taken over by the one or the other. On the whole, it might be said that the usefulness of the organization – besides its work in the field of human rights – lies mainly in the many contacts on ministerial level, as well as on the level of governmental experts on the one side and on the parliamentary level on the other, from which either initiatives in public health at national level may stem or useful international contacts may be initiated and co-ordination may be stimulated.

Its weakness, however, is in its very construction which hinders the decision-making process, and which is only partially neutralised by its function as a place for discussion on international level on public health subjects of current interest. Also the Committee of Ministers has only a limited decision-making power. This aspect of weakness finds expression in the numerous recommendations stemming from the Organization, which are only morally binding upon its member states.

On the other hand, it cannot be denied that these recommendations in the field of public health contribute largely to the policy-making on national level and that the Council of Europe contributes considerably to technical harmonization and standardization on many public health subjects and permits useful discussions at international level.

IV. Other organizations in Europe

1. Introduction

In the previous chapters the international organizations with major health functions in the European Region (the WHO and the Council of Europe) were analysed. There is also a certain number of international organizations with objectives which have consequences at random for the international health field and which are, as such, of importance for European co-operation in this respect. These organizations carry out activities in the field of health restricted to specific areas such as occupational health, health aspects of foodstuffs, health education and atomic radiation. The realization of the right to health care is not among the objectives of these organizations. Their activities which have some bearing on this human right are all part of other objectives.

Most of these organizations were mentioned before, when dealing with the task of co-ordination and co-operation of the WHO (Ch. I, para. 5., Ch. II, para. 2.5.) and of the Council of Europe (Ch. III, para. 2.5.). The co-operation of the WHO with members of the United Nations family, which have regional (European) activities (ILO, FAO, UNESCO and IAEA) was mentioned, as well as the co-operation on a European level with some other organizations (the UN institutions ECE, UNDP and the UN Children's Fund as well as the European Community).

The latter organization will be given more ample consideration in para. 2. below because of its very nature (supranational), which makes it suitable for contributing in an effective manner to the promotion of the human rights which are under discussion. Furthermore, the Organisation for Economic Co-operation and Development (OECD) and the North Atlantic Treaty Organization (NATO), will be briefly discussed (paras. 3. and 4.). These organizations, though not operating on a strictly European scale, are rather European oriented.

In para. 5. the European Free Trade Association (EFTA) will be dealt with, while in paras. 6. and 7. two regional arrangements with activities which have implications for the health sector, namely the Benelux Economic Union and the Nordic Council, will be given some attention.

2. European Community (EC)

2.1. INTRODUCTORY REMARKS

As a supranational organization the EC has in principle all the pre-requisites to contribute effectively to the promotion of public health in Europe. It is the only international body able to enact legislation directly binding on its member states and also, in some cases, on their citizens. It is therefore worth-while

194

to give some consideration to the activities of this Organization which bear on the field of health, despite the fact that it has not included in its Constitutionary texts health care and the promotion of health as a direct objective: the integration of a general, overall public health policy is not provided for in the Treaties establishing the three Communities composing the European Community: the European Coal and Steal Community (ECSC) of 1951, the European Economic Community (EEC) of 1957 and the European Atomic Energy Community (EAEC) of 1957.[94]

Moreover, the field of health care is certainly a field of concern to the Community, as is shown already by the fact that since 1977 the ministers for public health of the member states and the Commission of the European Communities have met once a year to discuss on various problems of major importance. [95]

The European Community covers the following member states: Belgium, Denmark, France, the Federal Republic of Germany, Ireland, Italy, Luxemburg, the Netherlands and the United Kingdom.

Since 8 April 1965 the three European Communities have a single Council of Ministers [96], a single Commission [96], a single European Parliament [97] and a single European Court of Justice. [97]

The Council of Ministers is composed of one representative for each member country. It is charged with the co-ordination of action of the member states and of the Community, in particular regarding the general economic policy of the member states. It has in most cases decision-making power (Article 26 of the ECSC Treaty, Article 145 of the EEC Treaty, Article 115 of the EAEC Treaty and Article 1 of the Merger Treaty of the EC).

The Commission, which is composed of thirteen members, is the daily executive body of the Organization (Article 1 of the ECSC Treaty, Article 155 of the EEC Treaty, Article 124 of the EAEC Treaty and Article 9 of the 1965 Treaty). It is responsible for drafting legislative acts and negotiates on the conclusion of agreements between the Community and other international organizations. Such agreements are concluded by the Council.

The European Parliament is the supervisory and advisory body, in which deliberations on all important subjects regarding the Treaties take place (Article 20 of the ECSC Treaty, Article 137 of the EEC Treaty, Article 107 of the EAEC Treaty and Articles 1 and 2 of the 1965 Convention).

Among the powers of the European Parliament are: the right to be consulted and informed about Community legislation; the right to question the Commission and Council (power of control) and the right to criticize the Commission and Council for the action they are taking or failing to take in pursuing Community policies. It has, moreover, the right to propose to the Council modifications to the draft budget of the Community and in some

94. Chapter III of the EAEC Treaty deals with 'health and safety', but it is limited to one aspect only, namely basic standards within the Community for the protection of the health of workers and the general public against the dangers arising from ionizing radiation.
95. See also Part C, Ch. II, para. 1.4.
96. Treaty establishing a Single Council and a Single Commission of the European Communities.
97. Convention on certain Institutions common to the European Communities.

cases a right of amendment in respect of expenditure other than that necessarily resulting from the EEC Treaty (see Articles 203 and 203a).

One of the twelve specialist committees of the European Parliament, in which a detailed analysis of the Commission's proposals is made, is the commission on environment, public health and consumer protection.

The European Court has been assigned the task of ensuring that in the interpretation and application of the Treaties the law is observed (Article 31 of the ECSC Treaty, Article 164 of the EEC Treaty, Article 136 of the EAEC Treaty and Articles 3 and 4 of the 1965 Convention).

To carry out their tasks, the Council and the Commission make regulations, issue directives, take decisions, make recommendations or deliver opinions (Article 14 of the ECSC Treaty [98], Article 189 of the EEC Treaty, Article 161 of the EAEC Treaty and Articles 1 and 9 of the 1965 Treaty).

Regulations have general application and are directly applicable in all member states. Directives are binding as to the results to be achieved, the form and methods of their implementation being left to the national authorities to which they are addressed. Decisions are binding upon those to whom whey are addressed, while recommendations and opinions have no binding force.

Relationships with other organizations are mainly covered by Articles 93 and 94 of the ECSC Treaty, Articles 229-231 of the EEC Treaty [99] and Articles 199-201 of the EAEC Treaty. The relations with the WHO regional office for Europe and the Council of Europe were dealt with previously (Ch. II, para. 2.5. and Ch. III, para. 2.5. respectively).

Article 233 of the EEC Treaty refers to the Benelux Economic Union (see also para. 6. below).

Of the countries participating in the Nordic co-operation (see para. 7.), Norway, Sweden, Iceland and Finland have separate agreements with the Community.

It would be outside the scope of the present study to describe at length the position, functions and methods of work of the various organs of the EC. The following is therefore limited to a general review of the various activities with implications for health and health care, undertaken in the framework of the three European Communities, of which those of the EEC are the most significant ones.

2.2. ACTIVITIES WITH IMPLICATIONS FOR HEALTH AND HEALTH CARE

The Three European Communities have some common broad objectives, among which are the following:
— promotion of the harmonious development of economic expansion;

98. The ECSC Treaty only knows decisions (binding in their entirety), recommendations (binding as to the aims to be pursued, the choice of the appropriate methods for achieving these aims being left to those to whom the recommendations are addressed) and opinions (no binding force).
99. See also part C, Ch. II, para. 2.3.

— raising of the standard of living (Article 2 of the Treaties of the ECSC and of the EEC and Article 1 of the EAEC Treaty).

These objectives are pursued through various activities, which include those given in Article 3 of the Treaties of the ECSC and of the EEC and Article 2 of the EAEC Treaty.

Activities in the field of health within the three Communities are not coherent, are mainly undertaken as marginal activities in the context of the objectives of the three Communities, and are, therefore, based on a variety of articles of the respective Treaties. Yet one may distinguish four broad categories of activities with implications for health and health care, starting from the objectives mentioned above and mainly on basis of the tasks given in the Articles indicated above. These categories of activities, which take primarily place in the framework of the EEC, are as follows:

Category I. Free circulation of goods

The protection of health calls for strict quality requirements for goods destined to circulate freely within the Community, in particular foodstuffs and pharmaceuticals. Therefore a whole range of directives has been issued for the purpose of approximation of laws based on Article 100 of the EEC Treaty.[100] These measures are also concerned with health and safety control for imports coming from third countries.

In the field of foodstuffs, harmonization of legislation includes, for instance, requirements for composition, packaging, labelling and distribution, so that foodstuffs conform to high uniform standards. Measures for the hygiene of foodstuffs and food additives (such as colouring matters, preservatives and antioxidants) are also laid down in some detail. A list of food additives which are permitted at Community level has, for instance, been elaborated. Furthermore, a directive on diet food has been issued (Directive 77/94/EEC, OJ 1977, L 26/55). A scientific committee for pesticides has been assigned the task of considering, among other matters, questions relating to health protection (Decision 78/436/EEC, OJ 1978, L 124/16).

The efforts which have been undertaken in the pharmaceutical sector have not yet resulted in a common market, though it was the intention to have such a market realized as early as the first of January 1970. The first Directive in this field dates from 1965: Directive 65/65/EEC (OJ 369/65)[101] relates to proprietary medicinal products. This Directive requires products to be authorized by a competent authority of a member state before they are marketed; it lays down the requirements to be satisfied for each product authorized; it

100. These activities may be seen as forming part of the efforts of the EEC for consumer protection. In this latter framework a preliminary programme for a consumer protection and information policy was adopted by the Council through its Resolution of 14 April 1975 (OJ 1975, C 92/1). (See also: Commission of the European Communities, consumer protection and information policy, first report, 1977.) This preliminary programme sets out principles, objectives and a general description of action to be taken in this respect at Community level. The right to the protection of health and safety is named as one of the five basic rights on which consumer protection is based. One of the objectives of Community policy towards consumers is to secure effective protection against hazards to consumer health and safety.
101. Amended by Directive 66/454/EEC (OJ 2658/66).

establishes the conditions for suspension and revocation and it lays down requirements for the labelling of products. In 1975 two further Directives were adopted, namely Directive 75/318/EEC (OJ 1975, L 147/1) and Directive 75/319/EEC (OJ 1975, L 147/13).[102] The first Directive lays down uniform rules for tests and trials, the compilation of dossiers and the examination of applications for authorizations to market products. For the purpose of quality control of the proprietary medicinal products the Council of Europe European Pharmacopoeia shall be applicable to all substances appearing in this Directive.

The second Directive aims to facilitate authorizations to market products in more than one member state. It establishes a committee for proprietary products to give opinions on whether particular products comply with the requirements of Directive 65/65/EEC; it lays down procedures to be followed for a product to be authorized for marketing in more than one country and it requires manufacturers and importers of products to be subject to authorizations and requires such manufacturers and importers to have at their disposal qualified persons with responsibilities to secure and certify that products manufactured or imported meet the quality standards required.[103] The international non-proprietary names recommended by the WHO should, in accordance with this Directive, be used, where such names exist, in the leaflets enclosed with the packaging of a proprietary medicinal product.

With Decision 75/320/EEC a pharmaceutical committee has been set up to examine any question relating to the application of Directives on proprietary medicinal products and any other questions in the field of proprietary medicinal products. The committee also advises on proposals for new Directives.

Directive 78/25/EEC (OJ 1978, L 11/18) relates to authorized colouring matters in respect of medicines. There are, moreover, various proposals pending before the Council of Ministers, such as one on advertising and one which relates to a new marketing procedure for proprietary medicinal products.

The classification of dangerous substances and the medical apparatus and equipment are other examples of subjects which are of concern to the EEC and which fall under the present category.

Category II. Free movement of persons

The free movement of workers is subject to Articles 48-51 of the EEC Treaty. Measures relating to the free movement of workers are relevant for those members of the medical, pharmaceutical and allied professions who are in employment. The free movement of the self-employed is subject to Articles 52-58 of the EEC Treaty (right to establishment).

Unlike the provisions covering employees, the provisions on the self-employed comprise the issue of directives for the mutual recognition of diplomas, certificates and other evidence of formal qualifications (Article 57, para. 1 of the Treaty). The progressive abolition of restrictions on the establishment of members of the medical, pharmaceutical and allied professions is, however,

---

102. Amended by Directive 78/420/EEC (OJ 1978, L 123/26).
103. See p. 37 of doc. SEC (78) 3864 on pharmaceutical consumption.

made dependent upon prior co-ordination of the conditions for the exercise of these professions in the various member states (Article 57, para. 3 of the Treaty).

In *Medisch Contact* (32, 1977, pp. 1192-1196) it is stated that the latter clause implies in the first instance the need for the co-ordination of systems of health care within equivalent systems of social security, then the equivalence, and finally the equality of these systems (p. 1193). I would not stress this point of view, because the 'co-ordination of conditions for exercise' as meant in Article 57, para. 3 in my view refers in particular to the co-ordination of requirements for taking up, and pursuing activities by the self-employed (Article 57, para. 2), and therefore refers in the first instance to the co-ordination of training systems. The paragraph under discussion only refers to facilitating the right of establishment, while guaranteeing at the same time the quality of services rendered. It cannot therefore be interpreted in such a way that the standardization of systems of health care (and social security) is first needed for ensuring the right of establishment to the professions involved, though it is recognized that the harmonization of social systems is one of the objectives of the social policy of the EEC (see, for instance, Articles 117 and 118 of the Treaty). In fact, this kind of standardization is in itself not a condition for exercising the medical, pharmaceutical and allied professions, which depends rather on the legal requirements for, for instance, qualification. This point of view is supported by various remarks of the Commission in the European Parliament. For example, it was stated during the session of the Parliament on 7 March 1977 that the Commission was 'seeking to achieve harmonisation in the area of social security, but this should not be interpreted as an attempt to standardise the various systems' and that 'the Commission has no intention of providing a comprehensive Community health service, which ... would have to replace existing national systems.
The Commission will, however, attempt to improve the health care of the citizens of the Community by co-ordinating and harmonising certain existing arrangements' (Official Journal of the EC, Annex, nr. 213, March 1977, debates of the European Parliament, 1976-1977 Session, report of proceedings on 7 March 1977). Furthermore, in reply to a written question (nr. 881/76) the Commission informed the European Parliament that it was not the objective to harmonize through the Directives relating to doctors (see below) the manner in which particular forms of medicine were practised in member states. The European Commission considered this primarily a matter of national conception on public health policy and does not consider it opportune to start the harmonization of the practice of medicine through the rules in the Treaty on the right to establishment and mutual recognition of diplomas.

Article 54, para. 3 of the Treaty stipulates that, as a general rule, priority will be given to those fields where freedom of establishment makes a particularly valuable contribution to the development of production and trade. The medical, pharmaceutical and allied professions can hardly be said to fall within this priority matter. However, directives concerning these professions have been issued as a priority matter. Van Nieuwenhuizen (*Medisch Contact* 28, 1973, pp. 605-615) presumes that this has been done to give a demonstration of European unity in this particular field which does not exist elsewhere, and which lies outside the (preponderant) economic activities of the Community. There might be other reasons, however, to explain this priority treatment, such as a shortage of the members of these professions in some member states, and a surplus in others, or just considerations of a mere practical, technical nature (such as shortterm feasibility).

Though employed doctors fall under the terms of the various directives and regulations issued under Articles 48-51 of the EEC Treaty, one of these regulations, namely Council Regulation EEC no. 1612/68 of 15 October 1968 (OJ 1968, L 257/2; free movement for workers within the Community), did not include specific provisions relating to subjects such as professional discipline or the use of title for the professions concerned for the very reason that these Articles did not contain such a condition. However, in member states such rules are or may be applicable both to employed and self-employed persons. Also in all member states the activities of doctors, either employed or self-employed, are subject to the possession of a diploma, certificate or other evidence of formal qualifications in medicine. Therefore, in order to encourage as far as possible the free movement of those professional persons within the Community and further to the advice of the European Parliament, Directives 75/362/EEC and 75/363/EEC of 16 June 1975 (OJ 1975, L 167/1 and L 167/14) on the right of establishment and freedom to provide services in respect of doctors in the Community, are equally extended to employed doctors. The first of these Directives, which both became effective on 1 January 1977, provides for the mutual recognition of diplomas, certificates and other evidence of formal qualifications in medicine, including measures to facilitate the effective exercise of the right of establishment and freedom to provide services. The second Directive pertains to the co-ordination of provisions laid down by law, regulation or administrative action in respect of the activities of doctors.

Also on 16 June 1975 two Decisions were taken: Decision 75/364/EEC setting up an advisory committee on medical training and Decision 75/365/EEC setting up a committee of senior officials on public health (OJ 1975, L 167/17 and L 167/19). The first committee is to help to ensure a high comparable level of training in the Community both for general practitioners and for specialists. To this end it exchanges information and holds consultations on all aspects of doctors' training. The second committee is responsible for noting and analysing any difficulties which might arise from the implementation of the Directive concerning the right of establishment of doctors, and for compiling information and delivering opinions on matters coming within the scope of the Directive. [104] The elaboration of the Directives has been much influenced by various international, non-governmental, European organizations of doctors, such as the European Union of general practitioners (UEMO), the European Union of Specialists, the European association of 'staff doctors' and the Hospital Committee of the International Hospital Federation. The objective of Directive 75/362/EEC is not to achieve the scientific equivalence of the educational level of doctors in the Community, but rather to give a European legal effect to national qualifications necessary for permission to practice the medical profession (*Europese Gemeenschap*, November 1976, p. 22).

Directive 75/363/EEC makes the mutual recognition of diplomas depen-

104. Decision 77/455/EEC of 27 June 1977 and Decision 78/689/EEC amended Decision 75/365/EEC with the effect of extending the terms of reference of that Committee to the activities of nurses and dental practitioners.

dent upon minimum training requirements: for the medical profession the acquisition of knowledge and length of training is made subject to very general conditions (it being understood that this applies to the general practitioner), whereas requirements for specialised medicine are much more detailed.

Efforts are being undertaken to make those directives relating to specialised medicine apply similarly to general practitioners, who have a recognized training of their own, so they will eventually be on an equal footing with the consultant.

There is so far no harmonization of training requirements in this respect.

The Council of Europe, through its Resolution (77) 30 on the general practitioner, his training and ways of stimulating interest in his vocation, has made a useful contribution to these efforts.

In respect of the profession of nurses, directives similar to those relating to doctors were also adopted. Directive 77/452/EEC of 27 June 1977 (OJ 1977, L 176/1) is concerned with the mutual recognition of diplomas, certificates and other evidence of the formal qualifications of nurses responsible for general care, including measures to facilitate the effective exercise of the right of establishment and freedom to provide services. Directive 77/453/EEC of the same date (OJ 1977, L 176/8) relates to co-ordination of provisions laid down by law, regulation or administrative action in respect of the activities of nurses responsible for general care.

As in the case of the Directives relating to doctors, these Directives extend for similar reasons also to employed nurses. Member states will have to comply with these Directives within two years of their notification.

A certain duplication of work in this respect with activities carried out by the Council of Europe cannot be denied.

European Agreement no. 59 (1967) on the instruction and education of nurses contains, for instance, the same training requirements. This Agreement has not yet been signed or ratified by all EC member states. On the expiration of the two year period stipulated in the Directives, there will be no obstacle in still adhering to this Agreement.

An advisory committee on training in nursing was also set up on 27 June 1977 (Council Decision 77/454/EEC), which was assigned tasks similar to those of the advisory committee on training of doctors.

Finally, Council Directive 78/686/EEC of 25 July 1978 (OJ 1978, L 233/1) deals with the mutual recognition of diplomas, certificates and other evidence of the formal qualifications of practitioners of dentistry, including measures to facilitate the effective exercise of the right of establishment and freedom to provide services. Council Directive 78/687/EEC of the same date (OJ 1978, L 233/10) is concerned with the co-ordination of provisions laid down by law, regulation or administrative action in respect of the activities of dental practitioners. Council Decision 78/688/EEC of 25 July 1978 sets up an advisory committee on the training of dental practitioners.

Directives relating to midwives and pharmacists are under preparation, while it is also to be expected that studies will be undertaken for other allied medical professions.

Category III. Safety, hygiene and health protection

Activities of the three Communities for the purpose of occupational accident and disease prevention and occupational hygiene fall outside the scope of this study (see Introduction).

Health protection against dangers arising from ionising radiation is one of the tasks of the EAEC (article 2b of the Treaty).

For this purpose uniform safety standards in the form of basic standards haven been laid down since 1959 in confirmity with Articles 30-39 of the Treaty. An entire revision of these basic standards was completed in 1976. The protection of patients against radiation applied in medical practice is presently under consideration.

Category IV. Studies and research

Studies within the EEC on matters relating to health and health care are based upon Article 118 of the Treaty, which provides the Commission with the possibility of making studies, delivering opinions and arranging consultations for the promotion of close co-operation in the social field between member states. Thus the Commission has, for instance, carried out studies on the cost of hospitalization, on pharmaceutical consumption and on the organization, financing and cost of health care in the European Community.

The EC also organizes study days on various subjects, such as epidemiology and alcoholism, the latter in close co-operation with the WHO and the International Council for Alcoholism and Drug Addiction.

Besides studies on specific subjects, the EC is also active in the field of research related to health matters. Leaving aside the research for occupational safety and hygiene within the ECSC, there is a whole range of research projects based upon Article 2a of the EAEC Treaty, including the applications of radio-isotopes in medicine and biology and studies of the harmful effects of radiation on living organisms.

Furthermore, a first programme of medical and public health research [105], which was prepared on the basis of the opinion of the Committee on Medical and Public Health Research (CRM) and of the Scientific and Technical Research Committee (CREST) was suggested in 1977 (Council Decisions 78/167/EEC, 78/168/EEC and 78/169/EEC), to be followed by a second programme, which was submitted for approval in 1978. [106]

The CRM was set up in 1972 by the working party on Scientific and Technical Research Policy of the Medium Term Economic Policy Committee and from 1974 was placed under the responsibility of the CREST (see OJ no. C7 of 29 January 1974, p. 3, Article 5). The

105. — the registration of congenital abnormalities
    — the cellular ageing and decreased functional capacity of organs
    — extra-corporal oxygenation.
(See for instance doc. 349/77).
106. — attempted suicide as a public health problem
    — detection of tendency to thrombosis
    — criteria for perinatal monitoring
    — common standards for quantitative electrocardiography. (See, for instance, OJ no. C. 213 of 7 September 1978, p. 3a.f.)

latter Committee is to assist the Commission and the Council in performing their tasks of co-ordinating national policies and defining Community projects in the field of research (Council Resolution of 14 January 1974, Article 2). The co-ordination of national policies aims at, for instance, eliminating unnecessary or unwarranted duplication of effort in national programmes; improving the efficiency or reducing the cost of national and Community projects by the sharing of tasks or by the concentration of resources or research teams and gradually harmonizing procedures for the formulation and implementation of scientific policies within the Community (Council Resolution of 14 January 1974, article 1.(a) 3).

In pursuance of the Council's Resolution of 14 January 1974 the CRM carried out a study on possible criteria and considerations involved in the implementation of gradual co-ordination between the medical and public health research organizations of the member states or in association with them.

Among the conclusions of the CRM were the following:
— the main objectives of European co-operation in the medical field should be the prevention and the early detection of disease and the rehabilitation;
— criteria for the choice of common action and for the selection of priorities should be:
  • the importance of the subject to the Community as a whole;
  • the practical importance of the subject, in particular from the social and economic point of view;
  • scientific grounds: either the project should need to be implemented jointly or at least could be carried out much more effectively on a Community basis than seperately in each member state;
  • the expectation of clear and reasonably early results;
— co-ordination of national policies should encourage coherence of methods of working of the national research organizations, thus laying the foundations for an effective scientific community. (See Document 230/77.)

These two beforementioned research programmes are in particular based upon Article 235 of the EEC Treaty.[107] As in the case of the environmental programme of the EEC, this Article has to be applied to action in the field of health care, because no other basis is found in the Treaty for undertakings in this particular field. The programme may be seen as a first attempt to combine resources at Community level, and is a first step towards the common development of research programmes. Form the point of view of rarity of resources, both scientifically and financially, this is a positive development.

2.3. THE EUROPEAN COMMUNITY AND HUMAN RIGHTS

It will be clear from the above review that the primary basis of the activities of the EC is not the realization of the right to health care of any of the other rights under discussion. The scope of the activities with implications for health or health care is much more limited; they may be seen as derivatives of the broad objectives of the three Communities, which have a primary aim

107. Article 235 of the EEC Treaty: 'If action by the Community should prove necessary to attain in the course of the operation of the common market, one of the objectives of the Community and this Treaty has not provided the necessary power, the Council shall, acting unanimously on a proposal from the Commission and after consulting the Assembly, take the appropriate measures'.

other than the promotion of health. The streamlining of medical provisions is, for instance, not provided for in the Treaties. The contribution to the protection and promotion of human rights, in particular through the application of the existing international instruments in this field, is, however, pursued by the three Communities. The Declaration on the importance of respecting fundamental human rights, which was signed by the European Parliament, the Council and the Commission on 5 April 1977, is but one example of this. In this text, special reference was made to the European Convention on the Protection of Human Rights and Fundamental Freedoms (OJ no. C 103 of 27 April 1977, p. 1). The European Parliament in particular is very alert on this subject (see, for instance, docs. 23/77, 69/77, 89/77, OJ no. C 299 of 12 December 1977, p. 26 and OJ no. C 108 of 8 May 1978, p. 42). It has, for instance, invited the Commission to take the necessary steps under Article 235 or possibly Article 236 of the EEC Treaty with a view to consider the European Convention on Human Rights as well as the International Covenant on Civil and Political Rights as an integral part of the Treaties establishing the EC. [108] The attention in this field is, however, entirely focused on the political and civil rights as well as on the economic rights and not on the social rights.

The European Court, in its preliminary ruling of 16 March 1978 (case 117/77) has greatly amplified the possibilities for the realization of the right to health care at Community level. (In this case the Court ruled that Article 22, para. 2 of Regulation 1408/72/EEC on treatment in an EC member state other than in the country of domicile, applies in every case where treatment for a specific disease is more adequate in another EC country than in the country of domicile. This implies that such treatment obtained in another EC country is chargeable to the social security system of the country of domicile, provided the treatment thus obtained is chargeable to the social security system of the country where the treatment is given)[109]

3. Organisation for Economic Co-operation and Development (OECD)

This Organization, set up by a Convention signed in 1960, was the successor of the Organization for European Economic Co-operation (OEEC). Unlike the OEEC, the OECD has ceased to be a European undertaking. (The members of the OECD are at present the following European countries: Austria, Belgium, Denmark, Finland, France, Federal Republic of Germany, Greece, Iceland, Ireland, Italy, Luxemburg, Netherlands, Norway, Portugal, Spain, Sweden, Switzerland, Turkey and the United Kingdom, as well as the non-European countries Australia, Canada, Japan, New Zealand and the United States of America; Yugoslavia has special status with the OECD). The Organization's governing body is the Council, which operates through various committees.

108. OJ no. C 299 of 12 December 1977, p. 26.
109. A request for further interpretation on this subject is pending before the Court.

The Organization undertakes miscellaneous activities in various fields in the framework of its major objective: harmonization of national economic policies.

The work of the OECD in this respect is performed through studies, publications, exchange of information, etc.

Thus, for instance, the Centre for Educational Research and Innovation, created in 1968, which functions within the OECD, has undertaken a study on education of the health professions in the context of the health care systems and on new directions in education for changing health care systems.

There is also a liaison bulletin between development research and training institutes in order to improve exchange of information in the field of economic and social development.

The Organization has also been involved with pharmaceutical questions, consumer protection (there is close co-operation with the European Community in this respect) and road safety.

The OECD Nuclear Energy Agency (NEA) was established in 1972 replacing the European Nuclear Energy Agency set up in 1959.

The NEA, which is a semi-autonomous institution, is involved with health and safety aspects of nuclear energy. In this context, attempts are made to draw up uniform atomic regulations, especially in the field of health and safety (the tasks of NEA are very similar to those of Euratom). The NEA works in collaboration with the International Atomic Energy Agency.

The OECD is at present more involved with environmental questions than with other health activities, though health policy is one of the main targets of a study project on 'integrated social policy'. In this framework a workshop was held in 1977 on 'public health policy as part of an integrated social policy'.

Moreover, several studies in the field of health have been undertaken, such as on the allocation of resources to health, approaches to the development of health indicators and new directions in education for changing health care systems.

4. North Atlantic Treaty Organization (NATO)

NATO was created in 1949, primarily for defence purposes. The members of NATO are at present the European countries Belgium, Denmark, Federal Republic of Germany, France, Greece, United Kingdom, Iceland, Italy, Luxemburg, Netherlands, Norway, Portugal, Turkey and the non-European countries Canada and the United States. In this framework the medical and health aspects of protection of the civil population are dealt with. Since 1954 a medical committee functions for this purpose.

NATO does not limit its scope of activities to defence purposes, but also covers a broader area for the purpose of co-operation towards the improvement of modern society in a more general way. This broader approach falls under the terms of Article 2 of the Treaty, which provides that member countries will contribute towards the further development of peaceful and friendly international relations by promoting conditions of stability and well-being. One area which is considered to be of special importance in this respect is that of science and technology. This has led in 1958 to the creation of the NATO science committee, which has an active programme of scientific and technical co-operation in, for instance, providing grants for research, in stimulating exchange of information, in providing opportunities for advanced instruction and in identifying specific areas which deserve special encouragement through grants, lectures, conferences, training programmes and other methods. NATO's science committee supports almost all fields of basic science through special programmes such as the research grant programme, which supports international collaborative research projects, the human factors programme and the system science programme. In the framework of these various programmes the health field is touched upon occasionally. Thus, in the framework of the latter two programmes, for instance, conferences were held on experimental and behavioural approaches to alcoholism, on human factors in health care and on system science in health care.

Another programme of NATO's science committee is the advanced study institute programme for the purpose of disseminating advanced scientific knowledge and increasing contacts among scientists from different countries. Proceedings of these advanced study institutes which are co-sponsored or sponsored by NATO are published.

One of the main scientific areas covered by these institutes is life sciences (including medical sciences).

In 1969 the committee on the challenges of modern society was established with the object of attacking practical problems already under study at the national level and by combining the expertise and technology available in a number of countries, arriving at valid conclusions and making recommendations for action.

The committee itself is not engaged in research but operates through 'pilot countries' which are responsible for the planning, funding and execution of a study.

Among the pilot studies which have been completed are a study on road safety and one on advanced health care. The object of the latter study was not to duplicate activities of the WHO, but rather to supplement these activities by coping with medical problems in developed countries. The study covers four areas: systematic assesment of health services, organized ambulatory health services, emergency medical services and automation of clinical laboratories. One of the on-going studies is the one on nutrition and health.

The committee receives strong support from the North Atlantic Assembly, in which parliamentarians from the member countries have seats, and which through its scientific and technical committee encourages the national implementation and follow-up of pilot studies, recommendations and resolutions.

There are also activities relating to public health in the framework of Eurogroup. Eurogroup is an informal grouping of European countries within NATO, established in 1968 to provide a stronger and more cohesive European contribution to the common defence. Eurogroup, which meets at ministerial

206

level, is operating through specialist sub-groups, among which since 1970 is one on co-operation in military medical services (EUROMED). EUROMED is assigned the task of exploring possibilities of closer co-operation in the military medical field, and has studied in this framework such items as the preservation and storage of red blood cells, and the notification and control of epidemic diseases, for which purpose special working groups were set up. NATO staff maintain contacts with other international organizations such as OECD, the European Community, IAEA and the Council of Europe, for the purpose of exchanging information and documentation.

5. European Free Trade Association (EFTA)

EFTA, which operates since 1960 on basis of the so-called 'Stockholm' Convention, is an arrangement between at present seven countries (Austria, Iceland, Norway, Portugal, Sweden, Switzerland and the associated member, Finland) to create a single market by the abolition of tariffs and all other restrictions on trade between the members, while leaving the members free to maintain their own tariffs and to follow their own commercial policies towards third countries.

If functions through a Council[110], which is the forum in which the member states consult and act together. The Council is composed of representatives of member states. Decisions are binding. The Council operates through several subordinate organs. EFTA parliamentarians have met regularly since its creation to discuss EFTA's work. Since 1977 there is a committee of members of parliaments to serve as a consultative body and as a channel of information.

External relations of EFTA include those with the Council of Europe (biennial debates on EFTA take place in the Parliamentary Assembly of the Council of Europe), the Nordic Council (representation at annual sessions) and the European Community (liaison meetings).

The health interests of EFTA lay mainly in the concern with requirements for pharmaceutical preparations. Thus, for instance, a Convention on mutual recognition of inspections in respect of manufacture of pharmaceutical products, which dates from 1970, is in force (as from December 1977) in the EFTA countries, as well as in Denmark, Hungary, Ireland, Liechtenstein and the United Kingdom.

The Convention provides for an exchange of information between the inspecting authorities and for the mutual recognition of inspections. Regular consultation takes also place under the Convention, for instance, in order to make recommendations and proposals for standards of good manufacturing practice, exchange experience on means and methods for achieving appropriate and effective inspections and promote co-operation between the competent authorities to facilitate the application of the Convention. For the purpose of this regular consultation a committee of officials is meeting several

110. There is also the Joint Council of EFTA and Finland.

times a year. This committee discusses items such as mutual training of inspectors, elaboration of guidelines for the stability of pharmaceutical products and for the geographical extension of the Convention. In fulfilling its tasks, the committee takes into account current development and work done in other organizations, in particular in the framework of the WHO, the Council of Europe and the European Community.

Besides the obligatory exchange of information under the Convention (relating to general or specific standards of manufacturing practice and quality control), there are also regular exchanges of views on various aspects involved, such as on safety aspects involved in the packaging and labelling of pharmaceutical products and modern methodology for the isolation, identification and qualification of drugs and related substances.

The Convention does not deal with requirements for the safety and effectiveness of pharmaceutical products. Therefore an ad hoc group of experts on registration procedures was set up in 1975 to study the difficulties caused by the existence of differing national procedures for the registration of pharmaceutical products and to study work being done on registration in the European Community and other international organizations. The expert group elaborated an international system for the exchange of reports on the evaluation of pharmaceuticals.

6. Benelux Economic Union (Benelux)

The Treaty of the Economic Union for the Benelux came into force in 1960 between Belgium, Luxemburg and the Netherlands.

It was preceded by the Benelux Customs Agreement of 1944 which became operative in 1948.

The Treaty of the Benelux Economic Union lays down minimum obligations for the participating countries, so that any activity falling within the primary objective of the Union (economic progress, leading to the promotion of personal and social well-being) may be expanded whenever necessary. Hence virtually all health activities may theoretically be undertaken in this framework. This regional co-operation on basis of an union is of importance because it may stimulate the European integration within the European Communities, including those activities which concern health. Thus the Treaty of the EEC in article 233 refers to the Benelux Union:

'The provisions of this Treaty shall not preclude the existence or completion of regional unions between Belgium and Luxemburg or between Belgium, Luxemburg and the Netherlands, to the extent that the objectives of these regional unions are not attained by the application of this Treaty'.

The Union's main body with decision making power, the Committee of Ministers, has delegated the preparatory work to ministerial working groups, among which is the ministerial working group on public health, which was created in 1973. In the frame of this working group, general exchange of ideas takes place on developments in the field of health with a view to attaining a common policy and co-operation. The special committee for public health (1956) is the committee which prepares through its various committees and working groups the discussions for the ministerial working group and carries out decisions taken by the Committee of Ministers. The fields of competence of this special committee for public health include the harmonization of national provisions on public health problems in order to eliminate obstacles to the free circulation between the three countries (Article 6 of the Treaty); the harmonization of national provisions concerning public health problems in order to eliminate obstacles to free competition (Article 7 of the Treaty); prior consultation on policy lines and commitments towards, or in the framework of international agencies and conferences of an economic nature (Article 9 of the Treaty). Working Groups include those on hygiene, biology, foodstuffs, sera and vaccins and toxicology.

There is also a 'Benelux hygiene committee' (since 1964) in which the (advisory) 'Health' (or 'Hygiene') Councils of the three member countries co-operate and which may also contribute to the work of the special committee for public health and there is a Benelux committee of experts in medicines (1964). Both these committees of a special nature were created for the purpose of speeding up and facilitating the harmonization of legislation and of activating co-operation among Benelux members.

In 1965 a Benelux committee of experts in pesticides was established to give effect to recommendations and decisions in this field.

The advisory interparliamentary Council (1955) deliberates and advises the three governments on problems which are related to the economic union. Yearly the three governments report on achievements and activities of the Union. The Council also advises on draft agreements prior to their signature. The activities of the Regional Union in the field of health are very similar to those undertaken in the frame of the EC: the free circulation of goods between the members has, for instance, led to harmonization of legislation on foodstuffs (for instance quality control, food additives, packaging).

Health control measures are furthermore removed to the outside frontiers. The major harmonization project is in the pharmaceutical sector. A Benelux service for the registration of medicaments was created in 1973 for the purpose of harmonizing and registring pharmaceutical products for human use. Since 1977 all prefabricated medicines for human use which enter the three countries fall within the competence of the common registration service of medicines. [111]

The Benelux service is the competent body for Benelux to deal with registration demands under EC Directive 75/319.

Also in 1973 a committee of the common Benelux service for the registration of medicines was created for the purpose of controlling information on medicines for which registration is requested and of advising on registration requests. This advice is binding upon national instances.

111. See decrees of the Committee of Ministers of 30 November 1977, M (77) 11, 12 and 13.

Harmonization of legislation for the purpose of free circulation of medicines within the three member countries should be completed by 1 January 1981. The Union strives at a common standpoint towards EC policies regarding pharmaceuticals.

In the framework of the free movement of persons, mutual recognition of diplomas of medical and allied personnel has been studied. Also in this respect a common viewpoint within the EC has been formulated.

Finally, there are elaborate common medical research programmes between national laboratories. A subcommittee on 'public health laboratory' of the special committee for public health is assigned the task of harmonizing laboratory research for public health purposes. This harmonization is pursued with a view to eliminating obstacles to the free circulation of goods which may result from using different research methods, biological norms or standards. Furthermore there is an exchange of experience and information enabling rapid action whenever necessary.

Most of the subjects in the public health sphere are dealt with by way of recommendations.

The first advantage of the Benelux in respect to international health activities is that the three participating states strive at presenting a common coordinated policy within the EC and other international organizations. This evidently facilitates decision-making on the one hand and may stimulate new undertakings and, or health policy and orientation on the other hand. Secondly, the Benelux forms a first platform for reciprocal use of medical facilities, research and other facilities, though on a geographically limited scale.

In this way there is a possibility of pooling resources on a smaller scale ('regionalization' within a larger organization), which contributes to the attempts to rationalize the use of scarce resources on a larger scale in the framework of an international organization.

7. Nordic Council

The Nordic Council was established in 1952 as an initiating and advisory body for Nordic co-operation. It is composed of elected members of the parliaments of Denmark, Finland, Iceland, Norway and Sweden, as well as of representatives of the respective governments (ministers), the latter not having a right to vote. Since 1973 the Council meets biennially. The Council, set up as a purely consultative interparliamentary body and not as a formal international organization, has no authority to make decisions that are binding on its individual members (Solem, 1977, p. 36). Its main duty is to discuss questions of common interest to the countries and to make recommendations to the governments or to the Nordic Council of Ministers. Thus any matter may be discussed and dealt with by the Nordic Council, whenever such a matter is of interest to two of the participating countries. In practice the Nordic Council has so far concentrated its activities on economic matters, legal questions, communications and transport, social issues and cultural affairs. To deal with the subjects falling within these broad categories of activities five committees have been set up, each with competence in one of the main areas of concern. The committee dealing with health matters is the social and environmental standing committee.

The Nordic Council is the most active element in Nordic co-operation. Up until 1962 the co-operation between the Scandinavian countries was rather informal, and not based upon any written international agreement — but upon five national documents. In 1962 a general agreement was concluded (the so-called Helsinki Treaty), in which some general principles and objectives of co-operation were set out. Articles 14-17 of this Treaty deal with social (including health) co-operation.

This Treaty was revised in 1971, when, with a view to strengthening the organization of Nordic co-operation and to giving the governmental level of Nordic co-operation a formal character among other provisions, provisions were included for the creation of a Nordic Council of Ministers with responsibilities and jurisdiction over the whole field of Nordic co-operation (Saxrud, 1976, p. 11). This Council of Ministers which is the main body of co-operation among the Nordic governments may take decisions (for which unanimity is required) to the extent provided for in the Helsinki Treaty and under other agreements between the members of the Nordic Council.

The Nordic Council of Ministers operates through committees of senior officials. It may submit proposals to the assembly of the Council.

The major goal of the Nordic Council in the social sector is to turn the Nordic states into one unit with respect to social rights (as regards health this implies to make possible full use of the medical and hospital facilities available throughout Scandinavia; Solem, 1977, p. 113).

In the health field co-operation on the executive and administrative levels existed already prior to the creation of the Nordic Council.

As early as 1909 public health services in the Nordic countries started co-operation for the purpose of planning elaborate legislation for the inspection of foodstuffs and regulating other matters within their competence. The national boards of health have been meeting regularly since 1929 at Director-General level, for discussions and consultations. In this setting special ad hoc working parties were created, for instance, on polio treatment and the testing of dental materials. These meetings also resulted in the setting up of two permanent bodies, the annual meeting of the chiefs of the pharmaceutical testing laboratories and the Nordic methodological committee of food inspection.

There is also extensive co-operation among the Nordic public health authorities through continuous exchange of medical information and statistical data. In this way the Nordic area is more or less a unit which operates on a concerted medical basis.

Since 1958 the ministers of public health of the Scandinavian countries have been meeting regularly again with a view to closer co-operation. Informal co-operation among medical research institutions and members of the medical profession also takes place at a large scale, mostly promoted by large Nordic specialist organizations.

In 1953 the Nordic Council requested a careful examination within the

211

field of health and hospital matters in order to identify problems for which joint Nordic action was indicated. This has led to the intensification of co-operation among the Scandinavian hospitals and to the exchange of medical specialists.

Some of the practical results of the co-operation in the field of health are the elaboration of a common Nordic pharmacopoeia (medicinal prescriptions are valid through Scandinavia), control of foodstuffs, including the elaboration of common Nordic methods of analysis through the committee for standardizing methods of food analysis and co-ordination of the control of epidemics, including the joint utilization of personnel and equipment and the elaboration of common principles of prophylactic measures. The Nordic countries have become an international quarantine area (at the frontiers between Nordic and other countries). There is also harmonization of social and medical legislation in respect of boundary medical services (frontier area co-operation), co-operation between public health laboratories through exchange of information and of personnel, and through mutual assistance. There is also an almost free circulation of medical practitioners, dental sergeons, nursing staff, physiotherapists and various other groups of allied medical professions within Scandinavia. Conditions to which practice in another Scandinavian country is subject are limited to some specific additional social and medical studies, which does not create difficulties, as training is based upon almost identical rules in the various countries. There are also joint Nordic institutions for such training, while there has been since 1962 a joint school of public health between Denmark, Finland, Norway and Sweden.

The latter is a continuation of activities which began in 1953, when joint courses for public health personnel started with WHO's assistance. The joint health service for sailors should also be mentioned.

Co-operation with a view to the development of a common statistical system includes an international classification of mental derangement and cancer registers (Nordic co-operation in the social and labour field, 1965, pages 29-35).

The present health co-operation programme includes in general items such as education, medical statistics, accident prevention, transplantation (Scandia-transplant, a kidney exchange organization established in 1969, receives financial support from the Nordic Council of Ministers), disability, medicines (in 1974 a Nordic Council of medicines was created for the purpose of harmonizing legislation and administration with regard to medicines in the Nordic countries) and research activities covering drugs and alcoholism (there is a joint Nordic liaison committee for research into narcotic drugs and a joint Nordic council for alcohol research). The action programme for continuous co-operation in the health sector is mainly directed towards comprehensive programmes and is focused upon subjects such as the full realization of a common Nordic labour market for various categories of medical staff, the introduction of a Nordic health card system, the development of a programme to deal with the misuse of heavy narcotic drugs, the merger of the research councils on drugs and alcoholism, the building up of a Nordic co-operation regarding the hazards of smoking and the drawing up of guidelines for measures to prevent the occurence of disabilities.

212

Whenever health matters are discussed within other international settings, in particular the WHO and the Council of Europe, a common Nordic policy is aimed at. For this purpose there are, for example, preparatory meetings for the Nordic representatives to the WHO since 1956. There is, moreover, a relationship with the European Community on the basis of separate agreements with the Nordic countries (except of course Denmark). In the framework of a joint Committee, responsible for the supervision of the proper functioning of the provisions, the extension of the relations to areas not covered by the Agreement may be investigated. As these Agreements which are essentially free trade arrangements, do not yet cover public health subjects there is hence a possibility for extension to fields such as pharmaceuticals and the free movement of the medical and allied professions.

8. Some conclusions

When reviewing the activities in the field of health which take place in the various international settings discussed in the present Chapter, it becomes clear that, as far as the European Community is concerned, there is not yet a common policy in the field of health. A proper basis to this end is not provided for in the respective Treaties and not every member state is willing to co-operate in the development of such a policy. For this reason the undertakings in the framework of the three European Communities which have a bearing on health are not coherent. As a consequence, the overall picture of activities of the EC pertaining to health and health care is confusing and obscure. Despite this fragmented approach there have been significant achievements which, though not directly undertaken for this purpose, yet contribute to the improvement of health care in the EC and hence to the realization of the right to health care.

Thus, the free movement of members of the medical and allied professions is a guarantee of a certain level of quality of health care within the Community through the minimum training requirements which are contained in the various Directives. A common policy regarding the content and duration of professional training for the purpose of laying down minimum standards will thus gradually be developed. Such a common policy may eventually lead to the harmonization of training programmes for the medical and allied professions.

The efforts in the pharmaceutical sector which take account of the achievements in this field of the WHO and the Council of Europe Partial Agreement in the field of public health are also of great importance. Yet, harmonization of laws in itself is not sufficient for the purpose to be achieved, if it is not followed by uniform implementation, application and interpretation.

Finally, the programmes in the field of medical and public health research may be seen as the start of a range of undertakings, necessary for pooling technical and scientific medical and public health resources, which have become both rare and costly in Europe.

It seems indicated to tune these research programmes to those of the WHO regional office for Europe and the Council of Europe.

Regarding the OECD, NATO and EFTA, activities relating to the field of health are marginal. Both OECD and EFTA are, or have been concerned with pharmaceutical matters, a subject which is apparently of interest to all international arrangements discussed, except NATO. Educational activities are also focused upon in the framework of these international settings, except for EFTA.

Research or its stimulation is also falling within the sphere of activities of almost all these organizations.

The co-operation within Benelux for health purposes has a singular aspect in that it has its own functions within the European Community. Undertakings which are more usefully started at a limited scale initially, may in this manner eventually lead to expansion at Community level. Also the formulation of a common Benelux policy within the EC and in other international settings is a special feature of such a regional setting, which may eventually lead to fuller realization of the right to health care at a broader level, provided the undertakings are primarily directed towards this end.

Finally, the Nordic co-operation is particular relevant for the realization of the right to health care primarily within Scandinavia. As far as the international regional co-operation on a restricted level in Europe is concerned, the achievements of the Nordic Council are the most relevant in this respect. The region is particularly suitable for such so-operation because of the close relationship between the Scandinavian countries regarding, for instance, their legal systems, social structures and level of development. In particular the rational utilization of resources through pooling medical facilities (technical, scientific and regarding manpower) is very much advanced in this region. As with the Benelux, the common Nordic approach towards health activities undertaken in the framework of other international settings is a constructive, though not always conscious, contribution towards the realization of the right to health care in Europe.

Part C - Frame for international European undertakings for the purpose of furthering the human right to health care

I. General aspects of international work related to the promotion of the right to health care

1. Further elaboration at an international level of the human rights which are under review

1.1. SOME GENERAL REMARKS

The principle that the present study is based upon, is that international organizations have a clear function with respect to the promotion at an international level of the right to health care.

This implies amongst other things that the international organizations that are active in the field of public health also have a task to further elaborate those human rights which play a role in furthering the right to health care. In fact new developments make it necessary to either formulate more precisely the standards which are sometimes elaborated in too vague or incomplete a manner, or draw up additional standards on particular aspects of the human rights, which were discussed in Part A.

The necessity for the drawing up of additional and, or more elaborate standards by way of formulating additional human rights instruments, imposes itself in particular where the advances, developments and evolution of concepts and techniques in medicine call for more elaborate legal rules to protect human beings. We only have to look at changes which have already taken place and which are still in the full process of further development in fields such as human experimentation, organ transplantation, sterilization, abortion, euthanasia, genetics and computer techniques.

It has been demonstrated in previous chapters[1] that various efforts have already been undertaken to further elaborate the human rights under review. On a worldwide basis, the UN in particular has been active in this field, assisted, whenever relevant, by the WHO; on a European level, the Council of Europe is the most relevant organization. In this context the international organizations are also responsible for the respectation of the various individual human rights, that are involved with the realization of the right to health care.

Here lies the full complexity of the subject matter, namely that during the process of guaranteeing the full exercise of the human right to health care it simultaneously touches upon human values, which are in particular formulated in the individual human rights instruments. International undertakings in this specific field should always take into account this process of interaction between social human rights on the one hand and individual human rights on the other.

---

1. See for instance Part A, Ch. II, paras. 3. and 5.

A neglect of this interaction between the two different categories of human rights becomes more serious, the more technical possibilities in medicine, which enlarge the scope of the social right to health care, entail interference in the human personality, which latter is protected by the international recognition of individual human rights. The very fact that in this respect the basic formulation of both categories of human rights is found in two distinct international human rights instruments, might well stand in the way of the optimal realization of the right to health care at the international level, because it might lead to a separate instead of an integrated approach to this particular right.[2]

1.2. ACHIEVEMENTS BY THE VARIOUS ORGANIZATIONS WHICH ARE UNDER REVIEW

— the World Health Organization

When reviewing the concrete legal achievements by the WHO with the intention to give further substance to the *right to health care*, it should be noted that the Organization itself has not yet taken any successful initiative to draft a distinct human rights instrument for this purpose.

The Organization confines its role in this respect to advising the United Nations, upon request, for the purpose of the elaboration by that organ of special declarations and other such instruments.[3] Like in the case of the right to health care, also in the field of the *individual human rights* the Organization has refrained so far from establishing particular human rights texts or even guiding principles for safeguarding the rights of the human subject whenever there is a possibility of conflicting human rights.

As was seen before (Part B, Ch. I, para. 4.), the WHO considers its role in the solution of particular problems which result from the interrelationship between individual human rights and the right to health care, which influences legislative provisions dealing with health protection, a very limited one.

Its role consists mainly of supporting and promoting directly or indirectly medical research, the organizing of international scientific conferences and dissimenating of knowledge.

The rights of the patients is an example of a particular field in which an unsuccessful initiative was made to draw up an international instrument at global level, covering a specific aspect of the right to health care.

A 'draft Declaration of the rights of the patient' was drawn up as a result of a WHO-seminarium, which was held in 1953. (The text of this Declaration, which was elaborated by professor dr. G. Kraus and professor dr. A. Querido, is reproduced in: *Katholiek Artsen Blad*, 1968, pp. 162-164.) This draft Declaration, which was mainly based upon the concept of the respect of the human personality, was never presented to the World Health Assembly, presumably because the possibilities of its acceptance at global level were considered to be minimal at that time. This is a good example of the disadvantage

2. See below, Ch. III, para. 2.4.1.
3. See Part B, Ch. I, para. 4.

of the Organization's functioning at a global level, without realizing a full process of decentralization.

— the Council of Europe

The activities of the Council of Europe which were indicated in Part B, Ch. III, paras. 3.3. and 4. are a demonstration of the fact that the Organization is endeavouring to enhance its involvement with the international aspects of the human rights under discussion. Thus, for instance, the Council of Europe is aware of the fact that the protection of the rights of the patients is suitable to be dealt with in a standard setting instrument.

The fact that the Organization's 1979 programme of work includes the (overall) subject 'legal problems in the field of medicine' is another demonstration of the policy of the Organization to further strengthen its intergovernmental policy in this particular field. Whether these efforts will be optimally successful in that they will result in concrete legislative instruments rather than in recommendations will entirely depend on the weight national governments are likely to give to these activities.

— the European Community

The European Community has not yet taken any direct action for the further elaboration of the human rights under discussion. The respective Treaties contain hardly any reference to the protection of these rights. The European Court of Justice, however, takes into account the necessary protection of the *individual* human rights. As was seen in Part B, Ch. IV, para. 2.3., the three institutions of the EC as well as the European Parliament have repeatedly drawn attention to the importance of the protection of the individual human rights. There is no obvious reason why the EC should not as an institution adhere to both European human rights instruments, or at least consider them as integral parts of the EC Treaty.

In a Resolution adopted in 1976, the Parliamentary Assembly of the Council of Europe insisted upon a system of consultation between the Court of Justice of the EC on the one hand and the European Commission and the Court of human rights of the Council of Europe on the other, in order to prevent complications resulting from the simultaneous interpretation by the Commission and the Court of human rights of the Council of Europe on the one hand and the Court of Justice of the EC on the other (Recommendation 791 (1976).[4]

2. *Operational activities with a view to promote the realization of the right to health care*

It is obvious that the further elaboration of the right to health care by international organizations through the drawing up of appropriate human rights instruments alone is not sufficient for the promotion of the realization of that right at the international level.

4. See also' 'Proceedings of the fourth international colloquy about the European Convention on Human Rights', Rome, 5 to 8 November 1975, Council of Europe, Strasbourg, 1976, pp. 59-60.

Legal rules of such a nature have to be made operational if the realization of the right to health care is to be progressively achieved. The necessity for international undertakings with a view to the achievement of the economic, social and cultural rights is explicitly recognized in the Universal Declaration of Human Rights, the International Covenant on Economic, Social and Cultural Rights as well as the European Social Charter.

In the Universal Declaration a clause pertaining to the taking of international measures is inserted in its Preamble. In Article 23 of the International Covenant on Economic, Social and Cultural Rights, states parties to the Covenant agree that 'international action for the achievement of the rights recognized in the present Covenant includes such methods as the conclusion of the conventions, the adoption of recommendations, the furnishing of technical assistance and the holding of regional meetings and technical meetings for the purpose of consultation and study organized in conjunction with the Governments concerned'.

In part I of the European Social Charter (statement of rights and principles) contracting parties accept 'to pursue by all appropriate means, including those of an *international* character, the attainment of conditions in which the rights covered by the Charter may be effectively realised'. There are many reasons for considering the practical implementation of the right to health care at an international level.[5] One of these reasons is that in order to cope with a particular problem which has international aspects (communicable diseases, dangerous drugs moving in commerce and other similar harmful events which do not stop at frontiers) international co-operation is needed.

Another reason is that the extraordinary advances in science and technology of the twentieth century have their consequences for the field of public health, not only on a national, but also on an international level. Because of this evolution and progress countries become more and more dependent upon international co-operation. The progress in science and technology brings about high costs, both in regard to research and application methods. Therefore there is a risk that only very few will benefit from it, if there is no international co-ordination and co-operation for the primary purpose of pooling of knowledge and resources, with a view to ensure the least waste of precious resources.[6]

Closely linked with the latter aspect is that with the simultaneous increase of disease technology, its technical complexity and rise in costs, a contradiction arises between technical potential and socio-economic ability to apply new acquirements to all who need it. Yet another reason for international endeavours in the field of public health is that it offers the possibility of finding adequate solutions for national problems by combining efforts at an international scale; the holding of study groups, the comparison of data are but some examples of possibilities at an international level.[7]

5. See the Introduction, para. 2.1. for some general remarks; in Part B background information on, and examples of international endeavours are given when discussing the various organizations.
6. An example of undertakings to this end at the international level is the collaboration between research centres and health laboratories.
7. See below, Ch. III, para. 2.3.2.

The need for mutual assistance, for instance, for the purpose of exchange of blood and blood products and the organization of organ banks with a view to transplantation, is also a reason for international co-operation. This mutual assistance, as was sufficiently shown in Part B, can be adequately organized and promoted by international organizations.

In short, it may be said that if one wants to deal adequately with public health problems of the present day, given the present social and economic situation, national efforts alone do not suffice anymore. On the contrary, matters that could previously be dealt with at a pure national level, are now forcefully raised to the international level.

3. Regionalization

3.1. GENERAL REMARKS

Public health is not a subject which ranks high on the priority list for international political attention. It is, moreover, considered as an issue of primarely a technical nature rather than that the emphasis lies on political aspects, so that discussions on international activities in this field are, in general, not politically controversial. And yet, we have seen that few real significant legislative achievements were made, at least at a global level. The reason for this relatively poor result at a global level is rather obvious: general agreement for a common approach other than a rather superficial one on a global level is hard to reach, because the great variation in regional conditions has a major impact on the establishment of commonly acceptable and applicable rules and tends to hamper their realization on a world wide scale.

Hence, the only real significant, legislative achievements of a global import in the field of public health are in those fields, where international public health started. These achievements are the International Sanitary Regulations and the Nomenclature Regulations, both covering fields in which there is an agreed necessity for worldwide action, without too much infringement of international sovereignty.[8] The development of regional arrangements confirms the (relative) shortcomings both of traditional law and of general international organization.

Regional arrangements are more apt to meet the needs of individual countries under the economic, social and political conditions prevailing in the world at a given time (Padelford, 1955, p. 25; Robertson, 1959, pp. 1-4).

Quantitatively, co-operation on a regional level is more practical, because the scope of action is geographically limited.

Qualitatively, regional co-operation can be given more content and depth, because social, economical and political circumstances of the various countries of a given region will be less diverse as in the case of an organization grouping countries all over the world.

8. Some of the shortcomings in the practical application of these regulations were mentioned in Part B, Ch. I, para. 3.5. under b). They are, for instance, that requirements for the compulsory notification of diseases lack international consistency and that there are notification problems in times of major health problems.

Regional organizations contain elements of flexibility not present in a central organization. The mutual interests of groups of countries are taken care of best at a regional level enabling (legal) systems to be developed which take into account the specific characteristics and problems common to a given region: this is a prerequisite for adaptation of a world programme to regional needs and for increasing the effectiveness of field activities.[9]

Decentralization through the process of regionalization appears to be an unavoidable necessity where international public health is concerned, if only because this is a field which is particularly susceptible to a regional approach.

Ever since the first international activities in this field, health programmes were adapted to the special needs of distinct areas. (Thus, for instance, the mediterranean area developed protection against the importation of pestiential diseases from South Africa; Berkov, 1957, p. 35.) Economic arguments also plead in favour of a regional rather than a global approach in public health. In particular in less favourable economic times, when there is no national self sufficiency, there is every reason to combine efforts in order to make optimal, rational use of material and immaterial possibilities in the pursuance of the realization of the right to health care. A regional approach will favour necessary priority setting in the international (regional) public health programme, which will thus be adapted to the specific needs of a given region and which, hence, will be the best possible way for success in this particular field.

It is also more likely that additional and, or more elaborate standards on particular aspects of the human rights which were discussed in Part A[10] can be drawn up relatively easily on a regional level, while global consensus on this subject in most cases appears to be very remote. The founders of the WHO have been aware of the fact that at a worldwide level there can only be an overall policy, a very general approach to public health and that, to be effective, the structure should be such that there is an efficient system of decentralization within the worldwide organization.

For this reason, the Constitution of the WHO provides for the process of regionalization. [11]

It is precisely through an approach of regionalization, whereby action is concentrated upon distinct regions with more or less similar economic, social, technical and moral conditions, that the right to health care can be fully realized. Such a process of regionalization does not necessarily imply a conflict with the worldwide organization. On the contrary, regional rules in the field of health which take full account of regional particularities, can usefully supplement worldwide rules, which, by necessity, are of a general nature. Moreover, regional achievements may in due course be useful to other regions. Ideally, when opting for one central health organization with regional branches, it would seem more effective to give the regional branches specific legislative powers of their own in order to perform those tasks which can be

9.   See WHO, Off. Rec., no. 46, 1953, p. 158 for some advantages and disadvantages of regionalization.
10.   See para. 1.
11.   See Part B, Ch. II, para. 1.1. See also below, Ch. II, para. 1.1.

dealt with regionally rather than on a universal level. The central body, on the other hand, would be left primarily with the overall co-ordinating and promotional tasks and all other activities which have to be carried out on a world-wide scale (eg. epidemiological intelligence).

Minimum standards drawn up in a regional context tend in practice to be of a higher level than those drawn up on a worldwide scale. The enforcement of such standards too tends to be far more efficient on a regional scale, since control is facilitated by the fact that there is easy access to the authority which established the rules. Only standards of a fundamental or more general nature should be established on a worldwide scale.

Certain basic standards might even be applied more effectively on a regional level. In principle a world organization should only interfere in regional matters when the regional organization fails in its task (Brecht, 1944, p. 23). This applies in particular to the realization of the right to health care, a right which can best be assured by accepting the idea of strong regional organizations [12], thus making it possible to pay due attention to regional conditions (economic and social criteria and climatic and other conditions).

Thus, the overall principle 'right to health care for all people' is formulated on a global level, the principles will be elaborated in accordance with regional needs and will have legal implications on a regional (and national) level.

3.2. EUROPEAN REGION

Previously (paras. 2.1. and 2.4. of Part B, Ch. II in particular refer), it was seen that the present economic, scientific and technological situation in the European region is such that effective and efficient international co-operation in the field of public health is essential to Europe.

It was also seen (Part B, Ch. II, para. 2.3.) that some main problem areas for health action in Europe are not yet of concern to every part of the world. They are to date problems such as chronic degenerative diseases, mental health and accidents (see also the work of WHO in the European Region, July to December 1977, Eur/RC 28/2). Moreover, in Europe, like in other parts of the world, there is an increased demand from limited resources. The decisions, which have to be made on the attribution of these resources, the choices which have to be made in this field will automatically put the highest limit to the realization of the right to health care. Although in the majority of countries in Europe there is a certain amount of very sophisticated methods for cure and treatment of diseases, the benefits of recent discoveries are still limited to a few people (some examples are transplantation of organs, hemodialysis, open heart surgery). This may bring about a disparity in access to some health resources within the European region (and among the various regions of the world). In Europe there is now a situation that in some cases a priority choice has to be made between the provision of very specialised health care to

12. The principle that international undertakings in the field of public health can best be performed on a regional basis finds some explicit support in Article 23 of the International Covenant on Economic, Social and Cultural Rights (see para. 2.).

the few, who need it most on the one hand, or the equal distribution of the maximum possible facilities for proper health care to all on the other. [13] The latter ultimately implies that for economical reasons a rather low priority will be given to efforts directed towards attempting to get the utmost of scientific advances of which only a few will profit. However, priority setting should take place on the basis of the existing needs, the available manpower and other resources. To this end co-operation at a European level, through a systematic European approach, is imperative, if one wants optimally to realize the right to health care, by making proper use of social, economic, scientific and technological possibilities.

Such co-operation should be directed towards common priority setting for European programmes, by evaluating national requirements and in concentrating on those fields in which international co-operation is most needed in Europe.

Pooling of knowledge, experience, resources and manpower, whenever indicated, should be the main target in this respect, so that the realization of the right to health care will be, as far as feasable, at a united and equal level in the European region. Whatever course is taken in this respect in Europe, eventually the European experience will be of profit to other regions.

In Europe, medical possibilities have evolved to such an extent, that the protection of the human being through a further elaboration of particular aspects of the human rights which were discussed in Part B, has become a most urgent matter. [14]

Moreover, international organizations in Europe at present focus much attention on human rights, so that, for a variety of reasons, as was already indicated in para. 3.1., it is to be expected that on a regional level in Europe common agreement can be reached on the means to further elaborate and fully implement the human rights which are under discussion. [15]

One of the conditions for the further elaboration of the right to health care as a social human right, and the further promotion of individual human rights in that connection, is to dispose of an adequate organizational structure and to develop an appropriate policy. This prerequisite having been recognized at the national level, the situation at the international (European) level is far from being ideal.

4. Some conclusions

The most suitable approach to the realization of the right to health care is the one on a regional basis. It is at a regional level, that agreement on action, be it in the form of the elaboration of human rights instruments or through practical measures, is easier to attain when compared with global efforts.

Co-ordination of public health activities at a European level requires a close

13. It should be borne in mind that according to the definition of the WHO the right to health care means the attainment of the highest possible level of health by all.
14. See also para. 1.1.
15. See also Part B, Ch. II, para. 2.4.

and substantial relationship, not only among the various countries, but also between the various international organizations involved. This relationship imposes itself for a variety of reasons, such as avoiding duplication of efforts, waste of financial possibilities and manpower and filling gaps, which exist where activities are most needed. [16] It requires an adequate structure at European level with a built-in system of policy development and planning through regular consultation and tuning in of respective working programmes. The strength of international European public health activities, focused upon the realization of the human rights under review, largely depends upon the strength of the mutual relations which exist between the international European settings. The review, in Part B, of public health activities in these various international European settings shows that, though many efforts are undertaken to face public health problems in Europe, these activities have not yet yielded optimal success, primarily because of the relative failure of co-operation between these settings. One can not avoid the impression that public health efforts of European organizations, whatever their scope, are rather fragmented and that coherency among the various schemes is often lacking. An effective structure and hence integrated action to respond to the needs of the region on an international level is still missing in this respect.

Failing an adequate structure, there will not be an overall European programme for the purpose of effectively tackling those items, which are suitable for international action.

There will also be no possibility to lay down minimum legal requirements, guidelines or principles for the full realization and respectation of health components of human rights.

A critical examination of some specific aspects of the present functioning of the international organizations in Europe that were reviewed in Part B, will make it possible to design an adequate structure for international European undertakings in the field of public health and to determine in which settings specific activities should preferably take place for the purpose of promoting the realization and respectation of the human rights involved.

16. See also paras. 2. and 3.1.

II. Critical marginnotes on the various international settings

1. Some aspects of the functioning of the international bodies

1.1. GENERAL REMARK

A special (negative) feature, common to the majority of the international organizations under review relates to the information side of the organizations. It appears that in general no publicity or at the least insufficient publicity is given to achievements of the organizations in the field of public health. Many of the studies carried out in the various settings can usefully be applied at the national level. Yet, the distribution area of the results of a specific undertaking is very limited. Also resolutions or recommendations in the public health field are not sufficiently made known, through, for instance, mass-media nor are they directed towards the appropriate health institutions and instances. This is most likely due to the fact that few direct and efficient publicity campaigns are undertaken by the organizations. Also competent national instances fail very often in this respect, as they rarely direct information to the appropriate places.

This shortcoming of the international organizations is difficult to understand, because the organizations themselves are the first to recognize the importance of making available relevant information. (See, for instance, Resolution 104 of 25 October 1956 of the Council of Europe Parliamentary Assembly relating to the committee on parliamentary and public relations.)

When considering that one of the methods to ensure the realization of the right to health care is to make known the achievements as widely as possible, it becomes clear that publicity efforts are insufficient, both at the national and the international level.

1.2. THE WORLD HEALTH ORGANIZATION IN EUROPE

The WHO, being the only worldwide Organization empowered to deal with all aspects of health and health care and hence the leading authority in this field, has as such the primary responsibility for public health undertakings in Europe. This responsibility includes the responsibility for the necessary co-operation and co-ordination whenever there are undertakings in the sphere of public health in the frame of other international European settings. This particular function of the Organization, which is mentioned in Article 50 under (d) of its Constitution, follows as a matter of course from the fact that the attainment of the (universal) right to health care is the primary objective of the Organization. As this human right calls for equitable distribution of health resources both quantitavely and qualitatively, the Organization's guiding prin-

226

ciple, by setting in 1977 as a social target 'the attainment by all the citizens of the world by the year 2000 of a level of health that will permit them to lead a socially and economically productive life' (Resolution WHA 30.43)[17] has become the greatest health benefit to the greatest number of people at the lowest cost.

Yet, it should not be overlooked that this guiding principle is but one part of the realization of the right to health care. However justified this guiding principle may be, the Organization itself stated in 1951 that the realization of the right to health care was based upon a 'dual principle'. The first is that efforts are directed towards raising the standard of health of the socially and economically less advanced, by making proper use of their own means. The second is that efforts are directed towards appropriate health care for the more advanced countries, having due regard to their greater possibilities in resources, technology and manpower (see Part A, Ch. II, para. 4.2.; doc. E/CN. 4/544 refers).

Hence, it is a constitutional duty of the WHO to also pay due regard to the specific circumstances of Europe, which, as an advanced region, requires its own particular concerted action at an international level, for purposes such as humanizing medical care, pooling of scarce resources, knowledge and manpower, in order to avoid the risk that only a small number of people in that region will benefit by the highly sophisticated and costly health care possibilities, which are available in that region.

By focusing attention primarily towards the developing countries there is a certain risk that the second part of the dual principle proclaimed by the WHO does not get enough attention, which in Europe might result in a certain neglect of the obligations of the Organization to that Region.

To meet adequately with this eventuality the WHO should carry through the process of decentralization, at least in respect of the European region.[18] Only when this process is fully realized, the WHO will be in a position to assume complete responsibility for public health undertakings within this region in accordance with its own Constitution as well as to assure that the structure of international health undertakings in that region functions optimally.

Though a certain degree of decentralization has taken place and regional offices have been given some real power[19], the difference in approach of the central Organization which focuses its overall policy on developing countries, and of the European office, which operates in a region that is technically and industrially advanced and where medical care is highly organized, makes further delegation of powers to that region of paramount importance.

Only complete decentralization will enable the regional office for Europe to be the suppreme co-ordinating forum for all regional health matters, to fully live up to its responsibility for co-operation and co-ordination between international European settings and to attain regional self-reliance in the field of public health.

Such a process of further decentralization should not only include further

17. See also WHO, Off. Rec., no. 241, 1977, pp. 475-477.
18. See also Ch. I, para. 3.
19. See Part B, Ch. II, para. 1.4.

delegation of managerial and technical responsibilities, but also of appropriate legislative (and budgetary) powers.

Though, as was indicated previously, the necessity to focus to a lesser degree on worldwide unity and university in favour of regional arrangements is recognized by the Organization [20], it has not yet made optimal use of its constitutional possibilities in this respect to fully realize the process of decentralization. Considering the WHO's present policy line, it is questionable whether it will decentralize further in the near future.

There are ample constitutional possibilities for delegating powers to the region. Thus, Article 50 of the Constitution states that the functions of the regional committee shall be:

(a) 'to formulate policies governing matters of an exclusively regional character;
....

(g) 'such other functions as may be delegated to the regional committee by the Health Assembly, the Board or the Director-General.'

The advantages of delegating *legislative* powers to the region were already indicated in Ch. I, para. 3.1. For the reasons set out in Ch. I, para 3.2., it is of particular importance to the European region to empower the regional committee to formulate rules of a legislative nature of a regional import (in accordance with Article 50 under (a) of the WHO Constitution).

In this manner only, can the objective of the WHO in the European region be fully promoted. Moreover, it should be taken into consideration that the WHO is the only organization with exclusive competence in the field of health and has, as such, leading authority in this field. And yet, unlike organizations such as the Council of Europe and the European Community, it has no legislative possibilities with respect to the European region alone.

It should also be borne in mind that the work of the other organizations, which are active in the field of public health in Europe, will be of a more limited scope than in the case of the WHO, because the nature of these organizations is a multifunctional one. Furthermore, the number of countries the European region of the WHO is composed of, by far exceeds the membership of those organizations which are of major importance for public health in Europe (the Council of Europe and the European Community). Finally, by delegating legislative powers to the European region, at least some of the limitations encountered by the central organization in respect of its legislative powers [21] are lifted.

Article 3 of the agreement between the World Health Organization and the Pan American Health Organization of June 1949 provides for the possibility that the Pan American Sanitary Conference (the suppreme governing authority of the Organization) adopts health and sanitary conventions, provided they are compatible with the WHO policy. This somehow constitutes a precedent of the delegation of legislative powers to a regional organization, although it is

20. See for instance *WHO Chronicle*, 29, 1975, pp. 253-256.
21. See Part B, Ch. I, para. 3.5.

recognized that this argument is based on historical, rather than on rational arguments. [22]

As far as the *budgetary* powers are concerned it was indicated previously [23] that regional committees determine to a large extent, how the money allotted to their region by the World Health Assembly shall be spent, though the approval of the programme budget remains with the World Health Assembly.

Yet the fact, that since the early seventies the WHO's major policy is directed towards strengthening health services in the developing countries might have implications on the budgetary allocations within the European region. Though the regions are rather independent in fixing priorities for their own programmes, pressure is sometimes exercised on the region to focus primarily upon those programmes which will be of direct benefit to developing countries. Ideally, the budgetary arrangements should be such, that once the money having been allocated, the region can set its own priorities entirely in accordance with the particular needs of the region. So far, the regional committees do not have much influence on the allocation to regions:

'The pattern of allocation to regions is particularly influenced by WHO's role as an intergovernmental organization charged with the constitutional function to assist governments, upon request, in strengthening health services' (para. 4.2. of a working paper on allocation of resources between regions submitted to the fifty-fifth session of the Executive Board in relation to the programme budget for 1976 and 1977). [24]

Para. 5.9. of the same working paper reads:

'Ideally, the allocation of WHO resources between regions should not be imposed by the central organs of the Organization but should, instead, be the natural result of the aggregation at the regional level of the priority needs of individual members as identified through country health programming. As the Organization through country health programming becomes more responsive to the evolution of needs of individual countries, the allocation of resources between regions should become merely part of the problem of re-allocating WHO's resources within the regions ...'. [25]

Difficulties for the European region, which might arise from the present pattern of allocation to regions as described above, can be overcome somewhat in applying Article 50 (f) of the WHO Constitution, which reads as follows:

Article 50: 'The functions of the regional committee shall be:
....
(f) to recommend additional regional appropriations by the Governments of the respective regions if the proportion of the central budget of the organization allotted to that region is insufficient for the carrying-out of the regional functions.'

22. See also Part B, para. 1.1. The Pan American Sanitary Organization was already in existence prior to the creation of the WHO. Although Article 54 of the WHO's Constitution provides for integration of the earlier regional health organizations with the WHO, this integration has not been completed. (See also Goodman, 1971, pp. 326-336.)
23. Part B, Ch. II, para. 1.4.
24. WHO, Off. Rec., no. 245, 1978, pp. 48-59.
25. See also WHO, Off. Rec., no. 46, 1953, pp. 157-184 and no. 52, 1954, pp. 61-73.

Thus the powers (and strength) of the WHO in Europe largely depend upon the extent to which its European members agree on the necessity of European co-operation in the field of public health through that Organization.

Yet another aspect of WHO's present line of policy should be mentioned. If the WHO does not pay enough attention to the second part of the above cited dual principle, there will be a tendency of other organizations to take over tasks of the WHO in the European region. This tendency is an unfavourable one, in the case of an organization that is less well equipped for the purpose, when the promotion of public health is very remote from the organization's primary objective(s). NATO, for example, expressly claimed the sponsoring of the pilot study on advanced health care, because the WHO's efforts for the most part are concerned with improving health care in developing countries. The same tendency, moreover, unduly promotes duplication of work among the various organizations involved.

Once the possibilities of the region are strengthened in such a way that the objective of the Organization can be fully implemented, there will be more chances that the role of the Organization will be more directly concentrated on action necessary for that region. This might not only yield effective results for the European region itself, but also at the same time contribute to the stimulating role the European office has at a global level.

This process of full decentralization requires a continuous evaluation of activities of the WHO, of its functioning and its structure. Only through the process of strengthening regional arrangements, while safeguarding at the same time the close relationship with the other regions and the global Organization, will the dual principle, on which the Organization's efforts towards the realization of the right to health care is based, be kept in proper balance.

1.3. THE COUNCIL OF EUROPE

The comparative shortcomings of the functioning of the WHO in the European region are partially met by the way in which the Council of Europe operates in the public health field. Since it started its activities in this field, it has operated in close consultation with the WHO's regional office in Europe. This often resulted in the taking over of the tasks of the WHO in Europe or in complementing the European undertakings of the WHO.

The Council of Europe, moreover, usefully makes up for the WHO regional office's lack of competence in legislative matters. Another positive element in the functioning of the Council of Europe is that it has established a procedure of 'direct consultation' under the Partial Agreement, which makes it, for instance, possible to those participating in the Partial Agreement, to act directly in cases of emergency. The lengthy procedures of drawing up resolutions and conventions inherent to the intergovernmental organization that the Council of Europe is, can, moreover, be cut short in this manner.

For various reasons the Council of Europe is the best placed organization in

Europe to complement WHO's action. The Council has the largest membership, as compared to the other organizations involved, though the total number of its member countries is less than the number of countries that the WHO's European region is composed of. It has a suitable parliamentary forum with adequate procedures to ensure the democratic acting of the Organization. The Council of Europe can, moreover, tackle in principle any matter in the field of public health in Europe, as long as this falls outside the military scope. (The two smaller regional settings, which operate on an union basis, the Benelux Economic Union and the Nordic Council [26] have in principle also the possibility to enter any subject in the public health field.) [27]

As in the case of the WHO, the Council of Europe has also some aspects of weakness.

Firstly, though the Committee of Ministers has the authority to conclude conventions and agreements, the Organization still often turns to the less binding resolutions, sometimes because a special public health subject is not suitable for the conclusion of an agreement, sometimes because it is the utmost result it can arrive at. The evaluation, at regular intervals, of the action taken by governments in pursuance of resolutions lacks any practical effect.

Secondly, whereas the public health programme is only part of the overall programme of the Organization, the Council of Europe can not, for obvious reasons, cope with every public health activity for which action is indicated. Moreover, because international political attention is to date only marginally focused upon health activities on the one hand and because there are apparent budgetary restrictions in present times of economic regress on the other, there is also a real possibility that the public health programme does not rank high in the overall priority setting of the Organization, which might be reflected in the financial facilities for that programme.

Hence, the governmental committee in charge of the public health programme has to carefully set its priorities, taking into consideration the possibilities of other international settings.

The programme of work of the Council of Europe in the field of public health clearly reflects these budgetary restraints by the fact that it concentrates on a limited area of activities for which the costs are relatively small. Notwithstanding these financial restraints it is of the utmost importance that the possibilities of the Organization are fully exploited through a just allocation of funds, particularly in technical fields, where other international European organizations can not produce the same results. An example of these possibilities is in the field of blood problems, in which many achievements have been [28] and can yet be made.

The fact that the governmental experts sitting on the various public health committees and working groups are mostly civil servants is somehow a negative element in this kind of international co-operation. Very often (certainly

26. See Part B, Ch. IV, paras. 6. and 7.
27. It will be recalled that the European Community does not have this subject among its constitutional objectives.
28. See Part B, Ch. III, para. 3.2.2. under b).

not always), these civil servants are, in their daily functions, as part of an ever increasing bureaucratic system, too remote from reality in the field. They are, by lack of practical experience, not sufficiently informed about the subject. It is of course understood that international work does not ask for local, regional or national detailed facts, but it is undeniable that public health trends, which are in full process of development, should be fully known and understood. Although the technical experts, who often prepare reports for discussion in the committees, are well informed of the situation in their countries, they are in many cases not sufficiently informed on the international impact of the respective problem. An exception should again be made for the work performed in the above mentioned technical fields, as well as on the pharmacopoeia; here we see the excellent combination of experts, internationally well known and well informed, and governmental experts who contribute to these activities from a general, international policy angle.

Despite the fact that initiatives for inclusion of activities in the programme of work may also be taken by the secretariat itself, not too much can be expected of this possibility.

The secretariat, not being appointed for its expertise in the field of public health, often lacks the technical capacity in this respect. (This fact is not encountered to the same extent within the WHO, which has a technical secretariat.)

Yet another element which might hinder optimal European co-operation in respect of public health activities is the existence within the Council of Europe of two governmental settings for furthering public health. [29] This co-existence has a built-in possibility for competence conflicts and even brings about a possibility of duplication of work. These negative factors are already prevalent among the various international organizations involved; they hinder optimal progress in international co-operation in the field of public health and bring about a waste of precious manpower and financial resources. They should at least not exist within one organization. A reconsideration of the usefulness of maintaining this present system could well be initiated, through, for instance, a parliamentary initiative.

The picture of the Council of Europe is even more complicated because there are two other governmental committees, which are involved with the legal aspects of public health.

The committee on legal co-operation, which acts at the level of all member states, is of late expanding its programme of work in this particular field. [30] Whereas the two 'public health committees' are concentrating their activities on general aspects of public health problems, the latter is concerned with the legal aspects. Though the 'legal committee' performs its activities in close co-operation with the European public health committee, competency ques-

---

29. Namely the European public health committee, acting at the level of all member states and the public health committee of the Partial Agreement, to which not all members of the Council of Europe have adhered (see Part B, Ch. III, para. 3.1.).
30. See Part B, Ch. III, para. 3.3.

232

tions still arise sometimes, and are often detrimental to a coherent approach to the whole public health field within one organization.

The European committee on crime problems is particularly dealing with matters relating to drug dependence. [31] In the latter field co-operation between the various competent governmental and parliamentary committees is rather satisfactory.

1.4. THE EUROPEAN COMMUNITY

The European Community could, in principle, usefully contribute to, and, or stimulate public health activities which take place on a larger scale, such as in the case of the WHO European office and the Council of Europe.

So far its undertakings in the field of public health are very fragmented for the very reason that this subject does not fall within the general objectives of the Organization (see Part B, Ch. IV, para. 2.). Nevertheless, there is an increasing amount of activities of the Organization in this sphere. In particular within the overall objective of the European Economic Community to create one single common market some major achievements have been made in the field of public health, of which not the least is the free movement of members of the medical and paramedical professions. This increasing interest in the sphere of public health, which is also shown by the European Parliament, might well bring about a need for a more coherent approach to public health within the European Community, including the necessary budgetary appropriations for this field of action. A more coherent approach would in any case meet with the requirement to improve the co-ordination and co-operation in the field of public health at a European scale. Whereas the co-operation in this field among the international organizations is already difficult to realize, if only because of the difference in membership of the various organizations involved, the realization of an adequate structure for such a co-operation in Europe becomes more difficult to attain the more the overall picture of public health activities of one of the organizations involved is confused and not clear.

Moreover, whereas health care policy forms a coherent unity at the national level, it should also be the objective of a coherent policy at the Community level. It should also be borne in mind that harmonization of laws will not produce any result, if there is also not a common administration and interpretation. The fact should also not be overlooked that the European Community as a supranational organization has some important advantages, which neither the WHO nor the Council of Europe have. This very structure gives the Organization ample possibilities for major legislative achievements, in particular because the legal instruments for the EC do not require signature or ratification by individual members, once they have been elaborated. These legislative possibilities can usefully complement the efforts of the Council of Europe when it comes to the drawing up of legislative instruments. It is recognized that these legislative acts of the EC still only cover a limited

31. Treatment of prisoners also falls under its responsibility.

number of countries. Yet, whenever agreement within the Council of Europe on the conclusion of a convention on a particular public health subject which is appropriate to be dealt with by a legislative instrument is remote, these legislative acts of the EC may constitute the first impetus for eventual action at a larger scale. The fact that the EC has at the moment a relatively small membership may in some cases even be a positive aspect, because agreement is easier to reach among a smaller group of countries.

A first step was made in the direction of a community policy in the field of health when the ministers of health of the member states met with the Commission for the first time at Community level on 13 November 1977 to hold a preliminary discussion on various problems of major importance existing in all the member states. Though this meeting was of an exploratory nature only, it did, however, provide an opportunity for strengthening the spirit of co-operation in a field of common interest. As a result of the meeting, the Commission was requested to make studies in certain specific health fields, to draw up suggestions for Community measures and to look into ways of improving information and co-operation between member states in these specific fields. [32]

It is the intention to have meetings of this kind annually, so that in this way, despite the fact that there can not be binding decision making in this framework, it can still be a useful contribution towards international public health. Thus, for instance, priority fields of action for the EC might be indicated. Though the scope of these undertakings within the EC is limited, both regarding the fields to be covered and in respect of the countries involved, the existing possibilities should not be underestimated.

To give the EC a formal mandate in the field of public health to improve the scattered way public health subjects are now dealt with, an amendment of the Treaties and in particular of the EEC Treaty, in application of Article 236 of that Treaty, would be necessary.

As there is an understandable restraint to undertake such a lengthy and complicated procedure, there is yet another, though less binding, possibility in applying Article 235 of the EEC Treaty to take action in the field of public health at community level.

(Article 235: 'If action by the Community should prove necessary to attain, in the course of the operation of the common market, one of the objectives of the Community and this Treaty has not provided the necessary powers, the Council shall, acting unanimously on a proposal from the Commission and after consulting the Assembly take the appropriate measures.')

This Article provides, for instance, the main, though rather insufficient, legal basis for the environmental policy of the Community. Nevertheless, in par-

32. 1475/77 (Presse 166). A second meeting was held on 16 November 1978 (see 1291/78 (Presse 146)). The central theme at both meetings was economic aspects of health. The advisability of creating an advisory committee on health is presently under study (see also Part B, Ch. IV, para. 2.1.).

ticular in this field the Community has achieved many important results. The research programmes in the medical and public health field are also based upon this Article (see Part B, Ch. IV, para. 2.2.).

Yet, for the time being, there is no apparent sign that EC member countries are unanimously willing to support community action in the field of public health.

1.5. THE EUROPEAN FREE TRADE ASSOCIATION, THE NORTH ATLANTIC TREATY ORGANIZATION AND THE ORGANISATION FOR ECONOMIC CO-OPERATION AND DEVELOPMENT

The OECD, the NATO and the EFTA are essentially mono-functional organizations with objectives that are entirely different from those of the WHO, the Council of Europe or the European Community. The undertakings of these organizations in the public health sphere are rather casual and are not part of a distinct public health programme. Though the European Community also lacks a coherent public health programme, its undertakings, which are performed in the framework of four broad categories of action (see Part B, Ch. IV, para. 2.2.), unlike those of the OECD, NATO or EFTA, have an important impact on the public health field. The incidental undertakings of the latter three organizations contribute to the fact that the overall picture of present public health undertakings on the international (European) level is rather fragmented. The necessity for such undertakings within these settings, as limited as their scope may be, becomes the more questionable because the membership of the various international bodies under review are to a great extent overlapping. Moreover, though the OECD and the NATO also have non-European members, the majority of their member states is European, so that they increase in fact the number of international organizations involved with public health in Europe. This only helps to obscure more the structure of international public health work in Europe.

The afore said does not imply that the undertakings of these organizations in the field of public health are of no importance, but they are rather remote from the objective of contributing to the realization of the right to health care. The fact that the activities of these organizations in this particular field consume precious financial resources, makes the usefulness of these undertakings in these particular settings more doubtful.

1.6. THE BENELUX ECONOMIC UNION AND THE NORDIC COUNCIL

The two regional unions which were previously discussed (see Part B, Ch. IV paras. 6. and 7.), the Benelux Economic Union and the Nordic Council, have both some clear functions in the public health field, though their activities are restricted to a geographical limited area in comparison with the other international settings.

They both form a coherent sub-region, a kind of micro-region within various international European settings. Both, for instance, are part of the WHO and the Council of Europe; the Benelux Union is also part of the European Community.

Legislative efforts within the regional unions are concentrated upon harmonization of legislation and on removing health control measures to the outside frontiers.

The action in the field of public health in the framework of the Benelux is less developed than that of the Nordic Council, in particular when it comes to the pooling of resources and to joint action. It is not unlikely that the participation in the European Community of the three countries that the Benelux Economic Union is composed of, plays a certain role in this respect, because the members of the Union will refrain from action, if it is undertaken in the framework of the EC (see Article 233 of the Treaty of the European Economic Community). [33] It is obvious that these regional unions, with their small geographical coverage, can not complement the work of the WHO in Europe nor the public health activities of the Council of Europe.

Their main feature is that the co-operation which takes place in these settings widens to some extent the scope of the single nation. These unions tend to create a coherent unity among a rather small number of countries, which facilitates in particular the common use of services and exchange of personnel. They dispose of the necessary powers to come to a public health policy common to their members. Their major function in the international European structure for public health is to form a useful platform for initiating undertakings, which can not yet be successfully undertaken on a larger scale.

1.7. PARLIAMENTARY INFLUENCE

Each international setting that was discussed in Part B, with the exception of the WHO and the OECD, has a parliamentary forum. Of these, the Parliamentary Assembly of the Council of Europe and the European Parliament of the European Community, which were established by virtue of the respective constitutional texts, have major functions within their own Organizations.

Both parliamentary bodies play a role in the field of public health through their respective committees.

The very structure of the Council of Europe offers, in theory, all assets for yielding optimal results in that it functions at two levels, the governmental one through the Committee of Ministers, meeting in private and having executive powers, and the parliamentary one through the Assembly, meeting in public and having advisory functions. Some of the positive aspects of the co-existence of these two bodies are that the Assembly in giving its opinion on the programme of work of the Organization (on its substance, implementation and future development) can carry out its parliamentary functions in regard to all intergovernmental work of the Council of Europe; that the Assembly may address recommendations to the Committee of Ministers, including sug-

33. See also Part B, Ch. IV, para. 6.

gestions for the programme of work; and that the Assembly may submit questions.

There are, for instance, examples of the Parliamentary Assembly having made suggestions for the intergovernmental programme of work in the field of health, which were taken over by the Committee of Ministers. [34] Despite the usefulness of such a system of simultaneous undertakings at two levels, there are some failures inherent to its functioning. This can be explained by the fact that the Parliamentary Assembly has deliberative functions only.

Although the Council of Europe was the first Organization to set up a democratic assembly, there is no question of a real political union, but merely of a rather close association between independent partners. Furthermore, there is a lack of balance between both organs of the Organization. The Parliamentary Assembly being primarily a political body, the Committee of Ministers on the contrary has gradually developed into a rather successful body for technical co-operation. These facts would not themselves be a reason to hinder optimal functioning of the system, provided the committees of governmental experts and, or the Committee of Ministers itself were sufficiently alert to developments and general policy lines appearing within the Assembly. Reality however shows that this is not, or at least insufficiently, the case, while the consultation and deliberation between both sides of the system is also often insufficient. [35] In the field of public health, the Parliamentary Assembly is increasingly adopting resolutions and recommendations on subjects of major importance.

The governmental committee in charge of public health and the parliamentary committee dealing with these matters could in principle usefully complement each other and interact in this respect. In practice contacts are only marginal.

Periodical encounters between both committees that deal with health matters (and not only at a secretarial level, the secretariat not being composed of technical staff) would much contribute to increase effectiveness and obtain maximum advantages of the system, which in itself contains all elements for optimal effectiveness of co-operation at an international level in the public health field. One of the positive examples of joint undertakings is the field of drugs. Parliamentarians played an active role in a symposium organized in 1972 on this subject, which formed the basis for a specific programme of work in this field.

As far as the European Parliament of the European Community is concerned, this body is much more alert to the functioning of the Council of Ministers

34. See Part B, Ch. III, para. 3.5.
35. The joint committee which is to co-ordinate the activities of, and conciliate relations between the Committee of Ministers of the Council of Europe and the Parliamentary Assembly has not responded to its purpose, mainly because from a governmental point of view, participation is not considered to be in a personal capacity, but rather on the basis of an authorised brief, so that a complete free exchange of views is hardly possible (Council of Europe, Consultative Assembly, 1973, p. 73). To overcome this deadlock, it has become the practice since 1961 to hold colloquis in private sessions on general policy matters between the Assembly and the Committee of Ministers.

(the main desicion making body) and the European Commission (the daily executive). In this respect it comes close to the functioning of national parliaments, though it is equally void of legislative and governing competences. The European Parliament has, moreover, some influence on the yearly proposed budget. It is also consulted on major issues, in particular on activities planned on basis of Article 235 of the EEC-Treaty, which is, as seen, the present basis for Community action in the environmental sphere and might become equally the basis for an eventual public health programme. [36]

The European Parliament makes frequent use of the question procedure in respect to public health matters.

The parliamentary bodies of the other international settings which make use of a parliamentary forum, though not void of interest, have much less influence, with the exception of the Nordic Council. Nordic co-operation is orginally based on this interparliamentary body, in which discussions take place on practically every matter in relation to Nordic co-operation. These discussions very often lead to recommendations on which governments have to report back. As such, the interparliamentary body acts not only as a forum for discussion of general Nordic or international problems of policy co-ordination, but also as an important pressure group both towards the Nordic Council of Ministers, established in 1971, and directly towards governments. The Nordic Council advises, moreover, on the programme of the Council of Ministers in that it states its views on the more important questions of Nordic co-operation.

2. Co-operation and co-ordination among the relevant international settings

2.1. THE WORLD HEALTH ORGANIZATION

It was seen before (Part B, Ch. I, para. 3.3. under a) that one of the major functions assigned to the WHO is co-operation and co-ordination with other international organizations. Regional offices should, in the views of the Organization, become the supreme co-ordinating forum for all regional health matters. [37]

This implies that at the regional level, the WHO should assume the task of co-ordinating public health activities of all those international organizations in the region that are somehow involved with public health, as well as the task of pursuing co-operation with these organizations.

Article 50 (d) of the Constitution of the WHO explicitly mentions co-operation as one of the functions of a regional committee. It was also seen before (Part B, Ch. II, para. 2.5.) that there exist several forms of co-operation among the regional office for Europe and other organizations, either formally

---

36. The European Parliament has in fact already been consulted on the basis of this Article, namely when the Council proposed a first research programme on medical and public health research (see Part B, Ch. IV, para. 2.2. under category IV).
37. See Part B, Ch. II, para. 1.5.

through relationship agreements, or informally by way of exchange of letters or through other methods. These forms of co-operation are primarily *bilateral* arrangements and therefore form the risk of being of a fragmented nature. *Multilateral* overall planning and programming is still falling short, mainly because the regional office for Europe of the WHO has so far not designed an appropriate structure for multilateral co-operation and co-ordination among the organizations concerned. Yet, there is no apparent reason why the European regional office should not also take the initiative for multilateral co-operation and co-ordination between international settings which are active in the field of public health in Europe.

2.2. THE COUNCIL OF EUROPE

The Statute of the Council of Europe does not lay down explicit rules on the relationship of the Organization with other international organizations [38], though this relationship can be inferred from the text. Article 1 (c) of the Statute specifies that participation in the Council shall not affect the collaboration of its member states in the work of the United Nations or of other international organizations or unions to which they are partners. Article 23 (b) imposes upon the Parliamentary Assembly to have regard, in drawing up its agenda, to the work of other European intergovernmental organizations to which some or all member states are parties.

In May 1951, the Committee of Ministers adopted a Resolution of a statutory character (eighth session; Statute of the Council of Europe with amendments) which conferred upon the Committee, on behalf of the Council of Europe, the competence to conclude agreements with any intergovernmental organization. The same Resolution specifies that the Council of Europe, or any of its organs, shall be authorized to exercise any functions coming within the scope of the Council of Europe which may be entrusted to it by other European intergovernmental organizations.

Like the WHO, the Council of Europe has established working arrangements with a number of organizations on a bilateral basis. [39] The Council of Europe also applies other procedures with a view to developing and maintaining mutual relations through a process of consultation and co-operation with other organizations that are active in the field of public health. Through its procedures applied to the drawing up of its programme of work, the Council of Europe may rationalize the repartition of tasks among the various international settings. In sending its programme of work for comment to other international bodies, tuning in of the respective programmes in the field of public health is a real possibility. Unfortunately this procedure is rarily reciprocal, so that a real dialogue on matters of mutual concern is not established.

---

38. Part V of 'The Council of Europe, the Consultative Assembly, Procedure and Practice', 1973, deals with the Council's place in relation to other international organizations (pp. 291-395).
39. See Part B, Ch. III, para. 2.5.4.

Moreover, the Parliamentary Assembly forms an important forum in its role as interlocutor for other intergovernmental organizations which do not have such a body and which can seek political support in the Parliamentary Assembly. Thus, for instance, in the case of the WHO regional office for Europe, memoranda are submitted to the Assembly, the latter of which expresses its views on these. Also in considering reports from the other organizations involved, the Parliamentary Assembly is well placed to make a cross-examination of the respective programmes so that it can determine gaps and, or record overlappings. In performing a cross-examination of the respective work-programmes, the Parliamentary Assembly is even in the position to attempt to guide respective programmes towards priority fields.

The fact remains, however, that if such cross-examinations take place at all, which is hardly the case, the Assembly cannot go any further than giving advice to the respective organizations. It may in principle make recommendations to the Committee of Ministers, when submitting its opinion on the organization's own programme of work, in order to ensure that at least as far as the Council of Europe is concerned the public health undertakings are tuned in with other programmes. These recommendations may be of the nature to assist in the undertaking of activities in fields, where there is a need for it and which are of no concern to other organizations, or to advise against the undertaking of action whenever there is a possibility of duplication of work.

2.3. THE EUROPEAN COMMUNITY

The competence of the European Community to conclude relationship agreements is based upon various articles of the EEC Treaty [40], depending on the nature of the relations of the Community. [41]

Articles 229-231 are particulary relevant for the relationship agreements which are under discussion. Article 229 makes the Commission responsible on behalf of the Community for its relations with the United Nations and its specialised agencies as well as for relations as are appropriate with all international organizations. Article 230 prescribes that the Community shall establish appropriate forms of co-operation with the Council of Europe; the scope of Article 231 concerning co-operation with the OECD is similar. The working arrangements of the EC are also on a bilateral basis. [42]

Because of the fact that the nine members that the EC is composed of, are also members of the Council of Europe, a double representation of the Community is present. For example, when the European public health committee

40. For practical reasons abstraction is made here from the ECSC and EAEC Treaties.
41. 'The European Community, international organizations and multilateral agreements' (Commission of the European Communities, 1977) analyses the relation between the Community and the international organizations. See also Doc. 567/77 of 8 March 1978 of the European Parliament on the position of the European Communities in public international law.
42. See Part B, Ch. IV, para. 2.

meets, there is a representation of the individual members of the Community and the Community itself. Sofar elements of divergence, which might stem from such a double representation have not occurred, because the Community has not as yet a proper Community health care policy. Therefore, the Community representation at, and contribution to the Council of Europe's work in the field of public health is somehow marginal. The moment this situation changes, a formula for Community representation should be choosen (see para. 3. of 'the European Community, international organizations and multilateral agreements' (1977) for the presently existing modes of 'dual representation').

Apart from the working arrangements, which are principally based upon Articles 229-231 of the EEC Treaty, there is still a whole range of other possibilities for entering international commitments. There is, for instance, Article 113 of the EEC Treaty, on the basis of which Article the Council may conclude tariff, commercial and co-operation agreements. [43]

Then there is Article 235 of the EEC Treaty, which may find application in the field of the Community's international relations. (The Article is applicable if action by the Community should prove necessary to attain, in the course of the common market, one of the objectives of the Community and if the Treaty has not provided the necessary powers.) The application of this provision as the legal basis for agreements with third states or international organizations was confirmed by the Court of Justice. [44]

Article 238 of the EEC Treaty also applies, on the basis of which the Community may conclude with a third state, a union of states or an international organization, agreements establishing an association involving reciprocal rights and obligations and special procedures. These association agreements are concluded by the Council, acting unanimously after consulting the Assembly (Article 238, second clause). Articles 235 and 238 apply, therefore, in particular, whenever the Community wishes to enter into relationship with other international organizations for the purpose of co-operation in the field of public health. The Court of Justice also pronounced on various occasions in the context of opinions that the Community's competence to enter international commitments may result not only from powers explicitly conferred by the Treaty, but may also derive implicitly from the Treaty's provisions. In particular 'whenever Community law has created for the institutions of the Community powers within its internal system for the purpose of attaining a specific objective, the Community has authority to enter into the international commitments necessary for attainment of that objective even in the absence of an express provision in that connection'. [45]

The above demonstrates that the European Community has ample possibilities either to join legislative acts in the field of public health which are

---

43. See Part B, Ch. IV, para. 7. for the agreements with the Nordic countries Finland, Iceland, Norway and Sweden.
44. Judgment of 31 March 1971 in case 22/70 ([1971], E.C.R., 263).
45. Opinion 1/76 of 26 April 1977 ([1977] E.C.R., 741-762 et. 755).

concluded by other international organizations [46] or to negotiate on international agreements within other international settings. Finally, the member states of the European Community recognized in a joint Declaration on 'co-operation with the States members of international organizations' which was made at the time of signature of the Treaties establishing the EAEC and the EEC, that 'by setting up a customs union and working closely together on the peaceful development of nuclear energy, they will be ensuring economic and social progress and thus contributing not only to their own prosperity but also to that of other countries'.

Where-upon they declared their readiness 'to conclude agreements with other countries, particularly within the framework of the international organizations to which they belong, in order to attain these objectives of common interest and to ensure the harmonious development of trade in general'. [47]

2.4. RELATIONS BETWEEN THE PARLIAMENTARY ASSEMBLY (COUNCIL OF EUROPE) AND THE EUROPEAN PARLIAMENT (EUROPEAN COMMUNITY)

The Parliamentary Assembly and the European Parliament maintain close relations which have been formalized in an 'exchange of letters'. Thus, joint sessions are held in such a manner that time is reserved for discussions in groups as well as for general debate. Regarding the latter, three subjects for discussion are selected under the present procedures and members of other international organizations may be invited to these meetings according to the subjects to be discussed. It will be clear that we have here in principle an important tool at European parliamentary level, which may be used within an appropriate structure for international public health activities in Europe, though it is recognized that with the present procedure there is not yet a permanent possibility for joint discussions at a European parliamentary level with the contribution of other international organizations involved, in particular the WHO. In principle the group meetings give ample possibilities for meetings between the respective committees dealing with public health, though in practice most of the time is devoted to general debate. Furthermore, the European Parliament yearly presents a progress report to the Parliamentary Assembly. This report is, however, not debated.

46. In its decision 77/75/EEC the Council, on behalf of the Community, approved the texts of the European Agreement on the exchange of tissue typing reagents and the additional protocol thereto. This action by the Council is not based upon a specific Article of the EEC Treaty, but on the fact that any derogation from the common customs tariff falls within the exclusive competence of the Community on the one hand, and on the additional protocol to the Agreement on the other. In this protocol the signatory states have agreed that the EEC may become a contracting party to the Agreement by virtue of signing it. See also 'The European Community, international organizations and multilateral agreements', 1977, para. 4. for the procedure which was applied in this instance.
47. Treaties establishing the European Communities; Treaties amending these Treaties; Documents concerning the Accession; 1973; European Communities, p. 497.

242

3. Some conclusions

The functioning of the various international organizations which are under review is not optimal when it comes to the practical realization of the right to health care. This applies both to the extent to which use is made of the constitutional powers of each organization as well as to the mutual co-operation and co-ordination of activities.

Regarding the first, the tools which are at the disposal of each organization, are not fully exploited. The legislative powers and parliamentary facilities in particular could be much better utilised. Regarding the latter, there is no efficient international structure or general international policy development to give concrete form to the human right to health care. This is the more regrettable, because at present there are only very few sectors of the public health field, in which one organization can assume sole responsibility. Therefore, a close relationship among the various international bodies is a prerequisite for the optimal practical realization of the right to health care in Europe.

In fact, most of the sectors of the public health field require complementarity of action. This complementarity of action can be brought about in different ways, such as through joint undertakings or by the taking over of responsibility at a given stage from one organization by the other. The present co-operation system between the various organizations that are wholly or partially concerned with health matters in Europe is mainly on a bilateral basis and lacks any overall planning and co-ordination. This situation facilitates the waste of precious resources, inefficacy and duplication of work and sometimes abstinence of action where this is most urgently needed. It is already recognized that at the national level it is hard to achieve a coherent overall policy in the field of public health. At the international European level the situation is even more complicated.

And yet, if taken together, there are sufficient potentialities to arrive at an efficient European overall structure for public health. For this purpose a critical assesment of the present situation in Europe should be made, in order to be able to determine in which manner the possibilities of each organization can best be used with a view to arriving at a coherent, constructive contribution to the practical realization of the right to health care in Europe.

III. Design for international European undertakings in the field of public health

1. Possibilities for an adequate overall structure

It is evident that none of the international settings discussed are similar in their functioning. This is due to various factors, such as the character of the organization (supranational or intergovernmental), the objective of the organization (mono-functional or multi-functional) and the membership (large or small). Yet, this dissimilarity in itself is not a factor which should prevent the realization of an adequate structure for international European undertakings for the purpose of improving the further elaboration and practical application of the human rights under review.

This dissimilarity in the functioning of the various international settings in Europe may even contribute to an adequate overall structure, provided full use is made of the particularities of each organization and the conditions for appropriate harmonization of policies, programme planning and priority setting, are fulfilled.

Failing a proper strategy for co-ordination and co-operation among the various international settings in Europe no common overall planning and programming can be expected. As was shown in Ch. II, para. 2. the present situation is such that relations among the various international organizations are merely based upon bilateral arrangements; already for that reason an adequate overall structure for international European public health undertakings is lacking.

Therefore, in order to initiate discussions on possibilities to improve the situation in respect of international European public health undertakings, it seems indicated to convene a European conference, in which at least the relevant international organizations as well as representatives of the European Parliament (EC) and the Parliamentary Assembly (Council of Europe) participate. The WHO regional committee for Europe could, for instance, take the initiative for the convening of such a conference. Another possibility is that a parliamentary initiative is taken, either in the European Parliament or in the Parliamentary Assembly.

When considering the available possibilities to reach the said objective it seems that the most appropriate method for realizing an adequate overall structure for international European public health undertakings is to opt for a solution at the level of the international organizations.[48] Only if such a solution turns out to be out of reach, should one turn to another possibility. This other possibility consists of an arrangement at the level of the national governments, for the purpose of ensuring international coherency and rationalization

48. See below, para. 2.

in the public health sphere. Such an arrangement among governments could well be based upon the statutory competence of the Council of Europe to take the initiative of instituting negotiations between the members with a view to the creation of a European Specialised Authority with competence in a particular field. [49] If such a Specialised Authority were to be created for the public health field, there would be a new (mono-functional) international (intergovernmental) organization, in addition to the already existing ones, in which governments and not international organizations will participate as partners.

Regarding the membership of such an Authority, in the absence of a specific indication in the relevant Resolution on this subject, it is possible that also non Council of Europe member states adhere to it.

The mandate of such a Specialised Authority could, for instance, be to draw up a kind of 'Charter for international European public health activities', to be endorsed by its members. In such a Charter members could express their consensus in principle on health problems which necessitate international undertakings; on priorities; on manners in which the problems should preferably be dealt with; and on the most appropriate international settings to assume responsibility for the various parts of the programme thus established.

As such a Charter can only bind the states participating in the Specialised Authority and not international organizations, much will depend on the willingness of member states to carry through the consequences of the arrangements they make in the framework of the Specialised Authority in their policies regarding the other international organizations.

The successful functioning of such an Authority will also much depend on its relationship with other international organizations in Europe.

Special agreements, to be concluded between the Authority and the relevent international organizations, should at least contain specific conditions on reciprocal representation; on exchange of information and documentation; and on consultation on the respective programmes of work. [50]

If such a Specialised Authority were to be created, it should preferably meet at the level of ministers of public health. The informal periodical meetings of ministers of public health in the frame of the European Community (see Ch. II, para. 1.4.) are already a certain proof of readiness of at least nine governments to proceed with reciprocal consultation on public health matters. It constitutes somehow a precedent which, in the suggested framework, could be given a formal, broader basis.

With a view to ensure the democratic functioning of such a Specialised Authority, there are two possibilities. Firstly, to set up a parliamentary body in the framework of the Authority. Secondly, to bring it in relationship with the Parliamentary Assembly of the Council of Europe, by making the neces-

---

49. See Part B, Ch. III, para. 2.5.5. (Resolution adopted by the Committee of Ministers at its eighth session, May 1951).
50. This is in accordance with the procedure applied by the Council of Europe, which, however, is not on a reciprocal basis (see Ch. II, para. 2.2). In making a specific rule in the relationship agreement on this subject, there is at least some chance of tuning in programmes in accordance with the policies of the Specialised Authority.

sary arrangements in a relationship agreement among the two organizations. At first view it seems more practical to make use of the existing possibilities, so that the latter solution be opted for.

2. Overall co-ordinating Body for international European public health undertakings

2.1. SOME GENERAL REMARKS

The first solution which was mentioned in paragraph 1. with a view to obtain optimal efficacy and efficiency of international endeavours in the public health field in Europe was to make the necessary arrangements at the level of the international organizations. Such an arrangement should consist of the creation of a single overall co-ordinating body (the Body), in which the relevant international organizations participate with a view to further elaborate at a European level the human rights under discussion, as well as to put them into practice.

The possibility of setting up such a co-ordinating Body at the European level exists through the explicit or implicit constitutional competences of the international organizations involved to conclude relationship agreements with other international organisations, which is the sole authority of these organizations. [51]

These relationship agreements, which have so far been based upon *bilateral* arrangements should be adjusted in such a manner that there is a *multilateral* arrangement among the various organizations which provides for co-operation in the framework of a central co-ordinating Body.

The purpose of the Body being to realize in the first instance the proper co-ordination among the various organizations which are active in the public health field in Europe, it might possibly be opposed to on grounds that the WHO has exclusive authority in this field in accordance with its Constitution, which states that one of the Organisation's functions shall be to act as the directing and co-ordinating authority on international health work' (Article 2 under (a) of the Constitution). [52]

Yet, this being a global function of the Organization, the regional committee's function which is mentioned in this respect is 'To co-operate with ... and with other regional international organizations having interests in common with the organization' (Article 50 under (d) of the Constitution). [53] Therefore, co-ordination and co-operation at a regional European level being pursued in the frame of an overall co-ordinating Body in which the WHO European office participates, does not seem to constitute an infraction of the WHO's Constitution. Moreover, whenever an international organization does not live up to its constitutional obligations, there is every reason to look for appropriate alternatives to reach the desired objective.

51. See also Ch. II, para. 2.
52. See Part B, Ch. I, para. 2.
53. See Part B, Ch. II, para. 1.3.

246

There is a particular aspect which should be taken into consideration, when setting up the Body, namely its membership.

The review in Part B has shown that, apart from the WHO regional office for Europe, the Council of Europe as well as the European Community, the Benelux Economic Union and the Nordic Council have (or are likely to have) their own functions with a view to further elaborating and putting into practice the human rights under discussion. In respect of the EFTA, the OECD and the NATO these functions are much less obvious. [54] It was seen in Ch. II, para. 1.5 that the somewhat fragmentary undertakings of these Organizations [55] are only likely to obscure the overall picture of public health in Europe. This, moreover, unnecessarily complicates the international co-ordination of activities and promotes inefficiency. There is, moreover, no reason why the activities that are undertaken by these latter three organizations should not be taken up by those organizations, which have proper functions in the field of public health. It, therefore, indicates the restriction of the membership of the overall co-ordinating Body to the WHO European office, the Council of Europe, the European Community, the Benelux Economic Union and the Nordic Council. The European Free Trade Association should be invited to partake in the discussions when pharmaceutical matters are involved. The North Atlantic Treaty Organization should limit its action in the field of public health to the medical defence sphere. The Organisation for Economic Co-operation and Development should preferably refrain entirely from activities in the public health field. In case there are any future intentions for public health activities of an international European reach outside the scope of the overall programme, drawn up at the level of the Body, this should first be discussed at the level of that Body. [56]

2.2. Functioning of the overall co-ordinating Body

The primary objective of the Body should be to co-ordinate the work of the relevant international organizations in Europe in such a manner that there is a maximum of effectiveness and efficiency from the organizational, the functional and the substantial point of view. The latter implies that the Body is not merely charged with the task of tuning in the respective programmes of work, but that it also serves as the central platform for designing an overall plan, on the basis of which undertakings can be promoted for the purpose of the further elaboration of the human right to health care, as well as the establishment of a policy to make this human right operational.

In other words, it will primarily be at the level of the Body that a common

54. With the exception of the NATO's activities in the sphere of medical defence.
55. With the exception of the EFTA's activities in the pharmaceutical field.
56. For practical reasons no particular mention is made of members of the UN family, other than the WHO. The responsibility for bringing them into the picture rests solely with the WHO. They are, moreover, in general not as decentralized as the WHO, so that their particular relevance for the European region is of comparatively less significance. It will still be the task of the Body to supervise and, if necessary, adjust the co-operation between the WHO European office and these other bodies in specific fields.

policy development for overall planning and programming of activities in the field of public health as well as a regular evaluation takes place.

For the purpose of designing an overall programme of activities it will be necessary to use a detailed survey of activities which are at present performed in the framework of the various international settings, including the specific objective of these activities, their scope and the methods used. Such a survey will determine fields in which up till now no international action, or insufficient international action has taken place. It will, furthermore, show in what fields there is undue duplication of efforts. [57]

To determine fields in which there is no action or insufficient action, it is necessary to have a common agreement among the participating organizations on fields in which action is most needed, as well as on the kind of action which might be most appropriate.

So far, the international organizations, when fixing their own programmes of work have not only paid too little attention to endeavours undertaken in the same field by other international organizations, they have also never paid attention to the need to come to a common overall priority programme planning at European level.

(There is some priority planning, such as in the framework of the WHO regional office for Europe, where since 1977 a consultative group on programme development meets at regular intervals. The possibilities of the Parliamentary Assembly of the Council of Europe in this respect were referred to in Ch. II, para. 2.2.) It will be the responsibility of the Body to make the necessary arrangements with a view to replacing apparent duplication of work and overlapping of activities, whenever relevant, by complementarity of action: the overall programme planning has to be focused upon adjusting the various separate undertakings of the international organizations in such a manner that they form an integrated part of a coherent overall European public health scheme.

Determinants for setting an overall strategy at the level of the Body will be the present situation and future outlook in respect of Europe as regards the socio-economic and cultural environment in which public health services function at present and will function in the future; the probable development of medical sciences and medical needs; the extent to which the human personality needs to be protected; the problems the public health services will face; as well as the extent to which, and by which methods international organizations have to be involved.

Once there is agreement on such a priority plan, the Body will have to assign, in common accord, separate tasks to the various organizations, having due regard to the respective operational and budgetary possibilities. To be rational and effective such an assignment should be based upon the principle that activities are preferably performed within those settings, which dispose of the most appropriate tools to achieve the special objective of any programme

---

57. Duplication of work occurs, for instance, in the fields of pharmaceuticals, foodstuffs, education and training, technical research and problems of the organization of health services.

part. This not only presupposes that there is absolute clarity about the operational methods through which a specific programme part can best be performed at a given time, but it also necessitates the exact determination of the objective, including the desired practical result of any programme part and the method through which the result can best be implemented.

This efficiency criterium should prevail over the criterium of having the undertakings performed in the international setting with the largest territorial reach, if the latter implies that in this larger setting the results are not optimal. The guiding principle should in fact be that major tasks in the field of international European public health work, including the drawing up of relevant human rights instruments, lie primarily with the WHO's European office, the Council of Europe and the European Community. The two Regional Unions (the Benelux Economic Union and the Nordic Council) occupy a specific position in serving as a first level at which activities can be undertaken in cases in which, at least for the time being, the set objective of a given programme can not be reached on a larger scale. When the moment appears appropriate, achievements thus reached at a limited scale can be expanded to a broader level.

If the WHO regional office for Europe is in a position to undertake a specific activity without putting pressure on the special objective of such an activity, in other words, if it produces the results desired for a given activity, preference should be given to that Organization, because it has the widest territorial reach. This will be the case when Eastern European countries are also positively interested in any given activity. If the desire to be fully cooperative is not present, or when it comes to the drawing up of a legislative instrument which is not within the powers of the European office of the WHO, the Council of Europe is the most appropriate organization to take responsibility for the carrying out of a given activity. The objective of a given action field will be determinant whether the European Community, because of its specific powers as a supranational organization, will take up any specific activity.

In case the Council of Europe proceeds to elaborate European agreements or conventions, a provision should be inserted in these instruments, enabling non member-states to adhere to such instruments. In this manner the negative aspect of the smaller membership of the Council of Europe in comparison with the coverage of the WHO European region, can be side-stepped.

In reaching agreement on the proper assignment of fields of attention, possibilities for joint undertakings or complementarity of activities can also be taken into account. This overall assignment will give each organization an appropriate place in the overall European institutional setting, taking into account the specific assets of each of them. The overall planning and programming and the assignment of special tasks should allow for the necessary flexibility so that adaptation can take place according to changing circumstances. The latter implies that a regular evaluation takes place at the level of the Body.

Such an evaluation should be of two kinds. The first one is concerned with the overall situation of the further elaboration of the right to health care and the putting into practice of that right at an international European level.

This kind of evaluation will permit the Body, and hence the organizations participating in it, to bring the respective programme parts in line with the requirements of the moment, so that the programme as a whole will function in a dynamic manner. The second kind of evaluation should be directed towards an assesment of measures taken by governments in respect of the recommendations and resolutions drawn up by the various international organizations in the framework of the overall programme, as well as of follow-up given by governments to measures of a legal nature (conventions and agreements). This kind of evaluation will enable the Body to put the necessary pressure upon governments whenever it becomes evident that governments do not (sufficiently) live up to their moral, or even legal obligations in this respect.

Both kinds of evaluation necessitate a stringent and efficient scheme, in order to avoid the shortcomings inherent to the assesment of results which has been performed hitherto in the frame of international organizations.

The role that one or other parliamentary forum might play in this respect could well contribute to the effectiveness of the various evaluation schemes.

The above procedure presupposes that decisions on the overall priority programme-planning, including the general repartition of work among the various organizations, that are reached in common accord among these organizations at the level of the Body, will be respected by each organization which participates in this scheme, when drawing up its own programme of work. It, therefore, is based upon the presumption that both governments and organizations support the necessity to come to an effective and efficient structure for international European undertakings in the field of public health, including the necessary efforts in this respect to further elaborate the human rights involved. Though, in general, in the absence of effective sanctions, every agreement at an international level stands or falls with the political willingness of governments (and international organizations) to live up to their obligations, there is still a possibility to limit to the minimum the chances that arrangements are not kept. This can be brought about by having the Body set up by agreement not only signed by the organizations which will participate in the Body, but also by the governments which are members of one or other organization. Such a system of double signature has yet another advantage, which is that in this way the risk that other organizations, not participating in the Body can still enter the subject field, is also brought down to the minimum, because the governments are at the least moraly, obliged to draw one line with the Body.

It is also possible to insert a special provision into the agreement setting up the Body, obliging the organizations participating in the Body to refer any dispute to arbitration. Finally, the Parliamentary Assembly of the Council of Europe could also be a forum of control of the proper functioning of the Body. If necessary, that parliamentary body can also put pressure upon the international organizations and eventually, through national parliaments, upon the governments.

The functions of the Assembly in respect of the Body, which could be laid down in the agreement setting up the Body, could be similar to the present functions of the Assembly in respect of other organizations. Provisions could be made, for instance, for a proper debate to take place yearly on the results obtained in the framework of the overall programme of the Body. The European Parliament of the European Community could also be associated with this debate. The purpose of such a debate should, however, not be limited to a 'control' function. On the contrary, an effective contribution towards the programme planning should also be expected from the parliamentary forum.

2.3. THE OVERALL CO-ORDINATING BODY AND THE PRACTICAL REALIZATION OF THE RIGHT TO HEALTH CARE

2.3.1. General remarks

The contribution of the international organizations towards the practical realization of the right to health care can roughly be put into two categories.

The first contribution consists of measures of a regulatory nature. This contribution will, for instance, aim at the setting of common standards for safety and control and the promotion of free movement of personnel and material, while guaranteeing at the same time a certain level of quality and safety. This kind of international collaboration will include international standardizations, protectionary health measures and, in general, the approximation and harmonization of provisions laid down by law, regulation or administrative action relating to various aspects of the right to health care.

The second contribution consists of the so-called 'promotional' or 'assistant' services. These services will mainly aim at the development of strategies and general policy lines or the tendering of advice. This kind of international collaboration in health matters will include organized exchange of experience and information and joint efforts to resolve health problems. Some of the methods used are expert committees, consultants, advisory panels, special technical conferences, the attribution of grants, training of staff and field work.

Broadly speaking, it can be said that the efforts of the WHO are mainly concerned with the 'promotional' and 'assistant' services, and to a lesser degree with measures of a regulatory nature. Its endeavours in the latter field concentrate mostly on safety criteria, standardization methods and international control of epidemics. These subjects are, moreover, preferably dealt with by way of recommendation.

These endeavours are not peculiar to the European situation, but are of worldwide concern, hence the responsibility of the WHO Headquarters. The contribution of the European Community is mainly the provision of regulatory measures of a legislative nature (harmonization and co-ordination of national rules). The Council of Europe, as well as the two regional arrangements are placed somewhere in between.

When attempting to indicate in some way various sectors of the public health field in which international action is needed, as well as the most appropriate setting(s) in which action can take place, it should be realized that the various sectors are closely interrelated and sometimes overlapping. Moreover,

251

the possible contribution of each organization to these sectors can take place through simultaneous undertakings, joint action, complementarity of action or successive action.

Furthermore, the programme planning and assignment of tasks will be a continued process of changes and adaptations to arising needs. Therefore any classification of programme areas which should be covered by international public health undertakings at the European level, of instruments to be used for various aspects of these programme areas and of international organizations which should be involved with a given programme section, will be arbitrary and incomplete. In the following, an attempt is made to give some indications on a possible programme design and the place each organization may take within each programme area.

This programme design takes account of the fact that sofar various functions have been carried out adequately by international organizations and that they should therefore remain the main responsibility of these organizations. Moreover, as most of the instruments that are used in the framework of the 'promotional' or 'assistant' services of international organizations are common to these organizations, the decision on the distribution of these tasks has been based on rational arguments.

2.3.2. Tentative design of various programme areas [58]

I. Communicable disease prevention and control

The international aspect of this programme area is obvious and the necessity for international co-operation in this field was already sufficiently indicated. This programme area which has important hygiene and sanitation aspects may be divided into two main categories.

   — quarantinable diseases

These are the diseases which are covered by the International Health Regulations (IHR) of the WHO. This category is the least complicated for the distribution of tasks at the international level. As this category is dealt with by the WHO (as a global responsibility) in the application of the IHR (international quarantine, epidemic intelligence and epidemiological serveillance) as well as through other efforts, such as studies by expert committecs on specific deseases (laboratory studies), there is no reason to change this course of action.

Yet, two remarks have to be made in this context. Firstly, it may be recalled that in accordance with article 92 [59] of the IHR within the frame-

58. For this design use has been made in particular of 'Prospective studies and future action in the public health field' (Aujaleu, 1972); 'International Health Organizations' (Goodman, 1971); 'Health services in Europe' (WHO regional office for Europe, 1975); Handbook of resolutions and decisions of the World Health Assembly and the Executive Board, Volumes I and II (1973; 1977).
59. Article 92 provides for the possibility of the conclusion of special treaties or arrangements between two or more states which have certain interests in common, owing to their health, geographical, social or economic conditions, in order to facilitate the application of the IHR.

252

work of the Council of Europe Partial Agreement on public health, administrative arrangements were made for the establishment of a so called 'excepted area' for the health control of sea, land and air traffic (see Part B, Ch. III, para. 3.4.2. under (b)); there is a similar situation in respect of the Nordic countries (see Part B, Ch. IV, para. 7.).

The possibilities for extension of these 'excepted areas' should be taken in consideration, so that co-ordination of efforts towards prevention of the introduction and spreading of quarantinable diseases, as well as the possibilities for quick and effective action if the situation so requires, may eventually be raised to a European level.

Secondly, possible side effects of the WHO policy to deal with various aspects of the quarantinable diseases by way of issuing texts of 'desirability' rather than of a mandatory nature should be subject to continued critical study at the level of the Body. Such a critical examination will draw the attention of the WHO in due course to negative aspects of this policy, so that the Organization might be urged to issue texts of a more binding nature. Failing such an action by the WHO, the Council of Europe could attemp to draw up regulatory rules, although it is recognized that within this programme area worldwide action is preferable.

Adequate measures to reduce to the minimum potential risks involved with the maintenance of stocks of virus and bacteria by laboratories have also to be taken.

— other communicable diseases

This category, which includes the parasitic, bacterial, and virus diseases which do not call for quarantine measures, also falls under the worldwide responsibility of the WHO. Assistance by that Organization may range from services such as international notification and surveillance, support to laboratory studies, training and education. So far the WHO has not taken legislative measures on this subject. Yet, as the communicable diseases which fall under the present category continue to pose a serious problem to the European region, due to the movement of migrant workers and tourists, urbanization and international trade, it might well become necessary to aim at harmonization of national legislations in some of the aspects (such as in fields of vaccination and food safety and standards). Moreover, notification in this area is often insufficient, and methods of investigation and diagnostic criteria often lack uniformity. There is ample reason to assess adequacy of epidemiological, statistical and operational information, made available under recommendations of the WHO, in order to be able to determine whether the present practice of voluntary government information needs a stronger basis, at the least in respect of those diseases, which present a major risk to public health in Europe. In regard to the distribution of tasks in this area, the primary responsibility for the 'assistant' and 'promotional' services should remain with the WHO.

Yet, whenever a conflict of responsibilities arises between the WHO headquarters and the European Office regarding the special requirements of the European region, the Council of Europe should take over responsibility for specific subjects. Such a conflict may arise by a combination of limited budgetary appropriations and priority orientation of Headquarters towards developing countries, which can put the European office into such a position, that it cannot cope adequately with the various aspects of these diseases in accordance with the priority planning of the Body.

The Council of Europe has already occasionally taken up this stand-by function, for instance, when dealing with sexually transmittable diseases. The latter Organization should moreover be entrusted with the responsibility of drawing up legislative measures in this area whenever such measures become preferable to the less obligatory recommendations issued sofar by the WHO. An example in this field is the Council of Europe Agreement on the transfer of corpses. The European Communities should also, where appropriate, perform legislative activities.

II. Non-communicable disease prevention and control

As health problems occur in very much the same form in almost all countries of the region, it is one of the tasks of the international organizations which are active in the field of public health to ensure regular, reliable and general applicable information on health events occuring, measures taken, methods used and results obtained. Moreover, serious problems arise almost simultaneously in various countries of the region, for which solutions are difficult to find and for which endeavours of a national scope will hardly suffice. Hence the need to combine efforts at the European level. In this programme area, which covers major categories of diseases such as chronic and degenerative ones, hereditary and congenital defects, mental illnes, dental defects and others, a sound system of international exchange of information and experience, as well as joint programmes for the purpose of reaching solutions acceptable to all, and applicable in every country, are needed. There is in some fields also a need to redefine some legal and medical guidelines.

The repartition of tasks can be similar to the one under 1.2.: appropriate arrangements for repartition of work among the WHO regional office for Europe and the Council of Europe, having due regard to the technical possibilities of each Organization. Although within the frame of the Council of Europe Partial Agreement in the public health field activities have been undertaken which concern this programme area, it is preferable that activities be undertaken at the broadest level possible, namely that of the twenty one member states of the Council of Europe.

The undertakings of the international organizations in this programme area will be mainly of a 'promotional' and 'assistant' nature, though there may sometimes also be a need for regulatory measures. The latter may be, for instance, the case when joint programmes on a specific subject matter involve multidisciplinary research for which purpose it will be recommendable to draw up international agreements or protocols, or safeguards for confidentiality of records that are made accessable for such research. The Council of Europe should take the responsibility whenever there is a need to draw up legal measures in this programme area. Yet another endeavour under this programme area is the promotion of the availability of human substances necessary for the cure of some diseases (see also under III b.). Under the auspices of the Council of Europe a European frozen blood bank of rare groups functions already. The next step could be the creation of organ banks, preferably also under the auspices of the Council of Europe, because of the legal aspects involved. It should also be considered whether activities such as those of Eurotransplant [60], which operates mainly as a mediator for the selection of recipients of organs, should be raised to a broader level, and should then function under the auspices of an international organization. [61]

III. Organization of medical care and preventive services

This programme area can roughly be devided into two main categories, namely the organization and structure of health services in a country for the purpose of ensuring the appropriate distribution of available facilities on the one hand, and the availibility of these services at a larger than national scale on the other.

a. national level
  The various countries in Europe face similar problems in this programme area, such as health planning, health policy and increasing costs.
  Therefore, the exchange of experience and information as well as the undertaking of efforts, with a view to finding solutions to common problems, are equally of international concern. Also here, it is most indicated to proceed with a repartition of work, based upon a sound priority planning and inspired by rational arguments. In this programme area in particular, the stand-by function of the Council of Europe is of importance. [62] The situation can be such, that at a given moment the Council of Europe takes primary responsibility for rendering 'promotional' and 'assistant' services in this programme area.
  Whenever there is a need for regulatory measures in this area, the Council of Europe should, in any case, assume responsibility. The European Community for its part could usefully contribute to this programme area in endeavouring to bring into line the various national public health systems. It could also promote the co-ordination of provisions of medical care (if necessary, to be initiated at the level of the Benelux Economic Union).

b international level
  One of the main targets of the realization of the right to health care is the equitable distribution of available possibilities for medical care. International attention should, therefore, also focus upon this aspect.

60. This (private) organization operates in Austria, Belgium, the Federal Republic of Germany, Switzerland and the Netherlands (where it is located). It also maintains close contacts with similar organizations such as those operating in the Scandinavian countries, the United Kingdom and France.
61. The capacity of organ banks and the availibility of organs has been discussed in the framework of the European Community. This has been done on the basis of a decision of the Council of Ministers of 22 July 1976 (OJ no. L. 223 of 16 August 1976). The possibility of the linkage of existing banks is presently under study by the Commission.
62. The Council of Europe has, for instance, thoroughly dealt with the subject of hospital organization.

It was already emphasized that in Europe, national governments are called upon to make priority choices in respect of the organization of their health care systems. Also the relative scarcity of particularly advanced and costly treatment methods makes it necessary that decisions be made both at governmental level and at the level of the medical professions. [63] On the governmental level decisions have to be taken on what kind of treatment facilities will be made generally available. At the level of the medical professions, individual choices have to be made on whom will benefit from very specialised and hence relatively scarce treatment facilities. In this respect there is an international responsibility to endeavour to prevent undue proliferation of highly intensive treatment facilities causing high costs on the one hand and to promote an objective, rational distribution of very specialised and relatively scarce treatment facilities [64] on the other.

To adequately face this situation, national availibility should in some cases be substituted by international availibility. This not only requires a sound international policy development, but also the acceptance at national level that some of the national public health is supplemented or even in some cases replaced by international undertakings.

Prior to the realization of such an international policy it is necessary to undertake an international study at the level of the Body to determine which fields are most indicated for international treatment facilities. International agreement also has to be reached in such a way that through 'international pooling' optimal use is made of the existing possibilities, taking into account the economic aspects in relation to the benefits which are expected from it.

The co-operation which exists among the Nordic countries is a constructive example in this field.

In view of the complexity of this specific subject, which, moreover, requires considerable effort and willingness on the part of national instances, it seems appropriate to start such a scheme, at first, on a limited scale, namely on that of the European Community. This Organization moreover has an advantage because of its supranational nature. It disposes of all prerequisites to carry through such a policy on the basis of a general plan for the spread of medical care provisions throughout the Community, to be developed at community level. The free movement of the medical and paramedical professions which is in the process of being realized within the European Community makes it moreover possible to put mutual recognized, qualified personel at the disposal of international treatment facilities within the EC.

Once such a scheme is operative at the level of the European Community, the possibility of offering treatment facilities at an even broader level, whenever the need arises, might be considered. In thus pooling at a European level very special treatment facilities, the international responsibility for this special aspect of the right to health care can be optimally realized.

It is recognized that in doing so, the problem of selection of recipients for very specialised treatment still remains. Decisions on the individual allocation

63. See also Ch. I, para. 3.2.
64. This is not limited to medical facilities, but equally applies to availibility of human substances (see under II) and to health manpower, which will be dealt with under IV.

of these specific international treatment facilities should be taken in accordance with a carefully worked out international set of objective and rational criteria, while there should be a built-in system for supervising the application of these criteria. The pooling at the European level is not limited, however, to very specialised treatment facilities. The research field is also very suitable for such international pooling and, in fact, easier to realize. This is supported by the fact that in some fields it has already been carried through. Yet, also here the risk of duplication of efforts and hence of waste of precious and scarce equipment and manpower and economic availibilities cannot be disregarded, so that amplification of pooling of research at an international level should be stimulated by the Body.

Finally, the question of mutual medical assistance in the event of catastrophies or particularly serious accidents or diseases should be mentioned. Within the EC mutual health assistance activities are studied, while the Council of Europe has deployed various activities in this field. A scheme for mutual medical assistance in case of catastrophies could be worked out in co-operation among both organizations.

IV. Health manpower

This programme area has several aspects for international concern. Those which relate to the necessity of pooling of manpower were already covered under III, when dealing with the organization of medical care and preventive services.

At the national level, there are many aspects of a general nature, such as questions about quality, quantity and proliferation of health professions to which the international exchange of information and experience might contribute with a view to solving national problems. There are also legal aspects involved, such as the problem of liability and the legal aspects of the free exchange of health professions. (The problem of liability naturally also arises in respect of institutions which operate in the health field.)

These legal aspects call for harmonization and, or approximation of national legal rules. Regarding the repartition of tasks in this programme area the WHO should concentrate primarily on the 'promotional' and 'assistant' services, while the Council of Europe could deal with harmonization and legal aspects inherent to the exercise of the profession (for instance: liability and harmonization of standards for the assesment of damages). The European Community should not only continue and expand its work on the mutual recognition of diplomas and the problems arising from it. It should also undertake planning at Community level of the number of staff required, so that the establishment policy is brought from the national to the Community level (see also under III).

V. Prophylactic, diagnostic and therapeutic substances

This programme area is of international concern for a variety of reasons.

Of these, the aspects of international trade, the international supply of products and substances, requires adequate standards for quality, safety and efficacy of pharmaceuticals. Registration requirements and manufacture practices are only some of the problems involved. Adequate standards for quality and safety are also needed in the field of blood and bloodproducts. Then there is the need for the adoption of international standards and units for biological substances used in prophylactic and therapeutic medicine, the standardization of diagnostic reagents and related reference methods. The question of availibility (quantitative aspect) of a great variety of medicines is also of international concern which in turn will have its influence on prevalent patterns of use and misuse. Regarding the field of pharmaceuticals in particular, the overall picture of international undertakings in Europe is very confusing. Practices of manufacture and registration requirements are dealt with in most of the international settings. Yet, this fact has hitherto not brought about adequate harmonization of control and registration systems.

Although it is recognized that some improvements in legislation have been made particularly in the field of drug control and in the field of developing and standardizing specifications and methods of examination (analytical, pharmacological, toxicological and clinical), the overall picture is far from being ideal. It is therefore one of the tasks of the Body on the basis of an overall picture of the various undertakings in this particular field in the different settings to lay down a scheme for a coherent European policy in this area, as well as to indicate fields for priority action through joint undertakings. Emphasis should be put, in particular, on legislative measures including early harmonization of control or even the introduction of European control to replace national controls. Endeavours in this respect of the European Community and the Council of Europe should be strengthened and brought to the largest possible level. The 'promotional' and 'assistant' services should preferably be left to the WHO European Office. Regarding the field of blood and blood products and other substances of human origin, the endeavours of the Council of Europe so far could well be expanded with a view to increasing the availibility at a European level.

VI. Health statistics and epidemiology

This programme area overlaps with most of the preceeding programme areas, whenever there is a need for easily accessable and reliable data. The WHO has worldwide responsibility in this respect, whereas in Europe the Partial Agreement of the Council of Europe is involved. Assesment of needs and shortcomings particularly relevant to the European region will determine whether or not the Council of Europe Partial Agreement should expand on these areas.

VII. Health and biomedical information

The distribution of practical tasks in order to meet with the constant need for intercountry transfer of knowledge through international data banks, clearing houses, journals and other publications, as well as the necessity for health information of the public, will largely depend upon the repartition of respon-

258

sibilities under the other programme areas discussed. The proliferation of information on results obtained within an international organization was already briefly critisized. The Body could both assist in bettering existing services as well as in evaluating existing needs and ways and means to respond to these needs.

The legal aspects which fall under this programme area, related to, for instance, the setting up of medical data banks and co-ordination of health legislation, call for action at the international level. Since 1977, the Council of Europe's committee on legal co-operation is studying the possibility of elaborating data bank regulations, particularly for medical data banks. In addition, a catalogue of other (regulatory) measures which should be taken, could be set up by the Council of Europe, so as to enable decision making at the level of the overall co-ordinating Body on priority programmes on this subject (see also below para. 2.4.2.).

VIII.   Public health endeavours directed towards specific groups

This programme area concentrates on certain groups of the population, that are specially at risk or require special health services. Examples of these are mothers of childbearing age, children, the handicapped, the old aged. International endeavours in this area will consist mainly of exchange of information and experience, and the undertaking of joint studies for setting guidelines for national policies.

Both the WHO and the Council of Europe Partial Agreement have been involved with this programme area, so here again a repartition of work should be based upon rationality, taking into consideration both existing possibilities and priority setting.

2.4.   THE OVERALL CO-ORDINATING BODY AND THE PROMOTION OF THE RIGHT TO HEALTH CARE

2.4.1. General remarks

The Body should not only have functions in regard to the practical realization of the right to health care. It should also have appropriate responsibilities for the further elaboration and implementation of the right to health care and those human rights which are closely related to this right. It was argued before (Ch. I, para. 1.1.) that there is a need at the international level to come to a more precise formulation of the standards which are covered by the relevant human rights as well as to elaborate additional standards on particular aspects of these rights. In many countries of the European region specific aspects of the right to health care, and particularly the rights of the patient, are presently under discussion. There is, moreover, also a growing interest for 'health law' which is increasingly being considered as a coherent entity of law in general. In this respect international undertakings are needed to cope with the evolution in this field in Europe. The achievements made so far at the European level in the framework of the various international settings were indicated briefly in Ch. I, para. 1.2.

It will be one of the tasks of the Body to come to a repartition of work in this field, on the basis of the present possibilities of each organization. The Body will have to take into account the fact that there is no outlook, for the time being, that the WHO is willing to embark itself on the drawing up of further instruments in the field of human rights, nor that it will delegate for this purpose appropriate legislative possibilities to the European region.

On the other hand the Council of Europe has all prerequisites to appropriately live up to its tasks of defending, protecting and furthering human rights in Europe. It has of living, moreover, proven to be capable to fulfil this task as it has already endeavoured successfully to draw up two human rights instruments and has, as far as the individual human rights are concerned, set up a rather adequate control machinery.

Furthermore, the foreign ministers of the Council of Europe member states have adopted in April 1978 a declaration in which they decide among other things 'to give priority to the work undertaken in the Council of Europe of exploring the possibility of extending the lists of rights of the individual, notably rights in the social, economic and cultural fields, which should be protected by European Conventions or any other appropriate means' (see B (78) 40 of 5 September 1978). [65] If it is, therefore, decided to confine primary responsibility for further elaborating the right to health care to the Council of Europe, this Organization should consider ways and means to further strengthen its present human rights instruments. It could, for instance, consider enlarging the field of application of the European Convention on Human Rights to include also economic and social rights, and revising and improving certain clauses of the European Social Charter, particularly the provisions relating to the implementation machinery, including the strengthening of the Parliamentary's role in the supervision procedure, as suggested by the Parliamentary Assembly's symposium on the European Social Charter and social policy today (Strasbourg, 7 to 9 December 1977). [66]

The contribution of the WHO to the further elaboration of the right to health care could consist of giving effective support and practical assistance to the Council of Europe's undertakings. Prior to undertaking any activity to further elaborate the right to health care, the Body should request the Council of Europe and the WHO regional office for Europe to jointly draw up an inventory of fields in which further human rights instruments at a European level are both indicated and necessary. In doing so, full use should be made of the studies so far made by the UN division of human rights on particular aspects of the right to health care, as well as of the occupations of the Council of Europe in this field, both at the governmental and parliamentary level.

There are various ways in which the different aspects of the right to health care as presently formulated in the European human rights instruments can be further elaborated. In making a choice about the method to be used with a view to obtain maximum protection and promotion of the right to health

65. See also for instance Parliamentary Assembly's doc. 4006 of 7 July 1977.
66. See doc. AS/COLL/Charte/CR.

care, due account should be given to the fact that this particular human right contains elements of various branches of law, such as civil, penal and administrative laws.

The interaction between social and individual human rights, when it comes to undertakings in the field of public health, was already referred to in Chapter I, para. 1. It may be recalled that, at the European level, the social human rights are formulated basically in the European Social Charter and the individual human rights in the European Convention on the Protection of Human Rights and Fundamental Freedoms. The Body should, therefore, not overlook this dual aspect of the human right to health care, when it comes to decisions on the further elaboration of that right. The exercise of the right to health care cannot be complete if both aspects, namely the relevant social human rights aspects and the relevant individual human rights aspects, are not taken care of.

Since these two closely interrelated human rights categories are broadly dealt with in two distinct European human rights instruments, it seems logical that the further elaboration and qualification of the right to health care and the various other rights involved takes place in the framework of the respective human rights instruments. This could, for instance, be done by adding a protocol to the respective human rights instruments, each dealing with the appropriate aspects of the right to health care. There is, however, a certain disadvantage in applying this procedure. The right to health care touches on so many branches of the law that there is a risk of the overall picture becoming obscure and hardly accessible to the individual, when the separation of the individual and the social human rights is categorically maintained. It might, therefore, be queried whether it is practical and efficient to incorporate into two distinct human rights instruments specific standards to be established for the right to health care, whereas this human right in question can be considered as forming the basis of one coherent branch of law (health law).

It is also possible to group all the relevant aspects of the right to health care into one single human rights instrument. There is no juridical objection to such a procedure, because a distinct human rights instrument which deals with a particular right, does not limit the rights that are broadly formulated in the two European human rights instruments. The advantage will be that these rights will be further qualified, if they are included in one single human rights instrument.

Regarding the implementation and control procedure for such an instrument, which covers two categories of human rights (individual and social) the possibility may be taken into consideration to provide for two distinct implementation procedures. Another possibility, which may be preferable, is to further look into the suggestions made at the already mentioned parliamentary symposium on the European Social Charter [67], and particularly into the suggestion to create a European social court or a social Chamber of the (existing) Court of human rights and to enable individuals, or groups of indi-

67. Strasbourg, 7-9 December 1977; doc. AS/COLL/Charte/CR, p. 79. See also doc. 4198 of the Parliamentary Assembly of 31 August 1978, p. 8.

viduals, to present petitions which can eventually be considered by the social Court (or social Chamber).

If such an institution were to be created with competence in the field of social rights, its competence in the field of individual human rights which play a predominant role in the realization of the right to health care should be taken into consideration: in other words, there may be a need to come somehow to a working arrangement with the already existing European Court of human rights, which is exclusively competent in the field of individual human rights.

Whatever method is chosen, it will be obvious that, once a possibility is created for individual appeal in relation to the right to health care, governments will be more or less obliged to give more content to this right, whenever necessary. This, in turn, will have a positive effect on the follow-up given by governments to resolutions and recommendations or conventions and agreements in the field of public health. It is, moreover, to be expected, that the parliamentary influence with respect to the further elaboration of the rights under discussion will become increasingly important, once the right to health care is stripped of its more or less non-committing nature.

2.4.2. Indication of aspects of the human rights that are suitable for further elaboration [68]

All the various human rights which were discussed contain standards which so far are not, or at least insufficiently, qualified. Also, various aspects of the right to health care should be further specified.

Though this particular field is subject to continuous change and adaptation as a result of the evolution, not only in medical science, but also in ethical, moral and legal concepts, this domain may still be given some indication on a possible programme design and repartition of work among the various international organizations.

When considering the European Convention on the Protection of Human Rights and Fundamental Freedoms there is, for instance, not yet a clearcut delineation of the moment of the beginning or ending of life, though the need of effective criteria in this field has been recognized. The Parliamentary Assembly of the Council of Europe, for instance, in its Resolution 613 (76) called upon the WHO regional office for Europe to establish universally valid guidelines for determining the moment of death (see, for instance, Part A, Ch. II, para 3.1.).

It does not, however, seem appropriate to include such guidelines into a proper human rights instrument. The very nature of the subject matter, which largely depends on advances in science and technology, does not lend itself to that purpose. It therefore seems indicated that the Body confines in the first instance the task of preparing such guidelines to the WHO European Office.

In assuming this responsibility, the WHO should take advantage of the support which non-governmental organizations such as the CIOMS and the WMA are likely to give, but it should not merely sponsor the actions of these

68. See: Leenen, Rechten van mensen in de gezondheidszorg, 1978.

262

non-governmental organizations, as it has done hitherto. It should be willing to seriously assume this responsibility as one of its own duties and establish European guidelines under its own authority.

There are also no decisive criteria for establishing the exact meaning of what one must consider to be torture, or inhuman and degrading treatment or punishment, although it is recognized that various cautious indications have been given by both the European Commission and the European Court for human rights. (The same applies to the international Covenant on Civil and Political Human Rights, despite the fact that this instrument is of a later date.)

In this context there is also a need to qualify the notion of 'informed consent'. This is of importance, not only with a view to putting into effect the right to information prior to undergoing medical treatment or an act of a preventive character, but also for the purpose of gaining consent whenever research involve human beings. International guiding principles which were already established should be amplified and given a proper legal basis, so that infrigment can be invoked by law. As the Council of Europe is the appropriate Organization to formulate human rights it should be given responsibility for this task, preferably in joint action with the WHO European office.

Whenever medical research involves human subjects, the application of the principles not only of ethical, but also of legal codes to actual specific situations in medical research should be guaranteed by independent and authorative advisory and guiding bodies.

National ethical review committees should be assisted in their work by an independent international European committee. Such a committee which could, for instance, be created under the auspices of the WHO European office, in close co-operation with the Council of Europe and the European Community, should be entrusted with the task to elaborate and constantly review guidelines for research at national or international level involving human subjects.

A system of obligatory notification of such research to this European committee will serve two purposes. Firstly it offers an opportunity to proceed in the correct manner with the required exchange of information and experience. Secondly, it enables the committee to draw attention to possible gaps in this field of research, as well as to duplications which should be avoided.

Yet another aspect which calls for international attention is to determine to what extent the state's interference in the individual human rights for the benefit of the community is permissable. Whereas various states are inclined to interfere more and more with the individual rights, there is clearly a need for international consensus on how far a state's interference by law (through compulsory measures) may go, for the benefit of public health, which appears throughout the two European human rights instruments as a possibility for limiting the full exercise of the human rights contained in these texts. The development of medical computing at national and international scale is but one of the concerns in this respect. In para. 2.3.2. reference was made to the necessity to pay attention to the legal aspects of the transfer of health and biomedical information (programme area no. VII). The right to privacy of the individual in particular calls for specific safeguards.

From among the other subjects which also call for international (European) attention, the professional secrecy and genetic questions may be mentioned. To some of these subjects attention is paid by the Council of Europe's committee on legal co-operation.

Various of the above mentioned examples of fields in which the standards enunciated in the relevant human rights instruments should be supplemented, and in some cases revised, are suitable for inclusion in an international human rights instrument dealing with the rights of the patient. If a general plan is formulated on such an instrument at the level of the Body, including the appropriate repartition of work, the question should also be studied as to whether some duties of the patient can be included. The latter aspect, an important element of human rights of a mainly moral nature, has hitherto been given hardly any attention in human rights instruments. [69]

And yet, it cannot be denied that whenever man has a claim as a consequence of the recognition of a human right, he also has some obligations, some duties in case he wants to make use of his claim, though it is recognized that generally enforcement will not be possible.

The most universal duty a person has in exchange of his right to health care is the merely moral duty to take care of his own health in such a manner that the risks which might endanger his health are reduced to the minimum. [70]

3. Some conclusions

The overall picture of international public health endeavours has clearly shown that the various areas of concern of international organizations are often overlapping, and that an overall planning and priority setting for European public health undertakings is most urgently needed.

The right to health care can only be appropriately further elaborated and put into practice at the international level if some conditions are fulfilled. The most important of these conditions is that there should be a proper basis for multilateral arrangements at the level of an overall co-ordinating Body, in which the international organizations decide the programmes to be performed and the repartition of work among the various international settings involved.

69. The American Declaration of human rights and duties (Bogota, 2 May 1948) is an example of a human rights instrument which contains some (very generally formulated) duties.
70. Leenen (1978, pp. 137-139) indicates some of the duties of the patient during the treatment process: the duty to give information necessary for the medical profession to carry out its work properly; to give suit to the doctor's opinion (within reasonable limits); to respect the privacy and to maintain secrecy of the doctor; to pay for services rendered (either directly or through the insurance system); to compensate damages and to partake in reasonable discussions whenever there is a particular problem.

The setting of overall guidelines for the repartition of tasks in each specific programme area should take place in such a manner that it is not based on the presumption that each organization takes fully advantage of its constitutional powers, but should preferably be based on realistic considerations. The latter implies that the practical functioning of each organization has to be taken into account, in order to be able to compensate shortcomings in the functioning of one organization by efforts of another organization. Very broadly speaking the repartition should be such that the World Health Organization European office, besides its traditional functions which come under the worldwide concern of the Organization, concentrates on 'promotional' and 'assistant' services for those problems, which are particular to the European region, and which require urgently solutions the Organization can offer. Preference should be given to thorough, intensive programmes instead of a broad overall approach to too many subjects. The Council of Europe should fulfil a 'stand-by' function in this respect. It should, moreover, assume responsibility for further elaborating the right to health care as well as for drawing up legislative instruments in any field of practical application of the right to health care, which necessitates such regulatory measures, including the relevant individual human rights. The Organization should also expand its activities in the field of blood and bloodtransfusion and activities related to the transplantation of organs, so that it can contribute to, and also promote, the pooling of resources where it is most urgently needed. If the Council of Europe wants to yield success in its endeavours for the practical realization of the right to health care, it should, however, critically examine its own structures and internal functioning.

In regard to the European Community, it is preferable that the Organization formally recognizes its competence in the field of public health so that its undertakings in this field may form part of a programme specially designed for that purpose. Its environmental hygiene programme may be held as an example in this respect. The European Community could primarily concentrate upon co-ordination of health systems and of available resources, as well as upon solving problems which arise from the free movement of health personnel.

As far as the Regional Unions are concerned, they should serve as a first level of co-ordination, harmonization and availibility, whenever this is needed, and stimulate action at a broader scale through a common approach.

Other international organizations which are active in Europe should not enter the field of public health, unless this matter has been thoroughly discussed at the level of the Body, with one exception, namely the activities falling under the medical defence programme of NATO.

The whole subject field in fact requires a reconsideration of the European situation at the level of the co-ordinating overall Body for the purpose of co-ordinating, adjusting and reorganizing at the European level, so that an optimal structure for international (European) public health undertakings will be realized. This includes a reorganization of the parliamentary contribution to public health policies in Europe, because not only the intergovernmental aspect, but also the parliamentary aspect requires a critical examination, so that at that level also a due process of co-ordination and control can take place and a useful contribution can be made to the Body. Moreover, the scarcity of some of the treatment facilities calls for a new (political) orientation towards the promotion of international availibility instead of unduly creating not justified, high cost, national possibilities.

Samenvatting

Het doel van deze studie is te onderzoeken op welke wijze op internationaal (Europees) niveau in het kader van internationale gouvernementele samenwerking de gezondheidszorg optimaal kan worden behartigd, met andere woorden, hoe in Europa in het kader van internationale samenwerking het recht op gezondheidszorg zo goed mogelijk verwezenlijkt kan worden. De gezondheidszorg is gebaseerd op het recht op gezondheidszorg als sociaal grondrecht alsmede op een aantal individuele grondrechten, met name het recht op leven en het verbod van mishandeling en experimenten op mensen (zgn. recht op fysieke en geestelijke integriteit). Nationale en internationale organisaties geven op basis van met name deze rechten gestalte aan op de gezondheidszorg gerichte activiteiten.

Teneinde te kunnen vaststellen wat de functie van internationale organisaties op het terrein van de gezondheidszorg is, hoe deze hun taken verrichten, c.q. zouden dienen te verrichten en waar de mogelijkheden en beperkingen in deze liggen, wordt in *deel A* inzicht gegeven in de genoemde mensenrechten en wel als volgt.

In Hfdst. I wordt een korte beschrijving van de volgende mensenrechtteksten gegeven:
— Universele Verklaring van de rechten van de mens (Verenigde Naties, 1948);
— Internationaal Verdrag inzake burgerrechten en politieke rechten (Verenigde Naties, 1966);
— Europees Verdrag tot bescherming van de rechten van de mens en fundamentele vrijheden (Raad van Europa, 1950);
— Internationaal Verdrag inzake economische, sociale en culturele rechten (Verenigde Naties, 1966);
— Europees Sociaal Handvest (Raad van Europa, 1961).

Vervolgens wordt in Hfdst. II ingegaan op de totstandkoming van de onderscheiden formuleringen van de verschillende individuele grondrechten (recht op leven: artikel 3 Universele Verklaring, artikel 2 Europese conventie, artikel 6 Internationaal Verdrag inzake burger en politieke rechten; verbod van mishandeling en experimenten: resp. artikel 5, 3 en 7) en het recht op gezondheidszorg (artikel 25 van de Universele Verklaring, artikel 11 van het Europees Sociaal Handvest, artikel 12 van het Internationale Verdrag inzake economische, sociale en culturele rechten).

De gedachtenontwikkeling ten aanzien van de verschillende mensenrechten alsmede de besluitvorming van de diverse organisaties inzake de onderscheiden teksten wordt beschreven teneinde inzicht te verkrijgen in de betekenis van deze rechten.

In *deel B* volgt een beschrijving van de ontstaansgeschiedenis, taken en bevoegdheden alsmede van het functioneren van die internationale vormen van samenwerking welke het meest van belang zijn voor de praktische uitvoering van het recht op gezondheidszorg, voor de verdere inhoudsbepaling en uitwerking van dit grondrecht. Deze organisaties zijn: de Wereldgezondheidsorganisatie (Hfdst. I: WGO, Hfdst. II: WGO, regionaal bureau voor Europa); de Raad van Europa (Hfdst. III); de Europese Gemeenschap, de Organisatie voor Economische Samenwerking en Ontwikkeling, de Noord Atlantische Verdrag Organisatie, De Europese Vrijhandels Associatie, de Benelux Economische Unie en de Noordse Raad (Hfdst. IV). Ook wordt ingegaan op de onderlinge relaties tussen deze organisaties, terwijl apart aandacht wordt besteed aan de resultaten van de verschillende vormen van internationale samenwerking ten aanzien van de verdere uitwerking van de in deel A beschreven mensenrechten.

Op grond van het organisatorische karakter van de verschillende organisaties en hun functioneren in het kader van de gezondheidszorg worden in *deel C* hun feitelijke mogelijkheden en tekortkomingen geanalyseerd. Deze analyse bestrijkt zowel de verdere inhoudelijke uitwerking van de verschillende rechten als de praktische toepassing van deze rechten door operationele aktiviteiten. Ook wordt de onderlinge relatie tussen de diverse internationale vormen van samenwerking, zowel op gouvernementeel als parlementair terrein onder de loep genomen. Hierbij wordt de opvatting ontwikkeld dat regionale samenwerking althans op het terrein van de gezondheidszorg de voorkeur verdient boven een uitsluitend mondiale aanpak (Hfdst. I en II).

Tenslotte wordt in Hfdst. III aan de hand van de in de beide voorgaande hoofdstukken verrichte analyse een 'blauwdruk' ontwikkeld voor de structuur en het functioneren van de gezondheidszorg in Europees verband. In principe worden twee mogelijkheden aangegeven. De eerste is het creëren van een nieuwe intergouvernementele organisatie, welke wordt belast met de organisatie en coördinatie van werkzaamheden van de verschillende vormen van internationale samenwerking op het gebied van de gezondheidszorg in Europa: verschillende intergouvernementele vormen van samenwerking zijn als zodanig van deze organisatie geen lid. De tweede mogelijkheid is het creëren van een zgn. overkoepelend orgaan, waarin alle betrokken vormen van intergouvernementele samenwerking in Europa participeren. Aan deze constructie wordt de voorkeur gegeven. Een aantal taken voor een dergelijk overkoepelend orgaan worden aangegeven, zoals, het plannen en programmeren van werkzaamheden, verdeling van werkzaamheden tussen de verschillende deelnemende instanties. Hierbij wordt uitgegaan van een pragmatische benadering: al naar gelang de doelstellingen van een specifiek programmaonderdeel en de functionele mogelijkheden van de deelnemende instanties, zal een programma, of een bepaald onderdeel daarvan, worden toegewezen aan een of meerdere van de participerende organisaties. Voor het opstellen van nieuwe, c.q. aanvullende mensenrecht-teksten wordt met name gedacht aan de Raad van Europa. De verdeling van werkzaamheden hangt in belangrijke mate af van de vraag of het al dan niet gewenst is een juridisch instrument in het leven te roepen. Met name de WGO zal bij behoefte aan juridische regelingen weinig of geen bijdrage kunnen leveren, zolang geen delegatie van wetgevende bevoegdheden naar de regio heeft plaatsgevonden.

In de studie zijn een aantal beperkingen ingebouwd. Om praktische redenen is uitgegaan van slechts één regio nl. Europa. Voorts zijn een aantal onderwerpen, zoals milieuvraagstukken, sociale verzekeringsvraagstukken en onderwerpen gericht op arbeidsomstandigheden buiten beschouwing gelaten. Het motief hiervoor is, dat deze vraagstukken weliswaar volksgezondheidsaspekten hebben, doch niet alleen in dat verband kunnen worden beschouwd.

Tenslotte is alleen ingegaan op de gouvernementele samenwerking omdat de niet-gouvernementele samenwerkingsvormen, hoewel incidenteel genoemd, geen juridische gevolgen hebben.

Litterature

Antheunissen, J.L., De gemeenschappelijke Benelux dienst voor de registratie van genees-middelen, Benelux 1, 1973, 30.

Arbab-Zadeh, A., Geschichte und Probleme Internationaler Gesundheitsgesetzgebung, Munch. Med. Wschr. 105, 1963, 2540.

Asbeck, F.M., Baron van, La Charte Sociale Européenne: sa portée juridique, la mise en oeuvre, in: Mélanges offertes à Henri Rollin, 1964 (Paris).

Asbeck, F.M., Baron van, International society in search of a transnational legal order, 1976 (Leyden).

Aujaleu, E., Prospective studies and future action in the public health field, Council of Europe, 1972 (Strasbourg).

Aujaleu, E., Des services irremplaçables, La santé du monde, Magazine de l'OMS, novembre 1974.

Benelux, Samenwerking op het gebied van de registratie van geneesmiddelen, Benelux 4, 1977, 3.

Benelux, Ministeriële werkgroep van volksgezondheid, Benelux 4, 1975, 4.

Berg, C., van der, Statuut van de WHO, in: Voorschriften Volksgezondheid, 1, V 20, 2, 1973, B.

Berkov, R., The World Health Organization: a study in decentralised international adminis-tration, 1957 (Geneva).

Beyrie-Menahem, C., La, Des institutions specialisées, 1953 (Paris).

Bouissou, R., Histoire de la médecine, 1967 (Paris).

Bowett, D.W., The law of international institutions, 1970 (London).

Brecht, A., in: Regionalism and world organization, post war aspects of Europe's global relationships, a symposium of the institute on world organization, American Council on Public Affairs, 1944 (Washington).

Brockington, F., The World Health Organization, in: The United Nations, the first ten years, ed. by B.E. Wortley, O.B.E., L.L.D., 1957 (Manchester).

Brockington, F., World Health, 1975 (Edinburgh, London, New York).

Calderwood, H.B., The founding of a single international health organization, WHO Chron-icle, 29, 1975, 435.

Campbell, A.V., Establishing ethical priorities in medicine, British medical journal, 1, 1977, 818.

Cartou, L., Organisations Européennes, 1965 (Toulouse).

Cassin, R., 20 years after, Journal of the International Commission of Jurists, Vol. VIII, no. 2, December 1967.

Castberg, F., The European Convention on Human Rights, ed. by T. Opsahl and T. Ouch-terlony, 1974 (Leyden).

Chapelle, Ph., de la, La Déclaration Universelle des Droits de l'Homme et le catholicisme, 1967 (Paris).

Chaumont, Ch.M., La signification du principe de spécialité des organisations internatio-nales, in: Mélanges offertes à Henri Rollin, 1964 (Paris).

Couvreur, L., De Raad van Europa en de Europese eenheidsgedachte, Internat. Spectator, 9, 1969, 758.

Council of Europe, European Convention on Human Rights, manual, 1963 (Strasbourg).

271

Conseil de l'Europe; l'Assemblée Consultative, procedure et pratique, 1965 (Strasbourg).

Council of Europe, Partial Agreement in the Social and Public Health field, Basic texts, 1971 (Strasbourg).

Council of Europe, Consultative Assembly, Parliamentary Conference on Human Rights; Vienna, 18-20 October 1971, 1972 (Strasbourg).

Council of Europe, The Consultative Assembly, procedure and practice, 1973 (Strasbourg).

Council of Europe; European co-operation in public health; collected resolutions adopted by the Committee of Ministers on the proposal of the European public health committee (1964-1974), 1975 (Strasbourg).

Council of Europe, civil liability of physicians, Proceedings of the fifth colloquy on European law, Lyons, 3-5 June 1975, 1975 (Strasbourg).

Council of Europe, Collected edition of the travaux préparatoires (prepared by E.H. Robertson), Vol. I and II, 1975 (The Hague).

Council of Europe, Proceedings of the fourth international colloquy about the European Convention on Human Rights, Rome, 5-8 November, 1975, 1976 (Strasbourg).

Council of Europe, Partial Agreement in the social and public health field, reports, recommendations, resolutions and other documents published, 1976 (Strasbourg).

Council of Europe, What is the Council of Europe doing to protect human rights, 1977 (Strasbourg).

Council of Europe, Drawing up and implementation of the European Social Charter, Symposium on the European Social Charter and social policy today, Strasbourg, 7-9 December 1977, proceedings, 1978 (Strasbourg).

Council of Europe, Parliamentary Assembly, Rules of procedure of the Assembly and Statute of the Council of Europe, 1978 (Strasbourg).

Crayencour, J.P., de, Le droit d'etablissement et les professions du domaine de santé, Revue du Marché Commun, 1967, 24.

Grayencour, J.P., de, La reconnaissance mutuelle des diplômes, un retentissant échec?, Revue du Marché Commun, 1973, 257.

Deliège-Rott, D., Le médecin face au Marché Commun, 1967 (Louvain).

Delon, P.J., The International Health Regulations, a practical guide, World Health Organization, 1975 (Geneva).

Drost, P.N., The crime of state, 1959 (Leyden).

Duclos, P., Le Conseil de l'Europe, 1964 (Paris).

The effectiveness of International decisions, papers of a conference of the American Society of International Law and proceedings, ed. by S.M. Schwebel, 1971 (Leyden).

Esveld, N.E.H., van, De sociaal-economische betekenis van de rechten van de mens, in: De rechten van de mens, 1968 (Leiden).

Ethics in medical progress with special reference to transplantation, Ciba Foundation Symposium, ed. by G.E.W. Wolstenholme, O.B.E., M.A., F.R.C.P., F.I. Biol. and Meave O'Connor, B.A., 1966 (London).

De EEG voor artsen kort verklaard, Medisch Contact 32, 1977, 1192.

Das Europa der Siebzehn; Bilanz und perspektiven von 25 Jahren Europarat, 1974 (Bonn).

European Communities (Commission), The European Community, international organisation and multilateral agreements, 1977 (Brussels, Luxemburg).

European Communities (Commission), Consumer protection and information policy, first report, 1977 (Luxemburg).

European Communities, European Parliament, Report on the position of the European Communities in public international law, drawn up on behalf of the legal affairs committee (rapporteur: mr. L. Jozeau-Marigné), 1978 (Luxemburg).

272

European Free Trade Association, Convention for the mutual recognition of inspections in respect of pharmaceutical products, 1970 (Geneva).

European Free Trade Association, Safety aspects involved in the packaging and labelling of pharmaceutical products, 1971 (Geneva).

European Free Trade Association, 1975-1976, sixteenth annual report of the European Free Trade Association, 1976 (Geneva).

Eyriey, F., Twenty years in the service of Europe; from the Brussels Treaty Organisation to the Council of Europe, Council of Europe, 1968 (Strasbourg).

Flacha, S., WHO and non-governmental organizations, WHO Chronicle, 31, 1977, 127.

Friedmann, W., The changing structure of international law, 1964 (London).

Gaudet, M., The European Communities, in: The effectiveness of international decisions, 1971 (Leyden).

Glaser, S., Les droits de l'homme a la lumière du droit international positif, in: Mélanges offertes à Henri Rollin, 1964 (Paris).

Glesner, A., Des medecins et des juristes, Journal des Tribunaux, 89, 1974, 561.

Golsong, H., Le Conseil de l'Europe et la souveraineté nationale, 1965 (Louvain).

Golsong, H., The Council of Europe, in: The effectiveness of international decisions, 1971 (Leyden).

Goodman, N.M., International health organizations and their work, 1971 (Edinburgh, London).

Goudsmit, C.J., Activiteiten op het gebied van de volksgezondheid in internationaal verband, T. Soc. Geneesk., 51, 1973, 485.

Gurvitch, G., La Déclaration des droits sociaux, 1946 (Paris).

Gutteridge, F., Notes on decisions of the World Health Organization, in: The effectiveness of international decisions, 1971 (Leyden).

Hobson, W., World health and history, 1963 (Bristol).

Hondius, F.W., J.W.G. de Jonge, A. Plate, H.D.C. Roscam Abbing, De Raad van Europa, Internat. Spectator, 2, 1975, 112.

Hoare, S., Sir, The UN Commission on human rights, in: The international protection of human rights, 1967 (London).

Hoare, S., Sir, Recent developments in the UN concerning the protection of human rights, in: Problèmes de protection internationale des droits de l'homme (René Cassin, Amicorum disciplinorumque Liber), 1969 (Paris).

Howard-Jones, N., The scientific background of the international sanitary conferences, 1851-1938, WHO Chronicle 28, 1974, 455, 495.

Howard-Jones, N., International Public Health. The organizational problems between the two world wars, WHO Chronicle 31, 1977, 391, 449; 32, 1978, 26, 63, 114, 156.

Humphrey, J.P., The UN Charter and the Universal Declaration of Human Rights, in: The international protection of human rights, 1967 (London).

Hutchison, A., The health of seafarers, WHO Chronicle, 29, 1975, 387.

International Classification of Diseases, World Health Organization, 1967, 1969, 1977 (Geneva).

International Health Conference, New York, June 19 to July 22, 1946, Report of the United States Delegation, 1946 (Washington).

International Labour Organisation, Comparative analysis of the International Covenants on Human Rights and international labour conventions and recommendations, official bulletin, LII, 1969, 181.

International medical care, a comparison and evaluation of medical care services throughout the world, ed. by John Fry and W.A.J. Farndale, 1972.

Jantzen, T., The operation of a free trade area, European Free Trade Association, 1964 (Geneva).
Jenks, C.W., Some constitutional problems of international organisations, the British Yearbook of International law, 1945, 11.
Jenks, C.W., Co-ordination in international organisation: an introductory survey, the British yearbook of international law, 1951, 29.

Koopmans, T., Vrijheden in beweging, Thorbeckecolleges nr. 2, 1976 (Leiden).
Kupke, K., International classification of diseases: ninth revision, WHO Chronicle, 32, 1978, 219.

Labeyrie-Ménahem, C., Des institutions spécialisées. Problèmes juridiques et diplomatiques de l'administration internationale, 1953 (Paris).
Lachs, M., Le rôle des organisations internationales dans la formation du droit international, in: Mélanges offertes à Henri Rollin, 1964 (Paris).
Lain Entralgo, P., Le médecin et le malade, 1969 (Madrid).
Landy, E., The effectiveness of international supervision, thirty years of ILO experience, 1966 (London, New York).
Ledeboer, L.V., Futurologische gedachten over gezondheidszorg, in: Volksgezondheid in ontwikkeling, 1971 (Assen).
Leenen, H.J.J., Sociale grondrechten en gezondheidszorg, 1966 (Hilversum).
Leenen, H.J.J., De rechten van de patiënt, Kath. Artsenblad, 47, 1968, 6, 162.
Leenen, H.J.J., Sociale grondrechten en recht op gezondheidszorg, in: Sociale Geneeskunde, 1968 (Utrecht).
Leenen, H.J.J., Milieuhygiëne recht, 1976 (Alphen aan den Rijn).
Leenen, H.J.J., Rechten van mensen in de gezondheidszorg, 1978 (Alphen aan den Rijn).
Leenen, H.J.J., Structuur en functioneren van de gezondheidszorg, 1979 (Alphen aan den Rijn).
Luard, E., The international protection of human rights, 1967 (London).
Lyon-Caen, G., Droit social Européen, 1969 (Paris).

Mahler, H., The constitutional mission of the WHO, WHO Chronicle 28, July 1974.
Mahler, H., Blueprint for health for all, WHO Chronicle 31, 1977, 491.
Martens, J.M.H.A., Farmacie en EEG, Pharmaceutisch weekblad, 112, 1977, 1156.
Maxwell, R., Health care the growing dilemma, 1974 (New York).
Melique, P., Le médicament dans la Communauté Européenne, les problèmes legislatifs et economiques, 1974 (Paris).
Muntendam, P., Gezondheidspolitiek als OESO-project, Medisch Contact, 32, 1977, 309.

Nagel, H., The Nordic Council: its organs, functions and judicial nature, A.A.A., 1956, 51.
Nationaal Ziekenhuisinstituut, Vrije vestiging van artsen in de EEG, een commentaar, Informatieblad MZ1, 1976 (Utrecht).
NATO, European defence, 10 years of the Eurogroup, 1978 (Brussels).
NATO handbook on standards and rules for the protection of the civil population against chemical toxic agents, NATO civil defence committee, 1973.
NATO, advanced health care, a pilot study of the Committee on the challenges of modern society, 1976.
Nicholas, H.G., The United Nations as political institution, 1962 (Oxford).

Nieuwenhuizen, C.L.C., van, Het nut der tegenspoeden: internationale aspekten van de strukturele ontwikkelingen in de gezondheidszorg, Het Ziekenhuis, 1974, 586.

Nieuwenhuizen, C.L.C., van, De vrije uitwisseling van artsen in EEG landen, Medisch Contact, 28, 1973, 605.

Nieuwenhuizen, C.L.C., van, Het Raadgevend Comité voor de medische opleiding, Medisch Contact, 32, 1977, 1197.

Nordic co-operation in the social and labour field, Ministry of Social Affairs, 1965 (Oslo).

Nordic Council for international organization in Europe, Nordic economic and social co-operation, second conference, 1968 (Stockholm).

Nordic Council for international organization in Europe, A regional approach a worldwide responsibility, sixth conference, 1975 (Stockholm).

Nordic organisations committee, The organisation of Nordic co-operation, proposals, 1970 (Stockholm).

Nordiska ministerradet, Berätelse rörande det Nordiska samarbetet i 1977, planer för det fortsatta samarbetet, 1978 (Stockholm).

OECD, Research innovation: Education of the health professions in the context of the health care systems, 1974 (Paris).

Activities of OECD in 1975, Report by the Secretary General, 1976 (Paris).

Padelford, N.J., Recent developments in regional organization, proceedings of the American Society of international law, 1955.

Pannenborg, Ch.O., van, A new international health order, 1978 (Alblasserdam).

Parry, C., The sources and evidences of international law, 1965 (Manchester).

Partsch, K.J., Die Rechte und Freiheiten der Europäischen Menschenrechts Konvention, 1966 (Berlin).

Percy, Senator, US calls for worldwide effort to eliminate torture and inhuman treatment of prisoners, Dep. of State bulletin, LXXI, 1974, 807.

Pfeffermann, H., F. Eyriey, Les travaux du Conseil de l'Europe dans le domaine de la santé publique, Annuaire Européen, Vol. XIII, 1965.

Pinto, E., Les organisations européennes, 1963 (Paris).

Rechten van de mens in mundiaal en europees perspectief, serie rechten van de mens, deel 1, 1978 (Nijmegen).

Reuter, P., Organisations Européennes, 1965 (Paris).

Regionalism and world organization, post war aspects of Europe's global relationships, a symposium of the institute on world organization, American Council on Public Affairs, 1944 (Washington).

Ribas, J.J., M.J. Jonezy, J.C. Seché, Droit social Européen, 1973 (Paris).

Robertson, A.H., European institutions; co-operation, integration and unification, 1959 (London).

Robertson, A.H., Human rights in Europe, 1963 (Manchester).

Robertson, A.H., The European Convention on human rights, in: The international protection of human rights, 1967 (London).

Robertson, A.H., De internationale bescherming van de rechten van de mens, 1974 (Groningen).

Rolland, M., Le respect de l'homme et l'experimentation medicale, in: Problèmes de protection internationale des droits de l'homme (René Cassin, Amicorum disciplinorumque Liber), 1969 (Paris).

Roscam Abbing, H.D.C., De Raad van Europa en de Volksgezondheid, T. Soc. Geneesk. 12, 1976, 391.

Roscam Abbing, H.D.C., Rechten van de mens, T. Gezondh. Recht, 1977, 128.

Saba, H., L'activité quasi legislative des institutions specialisées des Nations Unies, Academie de droit international, Receuil des cours, I, 1964, 607.
Saba, H., Les droits de l'homme et le problème de l'experimentation biomédicale sur l'homme, in: Mélanges offertes à Polys Modinos, Problèmes des droits de l'homme et de l'unification Européenne, 1968 (Paris).
Saxrud, G., Nordic co-operation: institution and activities, EFTA Bulletin, 4, Vol. XVII, 1976, 10.
Schachter, O., Towards a theory of international obligations, in: The effectiveness of international decisions, 1971 (Leyden).
Schambeck, H., Grundrechte und Socialordnung, Gedanken zur Europäischen Socialcharte, 1969 (Berlin).
Schermers, H.G., De gespecialiseerde organisaties, hun bouw en inrichting, 1957 (Leyden).
Schermers, H.G., Het Europees Verdrag tot bescherming van de rechten van de mens en de fundamentele vrijheden, 1964 (Zwolle).
Schermers, H.G., International institutional law, Vol. II, Functioning and legal order, 1972 (Leyden).
Schwelb, E., Notes on the early legislative history of the measures of implementation of the human rights Covenants, in: Mélanges offertes à Polys Modinos, Problèmes des droits de l'homme et de l'unification Européenne, 1968 (Paris).
Singh, N., in: The role of international organisations, Mélanges offertes à Henri Rollin, 1964 (Paris).
Sloot, H.A., Problemen rond de farmacie en de EEG, Pharm. Weekblad 1973, 748; 1975, 1270 and 1316.
Smyth, J.F., The implementation of the European Social Charter, in: Mélanges offertes à Polys Modinos, Problèmes des droits de l'homme et de l'unification Européenne, 1968 (Paris).
Snell, H., Ontwikkelingen in de besprekingen over de uitwisselingsmogelijkheid voor tandartsen in de EEG, Ned. Tandartsenblad, 33, 1978, 22.
Sohn-Harvard, L.B., Protection of human rights through international legislation, in: Problèmes de protection internationale des droits de l'homme (René Cassin, Amicorum disciplinorumque liber), 1969 (Paris).
Sohn-Harvard, L.B., Procedures developed by international organisations for checking compliance, in: The effectiveness of international decisions, 1971 (Leyden).
Solem, E., The Nordic Council and Scandinavian integration, 1977 (New York, London).
Spaander, J., De samenwerking in Benelux verband tussen de laboratoria op het gebied van de volksgezondheid, Benelux Publikatieblad, 1962, 30.
Stein, E., Application and enforcement of international organization law by national authorities and courts, in: The effectiveness of international decisions, 1971 (Leyden).
Stenson Clark, R., A United Nations High Commissioner for human rights, 1972 (The Hague).
Szabo, I., Remarques sur le developpement du catalogue internationale des droits de l'homme, in: Problèmes de protection internationale des droits de l'homme (René Cassin, Amicorum disciplinorumque liber), 1969 (Paris).

Tallec, G., 1e, Quelques aspects des rapports entre la CEE et les organisations internationales, Revue du Marché Commun, 1972, 636.
Taylor, C.E., Challenge to international agencies, Intern. Journal of Health Services, 1975, 489.
Teeling-Smith, G., Medicines in the 1990's, a technological forecast, United Nations Eco-

nomic Commission for Europe, Seminar on technological forecasting, Warsaw, 7-12 December 1970.

Tennfjord, F., The European Social Charter, an instrument of social collaboration in Europe, European Year Book, 1961, 71.

De toekomst van de huisartsengeneeskunde in Europa, Medisch Contact, 33, 1978, 819.

Tomaszunas, S., The Health of seafarers, WHO Chronicle, 29, 1975, 393.

Troclet, L.E., Elements de droit social Européen, 1963 (Bruxelles).

The United Nations, the first ten years, ed. by P.E. Wortley, O.B.E. L.L.D., 1957 (Manchester).

United Nations, Measures taken within the UN in the field of human rights, 20 June 1967, A/Conf. 3215.

Vasak, K., La Convention Européene des droits de l'homme, 1964 (bibl. constitut. et de science politique) (Tome X), (Paris).

Vasak, K., The European Convention on Human rights: A useful complement to the Geneva Convention, in: International review of the Red Cross, 53, 1965.

Vasak, K., Vers la création de Commissions regionales des droits de l'homme, in: Problèmes de protection internationale des droits de l'homme (René Cassin, Amicorum disciplinorumque liber), 1969 (Paris).

Vasak, K., Les problèmes specifiques en oeuvre internationale des droits économiques et sociaux; vers une protection des droits economiques et sociaux, 1973 (Bruxelles).

Vallance, E., Rights and social policy, The political quarterly, 45, 1974, 461.

Valticos, N., The International Labour Organisation, in: The effectiveness of international decisions, 1971 (Leyden).

Vedel, G., Les Déclarations des droits de l'homme (1789-1949), Etudes, tome 226, 1950, 66 (Paris).

Ven, J.J.M., van der; H.J.J. Beenen; J.F. Leekman, Human rights and social welfare; national report; National Council on Social Welfare, 1968 (The Hague).

Ven, J.J.M. van der, Sociale Grundrechte, 1957 (Utrecht).

Verdoodt, A., Naissance et signification de la Déclaration Universelle des droits de l'homme, 1964 (Louvain).

Vervolgnota op wetenschapsbudget 1978; deelname van Nederlandse zijde aan internationale wetenschappelijke samenwerking, Tweede Kamer der Staten Generaal, 1977-1978, 14801, no. 5-6.

Vinck, F., La politique sociale de la Communauté Européenne elargie (conférence), Europe – documents, no. 725, 1973.

Vries, J., de, Toelating van artsen uit de lid-staten van de EEG, T. Soc. Geneeskunde, 33, 1975, 627.

Vries, J., de, De wederzijdse erkenning van de artsdiploma's in de Europese Gemeenschappen, T. Gezondh. Recht, 1977, 27.

Wagenbauer, R., Où en est la reconnaissance mutuelle des diplômes de médecin dans la CEE, M. Trim. Dr. Eur., 1973, 426.

Wendt, F., The Nordic Council and co-operation in Scandinavia, 1959 (Copenhagen).

Weil, G.L., The European Convention on Human Rights; background, development and prospects, 1963 (Leyden).

World Health Organization, The first ten years of the World Health Organization, 1958 (Geneva); The second ten years of the World Health Organization, 1968 (Geneva).

World Health Organization, Handbook of resolutions and decisions of the World Health Assembly and the Executive Board, Volume I, 1948-1973, 1973 (Geneva); Volume II, 1973-1976, 1977 (Geneva).

World Health Organization, Glossary of mental disorders and guide to their classification for use in combination with the International Classification of Diseases, 1974 (Geneva).

World Health Organization regional office for Europe, Health services in Europe, 1975 (Copenhagen).

World Health Organization, Health aspects of human rights with special reference to developments in biology and medicine, 1976 (Geneva).

World Health Organization, Health aspects of human rights, WHO Chronicle, 30, 1976, 347.

World Health Organization, Towards more effective biomedical research, WHO Chronicle, 30, 1976, 375.

World Health Organization, The World Bank and Aid for health projects, WHO Chronicle, 31, 1977, 94.

World Health Organization, Controlling psychotropic substances, WHO's responsibilities under the new Convention, WHO Chronicle, 32, 1978, 3.

World Health Organization, The long-term future of the international health regulations, WHO Chronicle, 32, 1978, 439.

World Health Organization, Research development in WHO in retrospect, 1948-1978, WHO Chronicle, 32, 1978, 461.

Wiebringhaus, H., La Charte Sociale Européenne, Ann. Français de droit intern., 1963, 709.

Wiebringhaus, H., Het Europees Sociaal Handvest, Belgisch Tijdschrift voor sociale Zekerheid, 1977, 200.

Yemin, E., Legislative powers in the United Nations and specialised agencies, diss. 1969 (Leyden).

Zonneveld, R.J., e.a., Sociale Geneeskunde, 1972 (Utrecht).